D1572921

Advanced Programmer's Guide to the EGA/VGA

George Sutty
Steve Blair

Brady

New York London Toronto Sydney Tokyo Singapore

B R A D Y

Simon & Schuster
Gulf + Western Building
One Gulf + Western Plaza
New York, New York 10023

Distributed by Prentice Hall Trade

Manufactured in the United States of America

10 9 8 7 6 5 4 3

Library of Congress Cataloging-in-Publication Data

Sutty, George J.
    Advanced Programmer's Guide to the EGA/VGA

    System requirements for computer disk: IBM PC, AT, XT, PS/2, or compatibles; 512K;
DOS 2.0 or higher; C, Pascal, or Assembly; 1 disk drive; color monitor.
    1. Programming languages (Electronic computers)—Software. 2. Computer
graphics—Software. I. Blair, Steve. II. Title.
QA76.7.S87   1988   006.6′765   88-24977
ISBN 0-13-729039-X

Contents

Limits of Liability and Disclaimer of Warranty

Trademarks

Part I

Operating Principles

Introduction

Computer Graphics, like many other emerging technologies, promises to alter dramatically the way computers are used. By enhancing the interface between man and machine, this technology is changing the way we relate to computers, making them more accessible. This is especially true in personal computing where the user interface is (or should be) highly interactive.

Until recently, the expenses involved in graphics technology kept it in the realm of mini and mainframe computers. The graphics capabilities of personal computers were crude at best. Advances in memory technology, VLSI circuits, and CRT (Cathode Ray Tube) display design are now bringing high quality color graphics to personal computing.

The company that set the standard for personal computing has now set the standard for personal computer graphics. The IBM Enhanced Graphics Adapter (EGA) and its cousin, the Video Graphics Array (VGA) are fast becoming the most popular graphics display adapters available for the IBM PC and compatible machines. Over one million EGA compatible video adapters have been purchased from more than a dozen different vendors. The VGA, while much newer, is standard equipment on most of IBM's PS/2 computers.

The range of features available with the EGA has undoubtedly contributed to its phenomenal success. While the EGA is the first affordable adapter to bring high quality color graphics to the PC, its wide range of operating modes make it compatible with a large percentage of the huge software base that was written for the MDA (Monochrome Display Adapter) and CGA (Color Graphics Adapter.) In addition, many of the EGA compatible boards available today have been enhanced with other compatibility modes. (Compatibility claims can be deceiving, however, and this topic is covered in detail later.)

The versatility and features of the EGA unfortunately have served to complicate the lives of those who wish to develop software that can take advantage of the EGA's features. This problem has been compounded by a lack of adequate documentation. Programmers armed with little more than BIOS listings and brief register descriptions have puzzled over how to generate optimum EGA graphics software.

The information in this book is meant to take the guesswork out of trying to interpret the IBM EGA reference manual, as well as save you many hours of tedious trial and error. It also includes useful information on graphics algorithms for the EGA. No advanced programming skills are required, but a basic understanding of at least one programming language (Pascal, C or Assembly language) is needed. The text is organized so as to be readable as an EGA/VGA primer, but also to serve as a reference book where answers to EGA/VGA related questions can be found.

How the Book is Organized

Chapter 1 details the standard operating modes of the EGA and VGA. These include both color and monochrome graphics modes, and both color and monochrome text modes, at various screen resolutions. In this chapter you will find out how to identify the appropriate modes for a given video display and how to configure the EGA or VGA to operate in that mode. The standard EGA and VGA operating modes are compared with those of other popular video adapters for the PC.

In Chapter 2, the architectures of EGA and VGA are explained. Any graphics programming task that cannot be efficiently performed through the BIOS (Basic Input-Output System) Video Services must be performed by directly addressing the hardware of the display adapter. The information in this chapter provides an overall picture of what that hardware is, how it operates, and how it is addressed. A good understanding of the information in Chapter 2 is essential for the comprehension of the chapters that follow.

Chapter 3 provides detailed descriptions of all of the I/O registers of the EGA and VGA (there are over sixty in all.) The majority of these registers need only to be initialized by the BIOS to define the operating mode of the board and are not of serious interest to the application programmer. A small subset of the I/O registers can be used by the programmer to perform operations such as line drawing, BITBLTs (BIT oriented Block Transfers), panning, scrolling, and other functions.

Chapter 4 is dedicated to the EGA and VGA ROM BIOS. The BIOS firmware routines provide a relatively high level method of interfacing application software to the EGA and VGA adapters. The BIOS interface is, in fact, IBM's officially sanctioned method for programming the EGA and VGA. Unfortunately, the performance limitations that are incumbent with this approach make it impractical in most cases to rely solely on the BIOS interface. Still, the BIOS Video Services are a valuable resource that is available to the application programmer. EGA and VGA BIOS routines also provide some compatibility with the CGA and MDA video adapters. Chapter 4 details all the BIOS Video Services, with programming examples to show how they are used.

In Chapters 5-8 the information given in Chapters 1-4 is put to use in programming examples that demonstrate real world techniques for programming the EGA and VGA. Topics covered include the drawing of lines, arcs, and rectangles, text display and scrolling, color definition, and downloading of custom character sets. Many of the examples in this chapter can be used in real applications with little or no modification.

The appendices include useful technical reference data for the EGA and VGA, listed in a format that makes it easily accessible to the working programmer.

To assist you in determining which sections of the book will be most useful for your particular application, these symbols are used to identify important characteristics of the EGA/VGA:

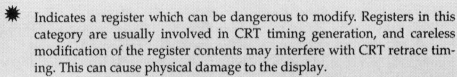

✳   Indicates a register which can be dangerous to modify. Registers in this category are usually involved in CRT timing generation, and careless modification of the register contents may interfere with CRT retrace timing. This can cause physical damage to the display.

Registers in this category are always initialized by the BIOS during display mode initialization, and there is usually no reason for software to modify them.

★   Indicates a register that can be very useful for performing some specific function (such as panning, scrolling, cursor movement, etc.)

▸   Indicates a feature of the EGA that will operate differently depending on the size of the EGA display memory. Almost all EGA compatible adapters sold have a full 256K bytes of display memory, but some have been sold with 64K bytes or 128K bytes. For more information on display memory size, see the section on Partial Memory Configurations in Chapter 1.

∅   Indicates a feature unique to the VGA. This feature will not operate on the EGA.

1

The Basics

Introduction

The Enhanced Graphics Adapter (EGA) was developed by IBM to be marketed together with the IBM Enhanced Color Display (ECD). This combination provides color graphics capabilities at resolutions as high as 640 pixels horizontally by 350 pixels vertically, and displays up to 16 simultaneous colors, which can be selected from the 64 possible colors that the display supports. Some third party vendors of EGA compatible products have included even higher resolution modes with their products.

The EGA is also compatible with almost every display in common use on IBM compatible personal computers, though it is compatible with only a fraction of the pre-existing software base that has been developed for those displays. This fact has forced most applications software developers to issue new EGA compatible versions of their programs.

The Video Graphics Array (VGA) was developed by IBM as an enhancement to the EGA, and is provided as standard equipment on most of IBM's PS/2 family of personal computers. It supports resolutions as high as 640 pixels horizontally by 480 pixels vertically, and can display more colors (as many as 256 simultaneous colors can be displayed, but only at a relatively low resolution.)

Unlike the EGA, the VGA is not compatible with a variety of displays. IBM provides one color display and one monochrome display that are VGA compatible. The VGA does, however, provide operating modes that simulate the performance of other displays and are partially software compatible. For more information on compatibility, see the section on Compatibility Modes in this chapter.

> Like all of the popular display adapters for the PC/AT family, the EGA and VGA are "dumb" adapters (they have no on-board processing capability.) The system processor is responsible for all drawing operations, writing directly to the bit-mapped display memory. Application programmers are left with the choice of either programming within the confines and limitations of a predefined graphics environment (such as Microsoft Windows, Digital Research GEM, or GKS), or writing their own graphics drawing routines.

Display Selection

Table 1-1. IBM PC compatible display.

Display	Compatible Adapters	Colors	Text Resolution	Graphics Resolution	Scan Rates
Mono-chrome	MDA Hercules EGA	2	80 x 25	640 x 350 720 x 350 720 x 348	Vert-50 Hz Hor-15.8 KHz
Color	CGA EGA	16	40 x 25 80 x 25	320 x 200 640 x 200	Vert-60 Hz Hor-15.8 KHz
Enhanced Color	CGA EGA	16 of 64**	40 x 25 80 x 25	320 x 200 640 x 200 640 x 350	Vert-60 Hz Hor-15.8 KHz or 21.8 KHz
Multisync digital *	CGA EGA	16 of 64**	40 x 25 80 x 25	320 x 200 640 x 200 640 x 350	Variable
Multisync analog	VGA	256 of 256K	80 x 25	640 x 480 800 x 600	Variable
VGA Color display	VGA	256 of 256K	40 x 25 80 x 25	320 x 400 640 x 400	Vert-70 Hz Hor-31.5 KHz
VGA Mono display				320 x 350 640 x 350 720 x 350 720 x 400 640 x 480	

* Multisync displays from NEC, and similar models from other vendors, offer extended modes with more colors and higher resolutions than the standard EGA can support.

** 16 of 64 means that at most 16 colors can be seen at one time out of a palette of 64 choices

256 of 256K means that up to 256 different colors can be seen out of a palette of 256,000.

MDA = Monochrome Display Adapter.

CGA = Color Graphics Adapter.

EGA = Enhanced Graphics Adapter.

VGA = Video Graphics Array.

Table 1-1 summarizes the display types that can be used with the EGA and VGA. Displays can be classified according to the type of interface they use. The following types of interfaces are commonly found on personal computers:

- **Digital (TTL) Displays** typically have from one to six color input lines. When a color line is asserted (ON), that color appears on the screen. The number of colors that can be displayed on a digital display is 2^n, where n is the number of color lines on the display. Most displays found on personal computers are digital. The EGA requires a digital display.

- **Composite Displays** have only one video input line. They may be either monochrome or color. All video information is encoded onto one line using the NTSC (National Television System Committee) encoding standard. Inexpensive monochrome composite displays are sometimes found in very low end systems. Such displays typically offer very poor resolution. The CGA (Color Graphics Adapter) is the only IBM video adapter that supports composite video (CGA also supports TTL video).

Composite color displays are commonly found in the television industry, but are not normally used as computer displays. The process of encoding all color data onto a single video line limits the resolution of the display. The resolutions required for even low-end computer graphics applications exceed the capabilities of even the highest quality television receivers.

- **Analog RGB Displays** have three analog color input lines (red, green, and blue). The voltage level on each input line determines the amount of that color that will appear on the screen. The number of colors that can be displayed is theoretically unlimited, but in reality is normally limited by the capabilities of the display adapter. Because of the limitless color capabilities, analog RGB is considered the superior display technology.

VGA requires an analog display. Analog color and monochrome displays are available for VGA that offer more flexibility than the older digital displays. Either display (monochrome or color) will support all operating modes of the VGA. If a color mode is invoked using a monochrome display, colors will be represented as shades of gray. A monochrome mode can also be invoked on a color display.

The selection of a display is in most cases governed by the application software that will be running (or developed) on the system. The common displays found on IBM compatible machines today are summarized in Table 1-1.

While it may not be obvious why anyone would buy an Enhanced Graphics Adapter (EGA) without also buying an Enhanced Color Display (ECD), there are at least two good reasons that are not uncommon. Some individuals have opted to pay the relatively small difference in adapter cost to have an EGA in their system, hoping that the much larger display cost will eventually shrink so as to bring enhanced color within their budget. This has proven to be a sound argument, as display prices have fallen considerably since the EGA was introduced. On the other hand, some corporate users have chosen the EGA as the standard video adapter for all their systems, from word processing systems to engineering workstations, allowing them to stock only one video adapter card for color as well as monochrome displays.

Monochrome Displays

The original IBM PC was sold with the IBM Monochrome Display (MD) and the Monochrome Display Adapter (MDA). The abbreviations MD and MDA will be found throughout this text. Even though the MDA has no graphics capabilities, this combination is still extremely popular today for text applications. The resolution of the MDA (720 x 350) is higher than that of the EGA (640 x 350). If colors and graphics are not required, the Monochrome Display with an MDA adapter offers crisp monochrome text at a relatively low price. Text quality is a weak point with many low end color displays.

Shortly after the introduction of the IBM PC, a number of companies took on the job of supplying the add-on options that IBM did not supply. One of these, a company called Hercules Computer Technology, Inc., introduced a monochrome display adapter for the IBM Monochrome Display that offered graphics capability as well as MDA compatibility. The Hercules graphics card quickly became the standard for monochrome graphics. Not until the EGA was introduced did IBM even offer a display adapter with monochrome graphics capability.

Displays that are compatible with the IBM Monochrome Display are available from a wide variety of vendors. These displays have a 50 Hz vertical refresh rate. (The display screen must be refreshed 50 times per second.)

The CGA (Color Graphics Adapter) includes an output jack for driving a monochrome composite display, and this configuration is found on some low end systems. It offers poor display quality, and usually does not receive serious attention from software developers.

The monochrome graphics modes of the EGA are not compatible with Hercules graphics. The resolution offered by the Hercules adapter (720 x 348) is superior to that offered by EGA (640 x 350). This fact, together with the large base of existing Hercules compatible software, has caused several third party manufacturers to add Hercules compatibility modes to their EGA compatible adapters. True compatibility is not easily achieved, however, and none of these adapters can claim true 100 percent Hercules compatibility. Most of them work well with a majority of the popular software packages, and this has been enough to secure them a large market share.

The quality of the Hercules emulations found on EGA compatible boards varies from vendor to vendor. Anyone to whom Hercules compatibility is important should invest some time investigating the degree of compatibility offered by different products before selecting an EGA vendor. This subject is discussed in detail later in this chapter (see Compatibility Modes).

Color Displays

IBM established the first important color standard for personal computers with the introduction of the IBM Color Display (CD) and Color Graphics Adapter (CGA). The CGA supports 4 color graphics and 8 color text. The display itself is capable of displaying 16 colors. However, the resolution of the Color Display leaves much to be desired (640 x 200). Looking at text on the Color Display is especially displeasing due to the small number of pixels in a character cell (8 pixels wide by 8 pixels high). The result is a grainy, poorly shaped character set.

To make matters worse, on the original IBM CGA board, a processor access to display memory can interfere with screen refresh operations. The result appears as "snow" on the display. To avoid this problem, most CGA software will "blank" the display (turn off display refreshing) while drawing functions are in progress. The result is an irritating flicker in some of the standard CGA operating modes (including the text mode, which is used by the MS-DOS console driver).

In spite of these limitations, the low price, colors, and graphics capability of the CGA have caused it to become a huge success. There is currently a vast installed base of CGA compatible hardware and software.

CD compatible displays are also available from a wide variety of vendors. The display has a 60 Hz vertical refresh rate.

Enhanced Color Displays

With the introduction of the EGA, IBM also introduced the ECD. This display is a marked improvement over the Color Display. Its resolution is higher (640 x 350), and it offers more colors (64 vs. 16). Text modes are improved by an enhanced character set which uses a character cell that is 8 pixels wide by 14 pixels tall, offering text that almost (but not quite) matches the quality of the monochrome MDA text. There are no screen flicker problems like those found with the CGA.

IBM took several steps in the design of both the EGA and the ECD to gain some backward compatibility with the CGA and CD. The EGA has operating modes that allow it to drive the Color Display and execute some CGA software. The Enhanced Color Display is a dual frequency display; besides operating at EGA resolution (640 x 350), the ECD can be connected to a CGA and it will automatically operate at CD resolution (640 x 200).

ECD displays are now available from several vendors. The display has a 60 Hz vertical refresh rate, with horizontal refresh rates of 15.75 KHz or 21.8 KHz.

Recognizing the trend toward higher resolutions, NEC Corp. created their Multisync line of displays. These displays are capable of operating over a wide range of horizontal and vertical sync frequencies, and are therefore able to support a wide range of screen resolutions. Other manufacturers, including Sony, Thompson, and Mitsubishi, have introduced similar variable frequency displays. Throughout this text, we will refer to this class of displays as multifrequency displays. These displays usually start at EGA resolution (640 x 350) and go up to 640 x 400, 640 x 480, 800 x 600, 1024 x 768, or even higher.

In addition to their superior resolution, multifrequency displays also offer more colors than the ECD. When operated in a digital mode, they have the same 64 color capability as the ECD. When switched to analog mode, a multifrequency display operates as an analog RGB display with virtually unlimited color capabilities. Most of the new multifrequency displays are also compatible with the VGA (an adapter cable may be required). The original NEC Multisync display is not VGA compatible.

Use of the higher resolution modes or extended color capabilities of a multifrequency display requires a display adapter that can support those resolutions and colors.

The EGA has the same compatibility problems with CGA that it has with the Hercules graphics adapter (and for mostly the same reasons.) This has created another opportunity for third party vendors to create new compatibility modes for their EGA compatible products. These CGA emulations share all the same limitations as the Hercules emulations discussed previously. If CGA compatibility is an important concern, it pays to do some research before selecting an EGA vendor. These problems are discussed in more detail later in this chapter (see Compatibility Modes).

VGA Displays ⊘

The introduction by IBM of the VGA was accompanied by the introduction of a new family of VGA compatible displays, including a high resolution analog RGB display and a high resolution monochrome analog display that shows color information as shades of gray. These two displays are interchangeable. Color applications can be run on the monochrome display, and monochrome applications on the color display.

Partial Memory Configurations ⟶

The vast majority of EGA compatible display adapters are configured with a full 256K bytes of display memory. The original EGA adapter from IBM, however, was sold in three memory configurations: 64K bytes, 128K bytes, and 256K bytes. Adapters with less than 256K bytes of display memory are limited in the number of display colors and/or the amount of display data they can support in some modes.

Because IBM shipped a significant number of EGA boards with less than the full complement of memory installed, we have documented throughout the book the limitations that are imposed when using a partial memory configuration.

Standard EGA Operating Modes

In order to standardize the video interface for applications software, IBM defined a set of standard operating modes for the EGA and VGA. These modes do not represent all configurations the display adapter can operate in, but there are few good reasons to stray from the defined standard modes. Some third party vendors of EGA compatible boards have implemented video device drivers that operate in nonstandard modes for two reasons: to implement emulations (such as CGA or Hercules) or to achieve higher resolutions than EGA is normally capable of (such as 640 by 480).

The modes listed below are found on both EGA and VGA. Many of these modes have been carried forward from the MDA and CGA video adapters.

Table 1-2. Standard IBM video modes.

Mode		Type	Colors	Resolution	Compatible Displays
0, 1		Color text	16	40 x 25 8 x 8 char cell	CD, ED, VGA Multifrequency
0*, 1*		Color text	16	40 x 25 8 x 14 char cell	ED, VGA Multifrequency
0+, 1+	⊘	Color text	16	40 x 25 9 x 16 char cell	VGA Multifrequency
2,3	➡	Color text	16	80 x 25 8 x 8 char cell	CD, ED, VGA Multifrequency
2*, 3*	➡	Color text	16	80 x 25 8 x 14 char cell	ED, VGA Multifrequency
2+, 3+	⊘	Color text	16	80 x 25 9 x 16 char cell	VGA Multifrequency
4, 5		Color graphics	4	320 x 200	CD, ED, VGA Multifrequency
6		Color graphics	2	640 x 200	CD, ED, VGA Multifrequency
7	➡	Monochrome text	2	80 x 25 8 x 14 char cell	Monochrome VGA
7+	⊘	Monochrome text	2	80 x 25 9 x 16 char cell	VGA only
8, 9, A		PC jr only			

(continued)

Table 1-2. Standard IBM video modes *(continued)*.

D	⇒	Color graphics	16	320 x 200	CD, ED, VGA Multifrequency
E	⇒	Color graphics	16	640 x 200	CD, ED, VGA Multifrequency
F	⇒	Mono graphics		640 x 350	Monochrome VGA
10	⇒	Color graphics	16	640 x 350	ED, VGA Multifrequency
11		Color graphics	2	640 x 480	VGA Multifrequency
12		Color graphics	16	640 x 480	VGA Multifrequency
13		Color graphics	256	320 x 200	VGA Multifrequency

Most multifrequency displays are VGA compatible.
The original NEC Multisync is not.

CD = Color Display.
ED = Enhanced Color Display.

Since the introduction of the IBM Color Graphics Adapter (CGA), all IBM display adapters have included 40 column text modes. These modes were created to allow text to be displayed on home television sets, which have much poorer resolution than computer displays and cannot display 80 columns of text. Other than a small number of computer games that have been written using 40 column text, these modes are not commonly used.

Special adapter circuitry is required to connect an IBM compatible computer to a television set.

Modes 0 and 1 (Color Text)

On the EGA and VGA there is no functional difference between Mode 0 and Mode 1. These two modes were brought forward from the CGA video adapter and the distinction between them disappeared with the CGA Composite Video output jack. Modes 0 and 1 display color text on either the Color Display (CD), Enhanced Color Display (ECD), VGA displays, or some multifrequency displays at a resolution of 40 character columns by 25 character rows. The CGA character set is used, with its 8 pixel by 8 pixel character cell, resulting in the same poor text quality that is inherent in the CGA.

CGA compatibility is not complete with either EGA or VGA, and not all CGA software will run properly in these modes. In general, software that makes use of BIOS video services and avoids any direct access to I/O registers on the video adapter will usually run without problems. Direct processor access to display memory does not cause compatibility problems. For more information, see the section on Compatibility Modes later in this chapter.

EGA and VGA both support 8 display pages in this mode. A BIOS call is the preferred method for selecting the page to be displayed, though the same result can be achieved by altering the Start Address register in the CRT Controller (see Chapter 3). The display pages can be accessed by the processor at the following memory locations:

Page 0 - B800:0000   Page 4 - B800:2000
Page 1 - B800:0800   Page 5 - B800:2800
Page 2 - B800:1000   Page 6 - B800:3000
Page 3 - B800:1800   Page 7 - B800:3800

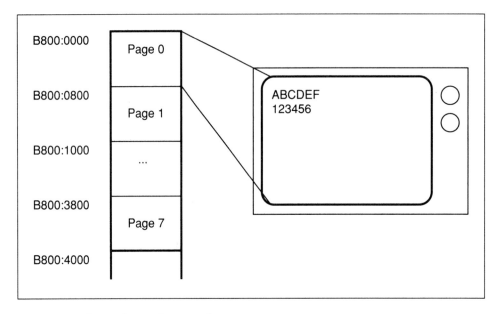

Figure 1-1. Pages in modes 0 and 1.

Eight standard display colors plus eight intensified colors are supported. Each character is independently programmable for foreground color and background color. Table 1-3 lists the standard color text attributes. For more information on text attributes, see Chapter 2.

Table 1-3. Standard text attributes.

Attribute	Standard Color	Intensified Color
000	Black	Gray
001	Blue	Light Blue
010	Green	Light Green
011	Cyan	Light Cyan
100	Red	Light Red
101	Magenta	Light Magenta
110	Brown	Yellow
111	Gray	White

Place First Class
Postage Here
Post Office
Will Not Deliver
Without Postage

Brady Books
15 Columbus Circle
New York, NY 10023

ATT: J. Padlad

Double Scanning   ⊘

When operating in CGA compatible modes, the VGA display adapter uses a technique known as Double Scanning to display the low resolution (200 scan line) CGA display on the high resolution (400 scan line) VGA display. Each of the 200 horizontal scan lines is displayed twice, increasing the vertical screen resolution from 200 scan lines to 400 scan lines. This improves the quality of the display, and helps compensate for the different aspect ratio of the VGA display. Double Scanning is used for modes 0, 1, 2, 3, 4, 5, 6, D, and E.

Modes 0* and 1* (Color Text)

Modes 0* and 1* are enhanced versions of modes 0 and 1. The display is formatted as 40 character columns by 25 character rows. The CGA 8 pixel by 8 pixel character set is replaced with the EGA enhanced 8 pixel by 14 pixel character set. This mode cannot be used with the standard CD; an ECD, multifrequency display, or VGA is required.

While this mode offers a more readable display than modes 0 and 1, the compatibility level with CGA is even lower due to the differences in the character sets. This can interfere with the operation of certain functions such as cursor display and character underlining.

As with modes 0 and 1, there are 8 pages of display memory that can be addressed by the processor at these addresses:

Page 0 - B800:0000   Page 4 - B800:2000
Page 1 - B800:0800   Page 5 - B800:2800
Page 2 - B800:1000   Page 6 - B800:3000
Page 3 - B800:1800   Page 7 - B800:3800

Eight standard display colors plus eight intensified colors are supported. Each character is independently programmable for foreground color and background color. Table 1-3 lists the standard color text attributes. For more information on text attributes, see Chapter 2.

Modes 2 and 3 (Color Text)   ⇒

Modes 2 and 3 are the 80 column counterparts to the 40 column modes 0 and 1. On the EGA, there is no functional difference between mode 2 and mode 3. As with modes 0 and 1, these two modes were brought forward from the CGA video adapter, and the distinction between them disappeared with the CGA Composite Video output jack. Modes 2 and 3 display color text on the CD, ECD, VGA display, or some multifrequency displays at a resolution of 80 character columns by 25 character rows. The CGA character set is used, with its 8 pixel by 8 pixel character cell and poor text quality.

EGA and VGA both support 8 display pages in this mode (except in the case of an IBM EGA with only 64K bytes of display memory installed, when only 4 display pages are supported). A BIOS call is the preferred method for switching display pages, though the same result can be achieved by altering the Start Address register in the CRT Controller (see Chapter 3). The display pages can be accessed by the processor at the following memory addresses:

Page 0 - B800:0000	Page 4 - B800:4000
Page 1 - B800:1000	Page 5 - B800:5000
Page 2 - B800:2000	Page 6 - B800:6000
Page 3 - B800:3000	Page 7 - B800:7000

Eight standard display colors plus eight intensified colors are supported. Each character is independently programmable for foreground color and background color. Table 1-3 lists the standard color text attributes. For more information on text attributes, see Chapter 2.

When operating in this mode, the VGA adapter uses a technique known as Double Scanning.

Modes 2* and 3* (Color Text) ➡

Modes 2* and 3* are enhanced versions of modes 2 and 3. The display is formatted as 80 character columns by 25 character rows. The CGA 8 pixel by 8 pixel character set is replaced with the EGA enhanced 8 pixel by 14 pixel character set. This mode cannot be used with the standard CD; an ECD, VGA, or multifrequency display is required.

While this mode offers a more readable display than modes 2 and 3, the level of compatibility with CGA is even lower due to the differences in the character set. This can interfere with the operation of certain functions such as cursor display and character underlining.

As with modes 2 and 3, there are 8 pages of display memory (except in the case of an IBM EGA with only 64K bytes of display memory installed, when only 4 display pages are supported). A BIOS call is the preferred method for switching display pages, though the same result can be achieved by altering the Start Address register in the CRT Controller (see Chapter 3). The display pages can be accessed by the processor at the following memory locations:

Page 0 - B800:0000   Page 4 - B800:4000
Page 1 - B800:1000   Page 5 - B800:5000
Page 2 - B800:2000   Page 6 - B800:6000
Page 3 - B800:3000   Page 7 - B800:7000

Eight standard display colors plus eight intensified colors are supported. Each character is independently programmable for foreground color and background color. Table 1-3 lists the standard color text attributes. For more information on text attributes, see Chapter 2.

Modes 4 and 5 (Four Color 320 x 200 Graphics)

Modes 4 and 5 are very popular CGA graphics modes that were also carried forward to EGA and VGA. The distinction between these modes disappeared with the CGA Composite Video output jack. Display resolution is 320 pixels horizontally by 200 pixels vertically. These modes are compatible with the CD, ECD, some multifrequency displays, or VGA displays.

Four colors can be displayed from either the standard color set or the alternate color set. Table 1-4 lists the standard and alternate colors.

As with all standard CGA modes, compatibility on the EGA and VGA is not complete. Software that writes directly to I/O registers of the CGA may not function properly on EGA. Software that makes use of BIOS calls to configure the registers will usually operate properly. For more information see the section on Compatibilty Modes later in this chapter.

Table 1-4. Standard colors - modes 4 and 5.

Standard Colors	Alternate Colors
Black	Black
Light Cyan	Green
Light Magenta	Red
White	Brown

Only one page of display memory is available, located at address B800:0000. Four color pixel data is stored in a packed pixel format with two bits per pixel (for details see section Display Memory in Graphics Modes in Chapter 2).

When operating in modes 4 and 5, the VGA adapter uses a technique known as Double Scanning.

CGA Graphics Modes present an unusual set of challenges for the graphics programmer. The CRT Controller used on the CGA (Motorola 6845) is limited to 128 scan lines of vertical resolution when operating in a graphics mode. To achieve 200 lines of vertical resolution, the CRT Controller is placed in a text mode and programmed to generate 100 rows of characters, each character being two lines tall. The bit-mapped display memory is then addressed as if it were a character generator. The result is that the display memory is not linearly mapped. A computation is required to translate from a pixel location on screen to a location in display memory. For an explanation of the CGA graphics memory map, see section Display Memory In Graphics Modes in Chapter 2.

Mode 6 (Two Color 640 x 200 Graphics)

Mode 6 is the highest resolution graphics mode of the CGA, carried forward to EGA and VGA. A screen resolution of 640 pixels horizontally by 200 pixels vertically is supported, but only in two colors. This mode is compatible with the CD, ECD, VGA displays, and some multifrequency displays.

As with all standard CGA modes on the EGA, compatibility is not complete. Software that writes directly to I/O registers of the CGA may not function properly on EGA. Software that makes use of BIOS calls to configure the registers will usually operate properly.

As explained for modes 4 and 5, the display memory is not linearly mapped. A computation is required to translate from a pixel position on the screen to an address in display memory. Details are given in the section on Display Memory in Graphics Modes in Chapter 2.

Only one page of display memory is available, accessible to the processor at memory address B800:0000.

When operating in mode 6, the VGA adapter uses Double Scanning.

Mode 7 (Monochrome Text)   ⏩

In Mode 7, the EGA and VGA are partially software compatible with the Monochrome Display Adapter (MDA). A monochrome display or VGA display is required for this mode. The display is formatted as 80 character columns by 25 character rows. The character set uses an 8-pixel wide by 14-pixel tall character cell. Each character is then padded to 9 pixels wide on the screen in order to fill the Monochrome Display's 720 horizontal pixels.

The insertion of a ninth column on the character cell creates an interesting problem for both MDA and EGA. The IBM character set includes block graphics (also called line graphics) characters that allow primitive graphics objects to be drawn on the screen (such as borders and boxes). These graphics objects should appear continuous. A blank ninth bit on each character would appear as holes in all such objects. IBM's solution for this is simple. If a block graphics character is displayed, all bits in the eighth bit position will be replicated in the ninth bit position (for that character only). This feature can be enabled or disabled through a control register. Block graphics characters are ASCII values between C0 hex and DF hex.

EGA supports 8 display pages in this mode (except in the case of an IBM EGA with only 64K bytes of display memory installed, when only 4 display pages are supported). A BIOS call is the preferred method for selecting pages for display, though the same result can be achieved by altering the Start Address register in the CRT Controller (see Chapter 3). The display pages can be accessed by the processor at the following memory locations:

Page 0 - B000:0000   Page 4 - B000:4000
Page 1 - B000:1000   Page 5 - B000:5000
Page 2 - B000:2000   Page 6 - B000:6000
Page 3 - B000:3000   Page 7 - B000:7000

In monochrome text mode, character attributes no longer control character color but represent other display characteristics. Monochrome text attributes include character blink, intensify, underline, and reverse video. For a description of monochrome text attributes, see Monochrome Text Attributes in Chapter 2.

Mode D (Sixteen Color 320 x 200 Graphics)   ⁞➡

Unlike modes previously described, this mode is not a backward compatibility mode for CGA or MDA. It is loosely patterned after mode 4 (CGA 4 color graphics), but offers more colors. The limited resolution of mode D (320 horizontal pixels by 200 vertical pixels) makes it undesirable for new software applications, yet it is not software compatible with any older applications. The result is a mode that is rarely used. Mode D is compatible with the CD, ECD, VGA displays, and some multifrequency displays.

For EGA adapters with a full 256K bytes of display memory, there are 8 pages of display memory available in mode D. For IBM EGA adapters with only 128K bytes of display memory installed, only 4 pages are available. With only 64K bytes of display memory, only 2 pages are available. Display pages are accessable by the processor at these addresses:

Page 0 - A000:0000   Page 4 - A000:4000
Page 1 - A000:1000   Page 5 - A000:5000
Page 2 - A000:2000   Page 6 - A000:6000
Page 3 - A000:3000   Page 7 - A000:7000

Mode D does not suffer from the nonlinear memory mapping that CGA compatible graphics modes do, and translating from a pixel position on the screen to a location in display memory is relatively straightforward. Details are given in the section on Display Memory In Graphics Modes in Chapter 2.

The standard colors supported by mode D are shown in Table 1-5.

When operating in mode D, the VGA adapter uses Double Scanning.

Mode E (Sixteen Color 640 x 200 Graphics)   ⟫

Mode E is not a CGA or MDA compatibility mode. It is loosely patterned after CGA mode 6 (2 color graphics), but offers more colors. Its limited resolution (640 horizontal pixels by 200 vertical pixels) makes it unpopular for new software development, and it is not compatible with any existing software. The result is that mode E is a rarely used mode. Mode E is compatible with the CD, ECD, VGA displays, and some multifrequency displays.

For EGA adapters with a full 256K bytes of display memory, there are 4 pages of display memory available in mode E. For IBM EGA adapters with only 128K bytes of display memory installed, only 2 pages are available. With only 64K bytes of display memory, only 1 page is available. These pages are accessible to the processor at these addresses:

Page 0 - A000:0000
Page 1 - A000:4000
Page 2 - A000:8000
Page 3 - A000:C000

This mode does not suffer from the nonlinear memory mapping that CGA compatible graphics modes do, and translating from a pixel position on the screen to a location in display memory is relatively simple. Details are given in the section on Display Memory In Graphics Modes in Chapter 2.

The standard colors supported by mode E are shown in Table 1-5.

When operating in mode E, the VGA adapter uses Double Scanning.

Mode F (Monochrome 640 x 350 Graphics)   ⟫

Graphics mode F is unique to the EGA and VGA. It is not a compatibility mode. A Monochrome Display or VGA display is required. Resolution in mode F is 640 horizontal pixels by 350 vertical pixels, which is less than the 720 horizontal by 348 vertical resolution of the Hercules monochrome graphics adapter.

Mode F does not suffer from the non-linear display memory address mapping of the Hercules adapter. The display memory is linearly mapped.

Two pages of display memory are available (except in the case of an IBM EGA with only 64K bytes of display memory installed, when only one page is supported). These pages are accessable to the processor at these addresses:

Page 1 - A000:0000
Page 2 - A000:8000

Two "color" planes of display memory are used, giving each monochrome pixel four attributes. These attributes are:

00 - black
01 - white
10 - blinking
11 - intensified

The memory planes can be enabled and disabled independently by writing to the plane enable register in the sequencer (see Chapter 3).

Mode 10 (Enhanced Color 640 x 350 Graphics)

Mode 10, which is unique to the EGA and VGA, is the most popular mode for new color graphics applications. It supports a resolution of 640 horizontal pixels by 350 vertical pixels. This mode is not compatible with the Color Display (an ECD, VGA, or multifrequency display is required). Four color planes are used, yielding up to 16 simultaneous colors (except in the case of an IBM EGA with only 64K bytes of display memory installed, when only two planes are supported). Color planes are enabled and disabled by writing to the plane enable register in the sequencer (see Chapter 3).

Two pages of display are available (except in the case of an IBM EGA with only 64K bytes of display memory installed, when only one page is supported). The display pages are accessable to the processor at addresses A000:0000 and A000:8000.

The standard color palette used with mode 10 is shown in Table 1-5. This color palette can be modified by reprogramming the palette registers of the attribute controller (see Chapter 3).

Table 1-5. Standard color palette for sixteen color modes.

Plane 3 2 1 0	Full (128K+) Colors	Partial (64 KB) Colors
0 0 0 0	Black	Black
0 0 0 1	Blue	Blue
0 0 1 0	Green	Black
0 0 1 1	Cyan	Blue
0 1 0 0	Red	Red
0 1 0 1	Magenta	White
0 1 1 0	Brown	Red
0 1 1 1	White	White
1 0 0 0	Dark Gray	Black
1 0 0 1	Light Blue	Blue
1 0 1 0	Light Green	Black
1 0 1 1	Light Cyan	Blue
1 1 0 0	Light Red	Red
1 1 0 1	Light Magenta	White
1 1 1 0	Yellow	Red
1 1 1 1	Intens. White	White

Additional VGA Modes ⊘

These modes are unique to the VGA. A VGA or multifrequency display is required.

Modes 0+, 1+ (Color Text) ⊘

These modes are enhanced versions of the standard CGA compatibility modes 0 and 1. The screen format is 40 character columns by 25 character rows. The standard CGA character set, which uses a character cell that is 8 pixels wide by 8 pixels tall, is replaced with a VGA enhanced character set in which the character cell is 9 pixels wide by 16 pixels tall.

This mode is subject to all the same compatibility problems that were described for compatibility modes 0* and 1*.

Modes 2+, 3+ (Color Text) ⊘

These modes are enhanced versions of the standard CGA compatibility modes 2 and 3. The screen format is 80 character columns by 25 character rows. The standard CGA character set, which uses a character cell that is 8 pixels wide by 8 pixels tall, is replaced with a VGA enhanced character set in which the character cell is 9 pixels wide by 16 pixels tall.

This mode is subject to all the same compatibility problems that were described for compatibility modes 2* and 3*.

Mode 7+ (Monochrome Text)   ⊘

This mode is a standard MDA text emulation, but uses the VGA 9 x 16 character set. It carries the same kinds of compatibility problems described for other modes that use enhanced character sets.

Mode 11 (Two Color 640 x 480 Graphics)   ⊘

While mode 11 supports the VGA at its highest resolution (640 horizontal pixels by 480 vertical pixels), it supports only two simultaneous colors. This mode can be used to display 30 rows of 80 column text. The base memory address for this mode is at A000:0000.

Mode 12 (Sixteen Color 640 x 480 Graphics)   ⊘

Mode 12 supports the VGA at its highest resolution (640 horizontal pixels by 480 vertical), with 16 simultaneous colors. Table 1-3 shows the standard colors supported in this mode. The base memory address is at A000:0000.

Mode 13 (256 Color 320 x 200 Graphics)   ⊘

This mode allows the use of 256 simultaneous colors, but at a very low resolution (320 pixels horizontally by 200 pixels vertically). The base memory address is at A000:0000.

EGA at Higher Resolutions

As an attempt to gain an edge in a highly competitive marketplace, some vendors of EGA compatible products provide software drivers that allow their video adapters to operate at higher resolutions (typically 640 horizontal pixels by 480 vertical, 800 x 600 and even 1024 x 768). A multifrequency display is required with drivers of this type.

These higher resolution modes are not always given full BIOS support by the manufacturer. They are often implemented as RAM resident device drivers and intended to support only a single application or environment. Such drivers have been written for Microsoft Windows, Digital Research GEM, Lotus 1-2-3, AutoCAD and other popular programs.

Compatibility Modes ➠

In the quest for a competitive edge, some manufacturers of EGA compatible display adapters have added new modes, claiming "true CGA compatibility" and "true Hercules compatibility." While these added modes usually work well with a majority of the most popular software packages, true 100 percent compatibility is not attainable. This subject has particular significance to the authors, who were responsible for the design of one of the first of these "enhanced EGAs."

The incompatibilities between EGA and the 6845 based adapters (MDA, CGA, and Hercules) are due to several factors. The internal register set of the EGA CRT controller is similar, but not identical to that of the 6845. Software that writes directly to I/O registers is therefore likely to have compatibility problems.

Many EGA compatible products with added compatibility modes use a series of CPU interrupts, with additional BIOS firmware, to try to straighten out these problems "on the fly" as they occur. This technique, while it works well for many cases, simply cannot handle all potential compatibility problems. A better technique, which is now being used by some vendors, requires that the VLSI circuitry of the EGA be modified so that it can operate identically to the 6845 CRT controller.

EGA compatible display adapters that rely on interrupt vectors usually cannot invoke their CGA or Hercules emulations until after the system BIOS has finished initializing the system vector table. On many machines (including the IBM AT), this means that the emulations cannot be invoked on power-up or reset, but must be enabled after DOS is loaded. This destroys any hope of compatibility with programs that execute without DOS (these are typically game programs, which require the user to insert the game disk into drive A, then reset the system).

Another set of compatibility problems are brought on by the architecture of the display memory on the EGA, which is plane oriented. Any software that changes the operating mode of the display adapter, and then makes assumptions about the content of display memory, may suffer from compatibility problems. Some programs exist that clear the display memory in one mode, then change modes, and assume that the display memory is still cleared.

Yet another potential compatibility problem is caused by the very existence of the EGA BIOS. Some application programs are designed to recognize the presence of this BIOS in the system and switch automatically into an EGA mode. These programs may yield unpredictable results if the EGA is configured to emulate a different display adapter.

The light pen circuits of the EGA are not compatible to those of the CGA. Light pen software will typically get erroneous light pen position readings.

The best advice we can offer to anyone who is concerned about the quality of the CGA or Hercules emulations on his or her EGA compatible adapter is to test the adapter with the software to be used before buying it.

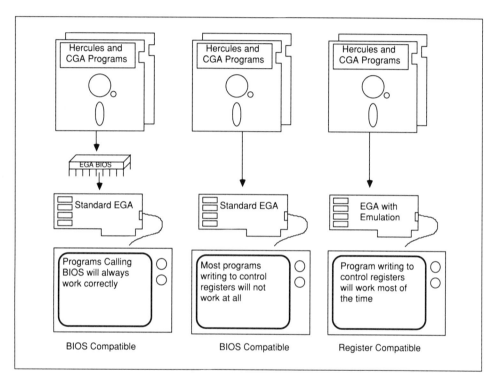

Figure 1-2. BIOS compatibility vs. register compatibility.

Dual Display Systems

The EGA is capable of co-existing with another display adapter, providing that certain guidelines are met:

• One display must be monochrome, and the other one color.

• Two EGAs cannot coexist.

If the EGA is driving a color display, it may co-exist with an MDA or Hercules adapter driving a monochrome display (the Hercules card must be configured in

HALF mode, not FULL mode, or its second page of display memory will overlay the EGA display memory). If the EGA is driving a monochrome display, it may co-exist with a CGA driving a color display.

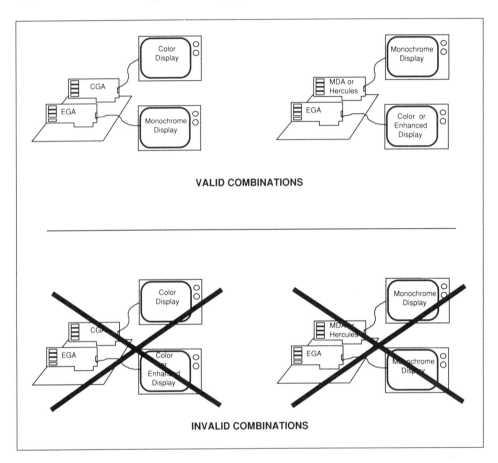

Figure 1-3. Dual adapter combinations.

The Primary Display is the display that is being used as the Console Device. This is the display to which MS-DOS directs all output. High level language librar-ies (such as C and Pascal) normally direct output to the console device. Either dis-play may be used as the primary system console device. The MS-DOS MODE CO80 and MODE MONO commands can be used to reassign the console device dynamically.

Some applications programs (such as Lotus 1-2-3 and Autocad) let the user select which display to use without regard to which display is primary.

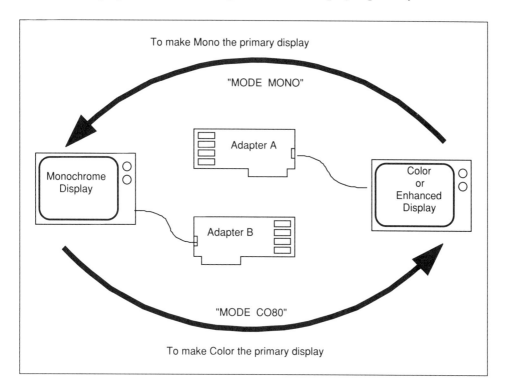

To make Mono the primary display

"MODE MONO"

Adapter A

Monochrome
Display

Color
or
Enhanced
Display

Adapter B

"MODE CO80"

To make Color the primary display

Figure 1-4. Changing primary adapter.

EGA Installation

Installation of an EGA involves a battery of configuration issues, such as how to configure the system board, which display to use, which operating mode(s) to select, and how to set the EGA configuration switches.

While most of the EGA compatible adapters on the market are closely patterned after the original IBM adapter, some EGA compatible products include features or installation requirements that are unique. It is important to study the installation instructions that are provided with the product. The installation procedure described here should be used as a general guideline only.

In the IBM XT, and many compatible machines, the system display device is defined by switches 5 and 6 on switch pack 1 of the system motherboard, according to the following format:

SW1-6	SW1-5	Display Adapter
OFF	OFF	MDA
OFF	ON	CGA (80 x 25)
ON	OFF	CGA (40 x 25)
ON	ON	EGA (or no display)

The switch setting used for EGA (switches 5 and 6 both ON) was originally defined by IBM to mean that no display adapter is present in the system. To the XT BIOS, there is no difference between these two conditions since the EGA adapter has its own on board BIOS to handle display initialization and video services.

Configuration of the IBM AT is very different. Instead of switches, a battery-backed memory is used to retain system configuration information. A menu driven utility program called SETUP is used to define the system configuration.

Table 1-6. EGA configuration switches.

S4	S3	S2	S1	Primary Adapter	Secondary Adapter
Off	Off	Off	Off	— INVALID —	
Off	Off	Off	On	— INVALID —	
Off	Off	On	Off	— INVALID —	
Off	Off	On	On	— INVALID —	
Off	On	Off	Off	EGA - Monochrome	CGA - 80 x 25
Off	On	Off	On	EGA - Monochrome	CGA - 40 x 25
Off	On	On	Off	EGA-80 x 25-Enhanced	Monochrome
Off	On	On	On	EGA-80 x 25-CGA Text	Monochrome
On	Off	Off	Off	EGA-80 x 25-CGA Text	Monochrome
On	Off	Off	On	EGA-40 x 25-CGA Text	Monochrome
On	Off	On	Off	CGA - 80 x 25	EGA - Monochrome
On	Off	On	On	CGA - 40 x 25	EGA - Monochrome
On	On	Off	Off	Monochrome	EGA-80 x 25-Enhanced
On	On	Off	On	Monochrome	EGA-80 x 25-CGA Text
On	On	On	Off	Monochrome	EGA-80 x 25-CGA Text
On	On	On	On	Monochrome	EGA-40 x 25-CGA Text

2

The Architecture of the EGA/VGA

Overview

Those readers who are familiar with either the CGA or Hercules display adapters will find similarities in the architecture of the EGA and VGA. In some ways, these newer display adapters represent an evolution of the technology used on the older adapters. EGA and VGA are more complex than their predecessors, however, and more effort will be required to fully understand how to use them.

Like their predecessors, the EGA and VGA are nonintelligent display devices; they have no on-board drawing or processing capability. The system processor is directly responsible for drawing directly into display memory. Essentially, writing a one bit into display memory is equivalent to lighting one pixel on the display screen. Most of the circuitry of the EGA and VGA is dedicated to the task of transferring the data in display memory onto the display screen. This process, called display refresh, must be performed 60 times a second for the EGA (70 times a second for VGA).

In color display systems, the number of colors that can be displayed is governed by the number of bits of display memory that are dedicated to color information for each pixel. If n bits per pixel are used, 2^n color combinations can be generated. EGA uses from one to four bits per pixel, permitting up to 16 (2^4) colors to be displayed on the screen at the same time. In other words, the EGA is capable of 16 simultaneous colors. The VGA has an added mode that supports 8 bits per pixel, or 256 (2^8) simultaneous colors.

Packed Pixels vs. Color Planes

Two common techniques for storing color information are the packed pixel method and the color plane method. EGA and VGA are color plane oriented devices, but both adapters, in addition to planar pixels, also support emulation modes that use packed pixels.

With packed pixels, all color information for a pixel is packed into one word of memory data. For a system with few colors, this packed pixel may require only part of one byte of memory; for very elaborate systems, a packed pixel might be several bytes long. Using 4 bits per pixel, a packed pixel looks as shown in Figure 2-1.

With the color plane approach, the display memory is separated into several independent planes of memory, with each plane dedicated to controlling one color component (such as red, green, or blue). Each pixel of the display occupies one bit position in each plane. This approach is shown in Figure 2-2.

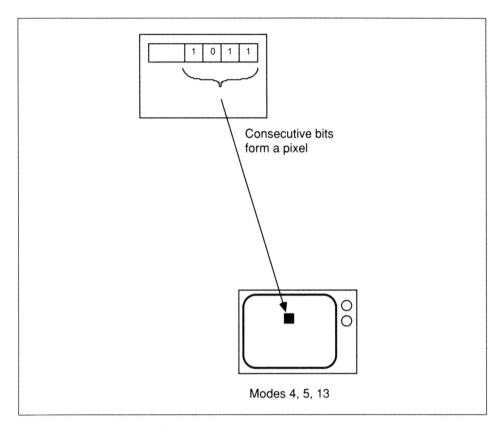

Figure 2-1. Packed pixels.

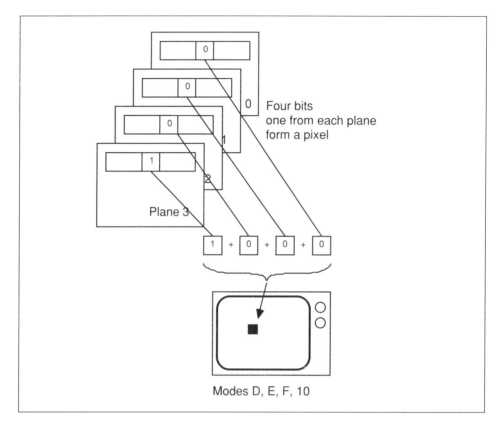

Figure 2-2. Planar pixels.

Text Modes vs. Graphics Modes

Two basic types of operating modes exist for the EGA and VGA: text mode and graphics mode. In graphics modes (which IBM frequently refers to as ALL POINTS ADDRESSABLE modes), a single bit in display memory represents a single pixel on the display screen. In text modes, however, a single byte ASCII character code placed in display memory causes an entire text character to be displayed on the screen. Text modes require much less display memory and place less burden on the system processor, but they are very limited in that only text and crude block graphics objects can displayed (see Figure 2-3).

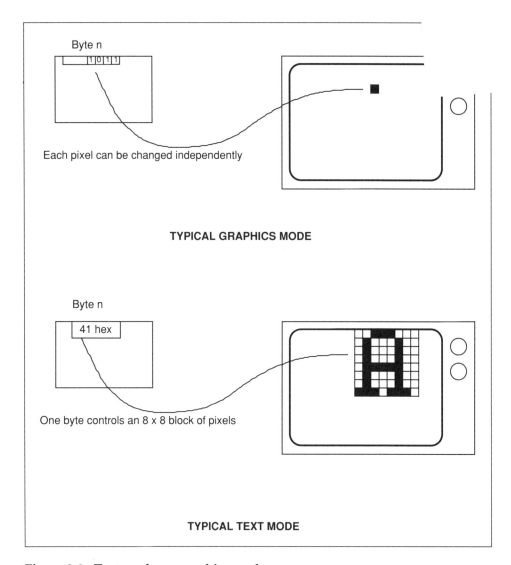

Figure 2-3. Text mode vs. graphics mode.

Architecture of EGA and VGA

Figure 2-4 illustrates the basic architecture of the EGA, which consists of six major pieces:

- The **Display Memory** is a bank of 256K bytes of dynamic random access memory (DRAM), divided into four color planes, which holds the screen display data.

- The **Graphics Controller** resides in the data path between the processor and display memory. It can be programmed to perform logical functions (such as AND, OR, XOR, or ROTATE) on data being written to display memory. These logical functions can provide a hardware assist to simplify drawing operations.

- The **CRT Controller** generates timing signals (such as syncing and blanking) to control the operation of the CRT Display and display refresh timing.

- The **Data Serializer** captures display information that is taken from display memory one or more bytes at a time, and converts it to a serial bit stream to be sent to the CRT display.

- The **Attribute Controller** contains the Color Look-up Table (LUT), which translates color information from the display memory into color information for the CRT display. Because of the relatively high cost of display memory, a practical display system will typically use a display that supports many more colors than the matching display adapter can simultaneously display. By programming a LUT on the display adapter, programmers can select which subset of the display's colors will be supported for their software. The EGA adapter supports 16 simultaneous colors, while the ECD can display 64 different colors. By programming the EGA Color Look-up Table, any 16 simultaneous colors can be selected from the palette of 64 colors.

- The **Sequencer** controls the overall timing of all functions on the board. It also contains logic for enabling and disabling color planes.

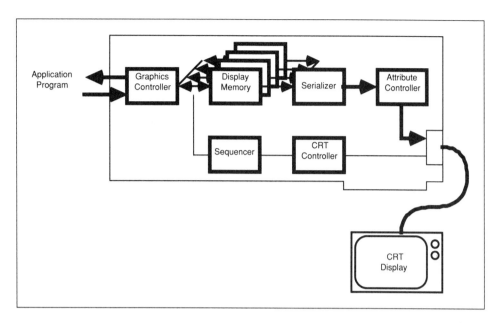

Figure 2-4. EGA/VGA Block diagram.

Unlike the CGA display adapter, the EGA adapter will allow the processor to access display memory while display refresh is in operation. The sequencer controls access to display memory, interleaving display refresh cycles with processor read/write cycles. For the IBM EGA operating in low resolution modes, the processor is allocated three out of every five memory cycles. In high resolution modes, display refreshing requires more data and the processor is allocated only one of every five memory cycles. Because of this interleaving of memory cycles, processor bus wait states are inserted during read or write operations.

Some EGA compatible products from third party vendors have been designed with improved memory timing to reduce the number of wait states that are generated by the board. With these products, the processor is typically allocated every other cycle of display memory while in high resolution modes.

Operation of CRT Displays

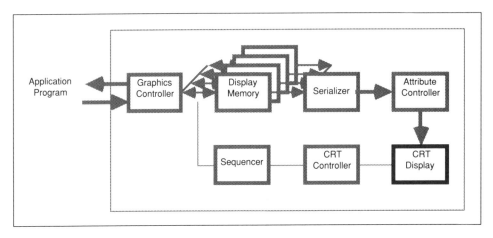

Figure 2-5. The display.

In Cathode Ray Tube (CRT) displays, colors are generated by a beam of electrons that strike the phosphorus coating on the back of the CRT screen and cause it to glow (see Figure 2-5). The electron beam is swept across the display screen from left to right in a series of horizontal lines. At the same time, its intensity is modulated to produce display patterns. The electron beam must continuously redraw the pattern on the screen 50, 60, or 70 times a second, depending on the display used (see Table 1-1). This process is called DISPLAY REFRESH or SCREEN REFRESH.

The sweep pattern of the electron beam on the display screen is called the RASTER. The beam begins in the upper left corner of the display and sweeps right. When it reaches the right edge of the screen, the beam is shut off *(horizontal blanking)* and then rapidly brought back to the left edge of the screen *(horizontal retrace)* to begin the next horizontal scan just below the previous one.

After all horizontal scans have been completed, the electron beam will end up in the lower right corner of the screen. At this point the beam is shut off *(vertical blanking)* and then rapidly brought back up to the upper left corner *(vertical retrace)* so the next raster can begin. This processes is represented in Figure 2-6.

The entire display pattern can be considered as a long serial string of bits that are fed to the electron beam as it passes over the display screen. The horizontal resolution of the display is equal to the number of bits that can be displayed on one horizontal scan line. The area of the screen that is lighted by a single bit in this data stream is called a *pixel*. The vertical resolution of the display is determined by the number of horizontal scans that are made.

Circuitry internal to the CRT display generates the electron beam (or beams, in color displays) and drives it across the display screen, but the display adapter must be capable of controlling the motion of the electron beam so it can be synchronized with the data stream. By pulsing the horizontal sync and vertical sync signals to the display, the adapter controls the timing of horizontal and vertical retrace cycles. By pulsing the blank signal to the display, the adapter performs horizontal and vertical blanking.

Many of the registers of the CRT Controller are dedicated to the task of controlling CRT blanking and retrace signals.

For more information on the CRT controller registers, see section CRT Controller in Chapter 3.

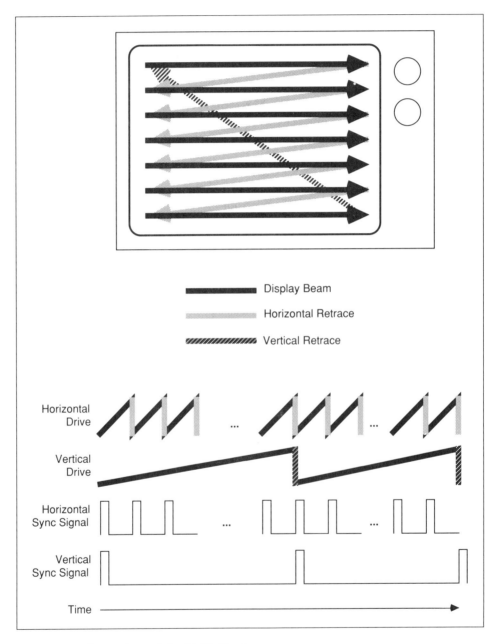

Figure 2-6. Operation of the CRT display.

Display Memory

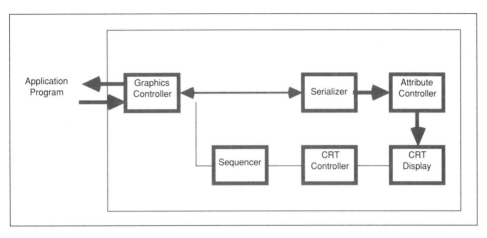

Figure 2-7. The display memory.

The EGA and VGA each contain up to 256K bytes of display memory, divided into four independent 64K byte sections of memory called color planes (see Figure 2-7). These memory planes all reside in the same processor memory space. Which color planes are being written to or read from at any time is determined by the settings of several I/O registers.

With all four memory planes residing in the same address space, the processor can write to all four planes (or any combination thereof) with a single memory write cycle. This capability can be very useful for some drawing operations, such as fast screen fills. In other drawing operations, it may be desirable to disable writing to all but a single memory plane. Color planes are enabled and disabled for writing via the Color Plane Write Enable Register of the Sequencer (see Chapter 3 for details).

Since it would not be meaningful for the processor to attempt to read data from more than one source at a time, only one memory plane may be enabled for reading. A color plane is enabled for reading via the Read Plane Select Register of the Graphics Controller (see Chapter 3). A special mode is provided, however, to read data from multiple color planes, compare it to some preset reference data, and return status to the processor declaring if the colors matched. The color compare function is useful for finding certain patterns in display memory during operations such as area fills. This mode is controlled by the Color Compare Register of the Graphics Controller (see Chapter 3).

In some operating modes, the organization of display memory will be altered. The best example of this is text mode, where even memory addresses (containing

ASCII data) are in color plane 0, odd memory addresses (containing text attributes) are in color plane 1, color plane 2 is reserved for the character generator, and color plane 3 is unused.

For many operating modes, the 64K byte address space of the EGA is divided into several display pages. Application software may then control which page is active (being viewed) at any time, and drawing operations can take place in off-screen display memory.

While the great majority of EGA adapters in use contain a full 256K bytes of display memory, IBM shipped some adapters with only 64K bytes or 128K bytes of display memory installed. These adapters, if not upgraded, have limitations on the number of colors or display pages they will support (see Partial Memory Configurations in Chapter 1).

The processor address space used by the EGA and VGA depends on the operating mode. This address space may begin at address A0000, B0000, or B8000, depending on mode.

Display Memory in Text Modes

Text mode displays have been in common use much longer than graphics displays, and are still very useful in applications that do not require graphics (or in which simple block graphics will suffice). Text modes place a much lower burden on the system processor, which only has to manipulate ASCII character codes rather than individual pixels.

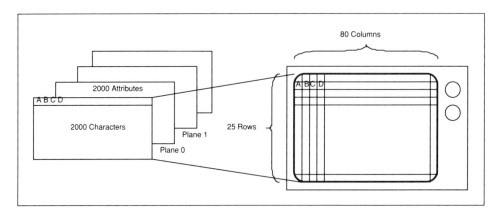

Figure 2-8. Display memory format - text modes.

In standard text modes, the display screen is divided into 25 lines of text, with either 40 or 80 columns of text per line. In 40 column modes, 1000 characters can be displayed on the screen; in 80 column modes, 2000 characters can be displayed (see Figure 2-8). Two bytes of display memory are used to define each character; the first byte, mapped at an even memory address, contains the ASCII character code, and the second byte, mapped at an odd memory address, contains color information called the Character Attribute. 2000 bytes of display memory are needed to define one 40 column page, or 4000 bytes to define one 80 column page. A page of display memory is 4096 bytes long, leaving 96 bytes unused at the end of each page.

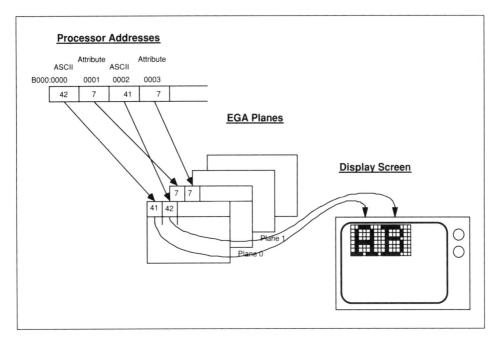

Figure 2-9. Processor addresses and EGA planes.

To convert an ASCII character code into an array of pixels on the screen, a translation table or Character Generator is used. On older display adapters such as MDA and CGA, the character generator is located in ROM (Read Only Memory). EGA and VGA do not use a character generator ROM; instead, character generator data is loaded into plane 2 of the display RAM. This feature makes it easy for custom character sets to be loaded. Multiple character sets (up to 4) may reside in RAM simultaneously. A set of BIOS services are available for easy loading of character sets. For more information on character sets, see the following section on Character Generators.

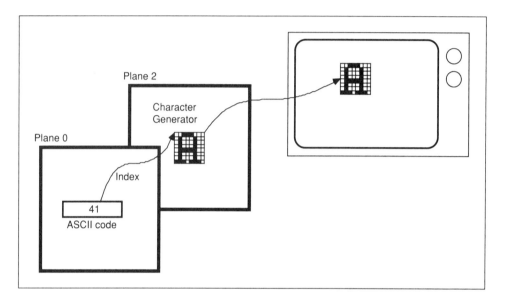

Figure 2-10. Character code as index into character generator.

Character Generators   ⟶

The EGA and VGA adapters provide a flexible mechanism for custom character sets to be loaded (see Figure 2-10). Rather than using a ROM based character generator, character data is stored in plane 2 of the display memory. Up to four character maps (eight for VGA) can be loaded into display RAM simultaneously, with up to 256 characters per map. Either one or two character sets may be active, giving EGA the capability to display up to 512 different characters on the screen simultaneously. When two character sets are active, a bit in each character attribute byte selects which character set will be used for that character. A register in the Sequencer is used to select the active character set.

Character width is fixed at eight pixels (this is stretched to nine for monochrome text). Character height is selectable from 1 to 32 pixels through an output register.

The standard character sets which are provided with the EGA are the CGA character set (8 pixels wide by 8 pixels tall), and the enhanced color character set (8 pixels wide by 14 pixels tall.) One of these character sets is automatically loaded by the BIOS when a text operating mode is selected. If a monochrome text mode is selected, the 8 x 14 enhanced color character set is used, but several characters in the set are replaced with characters that are optimized for the 9 pixel wide monochrome character cell. Because of its higher resolution capabilities, the VGA also includes a 9 pixel wide by 16 pixel tall character set. Custom character sets can be loaded using the BIOS video services (see Chapter 4).

The location of character maps in memory is shown in Table 2-1. Regardless of the character height being used, characters always begin on 32 byte boundaries. For instance, the 8 pixel by 14 pixel character set requires 14 bytes per character, so 18 bytes per character go unused in the character map. Figure 2-11 illustrates how a character map is designed.

Table 2-1. Location of RAM-resident character generators.

Character Map A	Character Map B
0000h to 001Fh - Char. 0	2000h to 201Fh - Char. 0
0020h to 003Fh - Char. 1	2020h to 203Fh - Char. 1
0040h to 005Fh - Char. 2	2040h to 205Fh - Char. 2
.	.
.	.
.	.
1FE0h to 1FFFh - Char. 255	3FE0h to 3FFFh - Char. 255
Character Map C	Character Map D
4000h to 401Fh - Char. 0	6000h to 601Fh - Char. 0
5FE0h to 5FFFh - Char. 255	7FE0h to 7FFFh - Char. 255

For VGA only:

Character Map E	Character Map F
8000h to 801Fh - Char. 0	A000h to A01Fh - Char. 0
9FE0h to 9FFFh - Char. 255	BFE0h to BFFFh - Char. 255
Character Map G	Character Map H
C000h to C01Fh - Char. 0	E000h to E01Fh - Char. 0
DFE0h to DFFFh - Char. 255	FFE0h to FFFFh - Char. 255

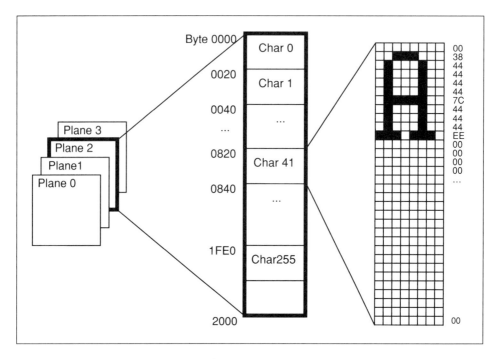

Figure 2-11. Character generator format.

To learn more about character generators, see:

• BIOS function 17 - Load Character Generator (Chapter 4).

• Character Generator Select Register of the Sequencer (Chapter 3).

• Maximum Scan Line Register of the CRT Controller (Chapter 3).

• READ_CHAR_GEN,   WRITE_CHAR_GEN,   ENABLE_512_SET,   and DISABLE_512_SET programming examples (Chapter 7).

Text Attributes

Each ASCII character being displayed on the screen has a corresponding attribute byte to define the colors and other attributes that character will have. The interpretation of text attributes depends on operating mode.

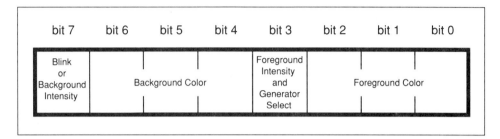

| bit 7 | bit 6 | bit 5 | bit 4 | bit 3 | bit 2 | bit 1 | bit 0 |

| Blink or Background Intensity | Background Color | | | Foreground Intensity and Generator Select | Foreground Color | | |

Figure 2-12. Attribute bits in a byte.

Standard Color Text Attributes

Figure 2-12 shows the bit definitions for text attribute bytes when operating in a standard color text mode. Bits D0-D2, Foreground Color, select the color for the body of the character. Bits D4-D6, Background Color, select the color for the rest of the character cell.

Attribute bit D3 can be used as a foreground color intensity control, effectively doubling the number of foreground colors from 8 to 16.

If two character sets are being used simultaneously (as defined by the Character Generator Select register of the Sequencer,) bit D3 selects which character set will be used. In this case, the color palette registers of the Attribute Controller should be modified to disable D3 from affecting color.

Attribute bit D7 can be used either as a foreground blink enable, causing the character to blink, or as a background intensity control, doubling the number of background colors from 8 to 16. The function of bit D7 is defined in the Mode register of the Attribute Controller. The default setting enables blinking.

Table 2-2 shows the standard colors used for both foreground and background.

Table 2-2. Standard color attributes.

Attribute	Standard Color	Intensified Color
000	Black	Gray
001	Blue	Light Blue
010	Green	Light Green
011	Cyan	Light Cyan
100	Red	Light Red
101	Magenta	Light Magenta
110	Brown	Yellow
111	Gray	White

Monochrome Text Attributes

Table 2-3 shows the bit definitions for a monochrome text attribute byte, which is similar in function to a color text attribute byte. Bits D0-D2 control foreground attributes, which can be normal, blanked, or underlined. Bit D3 will intensify the character foreground. Bits D4-D6 can select a reverse video character. Bit D7 can be used as either foreground blink enable or background intensity control; this function is controlled in the Mode Control register of the Attribute Controller. The default setting enables foreground blinking.

As with color attributes, bit D3 can be used to select between two active character sets.

As can be seen from Table 2-3, there are only a small number of valid text attributes in monochrome mode. All attribute values not shown in Table 2-3 should be considered invalid. Use of invalid attributes will create compatibility problems when software is run on different types of monochrome display adapters (MDA, EGA, and Hercules).

Table 2-3. Monochrome (MDA) text attributes.

Monochrome Display Attributes

00000000	Blank
00000111	Normal character
10000111	Blinking character
00001111	Intensified character
10001111	Blinking intensified character
00000001	Underlined character
10000001	Blink underlined character
00001001	Intensified, underlined character
10001001	Blinking, intensified, underlined character
01110000	Reverse video
11110000	Blinking reverse video

It should be noted that if a character is reverse video it cannot be underlined or intensified.

Custom Text Attributes

By reprogramming the Attribute Controller, the definitions of color attributes can be modified. Figure 2-12 shows how the attribute bits can be used to control color in the general case.

To learn more about text attributes, see:

- BIOS function 8 - read character and attribute (Chapter 4).

- BIOS function 9 - write character and attribute (Chapter 4).

- BIOS function 16 - set EGA palette registers (Chapter 4).

- WRITE_ATTRIBUTE programming example (Chapter 7).

Display Memory in Graphics Modes

Mode 6 (CGA Two Color Graphics)

At 640 pixels horizontally and 200 pixels vertically, Mode 6 is the highest resolution mode of the CGA adapter. It uses only one bit per pixel (8 pixels per byte). A pixel value of zero displays black, and a pixel value of one displays white. Pixel data is stored in color plane 0. Display data is serialized most significant bit first, so the first bit position in the upper left corner of the screen displays the data in bit D7 of byte 0 of display memory.

Limitations of the 6845 CRT Controller which was used on the CGA resulted in a non-linearly mapped display memory address space for all graphics modes. This complicates drawing algorithms, since a computation is required to translate between a pixel position on the display screen and a bit position in display memory.

Figure 2-13 illustrates the translation that occurs between the display memory and the display screen. The first half of display memory contains the data for all odd numbered CRT scan lines. The second half of display memory contains the data for all even numbered scan lines. To translate from a pixel position (x,y) on the display screen, where x is the horizontal coordinate in the range 0-639 and y is the vertical coordinate in the range 0-199, to a bit position in display memory use the following formula:

Byte address = 80 * (y/2) + (x/8)   if y is even
Byte address = 4096 + 80 * ((y-1)/2) + (x/8)   if y is odd
bit position (0-7) = 7 - (x modulo 8)

(The modulo operator is equivalent to taking the remainder of x/8).

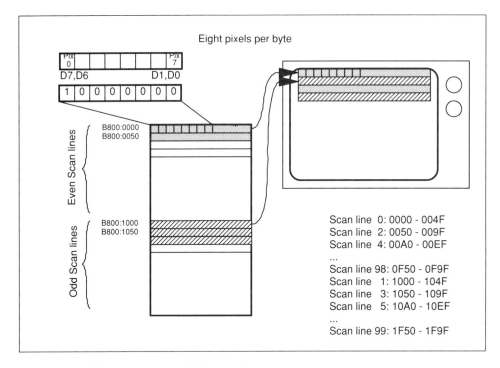

Figure 2-13. Memory map - CGA graphics mode 6.

Modes 4 and 5 (CGA 4 Color Graphics)

These are the most colorful, as well as most popular, graphics modes of the CGA adapter. The resolution is low; only 320 pixels horizontally by 200 pixels vertically. The display memory map uses packed pixels, two bits per pixel, packed four pixels per byte. Pixel data is stored in plane 0. Display data is serialized most significant bit first, so the first bit position in the upper left of the screen displays the data in bits D7 and D6 of byte 0 of display memory.

As with all CGA graphics modes, the display memory is nonlinearly mapped. A computation is required to translate from a pixel location on the display screen to a bit location in display memory. Figure 2-14 illustrates the memory map for modes 4 and 5. The first half of display memory contains the data for all odd numbered scan lines. The second half of display memory contains the data for all even numbered scan lines.

To translate from a pixel location (x,y) on the screen to a bit location in display memory, where x is a horizontal coordinate in the range 0-320 and y is a vertical coordinate in the range 0-199, use the following formula:

Byte address = 80 * (y/2) + (x/4)   if y is even
Byte address = 4096 + 80 * ((y-1)/2) + (x/4)   if y is odd
Bit position (0,2,4,6) = (x modulo 4) * 2

Two standard color sets are supported in modes 4 and 5. A BIOS call (BIOS function 11) is used to select colors. The standard colors for modes 4 and 5 are shown in Table 2-4.

Table 2-4. Standard colors-modes 4 and 5.

Pixel Value	Standard Color	Alternate Color
00	Black	Black
01	Light Cyan	Green
10	Light Magenta	Red
11	Intensified White	Brown

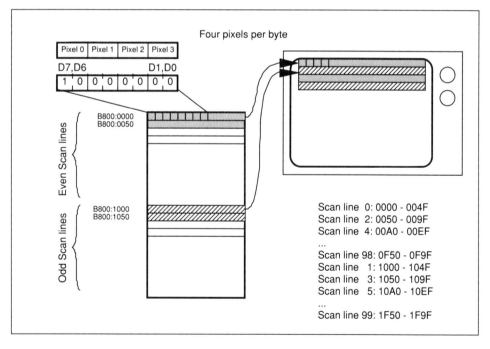

Figure 2-14. Memory map - CGA graphics modes 4 and 5.

Mode F - Monochrome Graphics   ⫸

Mode F, which is unique to EGA and VGA, does not suffer from the nonlinear addressing problems of CGA graphics modes. Resolution is 640 pixels horizontally by 350 pixels vertically. Two color planes are used (planes 0 and 1). Each pixel occupies one bit in each color plane. The four "colors" supported by these two-bit pixels are black, white, intensified white, and blinking. The two color planes are independently enabled and disabled for writing through the Color Plane Write Enable register of the Sequencer.

Figure 2-15 illustrates the memory map for mode F. To translate from a pixel (x,y) on the screen to a bit location in display memory, where x is a horizontal coordinate in the range 0-639 and y is a vertical coordinate in the range 0-349, use the following formula:

Byte address = y * 80 + x/8
Bit position (0-7) = 7 - (x modulo 8)

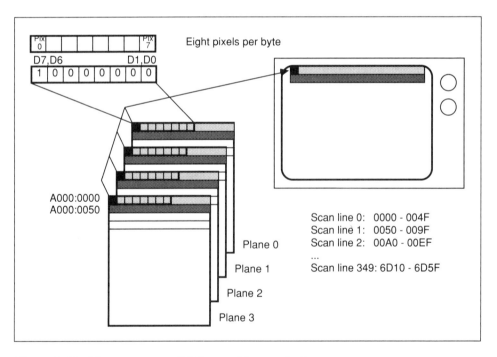

Figure 2-15. Memory map - EGA graphics mode F.

Mode 10 HEX - Enhanced Color Graphics Ⅲ➡

Mode 10, which is unique to EGA and VGA, is the most popular mode for new color graphics applications. Resolution is 640 pixels horizontally by 350 pixels vertically. All four color planes are used. Color planes are independently enabled and disabled for writing through the Color Plane Write Enable register of the Sequencer. Each pixel occupies one bit in each color plane. These four-bit pixels permit 16 simultaneous colors to be displayed.

Figure 2-16 illustrates the memory map for mode 10h. To translate from a pixel (x,y) on the screen to a bit location in display memory, where x is a horizontal coordinate in the range 0-639 and y is a vertical coordinate in the range 0-349, use the following formula:

Byte address = y * 80 + x/8
Bit position (0-7) = 7 - (x modulo 8)

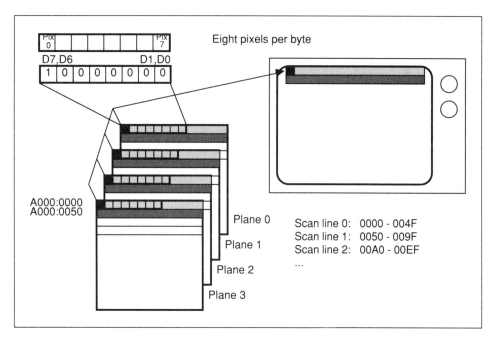

Figure 2-16. Memory map - EGA graphics modes D, E, 10, 12 (VGA).

Modes D and E (Sixteen Color Graphics) Ⅲ➡

Modes D and E are very similar to mode 10 in operation, differing only in screen resolution. Mode D operates at a resolution of 320 pixels horizontally by 200 pixels vertically. Mode E operates at a resolution of 640 pixels horizontally by 200 pixels vertically. These modes have not become popular because of the limited resolution they offer. However these are the only sixteen-color modes available for the Color Display (CD).

Mode 11 HEX - Two Color Graphics   ⊘

Mode 11 is unique to the VGA adapter. Resolution is 640 pixels horizontally by 480 pixels vertically, but only two colors are supported. Display data is stored in plane 0, and the other planes are unused. Each pixel occupies one bit in display memory.

Display memory is linearly mapped (as shown in Figure 2-17). To translate from a pixel (x,y) on the screen to a bit location in display memory, where x is a horizontal coordinate in the range 0-639 and y is a vertical coordinate in the range 0-479, use the following formula:

Byte address = (y * 80) + (x/8)
Bit position (0-7) = 7 - (x modulo 8)

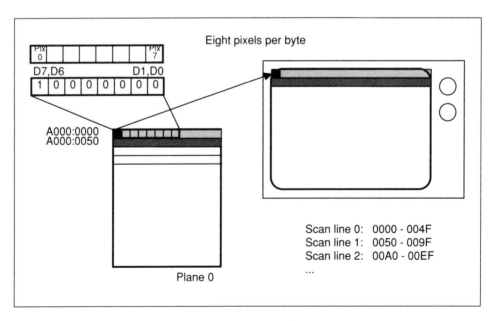

Figure 2-17. Memory map - VGA graphics mode 11.

Mode 12 HEX - Sixteen Color Graphics   ⊘

Mode 12, which is unique to VGA, is similar to mode 10 hex except that there are 480 lines displayed instead of 350. All four color planes are used; 16 simultaneous colors are supported.   The organization of memory is the same as in Figure 2-16.

Mode 13 HEX - 256 Color Graphics   ⊘

Mode 13, which is also unique to VGA, allows 256 simultaneous colors to be used at a low resolution (320 pixels horizontally by 200 vertically). Memory is linearly mapped as shown in Figure 2-18. To translate from a pixel (x,y) on the screen to a bit location in display memory, where x is a horizontal coordinate in the range 0-319 and y is a vertical coordinate in the range 0-199, use the following formula:

Byte address = (y * 320) + x

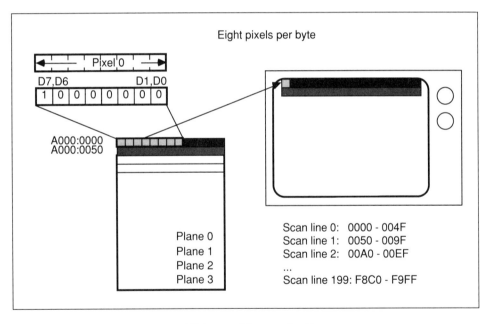

Figure 2-18. Memory map - VGA graphics mode 13.

Hercules Monochrome Graphics

Hercules graphics is not a standard mode for EGA or VGA adapters, but many third party EGA compatible products offer Hercules compatible modes. A discussion of Hercules graphics is therefore included here.

Hercules graphics uses just one bit per pixel (8 pixels per byte). Resolution is 720 pixels horizontally by 348 pixels vertically. The Hercules adapter is based around the 6845 CRT Controller; the Hercules graphics display memory is therefore burdened with a nonlinear address map that is even worse than that of the CGA. Scan line data in Hercules display memory is splintered into four sections as opposed to two for the CGA.

Figure 2-19 illustrates the memory map for Hercules graphics. To translate from a pixel (x,y) on the screen to a bit location in display memory, where x is a horizontal coordinate in the range 0-719 and y is a vertical coordinate in the range 0-347, use the following formula:

Byte address = 90 * (y/4) + (x/8)   if (y modulo 4) = 0
Byte address = 8192 + 90 * ((y-1)/4) + (x/8)   if (y modulo 4) = 1
Byte address = 16384 + 90 * ((y-2)/4) + (x/8)   if (y modulo 4) = 2
Byte address = 24576 + 90 * ((y-3)/4) + (x/8)   if (y modulo 4) = 3
Bit position (0-7) = 7 - (x modulo 8)

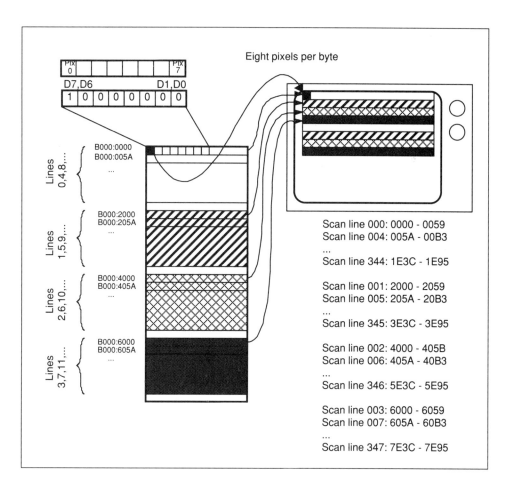

Figure 2-19. Memory map - Hercules graphics mode.

The Graphics Controller

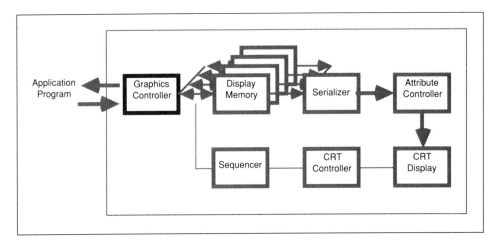

Figure 2-20. Graphics Controller.

The Graphics Controller is a VLSI integrated circuit that resides in the data path between the processor and display memory (see Figure 2-20). In its default state, the Graphics Controller is transparent. Data can be written to and read from display memory with no alterations. The Graphics Controller can, however, be programmed to assist in drawing operations by performing tasks that would otherwise have to be performed by the main processor. Chapter 3 describes the registers of the Graphics Controller in detail.

Processor Read Latches

Every time that the system processor reads data from display memory, the data is also latched into the EGA's on-board read latches. During write cycles, the data in these read latches can be logically combined with write data from the processor. If properly used, this function can assist the processor in performing drawing operations. While the processor can only read data from one plane at a time, the read latches latch data from all four planes simultaneously. This can be used to quickly copy data from one region of display memory to another.

Logical Unit

During display memory write cycles, the Graphics Controller can perform any of the following functions on the write data:

- Write data unmodified

- Logical OR write data with data in read latches

- Logical AND write data with data in read latches

- Logical XOR write data with data in read latches

- ROTATE write data

Logical AND/OR/XOR functions are useful for adding and removing foreground display elements over the background (such as graphics cursors and sprites).

Data rotation is useful when performing block transfers of nonbyte-aligned data.

The function of the graphics controller during write operation is illustrated in Figure 2-21.

To learn more about the proper use of the Read Latches and Logical Unit, see:

- Data Rotate And Function Select Register of the Graphics Controller (Chapter 3).

- Mode Register of the Graphics Controller (Chapter 3).

- Programming Examples - Graphics Operations (Chapter 8).

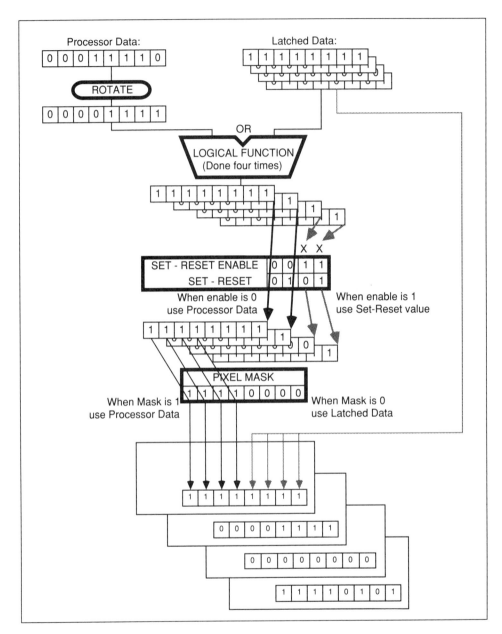

Figure 2-21. Graphics Controller write operations.

Color Compare

During processor read cycles, the Graphics Controller can perform a function called Color Compare, which is useful for drawing algorithms such as FLOOD FILL where a specific screen color or change in color must be detected. Using normal display memory read cycles, the processor may only interrogate one color plane at a time. With Color Compare, however, the processor enters a reference color into a register in the Graphics Controller. During a read cycle, the Graphics Controller compares the data in all four planes (or any selected subset of the four planes) against the reference color and indicates whether a color match was found.

Color Compare provides the ability to search display memory for an object of a specific color, especially when used with the 8086 REP SCASB instruction.

To learn more about the Color Compare function, see:

• The Color Compare Register of the Graphics Controller (Chapter 3).

• The Color Don't Care Register of the Graphics Controller (Chapter 3).

• The Mode Register of the Graphics Controller (Chapter 3).

Data Serializer

The Data Serializer, which is physically located in the same VLSI integrated circuit as the Graphics Controller, captures the data read from display memory during display refresh cycles and converts it into a serial bit stream to drive the CRT display. The only information the application programmer needs to know about the Data Serializer is that display data is serialized most significant bit first.

Attribute Controller

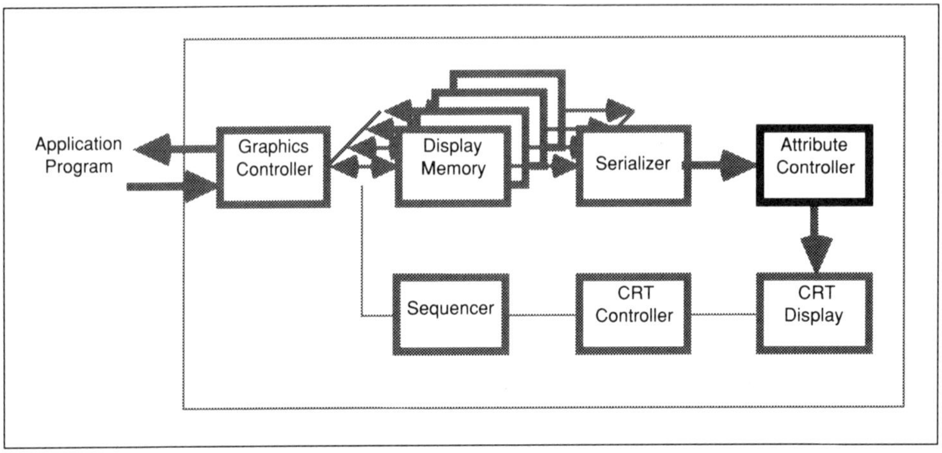

Figure 2-22. Attribute Controller.

The Attribute Controller determines which colors will be displayed for both text and graphics (Figure 2-22). The heart of the Attribute Controller is a Color Look-up Table that translates four bit information from display memory into 6 bit color information (EGA) or 12 bit color information (VGA). Chapter 3 describes the registers of the Attribute Controller in detail.

As part of a BIOS mode select operation, the Color Look-up Table is initialized with data appropriate for that mode. For monochrome modes, the table is initialized with only two colors. For CGA modes, the table is initialized to support the limited colors available with that adapter. For EGA and VGA modes, the table is initialized to support the richer colors of those adapters. Application software may at any time redefine the color palette by reprogramming the Color Look-up Table.

Figure 2-23 illustrates the function of the Color Look-up Table in the Attribute Controller during a screen refresh cycle. In the diagram, a pixel color value of 0111 (binary 7) has been read from the color planes. This color value is used as an address to select a register in the Color Look-up Table. Register 7 in the look-up table contains the binary data value 001001, and this becomes the color data that is output to the display (light blue for mode 10hex).

Note that the color (attribute) is represented in text modes differently than in graphics modes.

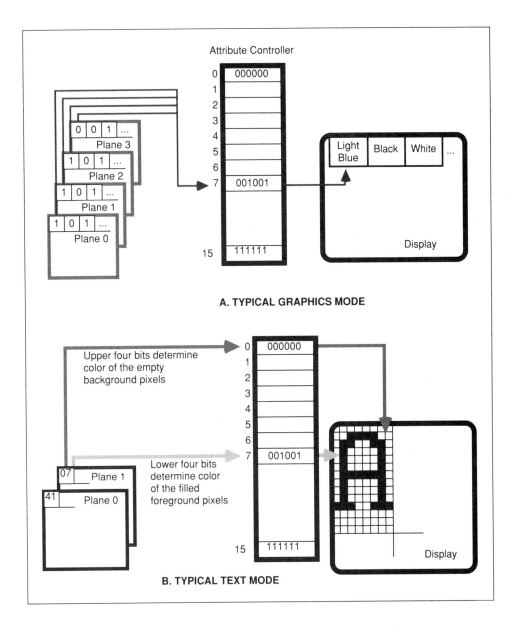

Figure 2-23. Attribute Controller Color Look-up Table (palette).

To learn more about the Color Look-up Table, see:

• BIOS function 11 - Set CGA Color Palette (Chapter 4).

- BIOS function 16 - Set EGA Palette Registers (Chapter 4).

- The Attribute Controller (Chapter 3).

- The WRITE_PALETTE programming example (Chapter 5).

CRT Controller

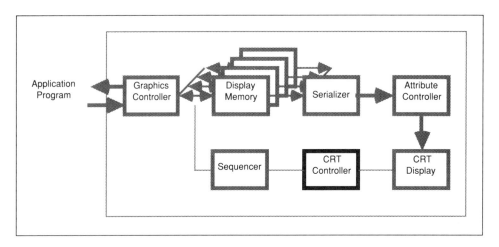

Figure 2-24. The CRT controller.

Most of the registers of the CRT Controller are dedicated to the task of generating the signals that control CRT Raster timing (CRT retrace and blanking). These registers are initialized during a Mode Select according to the display type and mode being used, and are generally not of interest to application programmers (Figure 2-24). Furthermore, modification of these registers can actually be dangerous since improper CRT timing can cause physical damage to the display.

Another set of registers in the CRT Controller are used to define the format of display data on the screen. These display parameters include the number of pixels per scan line, the number of scan lines, the pixel height of text characters, the starting location in display memory for screen refresh, and other related functions. These registers are also initialized by mode select for the mode being used, and in most cases do not require modification, Programmers who are defining custom character sets or modifying the screen format may require access to these registers.

Other CRT Controller registers define cursor shape and position, supply light pen information, and vertical scrolling (including smooth scrolling of text). The recommended method for accessing the cursor and light pen registers is through the BIOS video services.

Chapter 3 describes the registers of the CRT Controller in detail.

The CRT Controller is functionally very similar to the Motorola 6845 CRT Controller used on the MDA, CGA and Hercules display adapters, but it is not register compatible. Software that directly addresses 6845 registers will not, in general, run properly on the EGA or VGA (or vice versa). To make matters even more complicated, the CRT Controller of the VGA is not identical to that of the EGA. For the sake of compatibility, it is a good idea to use the BIOS functions when possible in order to avoid making direct accesses to registers in the CRT Controller.

Sequencer

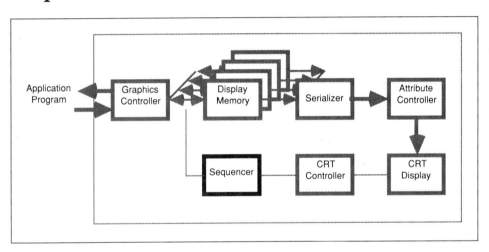

Figure 2-25. The sequencer.

As its name suggests, the sequencer controls the sequencing of all adapter functions (Figure 2-25). It generates the dot and character clocks that control display refresh timing. It controls the timing of display memory read and write cycles, and generates wait states to the processor when necessary.

The sequencer also contains logic for enabling and disabling processor access to specific color planes. It is this function that makes the sequencer interesting to programmers. It's action is illustrated in Figure 2-26. The register set of the sequencer is described in detail in Chapter 3.

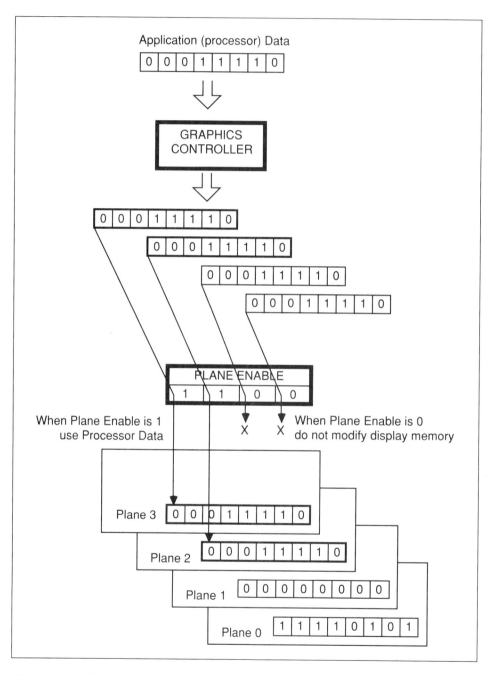

Figure 2-26. Plane write enable function of the sequencer.

3

The EGA Registers

Overview

The I/O mapped EGA register set is, in a word, intimidating. The VGA is even more so. The EGA contains nearly sixty registers, most of them write-only. This is a problem especially for multitasking applications that must save and restore the display state during task switches quickly. Because of this problem, some third party EGA compatible products have added read-back capabilities. The VGA contains even more registers than EGA, but a larger percentage of them are readable. For simplicity, it should be assumed that EGA information in this chapter applies equally to the VGA unless stated otherwise.

To avoid monopolizing a large piece of the processor I/O space, the registers of the EGA are multiplexed into a small number of I/O addresses. In most cases, register access is a two-step procedure of selecting a register through one I/O port, then reading or writing data through a second I/O port. (For information on changing registers, see Chapter 5.)

To further complicate matters, the I/O addresses used depend on the operating mode. To achieve compatibility with both the MDA and CGA display adapters, some I/O addresses must be mapped differently for color modes than for monochrome modes. Tables 3-1 and 3-2 list the I/O addresses used in color and monochrome modes.

Table 3-1. EGA/VGA monochrome I/O map.

I/O Address	Register
3C2	Miscellaneous Output Register
	Input Status Register 0
3BA	Feature Control Register
	Input Status Register 1
3BB	Clear Light Pen Latch
3BC	Set Light Pen Latch
3C4, 3C5	Sequencer
3B4, 3B5	CRT Controller
3CA, 3CC, 3CE, 3CF	Graphics Controller
3C0	Attribute Controller
3C3	VGA enable (VGA only)
3C6, 3C7, 3C8, 3C9	VGA Video DAC

Table 3-2. EGA/VGA color I/O map.

I/O Address	Register
3C2	Miscellaneous Output Register
	Input Status Register 0
3DA	Feature Control Register
	Input Status Register 1
3DB	Clear Light Pen Latch
3DC	Set Light Pen Latch
3C4,3C5	Sequencer
3D4,3D5	CRT Controller
3CA,3CC,	Graphics Controller
3CE,3CF	
3C0	Attribute Controller
3C3	VGA enable (VGA only)
3C6,3C7,	VGA Video DAC
3C8,3C9	

The memory space used by the EGA and VGA also varies depending on operating mode. Table 3-3 shows the address spaces used.

Table 3-3. EGA/VGA memory map.

Memory	Modes
B0000 - B7FFF	7
B8000 - BFFFF	0, 1, 2, 3, 4, 5, 6
A0000 - AFFFF	D, E, F, 10, 11, 12, 13

EGA I/O register addresses can be grouped logically according to function. The CRT Controller, Graphics Controller, Attribute Controller, and Sequencer each has its own set of addresses. Later sections will describe each of these in detail. The remaining registers, which do not belong to any of the major functional blocks, are described in the section on External Registers.

Most of the registers of the EGA are not of practical interest to programmers. Once they are properly initialized by the BIOS for the display mode being used, most registers require no further servicing and can be effectively ignored. In fact, some of these registers can be absolutely dangerous to modify. Many popular displays will literally burn up if driven with improper timing for any length of time as a result of improper register settings.

A small number of EGA registers can be used by the programmer to perform such functions as cursor control, panning and scrolling, split screen displays, and others.

While the chapters that follow will describe all of the EGA registers, a special effort has been made to point out those registers that are most useful, and how to use them, as well as those that are most dangerous. Registers that are dangerous to modify are labeled with the symbol ✳. Registers that are especially useful are labeled with the symbol ★.

When referencing the bits of a register or memory byte, the notation in Figure 3-1 will be used.

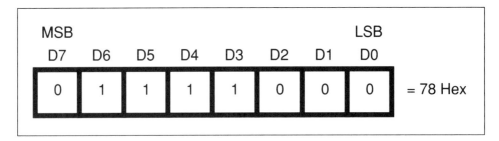

Figure 3-1. Bit annotation convention.

External Registers

These registers are called the external registers because they are not a part of any of the major VLSI functional blocks of the EGA (Sequencer, CRT Controller, Graphics Controller, or Attribute Controller).

Miscellaneous Output Register (Address 3C2)   ✳

Default Settings:	Mode 3	Mode3*	Mode 7	Mode F	Mode 10
	23h	A7h	A6h	A2h	A7

Care must be taken when addressing this register because it determines, among other things, the polarity of the sync outputs to the display and the video clock rate. There are a couple of register bits here, however, that may be of interest to some programmers.

This register is write-only on EGA. On VGA, it can be read back at I/O address 3CCh.

Bit Definitions:

D7 - Vertical Sync Polarity
D6 - Horizontal Sync Polarity
D5 - Odd/Even Page Bit
D4 - Disable Video
D3 - Clock Select 1
D2 - Clock Select 0
D1 - Enable Display RAM
D0 - I/O address select

To avoid damage, the Sync Polarity bits must be set properly for the display being used. A value of zero selects positive sync polarity, and one selects negative sync polarity. Table 3-4 shows the proper values for common display types. Dual frequency displays like the Enhanced Color Display use sync polarity to select their scan rate.

Table 3-4. Sync polarity vs. vertical screen resolution.

D7	D6	EGA	VGA
0	0	200 lines	invalid
0	1	350 lines	350 lines
1	0	invalid	400 lines
1	1	invalid	480 lines

- **D5: The Odd/Even Page** bit is used for those modes that send even addresses to plane 0 and odd addresses to plane 1 (all text modes use this function.) It selects one of two 64K byte pages.

- **D4: The Disable Video** bit, when set to one, disables the EGA video output driver. This can be used to permit a device on the feature connector to directly drive the display.

- **Note: The Disable Video** bit should not be used as a general purpose display on/off control, since it disables CRT sync signals as well as display data. The Attribute Controller provides the ability to safely enable and disable display data (see the section on Attribute Controller registers in this chapter).

- **D3, D2: The Clock Select** bits control the video clock rate. Table 3-5 shows the proper setting of these bits.

Table 3-5. Video clock selection bits.

D3 D2	Mode
0 0	640 columns (or 320 columns)
0 1	720 columns
1 0	external clock (from feature connector)
1 1	reserved

- **The External Clock** setting is used by some vendors who add a higher speed clock onto the feature connector to achieve higher screen resolutions. All timing registers have to be adjusted when this is done, and it is best left to the experts.

- **D1: The Display RAM Enable** bit may be used to disable processor access (reading or writing) to EGA display RAM. A zero disables the RAM, and a one enables it. This bit has no effect on display refresh.

- **D0: The I/O Address Select** bit, when set to zero, selects the monochrome I/O address space (3BX). When set to one, the color I/O address space (3DX) is selected.

Feature Control Register (EGA Only - Address 3BA/3DA)

Default Settings:	Mode 3	Mode3*	Mode 7	Mode F	Mode 10
	00	00	00	00	00

The I/O address of this register depends on the operating mode. In monochrome mode, it is mapped at I/O address 3BA. In color mode, it is at 3DA. For EGA, two bits of the register are used; these bits are tied directly to the EGA Feature Connector. This register is only used in applications where a piggyback board is mounted on the feature connector. This register is not used for VGA.

Bit Definitions:

D7 - D2 - reserved (0)
D1 - Feature control bit 1
D0 - Feature control bit 0

Input Status Register 0   (I/O Address 3C2)

This is a read-only register, mapped at the same I/O address as the Miscellaneous Output Register.

Bit Definitions:

D7 - Vertical retrace interrupt pending
D6 - Feature sense bit 1 (EGA only)
D5 - Feature sense bit 0 (EGA only)
D4 - Switch Sense
D3 - unused
D2 - unused
D1 - unused
D0 - unused

- **D7: The Vertical Retrace Interrupt Pending** bit can be polled by a interrupt handler to determine if vertical retrace was the cause of the interrupt (in case the IRQ2 interrupt line is being shared). This is a latched bit that is set at the start of vertical retrace and cleared through the Vertical Retrace End register of the CRT Controller. Vertical retrace is available as an interrupt source on IRQ2.

- **D6, D5: The Feature Sense** bits are inputs from the feature connector (EGA only).

- **D4: The Switch Sense** bit is used by the EGA BIOS to read the on-board EGA configuration switches. The four configuration switches are multiplexed onto this line. Switch selection is done via the two Clock Select lines on the Miscellaneous Register (3C2). Table 3-6 shows the relationship between Clock Select and Switch Sense. This switch data can also be found in the byte stored at memory address 0:488h.

The VGA uses the Switch Sense line to automatically sense the type of display being used (color or monochrome).

Table 3-6. Sense switches.

Clock Select	Sense Switch
00	Switch 1
01	Switch 2
10	Switch 3
11	Switch 4

To learn more about feature bits and switch settings, see also:

- BIOS function 18 Get EGA Status in Chapter 4.

- Read Register programming examples in Chapter 5.

Input Status Register 1 (I/O Address 3BA/3DA)

This is a read only register mapped at the same address as the Feature Control Register. It is located at I/O address 3BA for monochrome modes and 3DA for color modes.

Bit Definitions:

D7 - unused
D6 - unused
D5 - Diagnostic
D4 - Diagnostic
D3 - Vertical Retrace
D2 - Light Pen switch (EGA only)
D1 - Light Pen strobe (EGA only)
D0 - Display Enable

- **D0: The Display Enable** bit gives the real-time status of the CRT blanking signal, which goes active during horizontal or vertical retrace. A zero indicates that the video is blanked. By counting the number of horizontal blanking intervals that occur between Vertical Retraces (see bit D3), some conclusions can be drawn about the vertical resolution of the display. This can be useful for software that must adapt itself to different screen resolutions.

- **D1: A one on the Light Pen Strobe** bit indicates that the light pen has been triggered (EGA only). This bit will remain latched at a one until cleared by a write to I/O address 3BB (monochrome) or 3DB (color). For diagnostic purposes, this bit can also be forced to a one through a write to I/O address 3BC (monochrome) or 3DC (color).

- **D2: A zero on the Light Pen Switch** bit indicates that the light pen switch is closed (light pen is applied to CRT screen). It is usually preferable to interrogate the light pen through a BIOS function call, rather than directly accessing these light pen bits (see Chapter 4, BIOS function 4, Read Light Pen).

- **D3: A one on the Vertical Retrace** bit indicates that the CRT is in a vertical retrace.

- **D5, D4: The Diagnostic Bits** can be used to read back two of the six EGA video color output signals. Which colors are being read is determined by the value in the Color Plane Enable register (Index 12 of the Attribute Controller; see the section on Attribute Controller Registers in this chapter). Table 3-7 shows which register values yield which video output signals. Table 3-8 shows how this function can be used on the VGA to read back two of the eight VGA attribute controller outputs.

These diagnostic bits provide the only mechanism for reading the values of the EGA palette registers. By forcing known input data patterns into the attribute controller through its index register (see the section on Attribute Controller Registers in this chapter), then reading the video output lines, the contents of all sixteen EGA palette registers can be determined. Unfortunately, the diagnostic bits were implemented incorrectly in the chip set used on many popular EGA compatible products. Use of this method for reading palette registers may limit software compatibility with some vendors' products.

Table 3-7. Video read-back through diagnostics bits (EGA).

Color Plane Enable Register*	Input Status Register 1	
D5 D4	D5	D4
0 0	Red	Blue
0 1	Secondary Red	Secondary Green
1 0	Secondary Blue	Green
1 1	Unused	Unused

*On some EGA compatible products, D4 and D5 are reversed.

Table 3-8. Video read-back through diagnostics bits (VGA).

Color Plane Enable Register	Input Status Register 1	
D5 D4	D5	D4
0 0	P2	P0
0 1	P5	P4
1 0	P3	P1
1 1	P7	P6

To learn more about vertical retrace, also see Vertical Retrace programming examples in Chapter 5.

VGA Enable Register (I/O Address 3C3)

The VGA Enable Register is a one bit register. If D0 is set to zero, all VGA memory and I/O are disabled (except for writes to this register).

The CRT Controller

Overview

The CRT Controller does just what its name implies; it controls the CRT by generating the syncing and blanking signals that define the display raster. It also defines the format of display data on the screen. The register set of the CRT Controller is very similar to that of the Motorola 6845 CRT Controller that has been the standard for most earlier IBM compatible display adapters, including the MDA, CGA, and Hercules adapters.

Two I/O addresses are used by the CRT Controller. The first address is an index register which is used to select one of the 24 internal registers of the CRT Controller (see Table 3-9). The second address is used to read data from or write data to the selected register. On the EGA, most of the CRT Controller registers are write only.

As with many of the registers on the EGA and VGA, the addresses of the CRT Controller registers depend on operating mode. In monochrome modes, the index register is mapped at address 3B4 and the data register is at address 3B5. In color modes, the index register is at address 3D4 and the data register is at address 3D5.

Except for the rare case of a system developer who is using an unusual display device or who wants to create an unusual display format, most of the registers of the CRT Controller should not be modified by software. All timing control registers are initialized by the BIOS during a reset or Mode Select, and modifying these registers carelessly can actually damage your CRT display. For completeness, brief descriptions are included here of all timing registers. Registers that can be dangerous to modify are labeled with the symbol ✳.

Only a few of the registers of the CRT Controller are really of interest to the typical programmer. These registers are labeled with the symbol ★. Our primary goal in this chapter is first, to point out which registers are of greatest interest, and second, to explain how they are used.

Table 3-9. CRT Contoller Registers.

Index (3B4/3D4)		CRT Controller Registers (3B5/3D5)
0	✹	Horizontal Total
1	✹	Horizontal Display End
2	✹	Start Horizontal Blank
3	✹	End Horizontal Blank
4	✹	Start Horizontal Retrace
5	✹	End Horizontal Retrace
6	✹	Vertical Total
7 *	✹★	Overflow
8	★	Preset Row Scan
9		Max Scan Line
A	★	Cursor start
B	★	Cursor end
C	★	Start address (high byte)
D	★	Start address (low byte)
E	★	Cursor location (high byte)
F	★	Cursor location (low byte)
10	✹	Vertical Retrace Start
11	✹	Vertical Retrace End
10 (read only)		Light pen address (high byte)
11 (read only)		Light pen address (low byte)
12	✹	Vertical Display End
13	★	Offset
14	★	Underline location
15	✹	Start Vertical Blank
16	✹	End Vertical Blank

(continued)

Table 3-9. CRT Contoller Registers *(continued)*.

17	✸	Mode Control
18	★	Line Compare

✸ Indicates a register which may be dangerous to modify.
★ Indicates a register which can be especially useful.

*Unfortunately this is also needed for split screen.

Many of the compatibility problems that arise between EGA and CGA or MDA are due to the differences in the registers of the 6845 CRT Controller used on the older adapters versus the EGA CRT Controller. The differences are summarized in Table 3-10.

Table 3-10. CRT Controller on EGA vs 6845 CRT Controller.

Index	6845 Register	EGA/VGA Register
2	Horizontal Sync Position	Start Horizontal Blanking
3	Sync Width	End Horizontal Blanking
4	Vertical Total	Start Horizontal Retrace
5	Vertical Total Adjust	End Horizontal Retrace
6	Vertical Displayed	Vertical Total
7	Vertical Sync Position	Overflow
8	Interface Mode/Skew	Preset Row Scan

CRT Timing Registers   ✸

Registers in this group define the syncing and blanking signals that control the CRT display. They are initialized by the BIOS for any standard display mode. These registers should only be modified if a nonstandard display or display mode is being used. Careless modification of these registers can actually damage or destroy your display device.

Two counters internal to the CRT Controller, called Horizontal Count and Vertical Count, control timing generation. Horizontal Count is incremented on each character clock, and reset when Horizontal Count equals Horizontal Total. Vertical Count is incremented after each horizontal retrace, and reset when Vertical Count equals Vertical Total.

The values programmed into all the CRT timing registers described here are compared against either Horizontal Count or Vertical Count to determine the timing of CRT control signals.

Relation of the blanking and retrace timing is illustrated in Figure 3-20.

On the EGA, the CRT timing registers are all write-only registers.

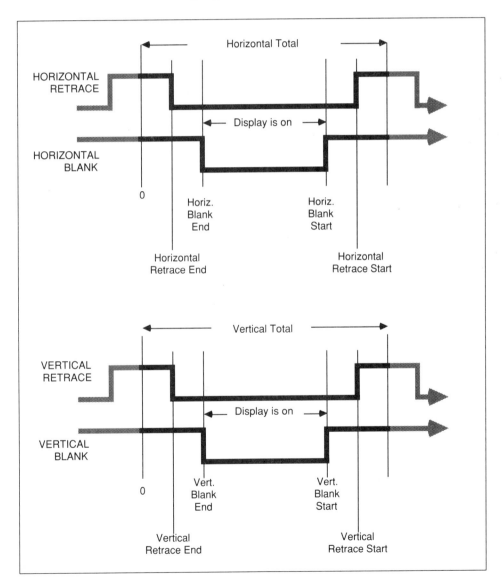

Figure 3-2. CRT Controller Timing Signals.

Horizontal Total (Index 0)

Default Settings:	Mode 3	Mode 3*	Mode 7	Mode F	Mode 10
	70h	5Bh	60h	60h	5Bh

The 8 bit value in this register defines the total number of 8 bit character clocks that occur during one horizontal CRT scan line, including blanking and retrace. For EGA, the number of character clocks per scan will be two greater than the 8 bit value in this register. For VGA, it will be five greater than the value of this register.

Horizontal Display Enable End (Index 1)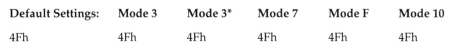

Default Settings:	Mode 3	Mode 3*	Mode 7	Mode F	Mode 10
4Fh	4Fh	4Fh	4Fh	4Fh	4Fh

This register determines the length of the Display Enable portion of a horizontal scan (the period when the display is not blanked). This defines the number of displayed character positions on the screen. The total number of 8 bit characters displayed per line is one greater than the 8 bit value in this register.

Start Horizontal Blanking (Index 2)

Default Settings:	Mode 3	Mode 3*	Mode 7	Mode F	Mode 10
5Ch	53h	56h	56h	56h	53h

The 8 bit value in this register determines the point during a horizontal scan at which horizontal blanking is asserted.

End Horizontal Blanking (Index 3)

Default Settings:	Mode 3	Mode 3*	Mode 7	Mode F	Mode 10
	2Fh	37h	3Ah	1Ah	17h

Bit Definitions:

D7 -Must be 0 for EGA
    Must be 1 for VGA
D6–D5 -Display Enable Skew Control
D4–D0 -End Horizontal Blanking

- **D4–D0:** When the 5 least significant bits of the horizontal character counter (Horizontal Count) equal this value, horizontal blanking will end.

- **D5, D6: Display Enable** skewing is used in text mode to allow time for display data to be fetched from the character generator at the start of a line before the display is enabled. If the skew value is too small, characters on the left edge of the screen may be lost; if it is too large, characters may appear more than once on the left edge of the screen.

```
00 = no skew
01 = skew 1 character clock
10 = skew 2 character clocks
11 = skew 3 character clocks
```

Start Horizontal Retrace (Index 4)

Default Settings:	Mode 3	Mode 3*	Mode 7	Mode F	Mode 10
	5Fh	51h	51h	50h	50h

This 8 bit value defines the point in a horizontal scan at which the horizontal retrace pulse begins.

End Horizontal Retrace (Index 5)

Default Settings:	Mode 3	Mode 3*	Mode 7	Mode F	Mode 10
	07	5Bh	60h	E0h	BAh

Bit Definitions:

```
D7 -     Start on Odd Memory Address (EGA only)
         End Horizontal Blanking Overflow bit (VGA only)
D6–D5 - Horizontal Retrace Delay
D4–D0 - End Horizontal Retrace
```

- **D7: Start On Odd Memory Address (EGA only)** is used for horizontal panning on EGAs with less than 256K bytes of display memory, when memory planes are chained. A zero causes the first screen refresh address after a retrace to be an even address. A one causes the first screen refresh address after a retrace to be an odd address. This bit should normally be set to zero.

- **D7: End Horizontal Blanking Overflow Bit (VGA only)** is the fifth bit of the End Horizontal Blanking Register.

- **D6, D5: Horizontal Retrace Delay** skews horizontal retrace with respect to display enable. This is required by the EGA in some modes.

00 - no delay
01 - delay one character clock
10 - delay two character clocks
11 - delay three character clocks

- **D4-D0: End Horizontal Retrace** When the five least significant bits of the horizontal character counter equal this value, horizontal retrace ends.

Vertical Total (Index 6)

Default Settings:	Mode 3	Mode 3*	Mode 7	Mode F	Mode 10
	04	6Ch	70h	70h	6Ch

This register defines the total number of horizontal scans that occur during one vertical scan, including vertical blanking and retrace.

On the EGA, this is a nine bit register. The ninth bit is located in the Overflow Register. On the VGA, there is also a tenth bit in the Overflow Register.

Overflow Register (Index 7)   ✳

Default Settings:	Mode 3	Mode 3*	Mode 7	Mode F	Mode 10
	11h	1Fh	1Fh	1Fh	1Fh

Several of the CRT timing registers of the EGA are nine bit registers. The Overflow Register is a collection of the ninth bits (most significant bits) from those registers. The VGA has an added tenth bit on some registers.

In most cases, the Overflow Register can be ignored. It is initialized by the BIOS during a Mode Select operation. Unfortunately, there is one bit in the Overflow Register (the Line Compare bit) that may be useful for some applications. Great care must be taken when using the Line Compare Register that the values of all other overflow bits are preserved. Appendix B-4 (Default Register Data) can be used to find the proper values of the Overflow Register for the standard operating modes not shown here.

Bit Definitions:

D7 - VGA only - Vertical Retrace Start (Bit 9)
D6 - VGA only - Vertical Display Enable End (Bit 9)
D5 - VGA only - Vertical Total (Bit 9)
D4 - Line Compare (Bit 8)
D3 - Start Vertical Blank (Bit 8)
D2 - Vertical Retrace Start (Bit 8)
D1 - Vertical Display Enable End (Bit 8)
D0 - Vertical Total (Bit 8)

To learn more about line compare operation also see Line Compare Register - 18hex in this chapter.

Vertical Retrace Start (Index 10H)

Default Settings:	Mode 3	Mode 3*	Mode 7	Mode F	Mode 10
	E1h	5Eh	5Eh	5Eh	5Eh

This register defines the point in a vertical scan when Vertical Retrace will begin. On the EGA, this is a 9 bit register; on the VGA, it is a 10 bit register. The most significant bit(s) are in the Overflow Register.

Vertical Retrace End (Index 11H)

Default Settings:	Mode 3	Mode 3*	Mode 7	Mode F	Mode 10
	24h	2Bh	2Eh	2Eh	2Bh

Besides determining the end of vertical retrace, this register also controls other functions that can be useful for some applications.

Bit Definitions:

D7 - Write Protect Index 0-7 (VGA only)
D6 - Alternate Refresh Rate (VGA only)
D5 - Enable Vertical Interrupt (0 = enable)
D4 - Clear Vertical Interrupt (0 = clear)
D3–D0 - Vertical Retrace End

- **D7: On the VGA only,** Write Protect Index 0-7 can be used to alleviate some of the compatibility problems between 6845 based adapters (MDA and CGA) and VGA. A one will write protect registers 0 through 7, assuring that software written for a 6845 will not corrupt the register settings. Many EGA compatible products that have enhanced emulation modes have a similar function incorporated in some proprietary fashion.

- **D6: Also on the VGA only,** Alternate Refresh Rate, when set to one, will generate 5 DRAM refresh cycles to the display memory during a horizontal retrace instead of the normal three. Though not currently used, this can permit the VGA to drive slower monitors (15.75 KHz horizontal scan frequency).

- **D5: A zero in Enable Vertical Interrupt** will cause an interrupt to be generated to the processor on interrupt line IRQ2 with every vertical retrace. This can be used as an accurate 60 Hz interrupt (for animation, for instance). Once a vertical interrupt is generated, the interrupt is latched on until it is acknowledged. Writing a zero to D4 (Clear Vertical Interrupt) will acknowledge the interrupt.

- **D4: Writing a zero to Clear Vertical Interrupt** will clear an interrupt and reset the Vertical Interrupt Pending flag.

- **D3-D0: Vertical Retrace End** Vertical retrace will end when the low order 4 bits of the horizontal scan counter equal this value.

Vertical Display Enable End (Index 12H)   ✸

Default Settings:	Mode 3	Mode 3*	Mode 7	Mode F	Mode 10
	C7h	5Dh	5Dh	5Dh	5Dh

The value in this register defines the point in a vertical scan at which vertical display enable ends and blanking begins. For the EGA, this is a nine bit register with its most significant bit in the Overflow Register. For the VGA, the Overflow Register also contains a tenth bit.

Start Vertical Blanking (Index 15H)   ✸

Default Settings:	Mode 3	Mode 3*	Mode 7	Mode F	Mode 10
	E0h	5Eh	5Eh	5Eh	5Fh

This register defines the point in a vertical scan at which vertical blanking will begin. For EGA, this is a nine bit register with the most significant bit in the Overflow Register. For the VGA, this is a ten bit register with the ninth bit in the Overflow Register and the tenth bit in the Max Scan Line register (Index 9).

End Vertical Blanking (Index 16H)

Default Settings:	Mode 3	Mode 3*	Mode 7	Mode F	Mode 10
	F0h	0Ah	6Eh	6Eh	0Ah

For the EGA, when the low order 5 bits of the horizontal scan counter equal the low order 5 bits of this register, vertical blanking will end. For VGA, a full 8 bit comparator is used.

Mode Control Register (Index 17H)

Default Settings:	Mode 3	Mode 3*	Mode 7	Mode F	Mode 10
	A3h	A3h	A3h	8Bh	8Bh

The mode control register is a collection of hardware specific control bits that configure the circuitry of the CRT Controller for a particular mode. In our opinion, this register should be avoided entirely by application software.

Bit Definitions:

D7 - Hardware Reset
D6 - Word/Byte Address Mode
D5 - Address Wrap
D4 - Output Control
D3 - Count by Two
D2 - Horizontal Retrace Select
D1 - CGA Graphics Compatibility Mode
D0 - Hercules Graphics Compatibility Mode

- **D7: Hardware Reset** must be set to one to enable horizontal and vertical retrace. When set to zero, retrace will be disabled.

- **D6: Word/Byte Mode,** when set to zero (word mode), causes the output bits of the Display Refresh Memory Address Counter to be rotated left one bit. Depending on the state of Address Wrap (D5), either counter output bit MA13 or MA15 appears on the least significant output. Table 3-11 shows the effect on the Memory Address Counter. Word Mode is used in some CGA compatible modes. Wrap is set to zero for EGA boards with only 64K bytes of memory installed; in all other cases, it is set to one.

Table 3-11. Word mode vs. byte mode.

Counter Outputs		
Byte Mode	**Word Mode** (WRAP = 0)	**Word Mode** (WRAP = 1)
MA0	MA13	MA15
MA1	MA0	MA0
MA2	MA1	MA1
MA3	MA2	MA2
MA4	MA3	MA3
MA5	MA4	MA4
MA6	MA5	MA5
MA7	MA6	MA6
MA8	MA7	MA7
MA9	MA8	MA8
MA10	MA9	MA9
MA11	MA10	MA10
MA12	MA11	MA11
MA13	MA12	MA12
MA14	MA13	MA13
MA15	MA14	MA14

- **D4: Output Control** must be set to zero during normal operation. When set to one, all CRT Controller outputs are disabled. This feature is used for test only.

- **D3: When Count By Two** is set to zero, the memory address counter is clocked on every character clock. When set to one, the memory address counter is clocked on every other character clock.

- **D2: When Horizontal Retrace Select** is set to zero, the Vertical Total counter is clocked by each Horizontal Retrace. When it is set to one, the Vertical Total counter is clocked by every other Horizontal Retrace. This bit can be used to double the number of scan lines the adapter can support, doubling the vertical resolution.

- **D1: CGA Graphics Compatibility Mode,** when set to zero, replaces memory address counter bit MA13 with Row Scan bit 0. This duplicates the fragmented memory map of the CGA graphics adapter (see Figures 2-13 and 2-14). For more information on this subject, see Compatibility Modes in Chapter 1. For a description of the Row Scan bits, see Text Modes in Chapter 2.

- **D0: Hercules Graphics Compatibility Mode,** when set to zero, replaces memory address counter bit MA14 with Row Scan bit 1. When CGA Compatibility Mode (D0) is also enabled (see above), this duplicates the fragmented memory map of the Hercules graphics adapter (see Figure 2-20).

Display Configuration Registers

The registers in this group are more interesting because of their potential for customizing the display format.

Preset Row Scan (Index 8)

Default Settings: 00 for all modes

Bit Definitions:

D7 -   reserved (0)
D6, D5 - byte panning control (VGA only)
D4–D0 - Preset Row Scan

- **D4-D0: Preset Row Scan** is used for smooth scrolling in text mode, so that character rows can be scrolled up or down one pixel at a time (see Figure 3-3). For the topmost row of text on the screen, this register defines which character scan line will be the first line displayed (so that the top character row shows only partial characters). Smooth scrolling is achieved by slowly incrementing or decrementing the value of this register.

- **D6, D5: The Byte Panning Control** augments the horizontal panning capability of the Horizontal Panning register of the Attribute Controller, which can pan horizontally up to 8 pixels. Beyond 8 pixels, panning is achieved by altering the start address register of the CRT Controller. Though not required by any current modes, VGA hardware can operate in modes so that incrementing the start address register pans the screen by 16 or 32 pixels. These byte panning control bits would permit smooth panning in such modes.

To learn more about smooth scroll, also see Panning and Scrolling examples in Chapter 5, and Smooth Scroll programming examples in Chapter 7.

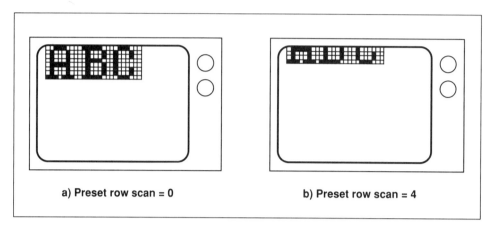

a) Preset row scan = 0   b) Preset row scan = 4

Figure 3-3. Preset row scan operation.

Maximum Scan Line/Text Character Height (Index 9)

Default Settings:	Mode 3	Mode 3*	Mode 7	Mode F	Mode 10
	07	0Dh	0Dh	00	00

IBM named this register Maximum Scan Line, but Text Character Height is more appropriate. Maximum Scan Line means the number of scan lines per text character, which is also equal to the pixel height of a character. It is used for text modes only.

Bit Definitions:

D7 -   Double Scan (VGA only)
D6 -   Bit 9 of Line Compare register (VGA only)
D5 -   Bit 9 of Start Vertical Blank register (VGA only)
D4–D0 - Maximum Scan Line

- **D7: The Double Scan Bit (VGA only)** permits VGA to run software written for CGA 200 line mode, but displays each line twice for a total of 400 lines. This improves the quality of the picture. It should be noted that when running CGA software on VGA, the Aspect Ratio will be different.

  For VGA, bit 9 of the Line Compare register and the Start Vertical Blank register are located in the Max Scan Line register presumably because there were no more bits available in the Overflow Register.

- **D6: Line Compare Bit 9 (VGA only)** is an overflow bit from the Line Compare Register (Index 18).

- **D5: Start Vertical Blank Bit 9 (VGA only)** is an overflow bit from the Start Vertical Blank Register (Index 15).

- **D4-D0: Maximum Scan Line** defines the number of scan lines in a character, which is the same as the height of a character in pixels. The character height is one greater than this value (Figure 3-4).

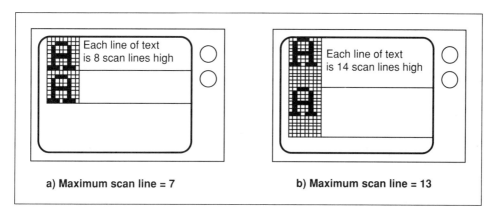

a) Maximum scan line = 7   b) Maximum scan line = 13

Figure 3-4. Maximum scan line operation.

To learn more about maximum scan line, also see 43 Line Text programming examples in Chapter 7.

Cursor Start (Index 0AH)   ★

Default Settings:	Mode 3	Mode 3*	Mode 7	Mode F	Mode 10
	06	0Bh	0Bh	00	00

Bit Definitions:

D7, D6 - reserved (0)
D5 -   Cursor Off (VGA only)
D4–D0 - Cursor Start

One of the few readable registers of the EGA, the cursor start register determines at which character row scan the cursor will begin. Together with the Cursor End register, this register defines the size of the cursor with respect to a character cell. For VGA, a Cursor Off bit was added. A one disables the cursor display. Setting a Cursor Start value that is greater than the Cursor End value will also blank the cursor for VGA, but with EGA this technique may yield unpredictable results.

Cursor End (Index 0BH)

Default Settings:	Mode 3	Mode 3*	Mode 7	Mode F	Mode 10
	07	0Ch	0Ch	00	00

Bit Definitions:

D7 -   reserved (0)
D6, D5 - Cursor Skew
D4–D0 - Cursor End

This register is the companion to Index 0AH (Cursor Start), and is also read-writable. It determines the character scan line at which the cursor display will stop.

The Cursor Skew control bits place a skew on the cursor relative to the character clock. This skew is required by EGA/VGA circuitry in some modes.

00 = no skew
01 = skew one character clock
10 = skew two character clocks
11 = skew three character clocks

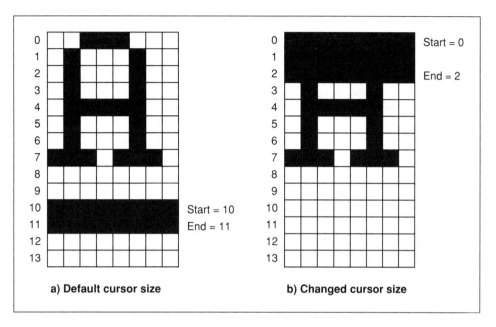

Figure 3-5. Cursor size operation.

To learn more about cursor size, also see:

- BIOS functions Set Cursor Size 1 and Get Cursor Size Position - 3, in Chapter 4.

- Write Register Programming examples in Chapter 5, Get Cursor Size in Chapter 6 and, Set Cursor Size in Chapter 7.

Start Address (High Byte) (Index 0CH)   ★

Start Address (Low Byte) (Index 0DH)   ★

Default Settings: 00 for all modes

This 16 bit read/write register defines the address in display memory of the data that will be displayed in the upper left corner of the screen (starting position). This register can be used to pan an image on the screen, or move between display pages in memory. It also plays a key role in establishing a split screen (see the Line Compare Register for details).

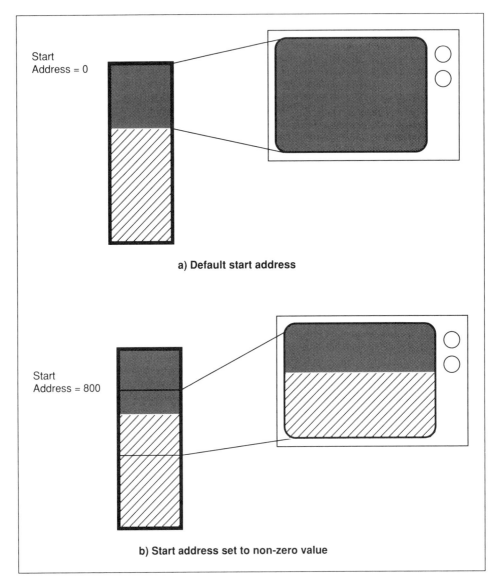

Figure 3-6. Start address operation.

To learn more about start address operation, also see:

- BIOS function 5, Select Active Page, in Chapter 4.

- Panning and Scrolling programming examples in Chapter 5, Split Screen and Smooth Scroll in Chapter 7.

Cursor Location (High Byte) (Index 0EH)   ★

Cursor Location (Low Byte) (Index 0FH)   ★

Default Settings: none

This 16 bit read/write register defines the position of the cursor on the screen. When the screen refresh memory address equals the cursor location register, the cursor will be displayed on the screen (Figure 3-7).

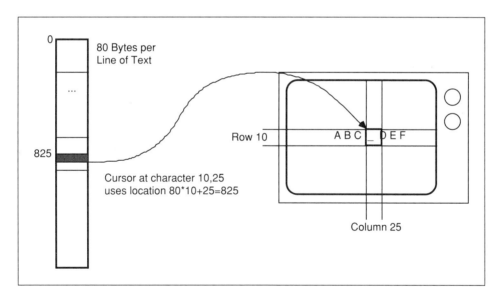

Figure 3-7. Cursor location operation.

To learn more about cursor location, also see:

• BIOS function 2 and 3, Set Cursor Position and Get Cursor Position in Chapter 4.

• Set Cursor Position and Get Cursor Position programming examples in Chapter 7.

Light Pen Register (High Byte) (Index 10H)

Light Pen Register (Low Byte) (Index 11H)

The 16 bit Light Pen register is a read-only register that is supported on EGA only. It latches the display memory address that was being accessed for screen refresh when the light pen was triggered, thus identifying where the electron beam was on the screen. This can be used to determine the physical location of the light pen.

The EGA light pen interface is not compatible with the CGA light pen interface.

Offset/Logical Screen Width (Index 13H)   ★

Default Settings:	Mode 3	Mode 3*	Mode 7	Mode F	Mode 10
	28h	28h	28h	14h	14h

IBM named this the Offset Register, but a better name for this register would be Logical Screen Width. In graphics modes, it defines the logical distance, in either 16 bit memory words or 32 bit double words, between successive scan lines. In other words, if the screen refresh data for scan line n begins at memory address m, refresh data for scan line n+1 will begin at address m+offset. In text modes, the offset is the logical increment between successive character rows.

In all standard operating modes, the logical screen width (offset) is equal to the physical screen width. For 80 column text or 640 pixel graphics, the offset is set to 40. For 40 column text or 320 pixel graphics, the offset is set to 20.

The most common reason for altering the offset value is to create a display that is logically wider than the display screen (for instance, a 132 column text format would use a value of 66). The EGA hardware panning features can then be used to view selected sections of the display.

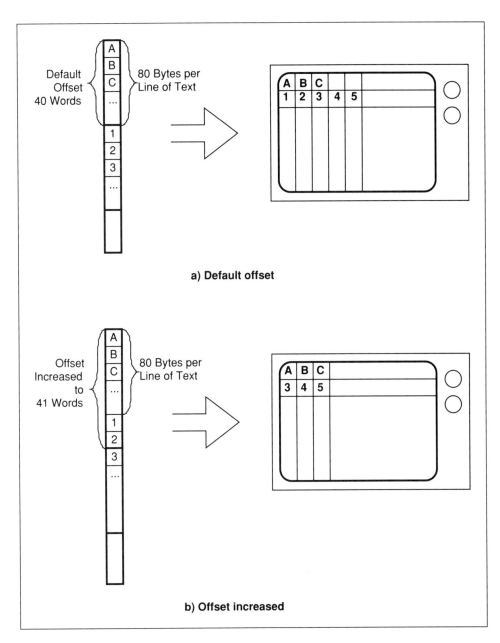

Figure 3-8. Offset register operation.

To learn more about offset operation, also see Panning and Scrolling programming Examples in Chapter 5 and Smooth Scroll programming examples in Chapter 7.

Underline Location Register (Index 14H)

Default Settings:	Mode 3	Mode 3*	Mode 7	Mode F	Mode 10
	08	0Fh	0Dh	0Dh	0Fh

In text mode only, Underline Location defines which line of a character cell will be illuminated when the underline attribute is set. This register is set during a BIOS mode select operation according to the font size being used.

Underlining is disabled in the standard color text modes by setting the value of this register to be greater than the character height.

For the VGA, two additional bits have been added to the Underline Register (Doubleword Mode and Count by 4).

Bit Definitions:

D7 -   reserved (0)
D6 -   Doubleword mode (VGA only)
D5 -   Count by 4 (VGA only)
D4–D0 - Underline Location

- **D6: Doubleword Mode (VGA only),** when set to one, selects double word memory addressing.

- **D5: Count by 4 (VGA only),** when set to one, causes the refresh address counter to be incremented once every four character clocks instead of every clock cycle.

- **D4-D0: Underline Location** determines the line number in a character cell where the underline attribute will be displayed.

For standard color text modes, the BIOS disables the underline attribute, by setting the underline location to the value F(hex) which is greater than the last line of a character. To enable the underline attribute in a color text mode, reprogram this register with a lower value (7 for a 200 line display, 0Ch for a 350 line display).

To underline a character, the character attribute must be set to 01, 09, 81h, or 89h.

Line Compare Register (Index 18H)

Default Settings: FFh for all modes

Used in combination with the Start Address register, the Line Compare register provides hardware support for a split screen display. When the horizontal scan counter (total number of horizontal scans) reaches the value of the Line Compare register, the display refresh memory address counter will be cleared. This has the effect of breaking the display screen into two separate windows. The upper window on the display screen displays the data that is pointed to by the Start Address register; the lower window on the display screen displays the data that starts at location zero in display memory. The upper window may be scrolled using the Start Address register while the lower window remains stationary.

On the EGA, this is a nine bit register with the most significant bit located in the overflow register. On the VGA, a tenth bit is located in the Max Scan Line register.

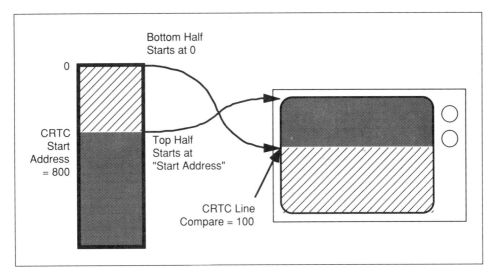

Figure 3-9. Line compare operation.

To learn more about line compare register, also see Split Screen programming examples in Chapter 7.

The Sequencer

Overview

The sequencer controls the overall timing of all EGA functions, and also performs some memory address decoding. It is controlled through five output registers that are write-only on the EGA, but are readable on the VGA. These five registers are multiplexed into two I/O addresses (3C4 and 3C5). At I/O address 3C4 is an index register that is used to select the active register. Data is output to that register at I/O address 3C5. Table 3-12 lists the sequencer registers and their indexes.

Table 3-12. Sequencer output registers.

Index (3C4)		Sequencer Register (3C5)
00	✺	Reset Register
01	✺	Clock Mode
02	★	Color Plane Write Enable
03*	★➠	Character Generator Select
04	✺	Memory Mode

✺   Indicates a register that can be dangerous to modify.

★   Indicates a register that is especially useful.

➠   Indicates a feature of the EGA that will operate differently

     depending on the size of the EGA display memory.

*This register is only of interest when using multiple character sets.

Reset Register (Index 0)   ✺

Default Settings: 03 for all modes

This register should be treated with great care. If set to a reset state, all timing on the EGA will be halted (including CRT timing). If left in this state for an extended period, damage to the display can result. The processor cannot access the display memory while the sequencer is in Reset. Bits D0 and D1 should both be set to one for normal operation.

Bit Definitions:

D7–D2 - reserved (0)
D1 -   Synchronous reset
D0 -   Asynchronous reset

- **D0: A zero in the Asynchronous Reset** bit will immediately halt and reset the sequencer. This can cause data loss in the display RAM, which may be interrupted in mid-cycle.

- **D1: A zero in the Synchronous Reset** bit will halt and reset the sequencer at the end of its current cycle, thus preserving the integrity of the data in the display RAM.

The sequencer should be placed in a synchronous reset before an access is made to the clock mode register.

The Clock Mode Register (Index 1)   ✸

Default Settings:	Mode 3	Mode 3*	Mode 7	Mode F	Mode 10
	01	01	00	05	05

The clock mode register configures the timing circuits of the sequencer. This register is initialized by the BIOS during a mode select operation. It is usually not necessary for software to modify this register.

There are a couple of bits in this register that may be of interest to some programmers. If these bits are used, care must be taken to preserve the state of other bits in this register.

Note: Before the Clock Mode register can be modified, the Sequencer must be placed in a reset state (see Reset Register above).

- **D5: On the VGA Only, a one in Display Off** will blank the screen and give the host CPU full access to the display memory. This minimizes the occurrence of wait states on the CPU bus, which slow down the processor and limit its throughput. Sync pulses are not interrupted.

- **D1: On the EGA Only, Bandwidth Control** controls how many cycles of the display memory are allocated to the processor for drawing operations. On low resolution displays (D1 = 1), the host CPU is granted 3 of every 5 available cycles. On high resolution displays (D1 = 0), because of the increase in data required for screen refresh, the host CPU is given only 1 of every 5 available cycles.

> If the host processor attempts to read or write to the display memory while a display refresh is in progress, the EGA will force the processor to "wait its turn" to access the display memory. The resulting processor wait states reduce the total system throughput (the rate at which the system can perform tasks). For the IBM EGA in text and low resolution graphics modes, display memory is busy performing display refresh only 40 percent of the time, leaving it available to the processor 60 percent of the time. In high resolution graphics modes display refresh uses the display memory as much as 80 percent of the time, leaving it available to the processor only 20 percent of the time.
>
> The VGA, as well as many second generation EGA compatible products, use improved memory timing, which grants the host more access and reduces the number of wait states imposed on the processor.

- **D0: A one in 8/9 Dot Clocks** causes character clocks to be 8 dots wide (normal mode). A zero causes character clocks to be 9 dots wide. This is used for monochrome text mode where characters are padded to 9 dots wide to fill the 720 column screen.

The Color Plane Write Enable Register (Index 2)

Default Settings:	Mode 3	Mode 3*	Mode 7	Mode F	Mode 10
	03	03	03	0Fh	0Fh

This is a very important register for graphics drawing operations. It controls the processor write enables of each color plane. Any combination of planes may be enabled for writing at any time. By selectively write enabling certain color planes, particular graphics objects or color components can be preserved on the display.

Bit Definitions:

D7–D4 - reserved (0)
D3 -   plane 3 write enable (1 = enabled)
D2 -   plane 2 write enable (1 = enabled)
D1 -   plane 1 write enable (1 = enabled)
D0 -   plane 0 write enable (1 = enabled)

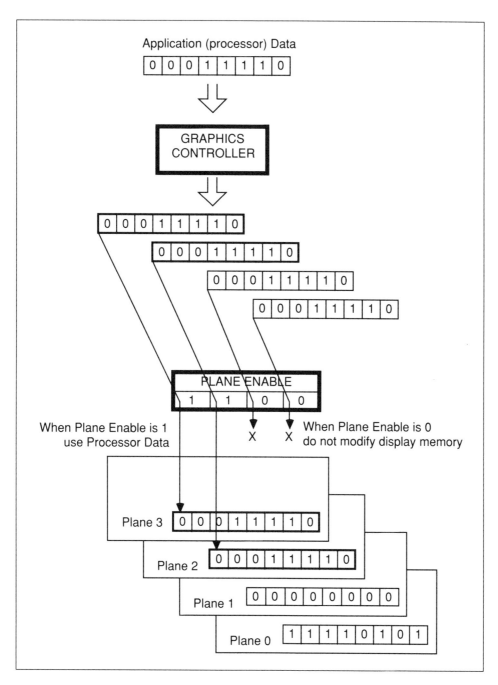

Figure 3-10. Color plane write enable.

To learn more about color plane write enable, also see Write Pixel programming examples in Chapter 8, and in particular assembly example procedure _Pixel_Write.

Character Generator Select Register (Index 3)

Default Settings: 00 for all modes

Bit Definitions:

D7 -   reserved (0)
D6 -   reserved (0)
D5 -   VGA only - Character generator table select A (MSB)
D4 -   VGA only - Character generator table select B (MSB)
D3–D2 - Character generator table select A
D1–D0 - Character generator table select B

This register is only of interest if your software will be using multiple character sets. It selects which RAM resident character set(s) will be displayed. The EGA can have up to four character sets loaded in RAM simultaneously (the VGA permits eight). Two character sets may be selected as active (character set A and character set B). If only one character set is needed, character set A select and character set B select can both contain the same value, and only one character set will be used.

As explained in Chapter 2, when two character sets are active, text attribute bit 3 selects which character set (A or B) will be used for that character. This facility permits up to 512 characters to be displayed simultaneously. Before enabling this function, the normal Foreground Intensify function of text attribute bit 3 should be disabled in the Attribute Controller. This is done by loading the second eight palette registers to equal the first eight palette registers (see Palette Registers description later in this chapter).

The preferred method for programming this register is through BIOS function 17 (see Chapter 4). Table 3-13 shows the register settings needed to enable each character generator. If only one character generator is to be active, the programmed value for Table A and Table B should be made equal.

At least 128K bytes of display memory is required to support two character sets. 256K bytes is required to support four character sets.

The Character Generator Select register is internally buffered so that no corrupted characters will result from dynamically changing this register in the middle of a screen refresh cycle.

Table 3-13. Selecting active character generators.

D5 D3 D2 - Used when text attribute bit 3 is 1
D4 D1 D0 - Used when text attribute bit 3 is 0

0   0   0   - Character Table 1
0   0   1   - Character Table 2
0   1   0   - Character Table 3
0   1   1   - Character Table 4
1   0   0   - Character Table 5 (VGA only)
1   0   1   - Character Table 6 (VGA only)
1   1   0   - Character Table 7 (VGA only)
1   1   1   - Character Table 8 (VGA only)

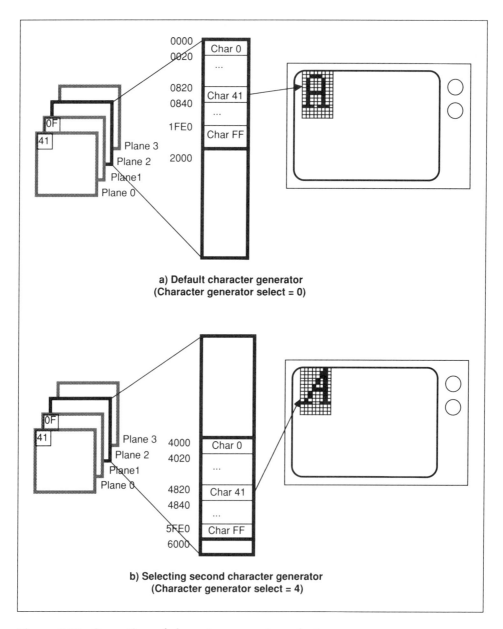

a) Default character generator
(Character generator select = 0)

b) Selecting second character generator
(Character generator select = 4)

Figure 3-11. Operation of character generator select.

To learn more about character generators, also see:

• Section on Character Generators, and Character Attributes in Chapter 2.

• BIOS function 17, Load Character Generator in Chapter 4.

• Write Attribute, Read Character Generator, Write Character Generator, 512
Character Set, and 43 Line Text programming examples in Chapter 7.

The Memory Mode Register (Index 4)   ✸

Default Settings:	Mode 3	Mode 3*	Mode 7	Mode F	Mode 10
	03	03	03	00	00

This register, which is initialized by the BIOS during a mode select operation, is
used by the sequencer to determine how the memory is structured for that mode. It
is not necessary to modify this register through software.

Bit Definitions:

D7–D3 - reserved
D2 -   Odd/Even
D1 -   Extended Memory
D0 -   Text Mode (EGA ONLY)

• **D2: The Odd/Even** bit must be set to zero in text modes to allow even memory
addresses to access color plane zero while odd memory addresses access plane
one.

• **D1: On the original IBM EGA,** as well as some compatible adapters, a one in
the **Extended Memory** bit instructs the sequencer that more than 64K bytes of
display memory are present on the adapter. Software compatibility problems
may result if this bit is modified by software.

• **D0: For EGA, the Text Mode** bit must be set to one to enable text mode Character Set Select functions. For VGA, this bit is normally set to zero.

The Graphics Controller

Overview

The Graphics Controller resides in the data path between display memory and
the system processor. In its default state, the Graphics Controller is transparent

and data passes directly between processor and display memory. In other configurations, the Graphics Controller can provide a hardware assist to graphics drawing algorithms by performing logical operations on data being written or read by the processor.

Nine internal Graphics Controller registers are multiplexed into two I/O addresses. At I/O address 3CE is an index register that is used to select a Graphics Controller register. I/O address 3CF is used to read or write data to the selected register (Table 3-14).

On the original IBM EGA board, as well as some EGA compatible adapters, two additional I/O addresses are used (3CA and 3CC). These are used during adapter initialization only and should never be addressed by software. 3CC should always be set to 0, and 3CA should be set to 1 before the first access to Graphics Controller registers.

A color plane must be write enabled via the Sequencer Color Plane Write Enable Register before any drawing operations can occur.

Table 3-14. Graphics Controller registers.

Index (3CE)		Graphics Controller Register (3CF)
00	★	Set/Reset Register
01	★	Set/Reset Enable Register
02	★	Color Compare Register
03	★	Data Rotate & Function Select
04	★	Read Plane Select Register
05	★	Mode Register
06	✹	Miscellaneous Register
07	★	Color Don't Care Register
08	★	Bit Mask Register

✹   Indicates a register that may be dangerous to modify.
★   Indicates a register that is especially useful.

The operation of Graphics Controller is summarized in Figure 3-12.

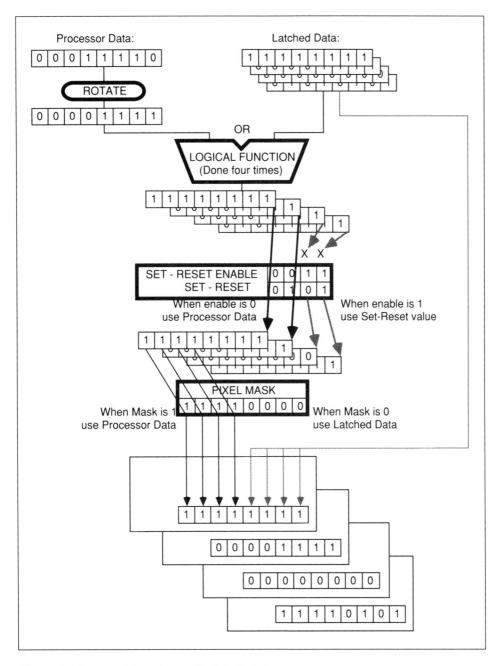

Figure 3-12. Graphics Controller block diagram.

Set/Reset Register (Index 0)   ★

Default Settings: 00 for all modes

A better name for this register would be Color Fill Data. It is used to define a fill color to be written to display memory during any display memory write operation. (The write data from the processor will be ignored.) Set/Reset mode is enabled for each plane individually through the Set/Reset Enable Register (Index 1 below).

Bit Definitions:

D7–D4 - reserved (0)
D3 -   fill data for plane 3
D2 -   fill data for plane 2
D1 -   fill data for plane 1
D0 -   fill data for plane 0

A single byte written to display memory defines 8 pixels in one or more planes (unless a pixel mask function is enabled). In Set/Reset mode, all 8 pixels of each plane will be filled with the fill data for that plane from the Set/Reset Register. The write mode must be set to zero (see Graphics Controller Mode Register - Index 5). The operation of Set/Reset and Set/Reset Enable is illustrated in Figure 3-13.

Individual memory bits may be write protected from a Set/Reset fill operation using the Bit Mask Register (Index 8). Other logical functions (such as Rotate, And Or, or Xor,) have no effect on Set/Reset operations. Planes that are not enabled for Set/Reset are under normal control of the other logical functions.

The Set/Reset register can be used to quickly fill regions of the display with a predefined color.

Set/Reset Enable Reset (Index 1)   ★

Default Settings: 00 for all modes

Set/Reset Enable defines which memory planes will receive fill data from the Set/Reset Register. Any plane that is disabled for Set/Reset will be written with normal processor output data.

Bit Definitions:

D7–D4 - reserved (0)
D3 - enable Set/Reset for plane 3 (1 = enable)
D2 - enable Set/Reset for plane 2
D1 - enable Set/Reset for plane 1
D0 - enable Set/Reset for plane 0

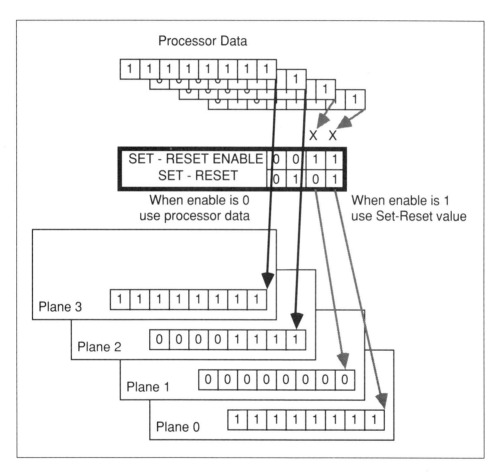

Figure 3-13. Operation of Set/Reset

To learn more about Set/Reset, also see Write Pixel programming examples in Chapter 8, and in particular assembly procedure _Pixel_Set.

Color Compare Register (Index 2)   ★

Default Settings: 00 for all modes

The Color Compare Register can be used to implement graphics drawing algorithms that must find and identify objects in display memory by their color. Without using Color Compare, a display memory read cycle will return data for only one color plane (the plane that is currently selected via the Read Plane Select Register). Rather than reading all four color planes one at a time to determine if a given color value is present, Color Compare allows a single display memory read cycle to compare the data of all four planes to a reference color and report whether a color match was found for each pixel position. In the result, for each bit position, a one indicates that the color data in all 4 planes matched the compare data.

The Color Compare function is enabled through the Mode Register (see below). The operation of the Color Compare and Color Don't Care is illustrated in Figure 3-14.

Bit Definitions:

D7-D4 - reserved (0)
D3 - Color Compare value for plane 3
D2 - Color Compare value for plane 2
D1 - Color Compare value for plane 1
D0 - Color Compare value for plane 0

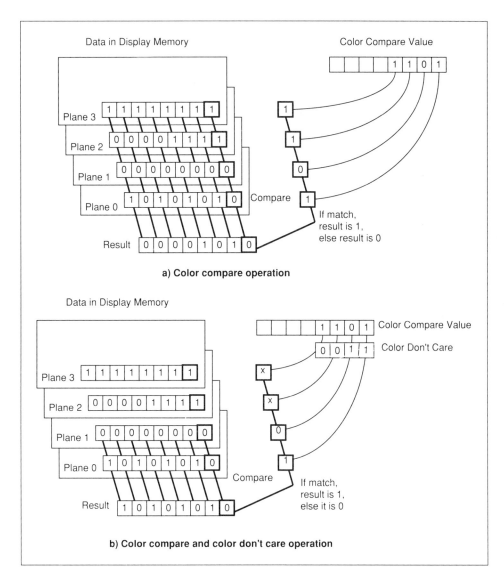

Figure 3-14. Color Compare and Color Don't Care operation.

Using Color Compare Function for boundary search

The color compare function is commonly used when searching through graphics memory for the edges of a polygon. This technique is useful in "seed fill algorithms" and "run length encoding" algorithms. These algorithms must be capable of finding the first pixel to the right or left of a given pixel in display memory that is of a different color than the given pixel.

To find a pixel that is not of a given color, successive reads are performed using the color compare function to compare to that color. A read value other then FF hex indicates a color difference. The following sequence searches for a color boundary to the right of a pixel:

```
... load graphics controller mode register and color don't care
register  ·
... load address of starting pixel into register DI
... load number of bytes to search into register CX

MOV    AL,0FFH         ;Want to search for zero bit
REPE   SCASB           ;Search for first zero bit (color does not match)

... look at the new value of register DI to compute address of the
different (boundary) pixel
```

Data Rotate/Function Select Register (Index 3)   ★

Default Settings: 00 for all modes

Bit Definitions:

D7–D5 - reserved (0)
D4, D3 - Function Select
D2–D0 - Rotate Count

This register controls two independent functions: write data rotation, and logical functions performed on write data.

Data can be rotated during a write cycle from 0 to 7 bit positions (as indicated in Table 3-15). Used with pixel masking, this function provides hardware support for functions such as BITBLTs (Bit oriented Block Transfers) that are not byte aligned. Write mode 0 must be selected to enable rotation.

Table 3-15. Data rotate bits.

D2	D1	D0	Right Rotation
0	0	0	none
0	0	1	1 bit
0	1	0	2 bits
0	1	1	3 bits
1	0	0	4 bits
1	0	1	5 bits
1	1	0	6 bits
1	1	1	7 bits

Function Select provides basic hardware support for read-modify-write operations on display memory. Each time a display memory read cycle is performed by the host processor, the read data is latched into a set of on-board latches called the processor latches. Function Select allows write data to be combined logically with the data stored in these latches. This can provide a fast means for doing read-modify-write operations, and can be especially useful for drawing and removing graphics cursors and sprites. Write mode 0 or 2 must be selected to enable logical functions. Functions are listed in Table 3-16.

Table 3-16. Function select bits.

D4	D3	Function
0	0	Write data unmodified
0	1	Write data AND processor latches
1	0	Write data OR processor latches
1	1	Write data XOR processor latches

Figure 3-15 illustrates the effects of logical operations and the rotate operation.

If both rotation and a logical function are enabled, the rotation occurs before the logical function is applied. Each color plane has its own byte wide processor latch, so that 32 bits may be latched into the processor latches during a single display memory read cycle.

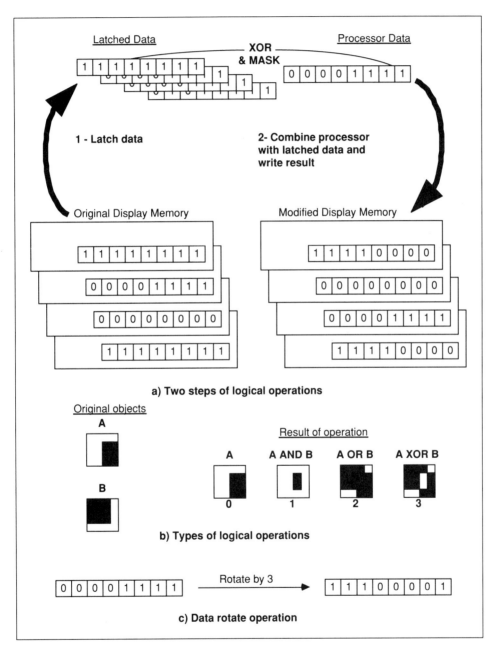

Figure 3-15. Logical functions and data rotate.

To learn more about logical operations and the data rotate, also see Block Transfer (BITBLT) programming examples in Chapter 8.

Read Plane Select Register (Index 4)   ★

Default Settings: 00 for all modes

The Read Plane Select register determines which color plane is enabled for reading by the processor (except in Color Compare mode.)

Bit Definitions:

D7–D2 - reserved (0)
D1, D0 - defines color plane for reading (0-3)

The operation of read select during a processor read access is illustrated in Figure 3-16.

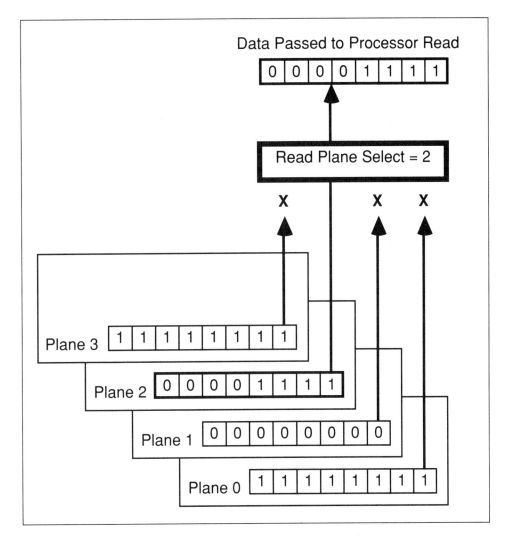

Figure 3-16. Read plane select operation.

To learn more about read plane select, also see Read Pixel programming examples in Chapter 8.

Mode Register (Index 5)

Default Settings:	Mode 3	Mode 3*	Mode 7	Mode F	Mode 10
	10h	10h	10h	10h	10h

Most of the bits in the Mode Register should not be modified after they are initialized by a BIOS Mode Select operation. Two fields that are of interest, however, are the Write Mode field, which can be used to control how processor data is written into display memory, and the Color Compare Mode Enable (see Color Compare Register).

If the mode register is altered by an application program, care must be taken to preserve the state of bits D4 through D7 or the operating mode of the board may be corrupted.

Bit Definitions:

D7 - reserved (0)
D6 - 256 color mode (VGA only)
D5 - Shift Register Mode
D4 - Odd/Even Mode
D3 - Color Compare Mode Enable (1 = enable)
D2 - reserved (0)
D1,–D0 - Write Mode

- **D1, D0: Write Mode** Selects current method of writing data into memory planes. There are three different write modes listed in Table 3-17.

Table 3-17. Write modes.

0 0	Direct processor write (Data Rotate, Set/Reset may apply)
0 1	Use content of latches as write data
1 0	Color plane n (0-3) is filled with the value of bit n in the processor write data
1 1	Not used

Write mode 0 (Direct Write) is most frequently used, and is the default state of the Graphics Controller. This mode allows direct processor writes to display memory, and also allows the use of other functions such as Set/Reset, Rotate, Bit Masking, AND, OR, and XOR.

Write mode 1 (Processor latches as write data) can be used to quickly copy a block of data from one place in display memory to another. A processor read from display memory will read one byte of data from each of the four color planes and latch the 32 bits of data into the processor latches. A processor write to display memory can then write all four bytes of data back to display memory at a different address (providing all four planes are write enabled). The MOVSB instruction of the Intel 8086 processor family can be used to perform this operation in minimum time.

Write mode 2 (Fill plane n with bit n,) when used with the mask register, will convert a packed pixel into a planar pixel and write it into the color planes.

The three types of write are illustrated in Figure 3-17.

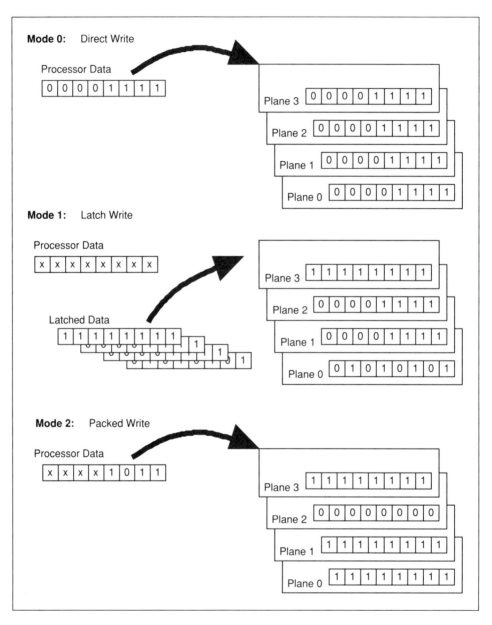

Figure 3-17. Write modes.

- **D6: 256 Color Mode (VGA only)** modifies the operation of the VGA attribute controller to accomodate the VGA 256 color mode.

- **D5: Shift Register Mode** alters the operation of the data serializer to operate in CGA modes 4 and 5, which use 2 bit packed pixels. Shift register operation must be modified to allow two bit pixels to be processed.

- **D4: Odd/Even Mode** must be set for text modes to map odd memory addresses into odd numbered planes and even memory addresses into even memory planes.

- **D3: Color Compare Mode Enable** selects the color compare read mode (for details, see the Color Compare Register (Index 2).

To learn more about write modes, also see Write Pixel programming examples in Chapter 8.

The graphics controller on the EGA/VGA offers three write modes, mode 0 the Direct Write, mode 1 the Latched Write, and mode 2 the Packed Pixel Write. Although in many cases functions can be performed using any of the three modes, there are distinct advantages in using a particular write mode for some functions.

Write One Pixel:

Mode 0 or Mode 2 are used for pixel write. Mode 0 is preferable since it is a default mode, and the Graphics controller does not have to be restored after the write. There are two ways to use this mode. It can be used either to write processor data into display memory, or it can be used with the Set/Reset function. The Set/Reset function allows all planes to be modified in one operation, which is faster then using processor write. With processor write, two operations are needed; one to clear planes, and second to set planes.

Writing several pixels with one color:

Mode 0, with Set/Reset is used for this function. Most drawing algorithms, such as line drawing, curve drawing, and polygon fill, should use write mode 0 with Set/Reset enabled.

Writing consecutive pixels of different colors:

Mode 2 should be used for this function. This mode is preferred over mode 0 because it does not require loading the Set/Reset or plane enable registers for each pixel.

Copying from display memory to display memory:

Mode 1 should be used to move data from one part of the display memory to another. Unfortunately this works only for byte aligned transfer (where one byte is moved to another byte). For example moving a scan line down by one line will work, however moving it right by one pixel will not. This is because in the second case 8 pixels from a byte are divided so that the right most pixel goes into one byte and the remaining pixels are moved into another byte.

The REP MOVSB instruction can be used to move data very quickly in this mode. However, do not use "REP MOVSW" Instruction in mode 1. With this instruction processor does two reads followed by two writes. Data latched in the second read is in the latch before the first write is performed. The data from the first read is lost. The MOVSB can be used safely.

Copying data from system memory to display memory:

Some programs keep "color" multiplanar data (like fonts and menu boxes) in four equal chunks of system memory, one chunk for each plane. For example MS-Windows does this. Copying such data into display memory is most efficiently done by using Mode 0, with plane select (not Set/Reset).

Using hardware rotate or logical functions:

When using data rotate and logical functions, mode 0 must be used. These are not supported in modes 1 and 2.

Miscellaneous Register (Index 6)   ✳ ⟶

Default Settings:	Mode 3	Mode 3*	Mode 7	Mode F	Mode 10
	0Eh	0Eh	0Ah	07	05

The Miscellaneous Register should normally not be modified after it is initialized by a BIOS mode select operation.

Bit Definitions:

D7 – D4 - reserved (0)
D3 – D2 - Memory Address Select
D1 - Chain Odd and Even Maps
D0 - Graphics Enable

- **D3, D2: Memory Address Select** selects the memory address range where the EGA display memory will be mapped to the host. This value is set by the BIOS during a Mode Select operation, and it is usually not necessary to modify this setting. Modification of this value can cause address conflicts with other display devices, or cause some BIOS functions to work incorrectly.

Table 3-18. Memory address select.

D3 D2	Address range
0 0	A0000 to BFFFF
0 1	A0000 to AFFFF
1 0	B0000 to B7FFF
1 1	B8000 to BFFFF

- **D1: Chain Odd And Even Maps** is used for some modes with EGA adapters that have only 64K bytes of display memory. When set to one, the four 16K byte memory planes will be chained into two 32K byte memory planes. For adapters with more than 64K bytes of display memory, this bit should always be set to zero.

- **D0: Graphics Enable** must be set to zero for text modes and one for graphics modes. This bit enables the address latches for the Character Generator.

To learn more about memory address select, also see:

- Memory map in Table 3-3 at the beginning of this chapter.

- Assembly procedures in Read Character Generator, and Write Character Generator programming examples in Chapter 5.

Color Don't Care Register (Index 7)   ★

Default Settings:	Mode 3	Mode 3*	Mode 7	Mode F	Mode 10
	00	00	00	0Fh	0Fh

Color Don't Care is used in conjunction with Color Compare Mode. This register masks particular planes from being tested during color compare cycles.

Bit Definitions:

D7–D4 - reserved (0)
D3 - Plane 3 don't care
D2 - Plane 2 don't care
D1 - Plane 1 don't care
D0 - Plane 0 don't care

To learn more about color compare operation, also see register Color Compare in this section.

Bit Mask Register (Index 8)   ★

Default Settings: FFh for all modes

Bit Definitions:

D7 - mask data bit 7
D6 - mask data bit 6
D5 - mask data bit 5
D4 - mask data bit 4
D3 - mask data bit 3
D2 - mask data bit 2
D1 - mask data bit 1
D0 - mask data bit 0

The Bit Mask register is used to mask certain bit positions from being modified during read-modify-write cycles. It must be noted, however, that the Bit Mask Register does not implement a true bit mask and it must be used very carefully to achieve the desired results.

A zero value in a particular bit of the bit mask register means that during a processor write to display memory, the data for that bit position will be taken from the processor latches rather than from the processor output data. For this to function as a mask operation, the processor latches must be properly loaded through a read operation before a write operation is performed. Thus the masking operation is a two-step process. First we must latch the original data, and second we write the new data. The second step is illustrated in Figure 3-18.

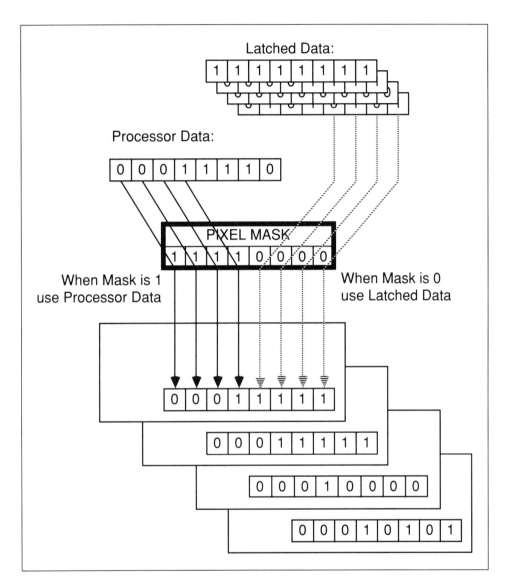

Figure 3-18. Bit mask register operation.

To learn more about bit mask register operation, also see Write Pixel programming examples in Chapter 8.

The Attribute Controller and Video DAC

Overview

The Attribute Controller, as its name suggests, controls display attributes. In some operating modes, color is the only attribute to be controlled. In other modes, attributes such as blinking and underlining also apply.

Internally, the Attribute Controller consists of twenty output registers that are multiplexed into one I/O address. The multiplexing scheme used by the Attribute Controller differs somewhat from other sections of the EGA that use an index register and a data register mapped at two separate I/O addresses. In the Attribute Controller, index register and data register are both mapped at address 3C0 HEX, with write cycles alternating between the two. An internal flip-flop, which toggles with each write operation, selects the index and data registers alternately. This flip-flop can be initialized by performing an I/O read operation at address 3BA (in monochrome mode) or 3DA (in color mode). After initialization, the first write cycle at address 3C0 will be directed to the index register of the Attribute Controller.

On the VGA, the Attribute Controller outputs drive a Video DAC (Digital to Analog Converter), which converts binary color information into analog voltages to drive the VGA analog display. The Video DAC circuit also includes an additional Color Look-up Table that expands the color palette from the 64 possible colors of EGA to the 256 thousand possible colors of VGA.

The Attribute Controller

The Index Register

D7 - reserved (0)
D6 - reserved (0)
D5 - Palette address source
0 = palette can be modified, screen is blanked
1 = screen is enabled, palette cannot be modified
D4-D0 - Register address (0-13H)

- **D0–D4: Index register bits D0–D4 (Register Address)** select which of the twenty internal registers of the Attribute Controller will be addressed by the next I/O write cycle.

.

Table 3-19. Attribute Controller registers.

Index (3C0)	Attribute Controller Register (3C0)
00	Color Palette Register 0
01	Color Palette Register 1
02	Color Palette Register 2
03	Color Palette Register 3
04	Color Palette Register 4
05	Color Palette Register 5
06	Color Palette Register 6
07	Color Palette Register 7
08	Color Palette Register 8
09	Color Palette Register 9
0A	Color Palette Register 10
0B	Color Palette Register 11
0C	Color Palette Register 12
0D	Color Palette Register 13
0E	Color Palette Register 14
0F	Color Palette Register 15
10	Mode Control Register
11	Screen Border Color
12	Color Plane Enable Register
13 ★	Horizontal Panning Register
14	Color Select Register (VGA)

★ Indicates a register that is especially useful.

- **D5: Index register bit D5 (Palette Address Source)** selects whether the color palette registers of the Attribute Controller are being addressed by the Index Register (for register programming operations) or by color plane data from display memory (for normal display refresh operations). When this bit is set to zero, the palette registers are addressed by the index register and the palette can be modified by writing to address 3C0 Hex. The display will be blanked at this time. When this bit is set to one, the palette registers are addressed by screen refresh data from the color planes. The display is enabled, and the palette registers cannot be modified.

The Palette Registers (Index 0 Through F)

Palette registers allow an application program to choose which colors will be displayed at any time. The four color planes of the EGA permit 16 (2^4) simultaneous colors to be used. The Enhanced color monitor, however, can display up to 64 different colors. The 16 palette registers of the Attribute Controller determine which 16 colors are currently usable.

Each palette register contains one bit for each of the six EGA video output lines. A one in a given bit position means that video output line will be active, and a zero means it will be inactive. When the EGA is used with other displays (such as the standard Color Display or Monochrome Display), fewer lines are used. The format of a palette register is shown below for each type of display device.

Table 3-20. Palette register definition for each display type.

D7 - Reserved (0)
D6 - Reserved (0)
D5 - Secondary Red
D4 - Secondary Green
D3 - Secondary Blue
D2 - Red
D1 - Green
D0 - Blue

Enhanced color display

D7 - Reserved
D6 - Reserved
D5 - Reserved
D4 - Intensity
D3 - Reserved
D2 - Red
D1 - Green
D0 - Blue

Standard color display

D7 - Reserved
D6 - Reserved
D5 - Reserved
D4 - Intensity
D3 - Video Out
D2 - Reserved
D1 - Reserved
D0 - Reserved

Monochrome display

(continued)

Table 3-20. Palette register definition for each display type *(continued)*.

D7 - Reserved
D6 - Reserved
D5 = P5
D4 = P4
D3 = P3
D2 = P2
D1 = P1
D0 = P0

VGA display

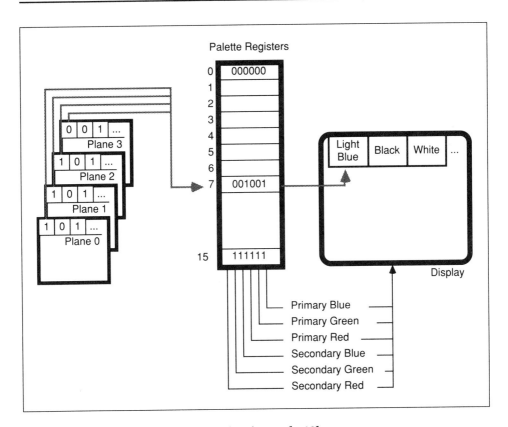

Figure 3-19. Palette register operation in mode 10hex.

To learn more about palette registers, also see:

- Standard color palette in Table 1-5 in Chapter 1.
- Text Attributes in Chapter 2.
- BIOS function 16, Set EGA Palette, in Chapter 4.
- Write Palette programming examples in Chapter 5.

Mode Control Register (Index 10)

Default Settings:	Mode 3	Mode 3*	Mode 7	Mode F	Mode 10
	08	08	0Eh	0Bh	01

In order to display attributes correctly, the Attribute Controller must be programmed for the appropriate operating mode. This is done via the Mode Control Register.

Bit Definitions:

D7 - P4, P5 Source Select (VGA ONLY) 🚫
D6 - Pixel Width (VGA ONLY) 🚫
D5 - Horizontal Panning Compatibility (VGA ONLY) 🚫
D4 - reserved (0)
D3 - Background Intensity/Enable Blink
D2 - Enable Monochrome Line Graphics
D1 - Display Type
D0 - Graphics/Text Mode

- **D0: Graphics/Text Mode** determines whether attributes are decoded as four bit graphics pixels or as byte wide text attributes. A zero enables text attributes, one enables graphics attributes.

- **D1: Display Type** determines whether monochrome or color attributes are generated. A zero selects color attributes, one selects monochrome.

- **D2: In Monochrome Text Modes,** where character cells are stretched to nine dots wide to fill the 720 dot screen, the **Enable Monochrome Line Graphics** bit will smooth block graphics by replicating the eighth dot of the character cell in the ninth dot position. The ninth dot position will otherwise be black. Block graphics characters are those characters in the monochrome character set that lie between ASCII C0 HEX and DF HEX inclusive. These characters allow the drawing of primitive graphics objects such as borders and lines.

- **D3: In all text modes, Background Intensity/Enable Blink** selects which of these two character attributes will be enabled by character attribute bit D7. A zero will allow the Background Intensity attribute to be enabled. A one will allow the Character Blink attribute to be enabled. This bit must also be set for those graphics modes that use a blinking attribute.

- **D5: Horizontal Panning Compatability (VGA only)** enhances the operation of the Line Compare register of the CRT Controller, which allows one section of the screen to be scrolled while another section remains stationary. When bit D5 is set to one, the stationary section of the screen will also become immune to horizontal panning. See Chapter 5 for a description of the Line Compare register.

- **D6: Pixel Width (VGA only)** is set to one for the VGA 256 color mode.

- **D7: P4, P5 Source Select (VGA only)** selects the source for video outputs P4 and P5. If set to zero, P4 and P5 are driven from the palette registers (normal operation). If set to one, P4 and P5 video outputs come from bits 0 and 1 of the color select register.

Screen Border Color (Index 11H)

Default Settings: 00 for all modes

In text modes, the Border Color register selects the color of the border that surrounds the text display area on the screen. This is also referred to by IBM as Overscan. The bit definitions for this register are identical to those of the 16 palette registers (see Figures 8-3 through 8-6).

Unfortunately, this feature does not work properly with many EGA adapters when the enhanced character set is used. The safest approach is to leave this register set to its default value of zero. For monochrome modes, this register should always be set to zero.

Color Plane Enable Register (Index 12)

Default Settings:	Mode 3	Mode 3*	Mode 7	Mode F	Mode 10
	0Fh	0Fh	0Fh	05	05

Bit Definitions:

D7, D6 - reserved (0)
D5, D4 - Video Status Mux
D3 - Enable color Plane 3
D2 - Enable Color Plane 2
D1 - Enable Color Plane 1
D0 - Enable Color Plane 0

- **D5, D4: The Video Status Mux** bits can be used in conjunction with the Diagnostic bits of Input Status Register 1 to read palette registers. See Chapter 4 (Input Status Register 1) for a description of how to use these bits.

- **D0–D3: Enable Color Planes** can be used to enable or disable color planes at the input to the color palette. A zero in any of these bits positions will mask the data from that color plane. The effect on the display will be the same as if that color plane were cleared to all zeros.

Horizontal Panning Register (Index 13)

Default Settings: 00 for all modes

Bit Definitions:

D7–D4 - reserved (0)
D3–D0 - Horizontal Pan

- **D3-D0: Horizontal Pan** allows the display to be shifted horizontally one pixel at a time. The start address register in the CRT Controller can shift the display by a multiple of 8 pixels at a time. Using these two registers together, an image can be smoothly panned horizontally by any amount. Panning can be used in either text or graphics modes.

Table 3-21. Pixel planning register values.

Left Pixel Shift D3 D2 D1 D0	Monochrome Text	VGA Mode 13	All other modes
0 0 0 0	8	0	0
0 0 0 1	0	invalid	1
0 0 1 0	1	1	2
0 0 1 1	2	invalid	3
0 1 0 0	3	2	4
0 1 0 1	4	invalid	5
0 1 1 0	5	3	6
0 1 1 1	6	invalid	7
1 0 0 0	7	invalid	invalid
1 0 0 1	invalid	invalid	invalid
1 0 1 0	invalid	invalid	invalid
1 0 1 1	invalid	invalid	invalid
1 1 0 0	invalid	invalid	invalid
1 1 0 1	invalid	invalid	invalid
1 1 1 0	invalid	invalid	invalid
1 1 1 1	invalid	invalid	invalid

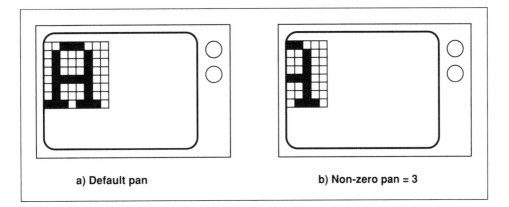

a) Default pan

b) Non-zero pan = 3

Figure 3-20. Pixel panning operation.

To learn more about pixel panning operation, also see Panning and Scrolling programming examples in Chapter 5 and Smooth Scroll programming examples in Chapter 7.

Color Select Register (Index 14)   ⊘

Bit Definitions:

D7–D4 - reserved (0)
D3 - color 7
D2 - color 6
D1 - color 5
D0 - color 4

* **D3, D2: Color 7 And Color 6** are normally used as the high order bits of the 8 bit video color data from the attribute controller to the VGA DACs. The only exception is 256 color mode.

* **D1, D0: Color 5 And Color 4** can be used in place of the P5 and P4 outputs from the palette registers. (See Mode Control register - Index 10.)

VGA Video DAC (I/O Addresses 3C6, 3C7, 3C8, and 3C9) ⊘

The VGA Video DAC is actually three video DACS (one each for Red, Green, and Blue), preceded by a Color Look-up Table. Each Video DAC converts six bits of binary color information into an analog voltage for driving the VGA analog monitor. The Color Look-up Table converts the 8 bits that are output from the VGA Attribute Controller into 18 bits (6 for each video DAC). This gives the VGA the capability of displaying 256 simultaneous colors from a palette of 256 thousand.

Five registers are used to access the Video DAC:

I/O Address	Register
3C6	Pixel Mask Register
3C7	DAC State Register (Read Only)
3C7	Look-up Table Read Index (Write Only)
3C8	Look-up Table Write Index
3C9	Look-up Table Data Register

Two separate index registers are used for selecting among the 256 internal color registers of the look-up table. The Read Index is used only when data is read from the look-up table, and the Write Index is used only when data is written to the look-up table. A color register, which is 18 bits wide, is programmed by writing an eight bit index to the Write Index Register (3C8), then writing three six-bit values to the Data Register (3C9). The index register will automatically increment after the third byte is written, so that a block of color registers can be programmed without repeatedly setting the index.

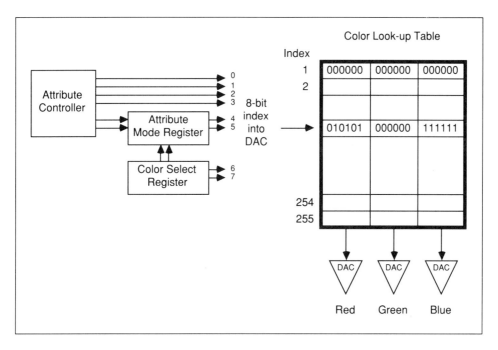

Figure 3-21. Video DAC's and Color Look-up Table.

A color register can be read by writing an eight bit index into the Read Index Register (3C7), then reading three six-bit values from the Data Register (3C9). The index register will automatically increment after the third byte is read, so that a block of color registers can be read without repeatedly setting the index.

The DAC State Register (3C7) can be read to determine whether the Color Look-up Table is currently configured for a register read operation or a register write operation. A value of zero in bits D0 and D1 indicates that the look-up table is in a read mode. A value of one in bits D0 and D1 indicates that it is in a write mode.

Unlike the Attribute Controller, processor accesses to the Color Look-up Table do not interfere with screen refresh.

IBM warns in the VGA reference manual that the Pixel Mask Register (3C6) should never be either written or read by application software.

4

The ROM BIOS

What is the ROM BIOS?

In IBM compatible microcomputers, the BIOS (Basic Input-Output System) is a set of low level firmware routines that make the resources of the system available in a standard fashion. BIOS services are provided for hard and floppy disks, serial and parallel ports, video display, and other functions. The system BIOS is located in ROM (Read Only Memory) on the system motherboard.

The standard PC/XT/AT BIOS includes a set of video services for driving the MDA and CGA display adapters. These services are accessed by executing a software interrupt instruction (INT 10H) with parameters specified in registers. Register AH specifies the function to be executed. For example:

```
mov     ah,0          ;load BIOS function number
mov     al,MODE       ;load parameter
int     10h           ;call  BIOS
```

In order to permit future system expansion, IBM defined a mechanism to permit add-in products to include their own extensions to the system BIOS. An add-in circuit board may include an on-board ROM, which will be recognized as an extension of the BIOS, providing it conforms to the IBM format. The EGA and VGA adapters both include on board BIOS extensions that take control of the INT 10H interrupt vector, supplying an expanded set of video services that are backward compatible with the standard video services. The older INT 10H vector for MDA/CGA video services is then re-installed as software interrupt INT 42H, so that the standard video services remain available in dual-display systems.

Throughout this chapter reference will be made to the EGA BIOS; unless stated otherwise, all information in this chapter applies equally to the VGA BIOS. The BIOS ROMs for EGA and VGA are 16K bytes long, and are located in the processor memory space from C000:0000h to C000:3FFFh.

Combining Text and Graphics

The text handling functions of the BIOS video services are available for use even if the EGA is configured in a graphics mode, in which case the processor must actually draw each text character into display memory. This feature can be useful for applications that combine text and graphics. For this purpose, interrupt vector INT 43H is configured as a pointer to a character generator table for drawing text. Initially, this vector points to a character set in the BIOS ROM; application programs may redirect the pointer to use a custom character set.

For CGA compatible graphics modes (modes 4, 5, and 6), the character generator pointed to by the INT 43H vector is assumed to contain only 128 characters

(ASCII 0 through 127). If additional characters are required, the application software must initialize the vector for INT 1FH to point to an additional 128 characters (ASCII 128 through 255).

Individual BIOS Functions

Mode Select – 0

BIOS function 0 can be used to initialize the display to any of the standard operating modes.

Input Parameters:

AH = 0
AL = Mode number (0 to 13H)

If AL register bit D7 equals 0, the display buffer will be cleared as part of the mode initialization. If bit D7 equals 1, the display buffer will be left unmodified.

Return Value: none

Default Setting:

EGA will default on reset to mode 0, 3, or 7, depending on the setting of the configuration switches. VGA will default to mode 3 or 7, depending on the type of display being used.

For a list of modes see Table 1-2 and the section Standard EGA Operating Modes in Chapter 1.

Example:

```
mov    ah,0
mov    al,3          ;select mode 3
or     al,80h        ;do not clear buffer
int    10h
```

To learn more about using this function, also see Set Mode programming example in Chapter 5.

Set Cursor Size – 1

The EGA cursor is a rectangle one character wide, and from one to 32 scan lines high. Its height cannot be greater than that of the character set being used. This

BIOS function defines how tall the cursor is, and where it appears with respect to a character cell. Figure 4-1 illustrates how scan lines are numbered for an 8 by 14 character cell.

Input Parameters:

AH = 1
CH = start scan line (0 - 31)
CL = end scan line (0 - 31)

Return Value: none

Default Setting:

Monochrome Display: start = 11, end = 12
Color Display: start = 6, end = 7
Enhanced Color Display: start = 11, end = 12

Example:

```
mov     ah,1            ;select cursor shape
mov     ch,0            ;cursor starts at scan line 0
mov     cl,12           ;and ends at scan line 12
int     10h             ;(full block cursor)
```

This function is one cause of the software compatibility problems that occur when different character sets are used (such as when CGA software is run using the EGA enhanced character set). In such cases, the cursor may appear in the wrong position relative to the character cell.

Some software has been written that disables the cursor by setting invalid start and end scan lines, but this technique is unreliable with products from some vendors.

To learn more about this function, also see Set Cursor Size programming examples in Chapter 7.

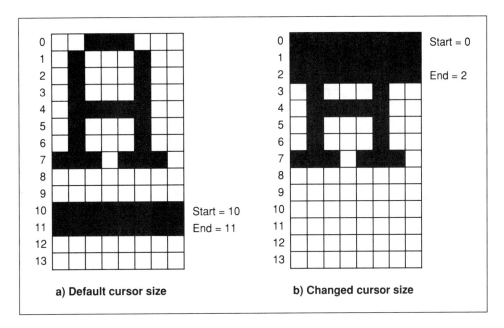

Figure 4-1. Defining cursor size.

Set Cursor Position – 2

BIOS function 2 will position the cursor at a specified location on the display screen. For modes that permit multiple display pages, a separate cursor is maintained for each display page. The cursor position function may address any display page, whether it is currently active (displayed) or not.

The position on the screen is defined in terms of row and column, this is illustrated in Figure 4-2.

Besides determining where the cursor will be displayed on the screen, the current cursor position also determines where on the screen the next character will appear when a BIOS character or string output function is executed.

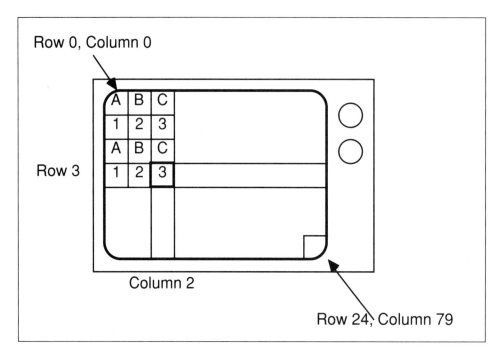

Figure 4-2. Defining position.

Input Parameters:

AH = 2
BH = display page number
DH = Row (0 - 24)
DL = Column (0 - 79)

Return Value: none

Default Setting: none

Example:

```
mov     ah,2                    ;set cursor position
mov     bh,ACTIVE_PAGE          ;on current display page
mov     dh,24                   ;bottom of screen
mov     dl,40                   ;middle column
int     10h
```

To learn more about this function, also see Set Cursor Position programming examples in Chapter 7.

Read Cursor Size and Position – 3

Data is returned regarding the current position of the cursor on the screen, and the start and end scan lines for the cursor (cursor shape). The cursor may be interrogated for any valid display page, whether it is currently active (displayed) or not.

Input Parameters:

AH = 3
BH = Display page number

Return Value:

CH = cursor start scan line
CL = cursor end scan line
DH = cursor row
DL = cursor column

Example:

```
mov     ah,3                    ;read cursor shape and position
mov     bh,1                    ;for page 1
int     10h
mov     crsr_row,dh             ;save result
mov     crsr_col,dl
```

To learn more about this function, also see Get Cursor Size and Get Cursor Position programming examples in Chapter 7.

Get Light Pen Position – 4

Information is returned regarding whether the light pen is in use, whether it has been triggered, and what its current position is on the screen. Position information is returned both in terms of pixel position (for graphics modes) and character position (for text modes).

The light pen of the EGA is not compatible with CGA. In general, CGA software that uses a light pen will not operate properly on the EGA.

The VGA adapter does not include light pen support.

Input Parameters:

AH = 4

Return Value:

AH = 0 means light pen is not down or was not triggered
AH = 1 means light pen is down and was triggered

CH = pixel row (0-348) (always a multiple of 2)
BX = pixel column
          (0-316 for 320 column modes; always a multiple of 4)
          (0-632 for 640 column modes; always a multiple of 8)

DH = char row (0-24)
DL = char column (0-39 or 0-79)

Example:

```
mov    ah,4
int    10h              ;read light pen
or     ah,ah            ;jump if not triggered
jz     no_trigger
mov    lpen_row,dh      ;save result
mov    lpen_col,dl
```

Select Active Page – 5

The specified page number, if valid, becomes the active page and is displayed on the screen. It is not necessary to select a page in order to write data to or read data from that page, or for the cursor to be addressed for that page.

Input Parameters:

AH = 5
AL = display page number

Valid page numbers are:

Modes 0, 1, 2, 3, D: pages 0 thru 7
Mode E: pages 0 thru 3
Modes F, 10:   pages 0 and 1

Return Value: none

Default Setting: page 0

Example:

```
mov     ah,5
mov     al,0                    ;select display page 0
int     10h
```

For a description of how display pages are mapped in memory, see the section on Standard Operating Modes in Chapter 1.

Scroll Text Window Up (Or Blank Window) – 6

A specified portion of the current active display page (the scroll window) is scrolled upward a specified number of lines. The empty lines created at the bottom of the scroll window are filled with spaces. All display area outside of the display window is left unchanged. Data that is scrolled past the top of the window is lost.

The scroll window is a rectangle that is defined by specifiying the screen coordinates of the upper-left corner and lower-right corner of the window. Figure 4-3 illustrates how a scroll window is specified.

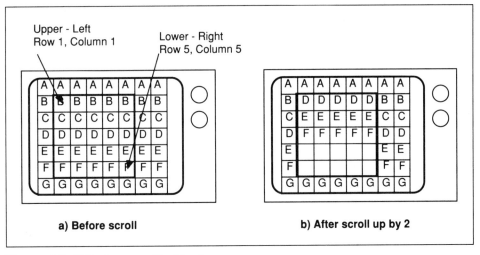

a) Before scroll   b) After scroll up by 2

Figure 4-3. Window scroll of text.

When the upper-left and upper-right corners of the window coincide with the screen corners, this function provides a convenient way to clear a screen (using scroll by 25 or 0 lines).

Input Parameters:

AH = 6
AL = number of lines to scroll
(AL = 0 blanks window to all spaces)
BH = text attribute to use when filling blank lines at bottom of window
CH = row number (0-24) of upper-left corner of window
CL = column number (0-79) of upper-left corner of window
DH = row # (0-24) of lower-right corner of window
DL = column # (0-79) of lower-right corner of window

Return Value: none

Example:

```
mov     ah,6                       ;scroll window up
mov     al,scroll_count            ;# of lines to scroll
mov     bh,7                       ;normal attribute

mov     ch,0                       ;window starts
mov     cl,0                       ;at top left

mov     dh,12                      ;window ends at midscreen,
mov     dl,79                      ;full screen width

int     10h
```

To learn more about scrolling also see the next function, Scroll Text Window Down in this chapter, and Chapter 7 programming examples Scroll Text Window and Scroll Page.

Scroll Text Window Down (Or Blank Window) – 7

A specified portion of the current active display page (the scroll window) is scrolled downward a specified number of lines. The empty lines created at the top of the scroll window are filled with spaces. All display area outside of the display window is left unchanged. Data that is scrolled past the bottom of the window is lost.

The scroll window is a rectangle that is defined by specifiying the screen coordinates of the upper left corner and lower right corner of the window. Figure 4-4 illustrates how a scroll window is specified.

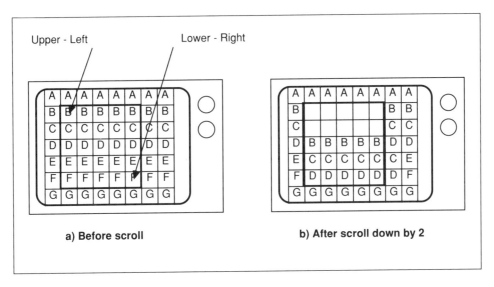

Figure 4-4. Window scroll of text.

When the upper-left and upper-right corners of the window coincide with the screen corners, this function provides a convenient way to clear a screen (using scroll by 25 lines).

Input Parameters:

AH = 7
AL = number of lines to scroll
(AL = 0 blanks window to all spaces)
BH = text attribute to use when filling blank lines at top of window
CH = row number (0-24) of upper-left corner of window
CL = column number (0-79) of upper-left corner of window
DH = row # (0-24) of lower-right corner of window
DL = column # (0-79) of lower-right corner of window

Return Value: none

Example:

```
mov     ah,7                    ;scroll window down
mov     al,scroll_count         ;# of lines to scroll
mov     bh,7                    ;normal attribute

mov     ch,12                   ;window starts
mov     cl,0                    ;at mid-screen
```

```
mov     dh,25                       ;window ends at bottom,
mov     dl,79                       ;full screen width

int     10h
```

To learn more about scrolling also see the previous function, Scroll Text Window Up, and Chapter 7 programming examples Scroll Text Window and Scroll Page.

Read Character and Attribute at Cursor Position – 8

BIOS function 8 returns the ASCII character at the current cursor position of any display page, as well as its character attribute.

Input Parameters:

AH = 8
BH = display page number

Return Value:

AL = ASCII character
AH = character attribute

Example:

```
mov     ah,8                        ;read character and attribute
mov     bh,active_pg                ;at cursor position-active page
int     10h
mov     ascii_data,al               ;al = ASCII
mov     attr_data,ah                ;ah = Attribute
```

To learn more about this function, also see Read Character and Read Attribute programming examples in Chapter 7 (_BIOS_Read_Char, _BIOS_Read_Attr and _BIOS_Invert).

Write Character and Attribute at Cursor Position – 9

An ASCII character and attribute value are written to display memory at the current cursor position of any valid display page. A repetition count may be specified, in which case the write operation will be repeated in sequential memory locations until the repetition count is reached. Results are not guaranteed if a repetition count is used that will attempt to write beyond the end of the current character row.

The cursor is not automatically incremented and will remain at its current location.

Input Parameters:

AH = 9
BH = display page number
AL = ASCII character
BL = attribute (text modes) or color value (graphics modes)
CX = repetition count (up to end of current row)

If the EGA is operating in a graphics mode and bit D7 of register BL equals 1, the character being written will be exclusive ored with the previous data in display memory.

Example:

```
mov     ah,9                    ;write char and attribute
mov     bh,active_page          ;to current page
mov     al,ascii_data
mov     bl,7                    ;standard attribute
mov     cx,1                    ;no repetition
int     10h
```

To learn more about character write, also see:

• BIOS functions Write Character and Attribute (9), Write Character and Advance Cursor (14) and Write Text String (19).

• Write Character, Write String and Write Attribute programming examples in Chapter 7 (_BIOS_Char_9, _BIOS_Char_A, _BIOS_Char_E, _BIOS_Write_String and _BIOS_Invert).

Write Character Only at Cursor Position – 10 (0A hex)

An ASCII character is written to display memory at the current cursor position of any valid display page. The previous character attribute is preserved. A repetition count may be specified, in which case the write operation will be repeated in sequential memory locations until the repetition count is reached. Results are not guaranteed if a repetition count is used that will attempt to write past the end of the current character row.

The cursor is not automatically incremented and will remain at its current location.

Input Parameters:

AH = 0Ah
AL = ASCII character
BH = display page number
BL = color value (graphics modes)
CX = repetition count

If the EGA is operating in a graphics mode and bit D7 of register BL equals 1, the character being written will be exclusive ored with the previous data in display memory.

Return Value: none

Example:

```
mov    ah,0ah              ;write character
mov    al,ascii_data       ;(attribute is not modified)
mov    bh,active_page      ;to current page
mov    cx,1                ;no repetition
int    10h
```

To learn more about character write, also see:

• BIOS functions Write Character Only (10), Write Character and Advance Cursor (14) and Write Text String (19).

• Write Character, Write String and Write Attribute programming examples in Chapter 7 (_BIOS_Char_9, _BIOS_Char_A, _BIOS_Char_E, _BIOS_Write_String and _BIOS_Invert).

Set CGA Color Palette (Modes 4, 5, 6) – 11 (0B hex)

This function call is included in the EGA BIOS for CGA compatibility. Function 0BH will configure the EGA to emulate one of the two standard CGA graphics color palettes. Table 4-1 describes the graphics color palettes of the CGA.

Table 4-1. CGA colors in modes 4 and 5.

Pixel value	Palette 0	Palette 1
0	Same as background	Same as background
1	Green	Cyan
2	Red	Magenta
3	Brown	White

Input Parameters:

AH = 0Bh

If BH = 0:
BL = graphics background color (0-15) or text border color (0-15)

If BH = 1:
BL = palette number (0 or 1)

Return Value: none

Example:

```
mov     ah,0Bh
mov     bh,0            ;select background color
mov     bl,bgnd_color
int     10h

mov     ah,0Bh
mov     bh,1
mov     bl,0            ;select palette 0
int     10h
```

Write Graphics Pixel – 12 (0C hex)

Function 0Ch provides a device independent, but very slow, method for ma-
nipulating pixels in graphics mode. Valid values for the various graphics modes
are summarized in Table 4-2.

Table 4-2. Legal pixel values for BIOS function 12.

Mode	Legal pixel values
4, 5	0 thru 3
6	0 and 1
D	0 thru 15
E	0 thru 15
F	0 and 1
10	0 thru 15

Input Parameters:

AH = 0Ch
AL = pixel value (See Table 4-2)
CX = pixel column number (0 - 639)
DX = pixel row number (0 - 349), (0-479 on VGA)

If bit D7 of register AL is set to one, the new pixel value will be exclusive-ored with the existing background color.

Return Value: none

Example:

```
mov     ah,0Ch
mov     al,line_color
mov     cx,pixel_column
mov     dx,pixel_row
int     10h
```

To learn more about this function, also see Write Pixel programming example _BIOS_Write_Pixel in Chapter 8.

Read Graphics Pixel – 13 (0D hex)

This function provides a device independent, but very slow, method for reading pixels in graphics modes.

Input Parameters:

AH = 0Dh
CX = pixel column number (0 - 639)
DX = pixel row number (0 - 349)

Return Value: AL = pixel value

Example:

```
mov    ah,0dh
mov    cx,pixel_column
mov    dx,pixel_row
int    10h                      ;read pixel value
mov    pixel_value,al           ;save result
```

To learn more about this function, also see Read Pixel programming example _BIOS_Pixel_Read in Chapter 8.

Write Character and Advance Cursor – 14 (0E hex)

This function is sometimes referred to as TELETYPE MODE, because its behavior is similar to an ASCII terminal when receiving a character. The character is displayed at the current cursor position, and the cursor is automatically advanced to the next character position. At the end of a line, the cursor will wrap around to the next line. ASCII BELL, BACKSPACE, CARRIAGE RETURN and LINEFEED are recognized and their functions are performed accordingly. Vertical scrolling is performed as required.

If the EGA is operating in a text mode, the character attribute is left unmodified. If operating in a graphics mode, the character color may be specified in the call.

Function 14 is used by the standard MS-DOS console driver for screen handling.

Input Parameters:

AH = 0Eh
AL = ASCII character
BH = page number (text modes only)
BL = character color (graphics modes only)

Return Value: none

Example:

```
mov    ah,0Eh
mov    al,ascii_char            ;display character
mov    bh,active_page           ;on current active page
int    10h
```

To learn more about character write, also see:

• BIOS functions Write Character and Attribute (9), Write Character Only (10), and Write Text String (19).

• Write Character, Write String and Write Attribute programming examples in Chapter 7 (_BIOS_Char_9, _BIOS_Char_A, _BIOS_Char_E, _BIOS_Write_String and _BIOS_Invert).

Get Current Display Mode – 15 (0F hex)

Function 15 can be used to determine the current operating mode of the EGA. Table 1-2 in Chapter 1 has a summary of all the valid modes.

Input Parameters:

AH = 0Fh

Return Value:

AH = number of display columns
AL = display mode (0-13h)
BH = active display page

Example:

```
mov    ah,0Fh
int    10h
mov    current_mode,al
mov    active_page,bh
```

To learn more about this function, also see:

• BIOS function Mode Select (0).

• Standard Operating Modes section in Chapter 1.

• Get Display Mode programming example _BIOS_Get_Mode in Chapter 6.

Set EGA Palette Registers – 16 (10 hex)

Function 16 is the preferred method for defining colors for the EGA, or for controlling the other functions of the Attribute Controller. It can be invoked in any one of four different forms:

Subfunction 0 - program a single palette register
Subfunction 1 - program the border color register
Subfunction 2 - program all palette registers
Subfunction 3 - enable foreground blink attribute or background intensify attribute

The following functions are available on VGA only:

Subfunction 7 - read a single palette register
Subfunction 8 - read the border color register
Subfunction 9 - read all palette registers
Subfunction 10h - program a single DAC register
Subfunction 12h - program multiple DAC registers
Subfunction 13h - select color subset
Subfunction 15h - read a single DAC register
Subfunction 17h - read multiple DAC registers
Subfunction 1Ah - read color page state
Subfunction 1bh - convert DAC registers to gray scale

To learn more about palette registers, also see:

- Text Attributes section in Chapter 2.

- Attribute Controller section in Chapter 2.

- Attribute Controller Registers in Chapter 3.

- Write Palette programming examples in Chapter 5.

Set a Single Palette Register – 0

Input Parameters:

AH = 10h
AL = 00h
BL = palette register number (0 thru F)
BH = color data

Return Value: none

Example:

```
mov     ah,10h
mov     al,0
mov     bl,reg_num
mov     bh,new_color
int     10h
```

Set Border Color – 1

This function sets the border color register of the Attribute Controller (sometimes called Overscan). This register must be used with extreme care, as border color does not work properly in some modes on many EGA compatible products.

Input Parameters:

AH = 10h
AL = 01h
BH = color data

Return Value: none

Example:

```
mov     ah,10h
mov     al,1
mov     bh,new_color
int     10h                 ;set border color
```

Set All Palette Registers – 2

This function provides a fast method of programming all of the EGA palette registers. Palette color data must be located in a 17 byte table somewhere in system memory. Bytes 0 through 15 contain data for palette registers 0 through 15. Byte 16 is the border (overscan) color.

Input parameters:

AH = 10h
AL = 02h
ES:DX = address of palette data

Return Value: none

Example:

```
mov     ax,ds
mov     es,ax                           ;get pointer
mov     dx,offset color_table           ;to color table
mov     ah,10h
mov     al,2
int     10h                             ;load palette registers
```

Also see Write Palette programming examples _BIOS_Palette in Chapter 5.

Blink/Intensity Attribute Control – 3

This function provides a convenient method of toggling the control bit that defines whether the blinking attribute is enabled or the intensified background attribute is enabled (See Chapter 2 - Attribute Controller).

Input Parameters:

AH = 10h
AL = 03h
BL = 0 - enable background intensify
BL = 1 - enable foreground blink

Return Value: none

Example:

```
mov     ah,10h
mov     al,3
mov     bl,1            ;enable blinking
int     10h
```

Also see Text Blink programming examples in Chapter 7.

Read a Single Palette Register – 7   ⊘

Taking advantage of the readable registers of VGA, this function returns the current contents of a palette register.

Input Parameters:

AH = 10h
AL = 7
BL = register number (0-15)

Return Value:

BH = palette register value

Example:

```
mov     cx,16
mov     bx,0            ;start with palette register 0
```

```
palette_read_loop:
mov     ah,10h
mov     al,7
mov     bl,0            ;read contents of palette registers
int     10h
mov     palette_data[bx],bh        ;and save
inc     bx
loop    palette_read_loop
```

Read Border Color Register – 8 ⊘

Taking advantage of the readable registers of the VGA, this function returns the contents of the Border Color (Overscan) Register.

Input Parameters:

AH = 10h
AL = 8

Return Value:

BH = border color register value

Example:

```
mov     ah,10h
mov     al,8
int     10h             ;read border color
mov     border_color,bh
```

Read All Palette Registers – 9 ⊘

Taking advantage of the readable registers of the VGA, this function reads all palette register.

Input Parameters:

AH = 10h
AL = 9
ES:DX = pointer to destination for 17 byte data table

Return Value: 17 bytes stored at [ES:BX]

Example:

```
mov     ah,10h
mov     al,9
les     dx,palette_data          ;set up pointer to destination
int     10h                      ;read palette registers
```

Set a Single DAC Register – 10 hex   ⊘

Set the 18 bit color value in a single DAC register.

Input Parameters:

AH = 10h
AL = 10h
BX = DAC register number (0-255)
DH = Red intensity level (6 bits)
CH = Green intensity level (6 bits)
CL = Blue intensity level (6 bits)

Return Value: none

Example:

```
mov     ah,10h
mov     al,10h
mov     bx,regnum                ;DAC register #
mov     ch,green_level
mov     cl,blue_level            ;color intensities
mov     dh,red_level
int     10h                      ;set DAC register
```

Set Block of DAC Registers – 12 hex   ⊘

Set the 18 bit color values in a block of DAC registers.

Input Parameters:

AH = 10h
AL = 12h
BX = starting DAC register (0-255)
CX = number of registers to set (1-256)
ES:DX = address of color table

The color table consists of 3 bytes per register (red, green, and blue.)

Return Value: none

Example:

```
mov     ah,10h
mov     al,12h
mov     bx,regnum                      ;set starting register #
mov     cx,regcount                    ;set # of registers
les     dx,color_table                 ;point to color data
int     10h                            ;load registers
```

Select Color Subset – 13 hex   ⊘

This function selects one of up to 16 color subsets.

Input Parameters:

AH = 10h
AL = 13h

    BL = 0: Select mode
        BH = 0: 4 subsets of 64 colors
        BH = 1: 16 subsets of 16 colors

    BL = 1: Select subset
        BH = subset (0-16)

Return Value: none

Example:

```
mov     ah,10h
mov     al,13h
mov     bl,1
mov     bh,3                           ;select color subset 3
int     10h
```

Read a Single DAC Register – 15 hex   ⊘

Read the contents of a single DAC register.

Input Parameters:

AH = 10h
AL = 15h
BX = DAC register number (0-255)

Return Value:

DH = red intensity level (6 bits)
CH = green intensity level (6 bits)
CL = blue intensity level (6 bits)

Example:

```
mov     ah,10h
mov     al,15h
mov     bx,regnum
int     10h                     ;read DAC register
mov     green_value,ch
mov     blue_value,cl
mov     red_value,dh            ;save results
```

Read Block of DAC Registers – 17 hex ⊘

Read the contents of a block of DAC registers.

Input Parameters:

AH = 10h
AL = 17h
BX = starting DAC register number (0-255)
CX = number of registers (1-256)
ES:DX = destination address for register data

Return Value:

Register data at destination address (3 bytes per register)

Example:

```
mov     ah,10h
mov     al,17h
mov     bx,regnum               ;get starting register
mov     cx,regcount             ;get # of registers
les     dx,dac_data             ;point to destination
int     10h                     ;read DAC registers
```

Read Subset Status – 1A hex ⊘

This subfunction returns the number of the current color subset.

Input Parameters:

AH = 10h
AL = 1ah

Return Value:

BH = number of current color subset

BL = 0 if 4 subsets are available
BL = 1 if 16 subsets are available

Convert DAC Registers to Gray Scale – 1B hex ⊘

This subfunction converts a block of DAC registers from color values to monochrome gray scale values. For each register, the color data is read and a weighted sum computed (30 percent red, 59 percent green, and 11 percent blue.) The result is then written back to all three color components of the register. The original register data is lost.

Input Parameters:

AH = 10h
AL = 1bh
BX = starting DAC register number (0-255)
CX = number of registers (1-256)

Return Value: none

Example:

```
mov     ah,10h
mov     al,1bh
mov     bx,0
mov     cx,256              ;convert all DAC registers
int     10h                 ;from color to monochrome
```

Load Character Generator – 17 (11 hex)

Function 17 is the recommended method to load a character generator (either standard or custom) into display memory for text mode operation. The adapter mode will be re-initialized, but the display memory will not be cleared. Either a partial or a complete character generator may be loaded. The following different forms can be used:

Subfunction 0 & 16 - Load custom character generator
Subfunction 1 & 17 - Load standard monochrome character set
Subfunction 2 & 18 - Load standard CGA character set
Subfunction 3 & 19 - Select active EGA character set(s) (0-3)
Subfunction 4 & 14 - Load VGA 16 line character set
Subfunction 32 (20H) - Initalize CGA graphics for custom character set
              (set INT 1FH vector)
Subfunction 33 (21H) - Initialize graphics mode to display text from custom character set
              (set INT 43H vector)
Subfunction 34 (22H) - Initialize graphics mode to display standard enhanced (8 x 14) text
              (set INT 43H vector)
Subfunction 35 (23H) - Initialize graphics mode to display standard CGA text
              (set INT 43H vector)
Subfunction 36 (24H) - Initialize graphics mode to display VGA 16 line text
              (set INT 43H vector)
Subfunction 48 (30H) - Return information about current character set

Setting bit D4 (10 hex) in register AL on calls of type 0 through 4 instructs the BIOS to recalculate certain CRT controller settings, such as Max Scan Line, Cursor Start and End, and Underline Location, based on the number of bytes per character (character height) specified. This can be useful for loading nonstandard character sets, though it is not guaranteed to work for all character sizes. If this feature is used, this function must follow immediately after a mode set command.

To learn more about character generators, also see:

- Display Memory in Text Modes section in Chapter 2.

- Character Generator Select Register of the Sequencer in Chapter 3.

- Read Character Generator, Write Character Generator, 512 Character Set and 43 Line Text programming examples in Chapter 7.

Load Custom Character Generator – 0

This form of function 17 will allow an application program to load a custom character set, or replace a portion of the standard character set with custom characters. The user character table must be loaded into system memory before this function is called; afterward, it may be deleted from system memory.

Input Parameters:

AH = 11h
AL = 0
ES:BP = address of character data in system RAM
CX = number of characters to load (1-256)
DX = character offset into character generator table
(0-255 - for loading a partial character set)
BL = which EGA character table to load (0-3), (0-7 for VGA)
BH = number of bytes per character (1-32)

Return Value: none

Example:

```
mov    ax,ds
mov    es,ax                ;point to char set to load
mov    bp,offset char_set
mov    cx,128               ;load 128 chars only
mov    dx,0                 ;starting at char 0
mov    bl,1                 ;load it as EGA char set 1
mov    bh,14                ;8x14 char = 14 bytes per char
mov    ah,11h
mov    al,0                 ;load custom character set
int    10h                 ;perform load
```

Also see Write Character Generator programming examples procedure _BIOS_Write_CG, and 512 Character Set programming examples procedure _BIOS_512_Set, in Chapter 7.

Load Monochrome Character Set – 1

This form of function 17 loads the standard EGA monochrome character set from the BIOS ROM to display memory plane 2.

Input Parameters:

AH = 11h
AL = 1
BL = which EGA character table to load (0-3), (0-7 for VGA)

Return Value: none

Example:

```
mov     ah,11h
mov     al,1            ;load monochrome character set
mov     bl,0            ;as EGA char set 0
int     10h
```

Load CGA Character Set – 2

This form of function 17 loads the standard CGA 8 x 8 character set from the BIOS ROM to plane 2 of EGA display memory.

Input Parameters:

AH = 11h
AL = 2
BL = which EGA character table to load (0-3), (0-7 for VGA)

Return Value: none

Example:

```
mov     ah,11h
mov     al,2            ;load CGA character set
mov     bl,3            ;as EGA char set 3
int     10h
```

Also see assembly programming example in 43 Line Text in Chapter 7.

Select Active Character Set(s) – 3

This form of function 17 allows the application to select which of the EGA's four internal character generator tables will be active. Before a table is made active, it must be loaded with character data using one of the other forms of function 17.

Input Parameters:

AH = 11h
AL = 3
BL (D0, D1) - Selects which character table will be active
                     for a text character with attribute bit 3 = 0
BL (D2, D3) - Selects which character table will be active
                     for a text character with attribute bit 3 = 1

Return Value: none

Example:

```
mov     bl,char_set_2                    ;select second char set
shl     bl,1
shl     bl,1
or      bl,char_set_1                    ;select first char set
mov     ah,11h
mov     al,3
int     10h
```

Also see 512 Character Set programming examples procedure _BIOS_512_Set in Chapter 7.

Load VGA 16 Line Character Set – 4   ⊘

Load the standard VGA 8 x 16 character set into plane 2 of display memory.

Input Parameters:

AH = 11h
AL = 4
BL = which VGA character table to load (0-7)

Return Value: none

Example:

```
mov     ah,11h
mov     al,4                             ;load VGA character set
mov     bl,3                             ;as VGA char set 3
int     10h
```

Initialize INT 1FH Vector (Modes 4, 5, and 6) – 20 hex

This function can be used in CGA compatible graphics modes (modes 4, 5, and 6) if more than 128 characters are required. The vector for INT 1FH is used to point to a table with an additional 128 characters (ASCII 128 through 255). The application must provide these additional characters. All characters must be 8 pixels in height.

Input Parameters:

AH = 11h
AL = 20h
ES:BP = Address in system RAM where characters are located.

Return Value: none

Example:

```
mov     ax,ds
mov     es,ax
mov     bp,offset char_table
mov     ah,11
mov     al,20h
int     10h                     ;initialize vector
```

Set Graphics Mode to Display Custom Char Set – 21 hex

This function can be used by applications that combine text and graphics. The adapter will be initialized to a graphics mode, and vectors initialized so that text can be drawn using a custom character set. The character set must remain resident in system memory, since it is not loaded into EGA display memory.

While normal text modes always operate with 25 rows of test, graphics modes permit the number of text rows to be varied. The CGA 8 x 8 character set can be displayed on an enhanced graphics display with 43 rows of text (see 43 Line Text programming examples in Chapter 7).

Input Parameters:

AH = 11h
AL = 21h
ES:BP = address of custom character table in system RAM
CX = bytes per character
BL = number of character rows to be displayed:

      BL = 1 - 14 character rows
      BL = 2 - 25 character rows
      BL = 3 - 43 character rows
      BL = 0 - DL contains number of character rows

Return Value: none

Example:

```
mov     ax,ds
mov     es,ax
mov     bp,offset char_set      ;get address
mov     cx,8                    ;8 bytes per char
mov     bl,3                    ;43 rows of text
mov     ah,11h
mov     al,21h
int     10h
```

Set Graphics Mode to Display Enhanced Text – 22 hex

This function will initialize the adapter to a graphics mode and configure it to display the standard EGA enhanced character set.

Input Parameters:

AH = 11h
AL = 22H
BL indicates number of character rows on screen
      BL = 1 - 14 character rows
      BL = 2 - 25 character rows

Return Value: none

Example:

```
mov     ah,11h
mov     al,22h          ;configure for enhanced text
mov     bl,2            ;25 character rows
int     10h
```

Initialize Graphics Mode to Display Standard CGA Text – 23 hex

This function will initialize the adapter to a graphics mode and configure it to display the standard CGA character set.

Input Parameters:

AH = 11h
AL = 23H
BL indicates number of character rows on screen
      BL = 2 - 25 character rows
      BL = 3 - 43 character rows

Return Value: none

Example:

```
mov     ah,11h
mov     al,23h          ;configure for CGA text
mov     bl,3            ;43 rows
int     10h
```

Initialize Graphics Mode to Display VGA Text – 24 hex

This function will initialize the adapter to a graphics mode and configure it to display the VGA 16 pixel high character set.

Input Parameters:

AH = 11h
AL = 24H
BL indicates number of character rows on screen
    BL = 1 - 14 character rows
    BL = 2 - 25 character rows
    BL = 3 - 43 character rows

Return Value: none

Example:

```
mov    ah,11h
mov    al,24h          ;configure for VGA text
mov    bl,3            ;43 rows
int    10h
```

Return Information About Current Character Set – 30 hex

The final form of function 17 can be used to read information about the current character set being used.

Input Parameters:

AH = 11h
AL = 30h
BH = Information type requested
    BH = 0: return current INT 1FH pointer
    BH = 1: return current INT 43H pointer
    BH = 2: return pointer to Enhanced (8 x 14) character set
    BH = 3: return pointer to CGA (8 x 8) character set
    BH = 4: return pointer to upper half of ROM 8 x 8 character set
    BH = 5: return pointer to alternate 9 x 14 monochrome characters
    BH = 6: return pointer to alternate 8 x 16 monochrome characters
    BH = 7: return pointer to alternate 9 x 16 monochrome characters

Return Values:

CL = character height (number of rows in a character)
DL = character rows on screen
ES:BP = return pointer

Example:

```
mov     ah,11h
mov     al,30h
mov     bh,0
int     10h                    ;get information on character set
mov     char_height,cl
mov     char_rows,dl
```

Also see Read Character Generator programming examples in Chapter 7.

Get EGA Status (Set Alternate Print Screen) – 18 (12 hex)

Function 18 is really a group of unrelated functions that share the same function number:

Subfunction 10h - returns information on the current EGA/VGA configuration.

This function can also be used to determine if an EGA is present in the system, allowing applications to automatically configure for the system (See Example below).

Subfunction 20h - selects an alternate print screen routine.

The following subfunctions are available on VGA only. They can also be used to check for the presence of a VGA in the system. If a VGA is present, the function call will return a value of 12h in register AL:

Subfunction 30h - set text mode scan lines (VGA only).
Subfunction 31h - enable/disable palette load on mode select (VGA only).
Subfunction 32h - enable/disable VGA adapter (VGA only).
Subfunction 33h - enable/disable gray scale conversion (VGA only).
Subfunction 34h - enable/disable CGA cursor emulation (VGA only).
Subfunction 35h - switch displays (VGA only).
Subfunction 36h - display on/off (VGA only).

Return Information on Current EGA/VGA Configuration – 10 hex

Besides returning useful information about the current state of the display adapter, this function can also be used to determine if an EGA or VGA is present in the system, allowing applications to automatically configure for the system.

Input Parameters:

AH = 12h
BL = 10h

Return Values:

BH = 1 if adapter is in monochrome mode
BH = 0 if adapter is in color mode

BL = 0 if EGA has 64KB of display memory
BL = 1 if EGA has 128KB of display memory
BL = 2 if EGA has 192KB of display memory
BL = 3 if EGA has 256KB of display memory

CH = Feature Control bits
CL = EGA configuration switches

If no EGA or VGA is present in the system, BH and BL will be unmodified by the function call. This can be used to test for presence of an EGA or VGA, as shown in the following example:

Example:

```
mov     bh,55h              ;known arbitrary BH value
mov     ah,12h
mov     bl,10h              ;read EGA status
int     10h
cmp     bh,55h
je      no_ega              ;is an EGA present?
mov     mode,bh
mov     memsize,bl          ;save result
```

Select Alternate Print Screen Routine – 20 hex

This function selects an alternate print screen routine that is capable of printing the screen while in 43 row text mode.

Input Parameters:

AH = 12h
BL = 20h

Return Value: none

Example:

```
mov    ah,12h
mov    bl,20h
int    10h                    ;enable alternate print screen routine
```

Set Text Mode Scan Lines – 30 hex   ⊘

This function improves VGA compatibility with CGA by setting the screen resolution that will be used when a text mode is initialized by a Mode Select. Enhanced
text modes can then be used with CGA software that uses Mode Select commands.

Input Parameters:

AH = 12h
BL = 30h

AL = 0: use double-scanned 200 line mode with CGA (8 x 8) text.
AL = 1: use 350 scan line mode with EGA enhanced (8 x 14) text.
AL = 2: use 400 scan line mode with VGA enhanced (9 x 16) text.

Return Value: AL = 12h

Example:

```
mov    ah,12h
mov    bl,30h
mov    al,0          ;next Mode Select will use double scanned CGA text
int    10h
```

Enable/Disable Palette Load on Mode Select – 31 hex   ⊘

This function can be used to prevent the palette from being initialized with default data during a mode select operation, which can be useful if a custom palette
has been programmed.

Input Parameters:

AH = 12h
BL = 31h

AL = 0: enable palette initialization on mode select
AL = 1: disable palette initialization on mode select

Return Value: AL = 12h

Example:

```
mov     ah,12h
mov     bl,31h
mov     al,1                    ;disable palette initialization
int     10h                     ;to preserve custom palette
```

Enable/Disable VGA Adapter – 32 hex   ∅

This function disables the VGA from responding to any I/O or memory reads or writes. The display is not affected.

Input Parameters:

AH = 12h
BL = 32h

AL = 0: enable VGA
AL = 1: disable VGA

Return Value: AL = 12h

Example:

```
mov     ah,12h
mov     bl,32h
mov     al,1                    ;disable VGA I/O and memory spaces
int     10h
```

Enable/Disable Gray Scale Conversion – 33 hex   ∅

This function will enable and disable the gray scale conversion feature of VGA. When enabled, a gray scale conversion will be performed when the DAC registers are loaded by a Mode Select or DAC Register Load function call.

Input Parameters:

AH = 12h
BL = 33h

AL = 0: enable gray scale conversion
AL = 1: disable gray scale conversion

Return Value: AL = 12h

Example:

```
mov     ah,12h
mov     bl,33h
mov     al,1              ;disable gray scale conversion
int     10h
```

Enable/Disable CGA Cursor Emulation – 34 hex

   This function addresses the cursor compatibility problem when CGA software
that sets cursor shape is used with EGA or VGA enhanced text. Because of the
larger character cell used with enhanced text, the cursor will appear in the wrong
part of the character cell unless CGA cursor emulation is enabled to translate the
cursor parameters (Cursor Start and Cursor End) to different values.

Input Parameters:

AH = 12h
BL = 34h

AL = 0: enable CGA cursor emulation
AL = 1: disable CGA cursor emulation

Return Value: AL = 12h

Example:

```
mov     ah,12h
mov     bl,34h
mov     al,1              ;disable CGA cursor emulation
int     10h
```

Switch Displays – 35 hex   ⊘

   This function can be used to switch between a VGA, which is located on the
system motherboard in PS/2 systems, and a plug-in display adapter, even if the

two adapters have conflicting memory and I/O spaces. The PS/2 will initialize with the plug-in adapter as the primary display; the four variations of this function must then be executed in proper order to perform display switching.

The calling program must supply a pointer to a 128 byte buffer for storage of display state data.

Input Parameters:

AH = 12h
BL = 35h
ES:DX = pointer to 128 byte state save buffer

AL = 0: turn off plug-in display adapter (Must Be Used First)
AL = 1: turn on VGA (Must Be Used Second)

AL = 2: turn off active display adapter (used for subsequent switches)
AL = 3: turn on inactive display adapter (used for subsequent switches)

Return Value: AL = 12h

Example:

```
;for first display switch:

mov     ah,12h
mov     bl,35h
les     dx,save_buffer
mov     al,0
int     10h                     ;turn off plug-in adapter

mov     ah,12h
mov     bl,35h
les     dx,save_buffer
mov     al,1
int     10h                     ;turn on VGA adapter

;for subsequent display switches:

mov     ah,12h
mov     bl,35h
les     dx,save_buffer
mov     al,2
int     10h                     ;turn off current display
```

```
mov     ah,12h
mov     bl,35h
les     dx,save_buffer
mov     al,3
int     10h                      ;turn on the other display
```

Display On/Off – 36 hex   ⊘

This function will blank and unblank the VGA display.

Input Parameters:

AH = 12h
BL = 36h

AL = 0: enable display
AL = 1: disable display

Return Value: AL = 12h

Example:

```
mov     ah,12h
mov     bl,36h
mov     al,1
int     10h                      ;blank VGA display
```

Write Text String – 19 (13 hex)

Function 19 allows an application to pass an entire text string to the BIOS for display. The text string may be straight ASCII data, or it may include embedded attribute data. The cursor may be advanced to the end of text, or it may be left unmodified. The ASCII characters for BELL (7), BACKSPACE (8), CARRIAGE RETURN (0D hex) and LINEFEED (0A hex) are recognized and their appropriate functions performed.

Input Parameters:

AH = 13h
BH = display page number
CX = character count (length of string)
DH = row number for start of string
DL = column number for start of string
ES:BP = address of source text string in system RAM
AL = mode

AL = 0: BL = Attribute for all characters. Cursor is not updated.
AL = 1: BL = Attribute for all characters. Cursor is updated.
AL = 2: String contains both ASCII and Attributes. Cursor is not updated.
AL = 3: String contains both ASCII and Attributes. Cursor is updated.

Return Value: none

Example:

```
string   db     "Hello there", 0Dh, 0Ah
string_end db   0

mov      ax,cs
mov      es,ax
mov      bp,offset string              ;get address of text
mov      bh,active_page                ;output to current page
mov      cx,string_end-string          ;get character count
mov      dx,0                          ;display at top of page
mov      al,1                          ;cursor will be updated
mov      bl,7                          ;normal attribute
int      10h
```

To learn more about character write, also see:

- BIOS functions Write Character and Attribute (9), Write Character Only (10), and Write Character and Advance Cursor (14).

- Write Character, Write String, and Write Attribute programming Examples in Chapter 7 (_BIOS_Char_9, _BIOS_Char_A, _BIOS_Char_E, _BIOS_Write_String and _BIOS_Invert).

Read or Write Configuration – 26 (1A hex)   ⊘

This function is used to read or modify information on the current configuration of display devices in the system. It consists of two subfunctions.

Read Display Configuration Code – 0   ⊘

Returns current display configuration.

Input Parameters:

AH = 1ah
AL = 0

Return Values:

AL = 1ah
BL = primary display
BH = secondary display

Display information is interpreted as follows:

    0 = no display
    1 = MDA
    2 = CGA
    3 = EGA with ECD display
    4 = EGA with CD display
    5 = EGA with Monochrome Display
    6 = PGC (Professional Graphics Controller)
    7 = VGA with monochrome display
    8 = VGA with color display
    0bh = MCGA with monochrome display
    0ch = MCGA with color display

Example:

```
mov     ah,1ah
mov     al,0
int     10h                     ;read display configuration
mov     primary,bl
mov     secondary,bh            ;save results
```

Write Display Configuration Code – 1   ⊘

Modifies current display configuration information.

Input Parameters:

AH = 1ah
AL = 1
BL = primary display info
BH = secondary display info

For an explanation of information codes, see subfunction 1.

Return Value: AL = 1ah

Example:

```
mov    ah,1ah
mov    al,1
mov    bl,primary
mov    bh,secondary
int    10h                    ;set configuration data
```

Return VGA Status Information – 27 (1B hex)   ⊘

Returns information about the state of the display.

Input Parameters:

AH = 1bh
BX = 0
ES:DI = pointer to 64 byte buffer for return data

Return Values:

AL = 1bh
The return buffer will contain the following information:

Byte	Size	Contents
0-3	dword	pointer to STATIC FUNCTIONALITY TABLE
4	byte	current display mode
5, 6	word	number of character columns
7, 8	word	size of video data area (REGEN BUFFER) in bytes
9, 0ah	word	address of REGEN BUFFER
0bh–1ah	8 words	Cursor positions for up to 8 pages
1bh	byte	Cursor start
1ch	byte	Cursor end
1dh	byte	current display page
1eh	word	CRT Controller address (3B4/3D4)
22h	byte	number of text rows
23h	byte	character height (in pixels)
25h	byte	Display Configuration Code (active display)
26h	byte	Display Configuration Code (inactive display)
27h, 28h	word	number of colors in current mode
29h	byte	number of display pages in current mode

2ah	byte	number of scan lines in current mode
		0=200 1=350 2=400 3=480
2bh	byte	Primary character map (0-7)
2ch	byte	Secondary character map (0-7)
2dh	byte	Miscellaneous state information:

D5 = 1 - blinking enabled
D5 = 0 - background intensify enabled
D4 = 1 - CGA cursor emulation enabled
D3 = 1 - default palette initialization disabled
D2 = 1 - Monochrome display attached
D1 = 1 - Gray scale conversion enabled

31h	byte	size of display memory
		0=64KB 1=128KB 2=192KB 3=256KB
32h	byte	Save Pointer State Information

D4 = 1 - Palette Override Active
D3 = 1 - Graphics Font Override Active
D2 = 1 - Alpha Font Override Active
D1 = 1 - Dynamic Save Area Active
D0 = 1 - 512 Character Set Active

The Static Functionality Table is formatted as follows:

Byte	Size	Contents
0-2	3 bytes	Table of video modes supported - one bit per mode:

Byte 0 Bit/Mode	Byte 1 Bit/Mode	Byte 2 Bit/Mode
D7 - 7	D7 - F	D7
D6 - 6	D6 - E	D6
D5 - 5	D5 - D	D5
D4 - 4	D4 - C	D4
D3 - 3	D3 - B	D3 - 13
D2 - 2	D2 - A	D2 - 12
D1 - 1	D1 - 9	D1 - 11
D0 - 0	D0 - 8	D0 - 10

Byte	Size	Contents
7	byte	Available resolutions

D2 - 400 scan lines
D1 - 350 scan lines

		D0 - 200 scan lines
8	byte	number of text mode character maps
9	byte maps	maximum number of active text mode character
0ah	byte	Miscellaneous functions
		D7 - multiple DAC color tables
		D6 - DAC palette
		D5 - EGA palette
		D4 - CGA cursor emulation
		D3 - Default Palette Loading
		D2 - Character Font Loading
		D1 - gray scale conversion
		D0
0bh	byte	Miscellaneous functions
		D3 - Display Configuration Codes
		D2 - Blinking enabled
		D1 - video state save/restore
		D0 - light pen support
0eh	byte	Save Pointer Functions
		D4 - Palette Override
		D3 - Graphics Font Override
		D2 - Alpha Font Override
		D1 - Dynamic Save Area
		D0 - 512 character set

Save/Restore Display Adapter State – 28 (1C hex)   ⊘

This function can be used to save and restore the state of the display, which is useful when the display must be quickly switched back and forth between different modes. It includes three subfunctions:

Subfunction 0 - Return required buffer size
Subfunction 1 - Save display adapter state
Subfunction 2 - Restore display adapter state

Return Required Buffer Size – 0   ⊘

Returns the required size of the buffer area that must be supplied by the host for storing state information.

Input Parameters:

AH = 1ch
AL = 0
CX = type of data to be saved
    0 = registers
    1 = BIOS data area
    2 = DAC registers

Return Value:

AL = 1ch
BX = required buffer size (in 64 byte blocks)

Example:

```
mov     ah,1ch
mov     al,0
mov     cx,2                    ;find the required buffer size
int     10h                     ;to save DAC registers
mov     size,bx
```

Save Display Adapter State – 1   ⊘

This subfunction saves adapter state data into a buffer area supplied by the calling program.

Input Parameters:

AH = 1ch
AL = 1
CX = type of data to be saved
    0 = registers
    1 = BIOS data area
    2 = DAC registers
    ES:BX = pointer to save buffer

Return Value: AL = 1ch

Example:

```
mov     ah,1ch
mov     al,1
mov     cx,1
les     bx,data_buffer
int     10h                     ;save BIOS data area
```

Restore Display Adapter State – 2   ⊘

This subfunction restores adapter state data from a buffer area supplied by the calling program.

Input Parameters:

AH = 1ch
AL = 2
CX = type of data to be restored
   0 = registers
   1 = BIOS data area
   2 = DAC registers
ES:BX = pointer to save buffer

Return Value: AL = 1ch

Example:

```
mov     ah,1ch
mov     al,1
mov     cx,0
les     bx,reg_buffer
int     10h                        ;restore VGA registers
```

The BIOS Data Area

Variables in Low Memory

BIOS maintains a set of variables to preserve important information such as the current display mode and cursor position. These are stored in system memory segment 0000 hex in bytes 400 - 500 hex. Programs that directly alter the status of the display should update these variables to avoid confusing BIOS.

0000:0410	BYTE	EQUIPMENT_FLAG

Bits D4 and D5 of this byte identify the current primary display device:

D5 D4	Adapter
0 0	EGA (or none)
0 1	CGA 40 x 25
1 0	CGA 80 x 25
1 1	MDA

0000:0449	BYTE	VIDEO_MODE	(current mode)
0000:044A	WORD	COLUMNS	(number of text columns)
0000:044C	WORD	PAGE_LENGTH	(length of each page in bytes)
0000:044E	WORD	START_ADDR	(Start Address Register value)
0000:0450	8 WORDS	CURSOR_POSITION	(cursor positions for all pages)
0000:0458	WORD	CURSOR_SHAPE	(Cursor Start and End Registers)
0000:045A	BYTE	ACTIVE_PAGE	(current active page number)
0000:045B	WORD	CRTC_ADDRESS	(3B4 or 3D4)
0000:045D	BYTE	MODE_REG_DATA	(CGA Mode Register setting)
0000:045E	BYTE	PALETTE	(CGA palette setting)
0000:0484	BYTE	ROWS	(number of text rows - 1)
0000:0485	WORD	CHAR_HEIGHT	(bytes per char)
0000:0487	BYTE	EGA_INFO_1	

D7 - equals bit D7 from AL register on most recent mode
      select. (A one indicates display memory was
      not cleared by mode select.)

D6, D5 - Display memory size (00=64K, 01=128K,
      10=192K, 11=256K)

D4 - reserved

D3 - A zero indicates EGA is the primary display.

D2 - A one will force the BIOS to wait for Vertical
      Retrace before writing to display memory.

D1 - A one indicates that EGA is in monochrome mode.

D0 - A zero means that CGA cursor emulation is
      enabled. The cursor shape will be modified if
      enhanced text is used.

0000:0488	BYTE	EGA_INFO_2	

D4-D7 - Feature Control Bits (from Feature Control
   Register)

D0-D3 - EGA Configuration Switch settings

0000:04A8	DWORD	ENVIRON_PTR	

ENVIRON_PTR contains a double word (four byte) pointer that points to the environment table, which is a table of pointers.

Environment Table

The environment table has eight double word pointers, defined as follows:

- **Pointer 1** (mandatory): Pointer to the Parameter Table, which contains the default EGA/VGA register values for the current mode.

- **Pointer 2** (optional): Pointer to the Dynamic Save Area, which is an optional 256 byte area used by the BIOS to save palette information during a mode select function. Since this data is simply copied from the Parameter Table, it can be considered redundant.

- **Pointer 3** (optional): Pointer to the Text Mode Auxiliary Character Set Table, which controls how user defined character sets are used in text modes.

- **Pointer 4** (optional): Pointer to the Graphics Mode Auxiliary Character Set Table, which controls how user defined character sets are used in graphics modes.

- **Pointer 5** (optional - VGA only): Pointer to the VGA Secondary Save Area, which is an expansion of the environment table.

- **Pointers 6, 7, and 8** are reserved. All optional pointers must be zero if not used.

At system initialization, the Environment Pointer is set to point to an Environment Table in ROM. This default Environment Table has only one entry (the Parameter Table Pointer). To modify the Environment Table, first copy it from ROM to RAM and then update the Environment Pointer.

Parameter Table

The Parameter Table is used for initialization of EGA/VGA registers. It has default register data for each of the standard adapter modes. The table contains 64 bytes per mode, arranged as follows:

Byte	Contents
0	Number of text columns
1	Number of text rows
2	Character height (in pixels)
3 and 4	Display page length (in bytes)
	Sequencer register values:
5	Clock Mode Register
6	Color Plane Write Enable Register

7		Character Generator Select Register
8		Memory Mode Register
9	Miscellaneous Register	
	CRT Controller register values:	
0ah		Horizontal Total Register
0bh		Horizontal Display End Register
0ch		Start Horizontal Blanking Register
0dh		End Horizontal Blanking Register
0eh		Start Horizontal Retrace Register
0fh		End Horizontal Retrace Register
10h		Vertical Total Register
11h		Overflow Register
12h		Preset Row Scan Register
13h		Maximum Scan Line Register
14h		Cursor Start
15h		Cursor End
16h-19h		Unused
1ah		Vertical Retrace Start Register
1bh		Vertical Retrace End Register
1ch		Vertical Display End Register
1dh		Offset Register
1eh		Underline Location Register
1fh		Start Vertical Blanking Register
20h		End Vertical Blanking Register
21h		Mode Control Register
22h		Line Compare Register
	Attribute Controller Register Values:	
23h		Palette Register 0
24h		Palette Register 1
25h		Palette Register 2
26h		Palette Register 3
27h		Palette Register 4
28h		Palette Register 5
29h		Palette Register 6
2ah		Palette Register 7
2bh		Palette Register 8
2ch		Palette Register 9
2dh		Palette Register 10
2eh		Palette Register 11
2fh		Palette Register 12
30h		Palette Register 13
31h		Palette Register 14

32h	Palette Register 15
33h	Mode Control Register
34h	Screen Border Color (Overscan) Register
35h	Color Plane Enable Register
36h	Horizontal Panning Register
	Graphics Controller register values:
37h	Set/Reset Register
38h	Set/Reset Enable Register
39h	Color Compare Register
3ah	Data Rotate & Function Select Register
3bh	Read Plane Select Register
3ch	Mode Register
3dh	Miscellaneous Register
3eh	Color Don't Care Register
3fh	Bit Mask Register

Modes are ordered in the parameter table as follows:

Table #	Mode	
0	0	
1	1	
2	2	
3	3	
4	4	
5	5	
6	6	
7	7	
8	8	
9	9	
10	A	
11	B	
12	C	
13	D	
14	E	
15	F	(EGA with 64K byte display RAM)
16	10	(EGA with 64K byte display RAM)
17	F	(more than 64K bytes)
18	10	(more than 64K bytes)
19	0*	
20	1*	
21	2*	
22	3*	

23	0+, 1+ (VGA only)
24	2+, 3+ (VGA only)
25	7+ (VGA only)
26	11 (VGA only)
27	12 (VGA only)
28	13 (VGA only)

Text Mode Auxiliary Character Set Table

This table controls the loading of user defined font tables in text modes. Its format is as follows:

Byte	Size	Contents
0	byte	Bytes per character
1	byte	Character Map number (0-3 for EGA, 0-7 for VGA)
2, 3	word	number of characters
4, 5	word	first character number
6, 7, 8, 9	dword	pointer to character set in system memory
10	byte	character height (in pixels)
11-n	bytes	list of modes this character set is compatible with, terminated by FFh

Graphics Mode Auxiliary Character Set Table

This table defines how to display a user defined character set in graphics mode.

Byte	Size	Contents
0	byte	number of character rows on display
1, 2	word	bytes per character
3, 4, 5, 6	dword	pointer to character set in system memory
7-n	bytes	list of modes this character set is compatible with, terminated by FFh

To learn more about using the BIOS Data Area, also see programming examples in Getting Information in Chapter 6.

Part II

Programming Examples

Introduction

The programming examples in Chapters 5–8 are meant to illustrate how the features of the EGA and VGA can be used to perform useful graphics and text operations. Examples are given in the form of a subroutine library, with source and object code included on the diskette, which is located in the back of the book.

While not intended as a comprehensive graphics library, the examples do illustrate real applications of the EGA and VGA. Two versions of the library are included; the first is compatible with Borland's Turbo Pascal and the second is compatible with the Microsoft C compiler. Where appropriate, sample code is included in both Pascal and C showing how each routine functions and how it can be used. Also where appropriate, assembly language code is shown to explain how each subroutine functions.

Most of the examples are written to be compatible with both EGA and VGA. The resulting code, while highly portable, may not in some cases be optimum for either. In some cases, for instance, the read back capability of VGA registers might permit a routine to be simplified if EGA compatibility is not required. For the sake of brevity, references made to EGA should be assumed to apply equally to VGA unless specifically stated otherwise.

Consideration is also given to the value of these examples as learning tools, and readability has taken precedence over optimization of code.

It should be noted that routines in the library will preserve the contents of processor registers as required by the Pascal and C compilers. Registers AX, BX, CX, and DX may not be preserved.

How To Read the Examples

Examples in Chapters 5–8 are grouped into four sections:

1.   Register Manipulation (EGA/VGA specific hardware control).

2.   Getting Information (Functions that return EGA/VGA status information).

3.   Text operations such as cursor control, scrolling, and so forth.

4.   Graphic operations such as line drawing, and the like.

In order to make these examples useful and easy to read for programmers of different experience levels, a layered approach is used for the documentation of each example:

At the highest level, the Library Function Descriptions and Examples describe the function performed by the library routine, how it is called from both Pascal and C, and the return value if any.

At the next lower level, the Theory section describes the inner workings of the library routine, showing algorithms in high level language and explaining the use of BIOS functions if they are used. References are made to other sections of the book where more detailed information can be found.

At the lowest level, the Assembly Code section shows the actual assembly language code that is used to control the hardware of the EGA/VGA. In all cases, complete source code is available on the diskette located in the back of the book.

Due to the low level interface of the EGA and VGA adapters, software will usually operate much more efficiently if some assembly language is used than if all tasks are performed in a high level language. In general, the programming examples will illustrate both how to perform a task in high level language and how to optimize it through the use of assembly language. Readers who are not comfortable with assembly language can ignore most of the assembly level examples if desired. A short tutorial on assembly language is included in the Appendix.

What's on the Diskette?

The diskette that is included with this book contains source and object code for all the programming examples shown in Chapters 5-8. For detailed information on the diskette contents, print the contents of the READ.ME file on the diskette, or display it using the DOS commands TYPE and MORE.

TYPE A:READ.ME | MORE

Two subdirectories are on the diskette. The PASCAL directory contains examples in a form that is compatible with Borland's Turbo Pascal, and the MSC directory contains examples that are compatible with the SMALL model of Microsoft C, and with Borland's Turbo C.

Each programming example is contained in its own source file. Files named PROGC###.C contain C source code. Files named PROGP###.PAS contain Pascal source code. Files named PROG###.ASM contain C compatible assembly language source code. Files named PROG###P.ASM contain Pascal compatible assembly language source code.

Due to the space limitiation on the diskette, all source code files for programming examples have been "packed". Read the READ.ME file on the diskette to find out which packed files contain the source code. The organization of the diskette is similar to that in Figure I-1.

File EGALIBP.TPU is a Turbo Pascal Unit file containing the subroutine library. EGALIBC.OBJ contains the library in C compatible format.

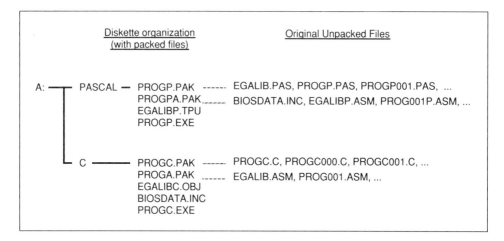

Figure I-1. Files on the diskette.

Using the Library Routines

Two approaches may be taken to using the subroutines provided; the source code may be incorporated into user programs, or the library object file may be linked with user programs.

Using Individual Programming Examples

To use the source code for assembly language library routines, use the INCLUDE directive of the assembler to include the source code in your program. The source files do not contain segment definitions so that you can include them in any assembly language program. Some of the library routines need definitions for BIOS data area variables; the file "BIOSDATA.INC" should therefore be included as well. For example, to include source file "PROG023.ASM" the following lines should be added to your program:

```
_TEXT   SEGMENT ...
        your code
        INCLUDE BIOSDATA.INC
        INCLUDE PROG023.ASM
        more of your code
_TEXT   ENDS    ...
        END
```

The data used in the "BIOSDATA.INC" file is described in the BIOS Data Area section of Chapter 3. The content of the file is:

File: BIOSDATA.INC

```
;********************************************************************
; Video BIOS Data Area Locations                                   *
;********************************************************************

BIOS_Mode        EQU    449H        ;Location of current mode
BIOS_CRT_Addr    EQU    463H        ;Address of CRT controller
BIOS_Rows        EQU    484H        ;Number of text rows
BIOS_Columns     EQU    44AH        ;Number of text columns
BIOS_Height.     EQU    485H        ;Character height
BIOS_Page_Size   EQU    44CH        ;Number of bytes in one page
BIOS_Curs_Mode   EQU    460H        ;Cursor start and end
BIOS_Equipment   EQU    487H        ;Type of equipment in system
BIOS_Switch      EQU    488H        ;Configuration switches
BIOS_Curs_Pos    EQU    450H        ;Current cursor address
BIOS_Curs_Start  EQU    460H        ;Current cursor shape
BIOS_Curs_Stop   EQU    461H
```

The C language source code examples and Pascal examples can be included in your source code in a similar manner. To include source code for the line drawing routine in file PROGC086.C in your C program, the following lines should be in your program:

```
...
your C code
#include "progc086.c"
more of your C code
...
```

For the Pascal programs the example source code can be included using the following lines as part of your program:

```
program my_program;
uses egalibp;
...
your code
{$I progp068.pas}
more of your code
...
end.
```

Building a Graphics Library for Microsoft C

To rebuild an object file containing all library functions, enter:

    MASM   EGALIBC;

The source file EGALIBC.ASM contains an include statement for each library function file PROG###.ASM, combining them into one object file called EGALIBC.OBJ. If you do not have an access to the MASM program, you can use instead the standard version of EGALIBC.OBJ provided on the diskette.

The object file EGALIBC.OBJ can be linked with user programs using the LINK utility:

    LINK MYPROG+EGALIBC;

or, if desired, it can be converted to a library module using the Microsoft LIB utility.

Also on the diskette are files PROGC.C and PROGC.EXE. This is a program that can be used to test all of the library functions.

Building a Graphics Library for Turbo Pascal

To build an object file containing all library functions, enter:

    MASM   EGALIBP;

The source file EGALIBP.ASM contains an include statement for each library function file PROG###P.ASM, combining them into one object file called EGALIBP.OBJ.

The Turbo Pascal compatible object file can be converted into a Turbo Pascal Unit file by entering:

    TPC EGALIBP

which builds a Turbo Pascal Unit file called EGALIBP.TPU, using the object file EGALIBP.OBJ and the Pascal source code file EGALIBP.PAS.

If you do not have access to the MASM utility, the standard version of EGALIBP.TPU is provided on the supplied diskette.

To make the library part of your Pascal program include the EGALIBP unit in the **uses** clause, using the following lines in your program:

```
program my_program;
uses egalibp;
...your code
...more of your code
end.
```

Also on the diskette are files named PROGP.PAS and PROGP.EXE. This is a program that can be used to test all of the library functions.

5

Register Manipulation

These library routines, which directly modify control registers on the EGA/ VGA, must be used with great care. Some registers can be safely modified at any time; others must be accessed in a particular order or initialized with particular data for the display to operate properly. Improper use of registers can interfere with display operation, and in some cases will actually cause physical damage to the display. Before attempting to modify a register, be sure to read carefully the register description provided in Chapter 3.

The examples included in this chapter are not intended to perform meaningful graphics functions. They simply illustrate the proper procedure to follow when modifying the contents of an EGA/VGA control register.

Write Register

Write a Value to an EGA Control Register

Pascal Library Procedure

procedure Write_Register(register:integer;data:byte);
                            {register to load, data value}

C Library Procedure

```
write_register(register, data)
int    register;                /* Register to load           */
char   data;                    /* Data value to load         */
```

Example

The following example, written in C, changes the text cursor from underline to full cursor by setting Cursor Start to a value of one. Note that two WRITE_REGISTER I/O operations are needed to load the register.

Listing 5-1. File: PROGC001.C

```
/***********************************************************************/
/* Write 1 into register 0A hex, CURSOR START, in the CRT controller   */
/***********************************************************************/

write_curs_start()
      {
      /* Change cursor start to 0 at both mono and color CRT addresses*/
      write_register(0x03D4, 0x0A);   /* Select register 07 in CRTC   */
      write_register(0x03D5, 0x01);   /* Load selected reg with 1     */
      write_register(0x03B4, 0x0A);   /* Select register 07 in CRTC   */
      write_register(0x03B5, 0x01);   /* Load selected reg with 1     */
      }
```

In Pascal, the procedure looks like this:

Listing 5-2. File: PROGP001.PAS

```
{/********************************************************************/}
{/* Write 1 into register 0A hex, CURSOR START, in the CRT controller   */}
{/********************************************************************/}

procedure write_curs_start;
begin
        Write_Register($3D4,$0A);        {/* Select register 07 in CRTC   */}
        Write_Register($3D5,$01);        {/* Load selected reg with 1     */}
        Write_Register($3B4,$0A);        {/* Select register 07 in CRTC   */}
        Write_Register($3B5,$01);        {/* Load selected reg with 1     */}
end;
```

Theory

The lowest level function that can be performed on the EGA/VGA is the loading of data into a selected register. For most (but not all) EGA registers, this is a two-step process; a control register is first selected by outputting a register index, using the processor's OUT DX,AL instruction, then data is output to the register.

Index and data registers are usually at sequential I/O addresses (for instance, 3C4 for sequencer index and 3C5 for sequencer data). In the IBM PC and AT, one 16 bit I/O write instruction will automatically be converted into two 8 bit I/O write operations at sequential addresses. Therefore, an 8 bit write to an index register, followed by an 8 bit write to a data register, can be reduced to one 16 bit I/O write, with the index in the low data byte and the data in the high data byte. For instance, the instruction sequence

```
        MOV     AL,Index
        MOV     DX,Port
        OUT     DX,AL
        MOV     AL,Data
        INC     DX
        OUT     DX,AL
```

can be converted to:

```
        MOV     AL,Index
        MOV     AH,Data
        MOV     DX,port
        OUT     DX,AX
```

The Attribute Controller of the EGA, which has both the index register and data register are mapped at 3C0h, has the same registers also mapped at 3C1h so that 16 bit I/O writes can be used. With the VGA, 16 bit I/O will work when reading the Attribute Controller but not when writing to it.

Another speed improvement can be gained by taking advantage of the fact that index registers retain their current value until modified. If a particular register is going to be written to or read from repetitively, the index only needs to be set once; the data register can then be written or read as many times as needed.

Before modifying any EGA/VGA registers, read the register description provided in this book carefully. In general, the following rules must be adhered to when modifying registers:

• Before modifying some of the registers in the Sequencer, the Sequencer must be placed into a reset condition using its Reset Register. While the sequencer is in a reset state, all functions of the EGA/VGA are halted.

• Before modifying the palette registers of the Attribute Controller, the Palette Address Source bit must be reset in the Attribute Controller index register. While this bit is reset, the display will be blanked.

• The I/O addresses of several EGA/VGA registers depend on the type of display being used (monochrome or color).

• CRT Controller registers that are involved in video timing require special care since incorrect register values may cause damage to the display. Any routine that loads video timing registers must be written in assembly language. A high level language (such as C or Pascal) will execute too slowly, possibly resulting in invalid display timing for an unacceptable length of time. It is also recommended that the display be blanked while timing registers are modified.

For the majority of applications that use the EGA/VGA in one of its standard operating modes, initialization of video timing registers should be left to the BIOS. Access to these registers can then be avoided entirely.

The important criteria to be considered when modifying EGA/VGA registers are summarized by the following pseudocode:

```
if (Miscellaneous Register is being modified)
        No special care needed, write directly to register

else if (CRT Controller register is being modified)
        {
        is CRTC in monochrome mode (address 3B4) or color mode (address 3D4)?

        is this a 'dangerous' register?

        output register index to address 3B4 or 3D4
        output register data to address 3B5 or 3D5
        }

else if (Attribute Controller register is being modified)
        {
        Is the current mode color or monochrome?

        Reset attribute controller Index/Data flip-flop by reading address 3BA
        or 3DA.

        If (this is a color palette register)
                {
                output register index, with PALETTE ADDRESS SOURCE bit clear, to
                address 3C0
                output register data to address 3C0
                output 20h to address 3C0 to re-enable video
                }
        else
                {
                output register index, with PALETTE ADDRESS SOURCE bit set, to
                address 3C0
                output register data to address 3C0
                }
        }

else if (Graphics Controller register is being modified)
        {
        output register index to address 3CE
        output register data to address 3CF
        }

else if (Sequencer register is being modified)
        {
        if (Clock Mode Register)
                {
                output 0 to index register (3C4)
                output 01 to data register (3C5) to synchronously halt the
                sequencer
                output register index to index register (3C4)
                output register data to data register (3C5)
                output 0 to index register (3C4)
                output 3 to data register (3C5) to re-enable sequencer
                }
        else
```

```
                    {
                    output register index to index register (3C4)
                    output register data to data register (3C5)
                    }
            }
```

To learn more about individual registers, see Chapter 3.

Assembly Code Examples

Listing 5-3. File: PROG001.ASM

```
;*********************************************************************
; Load register example                                             *
; Load CRTC register 0Ah with the value 20h                         *
;*********************************************************************

Change_Underline          PROC NEAR
        PUSH    ES
        XOR     AX,AX                   ;Set ES to point to BIOS data area
        MOV     ES,AX
        MOV     DX,ES:[BIOS_CRT_Addr]   ;Fetch CRTC address
        MOV     AL,0AH                  ;Fetch index
        OUT     DX,AL                   ;Select register
        INC     DX                      ;Increment register address
        MOV     AL,20H                  ;Fetch value
        OUT     DX,AL                   ;Load the register with value
        POP     ES
        RET
Change_Underline          ENDP
```

A faster way to output data to a register takes advantage of the fact that the Output Word instruction of the processor causes two bytes of data to be output to two sequential I/O addresses.

Listing 5-4. File: PROG002.ASM

```
;*********************************************************************
; Load CRT register 0Ah with the value 20h                          *
; Faster way (too fast for some chip sets)                          *
;*********************************************************************

Fast_Change_Underline   PROC NEAR
        MOV     DX,3D4H                 ;Fetch CRTC address (assumes color)
        MOV     AX,200AH                ;Fetch data and index
        OUT     DX,AX                   ;Select index and write data
        RET
Fast_Change_Underline   ENDP
```

A general routine which can be called from a higher level language, like C, is shown next.

Listing 5-5. File: PROG003.ASM

```
;****************************************************************************
; Write_Register                                                          *
; Write a value to a register                                            *
; Entry:         Register - Output port to write value to                *
;                Value    - Value to output                              *
;****************************************************************************

Register       EQU      [BP+4]
Value          EQU      [BP+6]

        PUBLIC   _Write_Register
_Write_Register PROC NEAR
        PUSH     BP
        MOV      BP,SP
        MOV      DX,Register              ;Fetch register address
        MOV      AL,Value
        OUT      DX,AL
        POP      BP
        RET
_Write_Register ENDP
```

Write Register Set

Load All EGA Control Registers

Pascal Library Procedure

```
procedure Write_Register_Set(table_seg,table_offset:integer);
                        {segment and offset of register data list}
```

C Library Procedure

```
load_register_set(list_ptr)
char    *list_ptr;                      /* Pointer to register data list      */
```

Example

To initialize the adapter to text mode (40 column for color, 80 column for monochrome).

Register values in the following example will not work with VGA displays. For VGA display use register values in Appendix B-4.

Listing 5-6. File: PROGC002.C

```
/***************************************************************************/
/* Load all control registers using a table                               */
/* First we determine type of display attached and then load register     */
/* with values for mode 3 (if Color display) or mode 7 (if Mono display)*/
/* Do not use with VGA Display                                             */
/***************************************************************************/

select_mode_x()
        {
        #define MONO    5
        #define VMONO   7
        #define VCOLOR  8

        static  char    mode_0[] = {
                0xD4,                               /* CRTC Address          */
                0x23,                               /* Miscellaneous Regs    */
                0x0B,0x03,0x00,0x03,                /* Sequencer             */
                                                    /* CRT Controller        */
                0x37,0x27,0x2D,0x37, 0x31,0x15,0x04,0x11,
                0x00,0x07,0x06,0x07, 0x00,0x00,0x00,0x00,
                0xE1,0x24,0xC7,0x14, 0x08,0xE0,0xF0,0xA3, 0xFF,
                                                    /* Graphics Controller   */
                0x00,0x00,0x00,0x00, 0x00,0x10,0x0E,0x00, 0xFF,
                                                    /* Attribute Controller  */
                0x00,0x01,0x02,0x03, 0x04,0x05,0x14,0x07,
                0x38,0x39,0x3A,0x3B, 0x3C,0x3D,0x3E,0x3F,
                0x08,0x00,0x0F,0x00};

        static  char    mode_3[] = {
                0xD4,                               /* CRTC Address          */
                0xA7,                               /* Miscellaneous Regs    */
                0x01,0x03,0x00,0x03,                /* Sequencer             */
                                                    /* CRT Controller        */
                0x5B,0x4F,0x53,0x37, 0x51,0x5B,0x6C,0x1F,
                0x00,0x0D,0x0B,0x0C, 0x00,0x00,0x00,0x00,
                0x5E,0x2B,0x5D,0x28, 0x0F,0x5E,0x0A,0xA3, 0xFF,
                                                    /* Graphics Controller   */
                0x00,0x00,0x00,0x00, 0x00,0x10,0x0E,0x00, 0xFF,
                                                    /* Attribute Controller  */
                0x00,0x01,0x02,0x03, 0x04,0x05,0x14,0x07,
                0x38,0x39,0x3A,0x3B, 0x3C,0x3D,0x3E,0x3F,
                0x08,0x00,0x0F,0x00};

        static  char    mode_7[] = {
                0xB4,                               /* CRTC Address          */
                0xA6,                               /* Miscellaneous Regs    */
                0x00,0x03,0x00,0x03,                /* Sequencer             */
                                                    /* CRT Controller        */
                0x60,0x4F,0x56,0x3A, 0x51,0x60,0x70,0x1F,
                0x00,0x0D,0x0B,0x0C, 0x00,0x00,0x00,0x00,

                0x5E,0x2E,0x5D,0x28, 0x0D,0x5E,0x6E,0xA3, 0xFF,
                                                    /* Graphics Controller   */
                0x00,0x00,0x00,0x00, 0x00,0x10,0x0A,0x00, 0xFF,
                                                    /* Attribute Controller  */
```

```
                    0x00,0x08,0x08,0x08, 0x08,0x08,0x08,0x08,
                    0x10,0x18,0x18,0x18, 0x18,0x18,0x18,0x18,
                    0x0E,0x00,0x0F,0x08};

        if (get_display_type() == VCOLOR)
                {
                write_register_set(mode_3);     /* Set VGA into mode 3    */
                getchar();
                set_mode(3);
                }

        else if (get_display_type() == MONO || get_display_type() == VMONO)
                {
                write_register_set(mode_7);     /* Set EGA into mode 7    */
                getchar();
                set_mode(7);
                }
        else
                {
                write_register_set(mode_0);     /* Set EGA into mode 0    */
                getchar();
                set_mode(3);
                }
    }
```

Listing 5-7. File: PROGP002.PAS

```
{/*******************************************************************/}
{/* Load all control registers using a table                       */}
{/* First we determine type of display attached and then load register */}
{/* with values for mode 3 (if Color display) or mode 7 (if Mono display)*/}
{/*******************************************************************/}

procedure select_mode_x;
const
MONO = 5;
VMONO = 7;
VCOLOR = 8;
mode_0 : array[0..60] of byte = ($D4,$23,$B,3,0,3,
                $37,$27,$2D,$37, $31,$15,$04,$11,
                0,7,6,7, 0,0,0,0,
                $E1,$24,$C7,$14,8,$E0,$F0,$A3, $FF,
                                                {/* Graphics Controller */}
                0,0,0,0,0,$10,$0E,0, $FF,
                                                {/* Attribute Controller */}
                0,1,2,3,4,5,$14,7,
                $38,$39,$3A,$3B, $3C,$3D,$3E,$3F,
                8,0,$0F,0,0);

mode_3 : array[0..60] of byte = ($D4,$A7,01,3,0,3,
                $5b,$4f,$53,$37, $51,$5b,$6c,$1f,
                0,$0d,$0b,$0c, 0,0,0,0,
                $5e,$2b,$5d,$28,$0f,$5e,$0a,$A3, $FF,
                                                {/* Graphics Controller */}
                0,0,0,0,0,$10,$0E,0, $FF,
                                                {/* Attribute Controller */}
```

```
                0,1,2,3,4,5,$14,7,
                $38,$39,$3A,$3B, $3C,$3D,$3E,$3F,
                8,0,$0F,0,0);

mode_7 : array[0..60] of byte = ($B4,$A6,0,3,0,3,
                $60,$4F,$56,$3A, $51,$60,$70,$1F,
                0,$0D,$0B,$0C,0,0,0,0,
                $5E,$2E,$5D,$28,$0D,$5E,$6E,$A3, $FF,
                                                {/* Graphics Controller */}
                0,0,0,0,0,$10,$0A,0, $FF,
                                                {/* Attribute Controller */}
                0,8,8,8,8,8,8,8,
                $10,$18,$18,$18, $18,$18,$18,$17,
                $0E,0,$0F,8,0);

var
table_seg : word;
table_offset: word;
c : char;
begin
        table_seg := seg (mode_7);
        if Get_Display_Type = VCOLOR then
                begin
                    table_offset := ofs (mode_3);
                    Write_Register_Set (table_seg,table_offset);
                    c := readkey;
                    Set_Mode(3);
                end

        else if Get_Display_Type = MONO then
                begin
                    table_offset := ofs (mode_7);
                    Write_Register_Set (table_seg,table_offset);
                    c := readkey;
                    Set_Mode(3);
                end

        else if Get_Display_Type = VMONO then
                begin
                    table_offset := ofs (mode_7);
                    Write_Register_Set (table_seg,table_offset);
                    c := readkey;
                    Set_Mode(3);
                end

        else
                begin
                    table_offset := ofs (mode_0);
                    Write_Register_Set (table_seg,table_offset);
                    c := readkey;
                    Set_Mode(3);
                end;

end;
```

Theory

This library procedure loads all EGA/VGA registers, as would be required to initialize a special (customized) display mode. Because of the interactions between different registers, registers cannot be initialized in any arbitrary order. For example, to change a Clock Mode register in the Sequencer Reset, the Reset register in the Sequencer must first be set to 01. The procedure described here illustrates how to properly load the registers.

The register data list pointer points to a string of 60 bytes, which are ordered as follows:

1 byte - Low byte of CRT Controller address (B4 for mono, D4 for color)
1 byte - data for Miscellaneous Register
4 bytes - data for Sequencer registers (Index 0 through 3)
25 bytes - data for CRT Controller registers (Index 0 through 18 hex)
9 bytes - data for Graphics Controller (Index 0 through 8)
20 bytes - data for Attribute Controller (Index 0 through 13h)

The following algorithm describes the sequence for loading all registers:

- Save address of CRT Controller (3B4 or 3D4)

- Disable video via the Attribute Controller

- To make sure graphics controllers are properly enabled,
  output 00 to address 3CC
  output 01 to address 3CA

- Load Miscellaneous Register

- Halt Sequencer by writing 01 to the Reset Register

- Load Sequencer Registers 1 through 3

- Start Sequencer by writing 03 to the Reset Register

- Load CRT Controller Registers

- Load Graphics Controller Registers

- Reset Index/Data Flip-Flop in Attribute Controller

- Clear Palette Address Source bit in Attribute Controller

- Load Attribute Controller registers

- Set Palette Address Source bit in Attribute Controller

- Enable video via the of the Attribute Controller

For most applications, register initialization is accomplished quickly and easily by performing a call to BIOS function 0, Mode Select, to select one of the standard modes.

Assembly Code Example

A control register loading procedure must be written in assembly language to be fast enough to avoid stressing the display with incorrect timing. The following routine implements the algorithm that was described above.

Listing 5-8. File: PROG004.ASM

```
;****************************************************************************
;                                                                          *
; Select mode on EGA adapter by loading all control                        *
; registers.  Register are read from a table pointed to by                 *
;                                                                          *
; Entry: [BP+4]-Pointer to the parameter table                             *
;               Parameter table should have the following format           *
;               1 byte  - 3BA for mono modes, 3DA for color modes          *
;               4 bytes - Sequencer values for register 1 - 4              *
;               25 bytes- CRT controller values                            *
;               9 bytes - Graphics controller values                       *
;               20 bytes- Attribute register values                        *
;                                                                          *
;****************************************************************************

        PUBLIC  _Write_Register_Set
_Write_Register_Set     PROC    NEAR
        PUSH    BP                      ;Standard entry from C call
        MOV     BP,SP
        PUSH    SI
        PUSH    DI

        ;- Select both graphics controllers

        MOV     DX,3CCH                 ;Load address
        MOV     AL,0                    ;Select controller 0
        OUT     DX,AL
        MOV     DX,3CAH                 ;Load address of second controller
        MOV     AL,1                    ;Select controller 1
        OUT     DX,AL

        ;- Get address of CRT controller from the parameter table
        ;    and turn the video off

        MOV     SI,[BP+4]               ;Fetch pointer to param table
        MOV     DI,SI                   ;Keep pointer to first parameter
        LODSB                           ;Fetch the crt controller address
```

```
        MOV     DL,AL
        MOV     DH,3
        ADD     DX,6                    ;Turn video off
        IN      AL,DX                   ;First reset data/index flip flop
        MOV     DX,3C0H                 ;Address of attribute controller
        XOR     AL,AL
        OUT     DX,AL                   ;Write 0 to turn video off

        ;- Load the Miscellaneous regiser

        MOV     DX,3C2H                 ;Fetch Misc register address
        LODSB                           ;Fetch value from parameter table
        OUT     DX,AL                   ;Load the Misc register

        ;- Load the Sequencer registers

        MOV     DX,3C4H                 ;Halt the sequencer
        XOR     AL,AL
        OUT     DX,AL
        INC     DX
        MOV     AL,1
        OUT     DX,AL
        DEC     DX

        MOV     CX,4                    ;Number of registers to load
        MOV     AH,1                    ;First register to load

LoopSeq:MOV     AL,AH                   ;Fetch index
        OUT     DX,AL                   ;Select index
        INC     DX                      ;Address of data register
        LODSB                           ;Fetch value from parameter table
        OUT     DX,AL                   ;Load data register
        INC     AH                      ;Update register index
        DEC     DX
        LOOP    LoopSeq                 ;Check if more to do

        MOV     AL,0                    ;Restart the sequencer
        OUT     DX,AL
        INC     DX
        MOV     AL,3
        OUT     DX,AL

        ;- Load the CRT controller registers

        MOV     DL,[DI]                 ;Fetch address of CRT controller
        MOV     CX,25                   ;Number of registers to load
        XOR     AH,AH                   ;Index of first register to load

LoopCRT:MOV     AL,AH                   ;Fetch index
        OUT     DX,AL                   ;Select register
        INC     DX                      ;Address of data register
        LODSB                           ;Fetch data
        OUT     DX,AL                   ;Load data register
        DEC     DX                      ;Address of index
        INC     AH                      ;Update index
        LOOP    LoopCRT
```

```
        ;- Load the Graphics controller registers

        MOV     DX,3CEH
        MOV     CX,9
        XOR     AH,AH

LoopGrf:MOV     AL,AH                   ;Fetch index
        OUT     DX,AL                   ;Select index
        INC     DX
        LODSB                           ;Fetch value from parameter table
        OUT     DX,AL                   ;Load value into data register
        INC     AH
        DEC     DX
        LOOP    LoopGrf

        ;- Load the palette registers in the Attribute controller

        MOV     DL,[DI]                 ;Reset data/index flip-flop
        ADD     DL,6
        IN      AL,DX

        MOV     DX,3C0H                 ;Address of index register
        MOV     CX,16                   ;Number of registers to load
        XOR     AH,AH                   ;First index

LoopVLT:MOV     AL,AH                   ;Fetch index
        OUT     DX,AL                   ;Select next index
        LODSB                           ;Fetch value from parameter table
        OUT     DX,AL                   ;Load the next data register
        INC     AH                      ;Update index
        LOOP    LoopVLT

        ;- Load Attribute registers beyond palette

        MOV     CX,4                    ;Number of register to load
        MOV     AH,30H                  ;Starting index is 10H and 20h is
                                        ;used to turn Attr. Ctrl on
LoopAtt:MOV     AL,AH                   ;Fetch next index
        OUT     DX,AL                   ;Select the index
        LODSB                           ;Fetch value from parameter table
        OUT     DX,AL                   ;Load register with the value
        INC     AH                      ;Update index
        LOOP    LoopAtt

        POP     DI                      ;Standard return to C
        POP     SI
        MOV     SP,BP
        POP     BP
        RET
_Write_Register_Set   ENDP
```

Read Register

Read a Value From an EGA Control Register

Pascal Library Procedure

function Read_Register(register:integer):byte;
                    {register address}

C Library Procedure

char read_register(register)   /* Read value of selected register */
char register;   /* Controller address for data   */

Example

Different registers require different procedures for reading. For many registers, an index must be used to select the register, as in the following:

Listing 5-9. File: PROGC003.C

```
/************************************************************************/
/* Get cursor position by reading CRTC registers E and F              */
/************************************************************************/

read_cursor_address()
        {
        #define MONO    5
        #define VMONO   7
        int     hi, lo, port;
        if (get_display_type() == MONO || get_display_type() == VMONO)
                port = 0x3B4;
        else
                port = 0x3D4;
        write_register(port, 0x0E);     /* Select register index       */
        hi = read_register(port+1);     /* Get register value          */
        write_register(port, 0x0F);     /* Select register             */
        lo = read_register(port+1);     /* Get register value          */
        printf("\nCursor is at %x hex", hi * 256 + lo);
        }
```

Listing 5-10. File: PROGP003.PAS

```
{/*******************************************************************/}
{/* Get cursor position by reading CRTC registers E and F         */}
{/*******************************************************************/}

procedure read_cursor_address;
const
MONO = 5;
VMONO = 7;
var
hi,lo,port: integer;
begin
        if Get_Display_Type = MONO then port := $3B4
        else if Get_Display_Type = VMONO then port := $3B4
        else port := $3D4;
        Write_Register(port, $0E);      {/* Select register index  */}
        hi := Read_Register(port+1);    {/* Get register value     */}
        Write_Register(port, $0F);      {/* Select register        */}
        lo := Read_Register(port+1);    {/* Get register value     */}
        writeln('Cursor is at ', hi * 256 + lo, ' (decimal)');
end;
```

Other registers can be read directly, as in this example:

Listing 5-11. File: PROGC004.C

```
/********************************************************************/
/* Get Feature bits from the external register                     */
/********************************************************************/

read_feature()
        {
        int     feature;
        feature = read_register(0x3C2);         /* Get external register*/
        feature = feature & 0x60;               /* Mask feature bits off*/
        printf("\nFeature bits are %x hex",feature);/* Print the value  */
        }
```

Listing 5-12. File: PROGP004.PAS

```
{/*******************************************************************/}
{/* Get Feature bits from the external register                   */}
{/*******************************************************************/}

procedure read_feature;
var
feature : word;
begin
        feature := Read_Register($3C2);         {/* Get external register*/}
        feature := feature and $60;             {/* Mask feature bits off*/}
        writeln('Feature bits are ',feature,' (decimal)'); {Print value}
end;
```

For some registers, the interpretation of the data being read depends on the value of another register, as in this procedure to read EGA configuration switches. This routine must alter the clock select lines of the Miscellaneous Register to select the four configuration switches.

Note: This routine MUST NOT BE SINGLE STEPPED. Leaving an improper clock select value in the Miscellaneous Register will interfere with CRT timing, and can damage your display. The routine ends with a SET_MODE function to be certain that display timing is properly restored.

Listing 5-13. File: PROGC005.C

```
/***********************************************************************/
/* Get configuration switches the external register                   */
/* This is a dangerous routine do not run!                             */
/***********************************************************************/

read_switches()
        {
        int     i, bits, switches = 0, old_mode;
        old_mode = get_mode();

        /* Writing to 3C2 disables video !                         */

        write_register(0x3C2,0x1C);    /* Select interpretation    */
        bits = read_register(0x3C2);   /* Get external register    */
        bits = (bits & 0X10) >> 4;     /* Isolate switch bit       */
        switches = bits | switches;    /* Add bit to switch        */

        write_register(0x3C2,0x18);    /* Select interpretation    */
        bits = read_register(0x3C2);   /* Get external register    */
        bits = (bits & 0X10) >> 3;     /* Isolate switch bit       */
        switches = bits | switches;    /* Add bit to switch        */

        write_register(0x3C2,0x14);    /* Select interpretation    */
        bits = read_register(0x3C2);   /* Get external register    */
        bits = (bits & 0X10) >> 2;     /* Isolate switch bit       */
        switches = bits | switches;    /* Add bit to switch        */

        write_register(0x3C2,0x10);    /* Select interpretation    */
        bits = read_register(0x3C2);   /* Get external register    */
        bits = (bits & 0X10) >> 1;     /* Isolate switch bit       */
        switches = bits | switches;    /* Add bit to switch        */

        set_mode(old_mode);            /* Restore 3c2 to proper value */
        printf("\nSwitch setting is %x hex", switches);
        }
```

Listing 5-14. File: PROGP005.PAS

```
{/**********************************************************************/}
{/* Get configuration switches the external register                 */}
{/* This is a dangerous routine because it turns off video clock      */}
{/**********************************************************************/}

procedure read_switches;
var
i,bits,switches,old_mode : word;
begin
        switches := 0;
        old_mode := Get_Mode;

        {/* Writing to 3C2 disables video !                           */}

        Write_Register($3C2,$C);      {/* Select interpretation       */}
        bits := Read_Register($3C2);  {/* Get external register       */}
        bits := (bits and $10) shr 4; {/* Isolate switch bit          */}
        switches := bits or switches; {/* Add bit to switch           */}

        Write_Register($3C2,$8);      {/* Select interpretation       */}
        bits := Read_Register($3C2);  {/* Get external register       */}
        bits := (bits and $10) shr 3; {/* Isolate switch bit          */}
        switches := bits or switches; {/* Add bit to switch           */}

        Write_Register($3C2,$4);      {/* Select interpretation       */}
        bits := Read_Register($3C2);  {/* Get external register       */}
        bits := (bits and $10) shr 2; {/* Isolate switch bit          */}
        switches := bits or switches; {/* Add bit to switch           */}

        Write_Register($3C2,$0);      {/* Select interpretation       */}
        bits := Read_Register($3C2);  {/* Get external register       */}
        bits := (bits and $10) shr 1; {/* Isolate switch bit          */}
        switches := bits or switches; {/* Add bit to switch           */}

        Write_Register($3C2,$A6);     {/* Select interpretation       */}

        Set_Mode(old_mode);               {/* Restore 3c2 to proper value */}
        writeln('Switch setting is ', switches, ' (decimal)');
end;
```

Theory

On the EGA, only a few of the registers can be read. On the VGA, almost all registers can be read. Most registers are read through a two-step process of outputting a register index and then reading the register data.

Registers that can be read on the EGA are:

- Input Status Register 0 (3C2)

- Input Status Register 1 (3BA/3DA)

In the CRT Controller (3B5/3D5):

- Cursor Start Register (Index 0Ah)

- Cursor End Register (Index 0Bh)

- Start Address Register (Index 0Ch and 0Dh)

- Cursor Location Register (Index 0Eh and 0Fh)

- Light Pen Address (Index 10h and 11h)

Assembly Code Examples

Listing 5-15. File: PROG005.ASM

```
;*************************************************************************
; Example of register read                                              *
; Read content of CRTC register 0E and 0F, the cursor address           *
; Exit: AX - Address of the cursor in display buffer                    *
;*************************************************************************

        PUBLIC  _Get_Cursor_Address
_Get_Cursor_Address     PROC NEAR
        PUSH    ES
        XOR     AX,AX                   ;Set ES to point to BIOS data area
        MOV     ES,AX
        MOV     DX,ES:[BIOS_CRT_Addr]   ;Fetch CRTC address
        MOV     AL,0EH                  ;Fetch index
        OUT     DX,AL                   ;Select index
        INC     DX                      ;Increment register address
        IN      AL,DX                   ;Read the register value
        JMP     $+2
        MOV     BH,AL                   ;Save high half of the address
        DEC     DX                      ;Fetch CRTC address
        MOV     AL,0FH                  ;Fetch index
        OUT     DX,AL                   ;Select index
        INC     DX                      ;Increment register address
        IN      AL,DX                   ;Read the register value
        JMP     $+2
        MOV     AH,BH                   ;Copy high half of the address
        POP     ES
        RET                             ;Return address in AX
_Get_Cursor_Address     ENDP
```

A general routine to read a register, suitable for calling from a high level language, like C, is shown next.

Listing 5-16. File: PROG006.ASM

```
;*************************************************************
; Read_Register                                             *
; Read a value from a register                              *
; Entry:          Register - Port to read value from        *
; Exit:           AX       - Value read in                  *
;*************************************************************

Register        EQU     [BP+4]

        PUBLIC  _Read_Register

_Read_Register  PROC NEAR
        PUSH    BP
        MOV     BP,SP
        MOV     DX,Register             ;Fetch register address
        IN      AL,DX                   ;Read value
        XOR     AH,AH
        POP     BP
        RET
_Read_Register  ENDP
```

Write Palette

Load a Palette Register

Pascal Library Procedure

procedure Write_palette(table_seg,table_offset:integer);
                {segment and offset of 16 element table of values}

C Library Procedure

write_palette(table)   /* Load palette registers   */
char table[16];   /* Pointer to 16 palette values */

Example

Listing 5-17. File: PROGC006.C

```
/***********************************************************/
/* Load palette registers from a table                    */
/* Which has BLACK and WHITE interchanged                  */
/***********************************************************/

invert_B_n_W()
        {
                                  /* Reverse video palette        */
        static  int     table[16] = {  15, 0, 2, 3, 4, 5, 6, 0,
                                         8, 9,10,11,12,13,14, 0};
```

```
        write_palette(table);
        }
```

Listing 5-18. File: PROGP006.PAS

```
{/*********************************************************************/}
{/* Load palette registers from a table                            */}
{/* Which has BLACK and WHITE interchanged                         */}
{/*********************************************************************/}
procedure invert_B_n_W;
const
table : array[0..15] of word = (15,0,2,3,4,5,6,0,8,9,10,11,12,13,14,0);
begin
        Write_Palette(seg(table),ofs(table));
end;
```

Theory

For EGA and VGA, the only method for altering display colors involves reprogramming the Color Palette Registers of the Attribute Controller. These sixteen registers define the sixteen simultaneous display colors that are available at any time. For display modes that use less than 16 colors, the Palette Registers are programmed with redundant data to reduce the number of available colors.

For a complete description of the operation of the color palette, also see:

- Attribute Controller (Chapter 2).

- Attribute Controller (Chapter 3).

- BIOS function 16 - Load Palette Registers (Chapter 4).

The recommended method for loading the Palette Registers is to use BIOS function 16 (Set Palette Registers), which is provided for this purpose. For CGA compatible modes, BIOS function 11 (Set CGA Color Palette) can be used. These functions are explained in Chapter 4.

Note that the BIOS service for loading all palette registers uses a 17 byte table, with the last byte being the overscan (border) color.

The palette registers can be directly loaded in software, and one of the examples provided below illustrates the process for doing so. The procedure for loading the Palette Registers is:

Initialize Index/Data Flip-Flop by reading address 3BA (mono) or 3DA (color).
Clear Palette Address Source bit (D5 in index register).
Load palette registers, keeping the Palette Address Source bit cleared.
Set the Palette Address Source bit.

Note that for the Attribute Controller, the index and data registers are mapped at the same address.

Assembly Code Examples

Listing 5-19. File: PROG007.ASM

```
;**********************************************************************
; Using BIOS service to load one palette register 3                  *
;**********************************************************************

        PUBLIC  _BIOS_1_Palette

_BIOS_1_Palette PROC NEAR
        MOV     AX,1000H               ;Function 10,subfunction 00
        MOV     BL,30H                 ;Load palette register 3
        MOV     BH,06H                 ;with value 6
        INT     10H                    ;Ask BIOS to load the palette
        RET
_BIOS_1_Palette ENDP
```

Listing 5-20. File: PROG008.ASM

```
;**********************************************************************
; Using BIOS service to load all registers in palette                *
;**********************************************************************
                                       ;Palette + Overscan value
Palette_table   DB      0, 1, 2, 3, 4, 5, 6, 7
                DB      8, 9,10,11,12,13,14,15, 0

        PUBLIC  _BIOS_Palette

_BIOS_Palette   PROC NEAR
        PUSH    ES
        MOV     AX,CS                  ;Load ES with Code segment
        MOV     ES,AX                  ;to get address of table into ES:DX
        LEA     DX,Palette_table       ;Load BX with offset of VLT
        MOV     AX,1002H               ;Function 10 and subfunction 02
        INT     10H                    ;Ask BIOS to load the palette
        POP     ES
        RET
_BIOS_Palette   ENDP
```

Listing 5-21. File: PROG009.ASM

```
;**************************************************************************
; Write palette registers from a table                                   *
;             Set the palette registers to the values in 'table'.        *
;             The palette registers are contained in the                 *
;             first 16 registers of the attribute controller.            *
;             Here the 16 registers are loaded using the values from     *
;             the parameter array.                                       *
;                                                                        *
; Entry:      [BP+4] - Pointer to register table (16 palette regs)       *
;                                                                        *
;**************************************************************************

        PUBLIC  _Write_Palette

_Write_Palette  PROC NEAR
        PUSH    BP
        MOV     BP,SP
        PUSH    SI
        PUSH    ES

        XOR     AX,AX                   ;Get address of CRT controller
        MOV     ES,AX                   ;From segment 0
        MOV     DX,ES:[BIOS_CRT_Addr]
        ADD     DX,6                    ;Compute address of Attrib Read reg
        IN      AL,DX                   ;Reset Attribute flip-flop

        MOV     SI,[BP+4]               ;Get pointer to the parameter table
        MOV     DX,03C0H                ;Address of Attribute controller
        MOV     CX,16                   ;Number of values to load
        XOR     AH,AH                   ;First index to load

PalLoop:MOV     AL,AH                   ;Fetch next index
        OUT     DX,AL                   ;Select next index
        LODSB                           ;Fetch next value from the table
        OUT     DX,AL                   ;Load register with value
        INC     AH                      ;Update index
        LOOP    PalLoop

        MOV     AL,20H                  ;Must turn controller back ON
        OUT     DX,AL

        POP     ES
        POP     SI
        MOV     SP,BP
        POP     BP
        RET
_Write_Palette  ENDP
```

Vertical Retrace

Wait for a Vertical Retrace Interval

Pascal Library Procedure

procedure Vertical_Retrace;

C Library Procedure

vertical_retrace()   /* Wait for next start of retrace   */

Example

Note that this routine first checks to see if a retrace is currently in progress. If it is, it waits for it to end before searching for a start of retrace. This technique is known as edge detection; it allows the software to synchronize to the beginning of a retrace interval.

Listing 5-22. File: PROGC007.C

```
/***********************************************************************/
/* Wait for start of next vertical retrace                           */
/***********************************************************************/

wait_4_vert()
      {
      int i;
      long int count, ticks();
      printf("\n...counting");
      count = ticks();                       /* Get current tick     */
      for (i = 0; i < 300; i++)
            vertical_retrace();              /* Wait for start of    */
                                             /* next vertical retrace*/
      count = ticks() - count;
      printf("\n300 vertical retraces took %ld ticks",count);
      printf("\nThat is %d cycle refresh rate",
            (300 * (long)91)/(5 * count));
      }
```

Listing 5-23. File: PROGP007.PAS

```
{/***********************************************************************/}
{/* Wait for start of next vertical retrace                           */}
{/***********************************************************************/}

procedure wait_4_vert;
var
i,count : word;
```

```
begin
        writeln('...counting');
        count := ticks;                             {/* Get current tick    */}
        for i := 0 to 299 do Vertical_Retrace;      {/* Wait for start of    */}
                                                    {/* next vertical retrace*/}
        count := ticks - count;
        writeln('300 vertical retraces took ',count,' ticks');
        writeln('That is a ',(300*longint(91)) div (5*count),' Hertz refresh
        rate');
end;
```

Theory

For some applications, it is useful to be able to sense when the CRT display is in a vertical retrace period. Counting retrace cycles can be used as an accurate time base. Many interactive games synchronize the motion of an object on the screen with horizontal or vertical retrace periods. This can be done either by polling a status register, or by enabling and processing vertical retrace interrupts.

For an explanation of CRT timing, including retrace intervals, see Operation of CRT Displays in Chapter 2.

The following procedure can be used when polling for retrace:

- Get display type (color or monochrome) and determine address of Miscellaneous Register (3DA for color, or 3BA for monochrome)

- Read Miscellaneous Register

- If retrace is already in progress, wait for it to end

- Wait for start of next retrace

- Return

Assembly Code Example

Listing 5-24. File: PROG010.ASM

```
;****************************************************************
; Wait for start of next vertical retrace                      *
;****************************************************************

        PUBLIC  _Vertical_Retrace

_Vertical_Retrace       PROC    NEAR
        PUSH    ES
        XOR     AX,AX                   ;Get address of STATUS register
        MOV     ES,AX                   ;From segment 0
        MOV     DX,3BAH                 ;Assume monochrome addressing
        TEST    BYTE PTR ES:[BIOS_Equipment],2  ;Is mono display attached?
```

```
        JNZ     VR_Address_Ok           ;...Yes, address is ok
        MOV     DX,3DAH                 ;...No, must set color addressing
VR_Address_Ok:

        IN      AL,DX                   ;Read in status
        JMP     $+2
        TEST    AL,08H                  ;Is retrace ON? (if ON bit = 1)
        JZ      Wait_For_On             ;...no, go wait for start
Wait_For_Off:                           ;...yes, wait for it to go OFF
        IN      AL,DX
        JMP     $+2
        TEST    AL,08H                  ;Is retrace OFF?
        JNZ     Wait_For_Off            ;...No, keep waiting
Wait_For_On:
        IN      AL,DX
        JMP     $+2
        TEST    AL,08H                  ;Is retrace ON?
        JZ      Wait_For_On             ;...No, keep on waiting
        POP     ES
        RET
_Vertical_Retrace       ENDP
```

Panning and Scrolling

Smoothly Move an Image on the Screen

Pascal Library Procedures

procedure Set_More_Columns(columns:integer);{Change logical page width}
procedure Vertical_Scroll(y:integer);   {scroll vertically y pixels}
procedure Horizontal_Scroll(x:integer);   {scroll horizontally x pixels}

C Library Procedures

| set_more_columns(width) | /* Set wider logical width | */ |
| int   width; | /* New width in columns | */ |

| horizontal_scroll(x) | /* Scroll horizontally | */ |
| int   x, | /* Number of pixels to scroll | */ |

| vertical_scroll(y) | /* Scroll vertically | */ |
| int   x, | /* Number of lines to scroll | */ |

Example

Listing 5-25. File: PROGC009.C

```
/**********************************************************************/
/* Scroll using arrow keys and quit if Escape is pressed             */
/**********************************************************************/

smooth_vertical()
        {
        #define KEY_ESC          0x011B
        #define KEY_UP           0x4800
        #define KEY_DOWN         0x5000
        #define KEY_LEFT         0x4B00
        #define KEY_RIGHT        0x4D00
        #define KEY_ENTER        0x1C0D

        int     y = 0, key;
        while((key = get_key()) != KEY_ENTER)
                switch (key)
                    {
                    case KEY_UP:
                        y = (-y) < 0 ? 0 : y;
                        vertical_scroll(y);                  /* Scroll up     */
                        break;
                    case KEY_DOWN:
                        vertical_scroll(++y);                /* Scroll down   */
                        break;
                    default:
                        break;
                    }

        vertical_scroll(0);
        }
```

Listing 5-26. File: PROGP009.PAS

```
{**********************************************************************}
{ Scroll using arrow keys and quit if Escape is pressed               }
{**********************************************************************}

procedure smooth_vertical;
const
KEY_ESC = $1B;
KEY_UP = 72;
KEY_DOWN = 80;
KEY_ENTER = $0D;
var
y : word;
key : char;
i : integer;
begin
    y := 0;
    key := ReadKey;
    i := integer(key);
    while i <> KEY_ENTER do
```

```
        begin
            case i of
                KEY_UP :    if y > 0 then y := y-1;  { Set for scroll up     }
                KEY_DOWN:  y := y+1;                 { Set for scroll down   }
                end;
            Vertical_Scroll(y);                      { Scroll to new value }
            key := ReadKey;
            i := integer(key);
        end;
Vertical_Scroll(0);                                  { Restore to 0 }
end;
```

Listing 5-27. File: PROGC010.C

```
/***********************************************************************/
/* Scroll in a loop by one pixel at a time                             */
/* Scroll using arrow keys and quit if Escape is pressed               */
/***********************************************************************/

smooth_horizontal()
    {
    #define KEY_ESC        0x011B
    #define KEY_UP         0x4800
    #define KEY_DOWN       0x5000
    #define KEY_LEFT       0x4B00
    #define KEY_RIGHT      0x4D00
    #define KEY_ENTER      0x1C0D

    int    x = 0, i, key;
    set_more_columns(100); /* Select 100 text column mode          */
    for (i = 0; i < 25;i++) /* Fill newly organized text buffer    */
            printf("\nThis is text line %2d in the new text buffer",i);
    while((key = get_key()) != KEY_ENTER)
            switch (key)
                {
                case KEY_RIGHT:
                    x = (++x) > 799 ? 799 : x;
                    horizontal_scroll(x);              /* Scroll right */
                    break;
                case KEY_LEFT:
                    x = (-x) < 0 ? 0 : x;
                    horizontal_scroll(x);              /* Scroll left  */
                    break;
                default:
                    break;
                }
    horizontal_scroll(0);
    }
```

Listing 5-28. File: PROGP010.PAS

```
{/**********************************************************************/}
{/* Scroll in a loop by one pixel at a time                          */}
{/* Scroll using arrow keys and quit if Escape is pressed            */}
{/**********************************************************************/}

procedure smooth_horizontal;
const
KEY_ESC = $1B;
KEY_UP = 78;
KEY_DOWN = 80;
KEY_LEFT = 75;
KEY_RIGHT = 77;
KEY_ENTER = $0D;
var
x : integer;

i : integer;

k : integer;
key : char;
begin
    x := 0;
    i := 0;
    Set_More_Columns(100);      {/* Select 100 text column mode        */}
    for i := 0 to 24 do         {/* Fill newly organized text buffer   */}
        writeln('This is text line ',i,' in the new text buffer');
    key := readkey;
    k := integer(key);
    while k <> KEY_ENTER do
        begin
            case k of
                KEY_RIGHT: if x < 800 then x := x+1;    {/* Scroll right */}
                KEY_LEFT:  if x > 0 then x := x-1;      {/* Scroll left */}
                end;
            Horizontal_Scroll(x);
            key := readkey;
            k := integer(key);
        end;
    Horizontal_Scroll(0);
end;
```

To permit horizontal scrolling, the Offset register of the CRT Controller must be modified to make the logical width of the display memory larger than the width of the display screen. This example operates in text mode, and configures display memory as a 100 column text buffer. The procedure Set_More_Columns() sets up a wider text buffer. A series of "print" commands fills the text buffer. The Set_More_Columns procedure is included in the Assembly Code section below. Two separate programs are shown; one scrolls vertically and the second pans horizontally. The keyboard "arrow" keys are used to control scrolling and panning.

A later example titled Smooth Scroll, included under Text Functions, incorporates both vertical scrolling and horizontal panning into a single routine.

This example was written assuming an 8 bit wide character cell. For monochrome modes that use 9 bit character cells, the procedure must be modified slightly.

Theory

The large display memory of the EGA/VGA can store much more data than can be displayed at one time on a standard display. The portion of display memory that is currently being displayed is referred to as the on-screen memory; the rest is referred to as off-screen memory.

A display image that is larger than the display screen can be stored in EGA/VGA memory. By redefining which section of memory is on-screen, different sections of this image can be displayed. Panning, the technique described here, allows the display screen to be moved smoothly around the image as if it were a camera lens panning around a landscape. This can be very effective for interactive systems where the operator uses a positioning device such as a mouse or trackball.

A similar application involves the display of large amounts of text on the screen. Text can be broken into pages, with one page displayed at a time, or it can appear as a continuous block (like a scroll). When text is scrolled upward, text lines disappear from the top of the screen as new lines appear at the bottom of the screen. When text is scrolled downward, lines disappear from the bottom of the screen as new lines appear at the top of the screen.

On most displays, scrolling will appear jittery as text moves upward or downward one full character row at a time. The EGA and VGA can support a technique called smooth scrolling, where text is scrolled up or down by one pixel at a time. This eliminates the annoying jitter.

The control registers used to implement panning include the Start Address and Offset registers of the CRT Controller and the Horizontal Panning register of the Attribute Controller. Their action is illustrated in Figure 5-1.

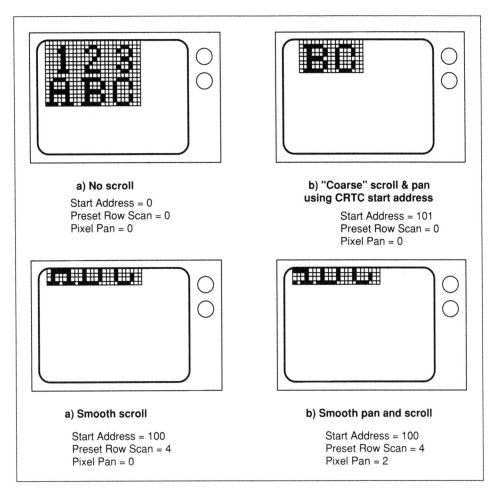

Figure 5-1 Panning and scrolling.

To learn more about registers involved in scrolling, see CRT controller registers Start Address and Offset, and Attribute controller register Horizontal Panning , in Chapter 3.

Panning 9-bit characters

Although the EGA with an EGA monitor always uses characters that are 8-bits wide, you should be warned that the monochrome text mode and most VGA text modes display 9-bit wide characters. This makes the smooth panning (using the Panning register in the Attribute controller) somewhat different than in the example shown here. Although the example here will work in all text modes, it will "jump" slightly when you reach a multiple of 8. In most cases it is not noticable. To do it properly, if a 9-bit mode is detected, two adjustments must be made. One, start address in the CRT controller is set to x/9 instead of to x/8, and two, the Panning register must be set to one of the nine values 8, 0, 1, 2,...,7 instead of the eight values 0, 1,...,7.

Assembly Code Examples

Listing 5-29. File: PROG012.ASM

```
;****************************************************************************
; Setup text mode with more addressable columns (80 visible)         *
; Entry:        [BP+4] - Number of columns to use (80 - 255)         *
;****************************************************************************

        PUBLIC   _Set_More_Columns

_Set_More_Columns  PROC     NEAR
        PUSH     BP                          ;Standard entry from C call
        MOV      BP,SP
        PUSH     ES

        XOR      AX,AX                       ;Get address of CRT controller
        MOV      ES,AX                       ;From segment 0
        MOV      DX,ES:[BIOS_CRT_Addr]
        MOV      AL,13H                      ;Index for OFFSET register
        OUT      DX,AL                       ;Select index
        INC      DX
        MOV      AX,[BP+4]                   ;Fetch new text line width
        MOV      ES:[BIOS_Columns],AX        ;Let BIOS know about new width
        SHR      AL,1                        ;Divide by 2 for OFFSET regiser
        OUT      DX,AL                       ;Set OFFSET register

        POP      ES                          ;Standard return to C
        MOV      SP,BP
        POP      BP
        RET
_Set_More_Columns ENDP
```

Listing 5-30. File: PROG013.ASM

```
;********************************************************************
; Smooth vertical scroll                                          *
; Assumes that line width is set correctly in the BIOS data area  *
; Entry:          Y_Offset- Current vertical offset               *
;********************************************************************

Y_Offset        EQU     [BP+4]

        PUBLIC  _Vertical_Scroll

_Vertical_Scroll PROC    NEAR
        PUSH    BP                      ;Standard entry from high level
        MOV     BP,SP
        PUSH    ES

        XOR     AX,AX                   ;Point ES to segment zero
        MOV     ES,AX

        ;- Wait for an end of vertical retrace

        MOV     DX,ES:[BIOS_CRT_Addr]   ;Get address of CRT controller
        ADD     DX,6                    ;Wait for retrace to change registers
VS_Wait1:                               ;Wait for vertical to start
        IN      AL,DX
        JMP     $+2
        TEST    AL,8
        JZ      VS_Wait1
VS_Wait2:                               ;Wait for vertical to end
        IN      AL,DX
        JMP     $+2
        TEST    AL,8
        JNZ     VS_Wait2

        ;- Set CRTC ADDRESS register to (columns * offset / char_height)

        MOV     AX,Y_Offset             ;Fetch new Y
        XOR     DX,DX                   ;Clear DX for divide
        MOV     BX,ES:[BIOS_Height]     ;Get character height
        DIV     BX                      ;Divide offset by character height
        MOV     BX,AX                   ;Save number of text lines to skip
        MOV     CX,DX                   ;Save number of scan lines to skip
        MOV     AX,ES:[BIOS_Columns]    ;Fetch number of bytes per text line
        MUL     BX                      ;Compute number of bytes to skip
        MOV     BX,AX                   ;Save it in BX
        MOV     DX,ES:[BIOS_CRT_Addr]   ;Get address of CRT controller
        MOV     AL,0DH                  ;Index for START ADDRESS register LO
        OUT     DX,AL                   ;Select index
        INC     DX
        MOV     AL,BL                   ;Fetch the scroll value we computed
        OUT     DX,AL                   ;Set START register
        DEC     DX
        MOV     AL,0CH                  ;Write the high byte of the start addr
        OUT     DX,AL
        INC     DX
```

```
        MOV     AL,BH
        OUT     DX,AL
        DEC     DX

        ;- Set CRTC PRESET ROW SCAN register to number of scan lines to skip

        ADD     DX,6
VS_Wait3:                               ;Wait for vertical to start
        IN      AL,DX
        JMP     $+2
        TEST    AL,8
        JZ      VS_Wait3
        SUB     DX,6

        MOV     AL,8                    ;Index of PRESET ROW SCAN register
        OUT     DX,AL                   ;Select PRESET ROW SCAN register
        MOV     AL,CL                   ;Fetch scan lines to skip
        INC     DX
        OUT     DX,AL                   ;Set PRESET ROW SCAN register

        POP     ES
        MOV     SP,BP
        POP     BP
        RET
_Vertical_Scroll ENDP
```

Listing 5-31. File: PROG014.ASM

```
;**********************************************************************
; Smooth horizontal scroll                                           *
; There is no error checking and it is assumed that new width was set *
; Entry:        X_Offset- Current horizontal offset                  *
;**********************************************************************

X_Offset        EQU     [BP+4]

        PUBLIC  _Horizontal_Scroll

_Horizontal_Scroll      PROC    NEAR
        PUSH    BP                      ;Standard entry from high level
        MOV     BP,SP
        PUSH    ES

        XOR     AX,AX                   ;Point ES to segment 0
        MOV     ES,AX

        ;- Wait for an end of vertical retrace

        MOV     DX,ES:[BIOS_CRT_Addr]   ;Get address of CRT controller
        ADD     DX,6                    ;Wait for retrace to change registers
HS_Wait1:                               ;Wait for vertical to start
        IN      AL,DX
        JMP     $+2
        TEST    AL,8
        JZ      HS_Wait1
```

```
HS_Wait2:                                ;Wait for vertical to end
        IN      AL,DX
        JMP     $+2
        TEST    AL,8
        JNZ     HS_Wait2

        ;- Set CRTC ADDRESS register to offset/8

        MOV     BX,X_Offset              ;Compute multiple of 8 offset to use
        SHR     BX,1                     ;in CRTC start address register 0D
        SHR     BX,1
        SHR     BX,1
        MOV     DX,ES:[BIOS_CRT_Addr]    ;Get address of CRT controller
        MOV     AL,0DH                   ;Index for START ADDRESS register LO
        OUT     DX,AL                    ;Select index
        INC     DX
        MOV     AL,BL                    ;Fetch the scroll value we computed
        OUT     DX,AL                    ;Set START register

        ;- Set Attribute PANNING register to (offset mod 8)

        ADD     DX,5                     ;Point to status port
HS_Wait3:                                ;Wait for vertical to start
        IN      AL,DX
        JMP     $+2
        TEST    AL,8
        JZ      HS_Wait3

        MOV     DX,3C0H                  ;Fetch address of Attr write register
        MOV     AL,33H                   ;Fetch index
        OUT     DX,AL                    ;Select PANNING register
        MOV     AX,X_Offset              ;Fetch offset
        AND     AL,7                     ;Keep last 3 bits (offset mod 8)
        OUT     DX,AL                    ;Set PANNING register

        POP     ES
        MOV     SP,BP
        POP     BP
        RET
_Horizontal_Scroll      ENDP
```

Clear Screen

Pascal Library Procedure

procedure Clear_Screen;

C Library Procedure

clear_screen();   /* Clear memory   */

Example

Listing 5-32. File: PROGC011.C

```
/*************************************************************************/
/* Clear screen using library function                                  */
/*************************************************************************/

cls()
        {
        clear_screen();                            /* Clear memory         */
        }
```

Listing 5-33. File: PROGP011.PAS

```
{*************************************************************************}
{ Clear screen using library function                                    }
{*************************************************************************}

procedure cls;
begin
    Clear_Screen;                              { Clear memory             }
end;
```

Theory

There are many possible methods that can be used to clear the display memory, including:

1. The BIOS Write Character function can be used to write space characters to each of the 2000 text positions of the screen.

2. The BIOS Write String function can be used to write a string of 80 blanks to the screen 25 times.

3. A BIOS Mode Select function can be used to clear the screen.

4. BIOS function 6 (Scroll Window Up) and function 7 (Scroll Window Down) can be used to clear the screen.

5. The processor can write directly to display memory.

Methods 4 and 5 are demonstrated below.

Assembly Code Examples

Listing 5-34. File: PROG015.ASM

```
;*********************************************************************
; Use BIOS call to clear memory                                     *
;*********************************************************************

        PUBLIC  _BIOS_Clear

_BIOS_Clear     PROC NEAR
        PUSH    ES                      ;Save ES
        XOR     AX,AX                   ;Load 0 into ES
        MOV     ES,AX
        MOV     CX,0                    ;Set upper left to 0,0
        MOV     DH,ES:[BIOS_Rows]       ;Get lower right corner
        MOV     DL,ES:[BIOS_Columns]
        DEC     DH
        DEC     DL
        MOV     BH,7                    ;Normal attribute
        MOV     AH,6                    ;Function = SCROLL UP
        MOV     AL,0                    ;Subfunction = whole screen
        INT     10H                     ;Ask BIOS to scroll screen
        POP     ES                      ;Restore ES
        RET
_BIOS_Clear     ENDP
```

The method that must be used to clear display memory depends on the current display mode. The example given here is generalized to determine the current display mode and act accordingly. In text modes, clearing the screen means setting all ASCII bytes (even addresses) to 20h and all attribute bytes (odd addresses) to 07. In graphics modes, all planes used by that mode must be cleared to zeros.

To learn more about display memory organization see Display Memory section in Chapter 2.

Listing 5-35. File: PROG016.ASM

```
;*********************************************************************
; Clear memory according to the current mode                        *
;*********************************************************************

        PUBLIC  _Clear_Screen

Clear_Table     DW      OFFSET  Clear_Col_Text          ;mode 0
                DW      OFFSET  Clear_Col_Text          ;mode 1
                DW      OFFSET  Clear_Col_Text          ;mode 2
                DW      OFFSET  Clear_Col_Text          ;mode 3
                DW      OFFSET  Clear_One_Plane         ;mode 4
```

```
                    DW      OFFSET  Clear_One_Plane         ;mode 5
                    DW      OFFSET  Clear_One_Plane         ;mode 6
                    DW      OFFSET  Clear_Mono_Text         ;mode 7
                    DW      OFFSET  Clear_All_Planes        ;mode 8
                    DW      OFFSET  Clear_All_Planes        ;mode 9
                    DW      OFFSET  Clear_All_Planes        ;mode a
                    DW      OFFSET  Clear_All_Planes        ;mode b
                    DW      OFFSET  Clear_All_Planes        ;mode c
                    DW      OFFSET  Clear_All_Planes        ;mode d
                    DW      OFFSET  Clear_All_Planes        ;mode e
                    DW      OFFSET  Clear_All_Planes        ;mode f
                    DW      OFFSET  Clear_All_Planes        ;mode 10

_Clear_Screen       PROC NEAR
          PUSH      ES
          PUSH      DI

          XOR       AX,AX                 ;Point ES to segment zero
          MOV       ES,AX
          MOV       BL,ES:[BIOS_Mode]     ;Fetch current video mode
          XOR       BH,BH
          CMP       BX,10H
          JA        Clear_Done
          SHL       BX,1
          JMP       Clear_Table[BX]       ;Select clear according to mode

Clear_Mono_Text:                          ;Load constants for mode 7
          MOV       CX,ES:[BIOS_Page_Size]
          MOV       AX,0B000H
          MOV       ES,AX
          MOV       AX,0720H
          JMP       Clear

Clear_Col_Text:                           ;Load constants for modes 0-3
          MOV       CX,ES:[BIOS_Page_Size]
          MOV       AX,0B800H
          MOV       ES,AX
          MOV       AX,0720H
          JMP       Clear

Clear_One_Plane:                          ;Load constants for graphics modes
          MOV       CX,ES:[BIOS_Page_Size] ;4,5 and 6
          MOV       AX,0B800H
          MOV       ES,AX
          MOV       AX,0
          JMP       Clear

Clear_All_Planes:                         ;Load constanst for all new graphics
          MOV       CX,ES:[BIOS_Page_Size] ;modes D,E,F,10
          MOV       AX,0A000H
          MOV       ES,AX
          MOV       AX,0
          MOV       DX,3C4H               ;Address of Sequencer
          MOV       AL,2                  ;Index for PLANE ENABLE register
          OUT       DX,AL                 ;Select register
          INC       DX
```

```
          MOV      AL,0FH                    ;Fetch value to enable all 4 planes
          OUT      DX,AL                     ;Set PLANE ENABLE register
          MOV      AX,0
          JMP      Clear

Clear:                                       ;Using pre-loaded constants
          XOR      DI,DI                     ;for segment, count, and value
          REP      STOSW                     ;clear the display memory
Clear_Done:
          POP      DI
          POP      ES
          RET
_Clear_Screen   ENDP
```

Set Mode

Initialize a Standard Display Mode

Pascal Library Procedure

procedure Set_Mode(mode:integer);
           {mode # to select}

C Library Procedure

set_mode(mode);	/* Select mode	*/
int mode;	/* One of the legal modes	*/
	/* 0 - 7, D - 13 hex	*/

Examples

Listing 5-36. File: PROGC014.C

```
/**********************************************************************/
/* Set mode                                                           */
/**********************************************************************/

test_set_mode()
    {
    #define MONO    5
    #define VMONO   7
    if (get_display_type() == VMONO ||
        get_display_type() == MONO) set_mode(7);
    else                            set_mode(3);
    }
```

Listing 5-37. File: PROGP014.PAS

```
{*********************************************************************}
{ Set mode                                                          }
{*********************************************************************}

procedure test_set_mode;
const
MONO = 5;
VMONO = 7;
begin
    if Get_Display_Type = MONO then Set_Mode(7)
    else if Get_Display_Type = VMONO then Set_Mode(7)
    else Set_Mode(3);
end;
```

Theory

This function will initialize the display adapter to any of the standard display modes. The display buffer will be cleared. In text mode, the cursor will be moved to its "home" position in the upper left corner of the screen. Standard display modes of the EGA and VGA are summarized in Table 1–2 in Chapter 1.

Assembly Code Example

Listing 5-38. File: PROG017.ASM

```
;*********************************************************************
; Select video mode                                                 *
; Entry: Mode - Mode to be selected                                 *
;*********************************************************************

Mode      EQU     [BP+4]

          PUBLIC  _Set_Mode

_Set_Mode         PROC NEAR
          PUSH    BP
          MOV     BP,SP
          MOV     AL,Mode           ;Fetch mode number
          XOR     AH,AH             ;Function = SELECT MODE
          INT     10H               ;Ask BIOS to set the mode
          POP     BP
          RET
_Set_Mode         ENDP
```

BIOS Interface

Call BIOS Video Service From High Level Language

Pascal Library Procedure

procedure Video_BIOS(ax,bx,cx,dx,es,bp:integer);
　　　　　　　{register values to load before call}
　　　　　　　{NOTE:video services that return values are not supported}

C Library Procedure

Video_BIOS(AX,BX,CX,DX,ES,BP) /* C interface to video BIOS　　　*/
int　　AX,BX,CX,DX,ES,BP;　　　　/* Values to be used in　　　　　*/
　　　　　　　　　　　　　　　　 /* corresponding registers　　　*/
　　　　　　　　　　　　　　　　 /* NOTE: Video services　　　　 */
　　　　　　　　　　　　　　　　 /* that return values are　　　 */
　　　　　　　　　　　　　　　　 /* not supported　　　　　　　　*/

Examples

Listing 5-39. File: PROGC012.C

```
/*************************************************************************/
/* Test low level example: Use Video_BIOS library function to use BIOS  */
/*************************************************************************/

test_video_BIOS()
        {
        int     i;
        static char     string[] = "Print string using BIOS function E";

        /* Move cursor to row Ahex column 20hex using function 2        */
        video_BIOS(0x0200, 0, 0, 0x0A20);

        /* Print a string at current cursor position using function E   */
        for (i = 0; string[i] != NULL; i++)
                video_BIOS(0x0E00 + string[i]);
        }
```

Listing 5-40. File: PROGP012.PAS

```
{*************************************************************************}
{ Test low level example: Use Video_BIOS library function to use BIOS   }
{*************************************************************************}

procedure test_video_BIOS;
const
str : array[0..33] of char = 'Print string using BIOS function E';
var
i : integer;
begin
    { Move cursor to row Ahex column 20hex using function 2 }
    Video_BIOS($200,0,0,$A20,0,0);
    { Print a string at current cursor position using function E }
    for i := 0 to 33 do Video_BIOS($E00 + integer(str[i]),0,0,0,0,0);
end;
```

Listing 5-41. File: PROGC013.C

```
/*************************************************************************/
/* Use C library function to select text mode                          */
/*************************************************************************/

set_mode_x()
        {
        #define MONO    5
        #define VMONO   7
        union   REGS regs;
        regs.h.ah = 0;                      /* Function = MODE SELECT     */
        if (get_display_type() == MONO  /* Get display type           */
          ||get_display_type() == VMONO)
                regs.h.al = 7;          /* With mono display use mode 7 */
        else
                regs.h.al = 3;          /* With color display use mode 3*/
        int86(0x10,&regs, &regs);       /* Call INT 10H               */
        }
```

Theory

This library procedure permits BIOS Video Services to be called from C or Pascal programs. Those BIOS functions that return status information are not supported.

The same function can be performed using the INT86 function in the standard C library.

Assembly Code Examples

Listing 5-42. File: PROG018.ASM

```
;***************************************************************************
; C interface to BIOS video services.  This routine will not              *
; return any values passed by BIOS service.                               *
; Entry:          [BP+4], [BP+6], ... - Values for AX,BX,CX,DX,ES,BP       *
;***************************************************************************

            PUBLIC   _Video_BIOS

_Video_BIOS     PROC     NEAR
        PUSH    BP                      ;Preserve BP
        MOV     BP,SP                   ;Use BP as index into stack
        PUSH    ES                      ;Preserve ES

        MOV     AX,[BP+4]               ;Copy values from stack into
        MOV     BX,[BP+6]               ;registers
        MOV     CX,[BP+8]
        MOV     DX,[BP+10]
        MOV     ES,[BP+12]
        MOV     BP,[BP+14]
        INT     10H                     ;Perform the BIOS service

        POP     ES                      ;Restore ES and BP
        POP     BP
        RET
_Video_BIOS     ENDP
```

6

Getting Information

These library procedures can be used to obtain useful information about the current state of the EGA/VGA display adapter, such as the current mode, current screen resolution, current display type, cursor position, or the values of other BIOS state variables that are stored in system memory in a 256 byte data area at address 0040:0000h (or 0000:0400h).

To learn more about BIOS state variables see the section on The BIOS Data Area in Chapter 4.

Get Display Mode

Return the Current Operating Mode of the EGA

Pascal Library Procedure

function Get_Mode:byte;

C Library Procedure

char get_mode()   /* Get current display mode   */

Example

Listing 6-1. File: PROGC020.C

```
/******************************************************************************/
/* Getting current video mode                                               */
/******************************************************************************/

print_mode()
        {
                                        /* Print current video mode      */
        printf("\nCurrent video mode is %x hex", get_mode());
        }
```

Listing 6-2. File: PROGP020.PAS

```
{******************************************************************************}
{ Getting current video mode                                                 }
{******************************************************************************}

procedure print_mode;
var
i : integer;
begin                                    { Print current video mode   }
    i := Get_Mode;
    writeln('Current video mode is ', i);
end;
```

Theory

The GET_MODE procedure returns the current display mode of the EGA, providing that mode was selected via BIOS function 0 (Set Mode). The current mode number is stored by the BIOS at byte address 0040:0049h (or 0000:0449h) in system memory. BIOS function 15 (Get Current Mode) will return the mode number, or the mode can be obtained directly by reading the byte value at memory address 0040:0049h (or 0000:0449h).

To learn more about standard modes see the section on Standard Operating Modes in Chapter 1, and programming example Set Mode in Chapter 5.

The following C routine will return the mode byte:

Listing 6-3. File: PROGC021.C

```
/****************************************************************************/
/* Fetch current mode using BIOS data area constant at 0000:0449          */
/****************************************************************************/

print_data_mode()
        {
        char far        *p = 0;          /* Declare far pointer           */
        printf("\nCurrent video mode is %x hex", p[0x449]);
        }
```

Assembly Code Examples

Listing 6-4. File: PROG020.ASM

```
;****************************************************************************
; Use BIOS function to get the current video mode                         *
; Exit: AX - Current operation mode                                       *
;****************************************************************************

        PUBLIC  _BIOS_Get_Mode

_BIOS_Get_Mode  PROC NEAR
        MOV     AH,0FH                  ;Function = GET DISPLAY MODE
        INT     10H                     ;Ask BIOS to fetch mode
        XOR     AH,AH                   ;Return mode in AX
        RET
_BIOS_Get_Mode  ENDP
```

Listing 6-5. File: PROG021.ASM

```
;******************************************************************
; Get current video mode from segment zero                        *
;******************************************************************

        PUBLIC   _Get_Mode

_Get_Mode        PROC NEAR
        PUSH     ES                      ;Point ES to segment 0
        XOR      AX,AX
        MOV      ES,AX
        MOV      AL,ES:[BIOS_Mode]       ;Fetch current video mode
        XOR      AH,AH                   ;Clear rest of AX for return to C
        POP      ES
        RET
_Get_Mode        ENDP
```

Get Text Resolution

Return the Number of Text Rows and Columns

Pascal Library Procedure

procedure Get_Rows_n_Cols(x_seg,x_offset,y_seg,y_offset:integer);
                    {segment and offset of destination for result}
                    {x = # of columns, y = # of rows}

C Library Procedure

```
get_rows_n_cols (x, y)          /* Get current resolution    */
int   *x;                       /* Number of columns         */
int   *y;                       /* Number of rows            */
```

Example

Listing 6-6. File: PROGC022.C

```
/******************************************************************/
/* Get number of rows and column using library function          */
/******************************************************************/

print_rows_cols()
        {
        int     x, y;
        get_rows_n_cols(&x, &y);        /* Get number of rows and cols */
                                        /* and print it                */
        printf("\nNumber of rows = %d and columns = %d", x, y);
        }
```

Listing 6-7. File: PROGP022.PAS

```
{*****************************************************************}
{ Get number of rows and column using library function           }
{*****************************************************************}

procedure print_rows_cols;
var
x : integer;
y : integer;
begin
    x := 0;
    y := 0;
    Get_Rows_n_Cols(seg(x),ofs(x),seg(y),ofs(y));{Get number of rows and cols}
                                                 { and print it              }
    writeln('Number of rows = ',x,' and columns = ', y);
end;
```

Theory

For text modes, the Get_Resolution procedure returns the current display resolution (number of text rows and columns), providing the current resolution was
established by the BIOS via a mode select (or by a 'well-behaved' video device
driver, which updated the BIOS data area). The current number of text rows is
stored by the BIOS at byte address 0040:0084h (or 0000:0484h) in system memory,
and the number of columns is stored at word address 0040:004Ah (or 0000:044Ah).
Customized display modes, implemented through RAM resident device drivers,
should update these variables when changing screen resolution to assure compatibility.

See Chapter 4 (The Rom BIOS) for a complete list of variables stored in the BIOS
data area.

The following C routine will print the text resolution using the values in the
BIOS data area.

Listing 6-8. File: PROGC023.C

```
/*****************************************************************************/
/* Fetch current number of rows and columns                                 */
/* from segment zero and print it                                           */
/*****************************************************************************/

print_data_rc()
      {
      char far      *p = 0;                      /* Declare far pointer */
      printf("\nCols  = %X hex", p[0x44A]);   /* Print columns       */
      printf(", Rows  = %X hex", p[0x484]+1);/* Print rows          */
      }
```

Assembly Code Example

Listing 6-9. File: PROG022.ASM

```
;**************************************************************************
; Get current number of rows and columns                                *
; Entry:Rows - Pointer to number of rows                                 *
;       Cols - Pointer to number of columns                              *
; Exit: Values at the pointer will be set                                *
;**************************************************************************

Rows    EQU     [BP+4]
Cols    EQU     [BP+6]

        PUBLIC  _Get_Rows_n_Cols

_Get_Rows_n_Cols PROC NEAR
        PUSH    BP
        MOV     BP,SP
        PUSH    ES                      ;Preserve ES
        XOR     AX,AX                   ;Set ES to segment zero
        MOV     ES,AX
        MOV     DL,ES:[BIOS_Rows]       ;Fetch current rows
        INC     DL                      ;Adjust (since row-1 is stored)
        MOV     BX,Rows                 ;Fetch pointer
        XOR     DH,DH                   ;Clear upper half of DX
        MOV     [BX],DX                 ;Save number of rows
        MOV     CX,ES:[BIOS_Columns]    ;Fetch current columns
        MOV     BX,Cols                 ;Fetch pointer
        MOV     [BX],CX                 ;Save number of columns
        POP     ES
        POP     BP
        RET
_Get_Rows_n_Cols  ENDP
```

Get Cursor Size

Determine the Current Size of the Cursor

Pascal Library Procedure

procedure Get_Cursor_Size(start_seg,start_offset,stop_seg,stop_offset:integer);
            {segment and offset of destinations for return data}
            {returns values of CURSOR START and CURSOR END}

C Library Procedure

get_cursor_size(start, stop)	/* Get cursor shape */
int start;	/* First scan line */
int stop;	/* Last scan line */
	/* within each character */

Example

Listing 6-10. File: PROGC024.C

```
/***********************************************************************/
/* Get current cursor size using library function                     */
/***********************************************************************/

print_cursor_size()
        {
        int     start, stop;                    /* Declare variables   */
        get_cursor_size(&start, &stop);         /* Get shape           */
        printf("\nCursor starts at %d and stops at %d",
                start, stop);                   /* Print the values    */
        }
```

Library 6-11. File: PROGP024.PAS

```
{***********************************************************************}
{ Get current cursor size using library function                       }
{***********************************************************************}

procedure print_cursor_size;
var
start : integer;
stop : integer;
begin
    Get_Cursor_Size(seg(start),ofs(start),seg(stop),ofs(stop));
    writeln('Cursor starts at ',start,' and stops at ',stop);
end;
```

Theory

Many text editors and word processors change the shape of the cursor, some-times using cursor shape as a flag to indicate the current edit mode. This library procedure will permit an application program to read the current cursor shape, providing the cursor shape was set via a BIOS call (or a "well-behaved" video device driver that updated the BIOS data area). The cursor shape is defined in terms of starting character scan line and ending character scan line. The BIOS stores the cursor shape in system memory at word address 0040:0060h (or 0000:0460h).

Unfortunately, the orignal IBM EGA BIOS does not properly set this informa-tion when the EGA enhanced (8 x 14) character set is used. Other BIOS suppliers have duplicated the bug to insure total compatibility with IBM. For an 8 x 14 char-acter cell, the cursor normally starts at scan line 11, and stops at scan line 12. The EGA BIOS sets the values in the data area to start = 6, and stop = 7, instead.

To learn more about cursor operation, also see:

• Description of registers Cursor Start and Cursor End of CRT controller in Chapter 3.

• BIOS functions Set Cursor Size and Get Cursor Size in Chapter 4.

• BIOS Data Area section in Chapter 4.

• Programming examples Set Cursor Size in Chapter 7.

Assembly Code Examples

Listing 6-12. File: PROG023.ASM

```
;***********************************************************************
; Using BIOS to obtain cursor start and end                          *
; Exit: AH - Cursor start                                            *
;       AL - Cursor end                                              *
;***********************************************************************

        PUBLIC  _BIOS_Get_Curs_Size

_BIOS_Get_Curs_Size    PROC NEAR
        MOV     AH,3               ; Select BIOS service 3
        MOV     BL,0               ; Set page
        INT     10H                ; Call BIOS
        MOV     AH,CH              ; Save starting value
        MOV     AL,CL              ; Save ending value
        RET
_BIOS_Get_Curs_Size    ENDP
```

Cursor shape is defined by the Cursor Start and Cursor End registers of the CRT Controller (indexes 0Ah and 0Bh). On the EGA, these registers cannot be read back; the BIOS and other well- behaved programs store the current cursor shape in the BIOS data area at word address 0040:0060h (or 0000:0460h).

Listing 6-13. File: PROG024.ASM

```
;***********************************************************************
; Get current size of the cursor from the BIOS data area             *
; Entry: Start - Pointer to where to save the starting value         *
;        Stop  - Pointer to where to save the ending value           *
; Exit:  Values at the pointers are set to proper values             *
;***********************************************************************

Start   EQU     [BP+4]
Stop    EQU     [BP+6]

        PUBLIC  _Get_Cursor_Size
```

```
_Get_Cursor_Size PROC NEAR
        PUSH    BP
        MOV     BP,SP
        PUSH    ES                      ;Preserve ES
        PUSH    SI
        XOR     AX,AX                   ;Set ES to segment zero
        MOV     ES,AX
        MOV     BX,ES:[BIOS_Curs_Mode]  ;Fetch cursor size
        MOV     SI,Start                ;Fetch pointer to save
        MOV     AL,BH                   ;Fetch start value
        MOV     [SI],AX                 ;Save starting value
        MOV     SI,Stop                 ;Fetch pointer to save
        MOV     AL,BL                   ;Fetch stop value
        MOV     [SI],AX                 ;Save ending value
        POP     SI
        POP     ES
        POP     BP
        RET
_Get_Cursor_Size ENDP
```

Get Page Size

Return the Number of Bytes Per Page

Pascal Library Procedure

function Get_Page_Size:integer;

C Library Procedure

get_page_size()   /* Get number of bytes in each page */

Example

Listing 6-14. File: PROGC025.C

```
/**************************************************************************/
/* Get current page size using the library function and print it        */
/**************************************************************************/

print_page_size()
        {
        printf("\nPage size = %d",              /* Print page size      */
                get_page_size());               /* Get page size        */
        }
```

Listing 6-15. File: PROGP025.PAS

```
{*************************************************************}
{ Get current page size using the library function and print it }
{*************************************************************}

procedure print_page_size;
var
i : integer;
begin
    i := Get_Page_Size;
    writeln('Page size = ',i);
end;
```

Theory

In some display modes, EGA display memory is sectioned into multiple pages. For example, 80 column text modes support 8 pages of display. Only one page can be displayed at a time.

This library procedure returns the number of bytes of data that can be displayed on the screen in the current mode, providing the current display mode was set by the BIOS (or by a "well-behaved" video device driver that updated the BIOS data area). The current page size is stored by the BIOS in system memory at word address 0040:004Ch (or 0000:044Ch).

To learn more about pages, also see

• Standard Operating Modes section in Chapter 1.

• BIOS Data Area variables in Chapter 4.

The following C routine will also return the page size:

Listing 6-16. File: PROGC026.C

```
/***************************************************************************/
/* Get current page size from BIOS data area and print it               */
/***************************************************************************/

print_data_page_size()
    {
    char    far    *p = 0;                  /* Declare far pointer  */
    int     size;
    size = p[0x44C] + 256 * p[0x44D];
    printf("\nPage Size = %X hex",size);    /* Print page size      */
    }
```

Assembly Code Example

Listing 6-17. File: PROG025.ASM

```
;**********************************************************************
; Fetching page size from BIOS data area                             *
; Exit: AX - Page size                                               *
;**********************************************************************

        PUBLIC   _Get_Page_Size

_Get_Page_Size  PROC NEAR
        PUSH     ES                         ;Preserve ES
        XOR      AX,AX                       ;Set ES to segment zero
        MOV      ES,AX
        MOV      AX,ES:[BIOS_Page_Size]      ;Fetch page size
        POP      ES                          ;Restore ES
        RET
_Get_Page_Size  ENDP
```

Get Display Type

Return the Current Display Type

Pascal Library Procedure

function Get_Display_Type:integer;

C Library Procedure

```
get_display_type()          /* Get current display type      */
                            /* Returns an integer            */
                            /*    0 - none                   */
                            /*    3 - Enhanced Display        */
                            /*    4 - Color Display           */
                            /*    5 - Monochrome Display      */
                            /*    7 - VGA Monochrome          */
                            /*    8 - VGA Color               */
```

Example

Listing 6-18. File: PROGC027.C

```
/*************************************************************************/
/* Fetch type of display attached to EGA and print it                  */
/*************************************************************************/

print_display_type()
        {
        static  char    *types[] =
                        {"Unknown", "Unknown", "Unknown", "Enhanced",
                         "Color",   "Monochrome", "Unknown", "Monochrome",
                         "Color"};
        int     index;
        index = get_display_type();              /* Get display type    */
                                                 /* Print the type      */
        if (index < 7)
                printf("\n%s Display attached to EGA", types[index]);
        else if (index < 9)
                printf("\n%s Display attached to VGA", types[index]);
        else
                printf("\EGA/VGA are not installed");
        }
```

Listing 6-19. File: PROGP027.PAS

```
{*************************************************************************}
{ Fetch type of display attached to EGA and print it                    }
{*************************************************************************}

procedure print_display_type;
var
index : integer;
begin
        index := Get_Display_Type;               { Get display type    }
                                                 { Print the type      }
        case index of
                3 : writeln("Enhanced Display attached to EGA");
                4 : writeln("Color Display attached to EGA");
                5 : writeln("Monochrome Display attached to EGA");
                7 : writeln("Monochrome Display attached to VGA");
                8 : writeln("Color Display attached to VGA");
        else
                writeln("Unknown display attached");

        end;
end;
```

Theory

Many application programs use different text attributes for monochrome displays than for color displays. Some graphics programs will operate differently with an Enhanced Color Display than with a standard Color Display. This library procedure identifies whether the current operating mode is color or monochrome.

BIOS function 18, Get EGA Status, will report whether the display is color or monochrome, and also return the current settings of the EGA configuration switches. If the display type is found to be color, the setting of the configuration switches must be examined to determine if the display is standard Color or Enhanced Color.

Assembly Code Examples

Listing 6-20. File: PROG026.ASM

```
;**********************************************************************
; Using BIOS to determine display type, and save type in AX         *
; Exit: AX - Display type                                           *
;          0 => None                                                *
;          3 => Enhanced Display (or Multi-scan)                    *
;          4 => Color Display                                       *
;          5 => Monochrome Display                                  *
;          7 => VGA Monochrome                                      *
;          8 => VGA Color (or Multi-scan)                           *
;**********************************************************************

          PUBLIC  _BIOS_Get_Display

_BIOS_Get_Display PROC    NEAR
          MOV     AX,1A00H                ;First look for VGA by trying fn=1A
          INT     10H
          CMP     AL,1AH                  ;There is no VGA if AL not 1A
          JNE     VGA_Not_In              ;...so go look for EGA
          MOV     AL,BL                   ;Return primary display info
          JMP     Type_Found

VGA_Not_In:
          MOV     AH,12H                  ;Select function 12hex
          MOV     BL,10H                  ;        subfunction 10hex
          INT     10H                     ;Call BIOS to get display type
          MOV     AL,5                    ;Assume that mono is attached
          OR      BH,BH                   ;Was display mono (BH = 1)?
          JNZ     Type_Found              ;...Yes, we are done
                                          ;...No, must look at switches
          MOV     AL,3                    ;Assume Enhanced display
          CMP     CL,9H                   ;Is switch "off on on off"?
          JE      Type_Found              ;...Yes, we are done
          CMP     CL,3                    ;Is switch "off off on on"?
          JE      Type_Found              ;...Yes, we are done
          MOV     AL,4                    ;...No, must be color display
```

```
Type_Found:
        XOR     AH,AH                    ;Clear AH
        RET
_BIOS_Get_Display ENDP
```

Listing 6-21. File: PROG027.ASM

```
;*************************************************************************
; Determine display type from BIOS variables in segment zero           *
; and return value in AX                                                *
; Exit: AX - Display type                                               *
;       0 => None                                                       *
;       3 => Enhanced Display (or Multi-scan)                           *
;       4 => Color Display                                              *
;       5 => Monochrome Display                                         *
;       7 => VGA Monochrome                                             *
;       8 => VGA Color (or Multi-scan)                                  *
;*************************************************************************

        PUBLIC  _Get_Display_Type

_Get_Display_Type       PROC NEAR
        PUSH    ES                       ;Preserve ES
        MOV     AX,1A00H                 ;First look for VGA by trying fn=1A
        INT     10H
        CMP     AL,1AH                   ;There is no VGA if AL not 1A
        JNE     VGA_Not_There            ;...so go look for EGA
        MOV     AL,BL                    ;Return primary display info
        JMP     Found_Type

VGA_Not_There:
        XOR     AX,AX                    ;Move segment zero into ES
        MOV     ES,AX
        MOV     AL,5                     ;Assume monochrome display
        TEST    BYTE PTR ES:[BIOS_Equipment],2   ;Test if mono bit is ON
        JNZ     Found_Type               ;...Yes, we are done
                                         ;...No, must look at switches
        MOV     CL,ES:[BIOS_Switch]      ;Fetch switch settings
        AND     CL,0FH                   ;Isolate config switches
        MOV     AL,3                     ;Assume enhanced display
        CMP     CL,9H                    ;Is switch "off on on off"?
        JE      Found_Type               ;...Yes, we are done
        CMP     CL,3                     ;Is switch "off off on on"?
        JE      Found_Type               ;...Yes, we are done
        MOV     AL,4                     ;...No, must be color display
Found_Type:
        XOR     AH,AH                    ;Clear AH
        POP     ES                       ;Restore ES
        RET
_Get_Display_Type       ENDP
```

Get Scan lines

Get the Total Number of Scan Lines on the Display

Pascal Library Procedure

    function Get_Scanlines:integer;

C Library Procedure

    get_scanlines()   /* Get total number of scan lines   */

Example

Listing 6-22. File: PROGC028.C

```
/***********************************************************************/
/* Fetch maximum number of scanline and print it                       */
/***********************************************************************/

print_scanlines()
       {
                                          /* Print the type      */
       printf("\nMaximum number of scanlines is %d", get_scanlines());
       }
```

Listing 6-23. File: PROGP028.PAS

```
{*************************************************************}
{ Fetch maximum number of scanline and print it             }
{*************************************************************}

procedure print_scanlines;
var
i : integer;
begin
i := Get_Scanlines;
       writeln('Maximum number of scanlines is ',i);
end;
```

Theory

In some situations, application software may need to determine the total number of scan lines, or vertical resolution, of the display. For example:

• To set limits on the movement of a graphics cursor;

• To control split screens;

• To determine the aspect ratio of the display. Some graphics drawing routines compensate for aspect ratio (see Arc Drawing under graphics programming examples).

The Color Display has 200 scan lines, The Monochrome and Enhanced Color Displays have 350 scan lines, and the VGA displays can use either 350, 400, or 480 scan lines depending on mode.

Assembly Code Example

Listing 6-24. File: PROG028.ASM

```
;*******************************************************************
; Determine maximum number of scan lines using the display type    *
; from BIOS variables in segment zero                              *
; Exit: AX - Maximum number of scanlines (200, 350, 480)           *
;*******************************************************************

        PUBLIC  _Get_Scanlines

_Get_Scanlines  PROC NEAR
        PUSH    ES                      ;Preserve ES
        MOV     AX,1A00H                ;Look for VGA (using BIOS)
        INT     10H
        CMP     AL,1AH                  ;Is VGA there? (AL=1A)
        JNE     No_VGA                  ;...No, go check EGA
        MOV     AX,480                  ;...Yes, must be 480 lines
        JMP     Found_Lines
No_VGA:
        XOR     AX,AX                   ;Move segment zero into ES
        MOV     ES,AX
        MOV     AL,ES:[BIOS_Equipment]  ;Fetch mono/color bit
        AND     AL,2                    ;Isolate bit1 and move it
        SHR     AL,1                    ; into bit0
        CMP     AL,1                    ;Was display type 1 (mono)?
        MOV     AX,350                  ;...assume so
        JE      Found_Lines             ;...Yes, we are done
                                        ;...No, must look at switches
        MOV     CL,ES:[BIOS_Switch]     ;Fetch switch settings
        AND     CL,0FH                  ;Isolate config switches
        MOV     AX,350                  ;Assume Enhanced display
        CMP     CL,9H                   ;Is switch "off on on off"?
```

```
            JE      Found_Lines            ;...Yes, we are done
            CMP     CL,3                   ;Is switch "off off on on"?
            JE      Found_Type             ;...Yes, we are done
            MOV     AX,200                 ;...No, must be color display
Found_Lines:
            POP     ES                     ;Restore ES
            RET
_Get_Scanlines  ENDP
```

Get Memory Size

Pascal Library Procedure

function Get_Memory_Size:integer;

C Library Procedure

```
get_memory_size()                  /* Get amount of RAM on EGA    */
                                   /* Return values:              */
                                   /*    64  = 64K bytes          */
                                   /*    128 = 128K bytes          */
                                   /*    256 = 256K bytes          */
```

Example

Listing 6-25. File: PROGC029.C

```
/**********************************************************************/
/* Get amount of RAM on EGA, using library function and print it     */
/**********************************************************************/

print_memory_size()
        {
        int     memory;                /* Declare variables        */
        memory = get_memory_size();    /* Get memory size          */
        printf("\n%dKBytes of Memory Available", memory); /*Print it */
        }
```

Listing 6-26. File: PROGP029.PAS

```
{*****************************************************************}
{ Get amount of RAM on EGA, using library function and print it }
{*****************************************************************}

procedure print_memory_size;
var
memory : integer;
begin
    memory := Get_Memory_Size;  { Get memory size            }
    writeln(memory, 'KBytes of Memory Available'); {Print it  }
end;
```

Theory

The original IBM EGA adapter was shipped in several memory configurations (see Partial Memory Configurations in Chapter 2). Partial memory configurations limit the capabilities of the EGA in some display modes. Some application programs check the EGA to be sure it has sufficient memory before running.

This library procedure returns the amount of display memory on the adapter. Except for the original IBM adapter, all EGAs have a full 256K bytes of display memory. The BIOS determines the size of display memory by running a memory size check during Power-on Self Tests, and stores this value in the Equipment Byte at address 0040:0087h (or 0000:0487h) in system memory.

For a complete description of the variables stored in the BIOS data area, see BIOS Data Area in Chapter 4.

BIOS function 18, Get EGA Status, returns the size of display memory. The value returned by this service is packed into two bits indicating 64K bytes, 128K bytes, 192K bytes or 256K bytes.

Assembly Code Examples

Listing 6-27. File: PROG029.ASM

```
;*********************************************************************
; Using BIOS to determine amount of installed EGA memory            *
; Exit: AX - Number of Kilobytes installed                          *
;       64  =>  64K bytes                                           *
;       128 => 128K bytes                                           *
;       256 => 256K bytes                                           *
;*********************************************************************

        PUBLIC  _BIOS_get_mem

_BIOS_Get_Mem PROC NEAR
        MOV     AH,12H              ;Select function 12hex
        MOV     BL,10H              ;        subfunciton 10hex
        INT     10H                 ;Call BIOS to get memory size
        MOV     AL,64               ;Convert memory size in BL to
        INC     BL                  ; remap BL from 0-3 into 1-4
        MUL     BL                  ; a multiple of 64
        RET
_BIOS_Get_Mem ENDP
```

Listing 6-28. File: PROG030.ASM

```
;************************************************************************
; Determine amount of installed EGA memory using constants in segment 0 *
; Exit: AX - Number of Kilobytes installed                              *
;       64  => 64K bytes                                                *
;       128 => 128K bytes                                               *
;       256 => 256K bytes                                               *
;************************************************************************

        PUBLIC    _Get_Memory_Size

_Get_Memory_Size PROC NEAR
        PUSH    ES                      ;Preserve ES
        XOR     AX,AX                   ;Move segment zero into ES
        MOV     ES,AX
        MOV     AL,ES:[BIOS_Equipment]  ;Fetch info byte
        AND     AX,60H                  ;Isolate bit1 and bit2 and
        MOV     CL,5
        SHR     AX,CL                   ; move it onto bit0 and 1
        INC     AX                      ; map 0-3 into 1-4
        MOV     CL,6                    ;Convert to multiple of 64
        SHL     AX,CL
        POP     ES                      ;Restore ES
        RET
_Get_Memory_Size ENDP
```

Get Primary Adapter

Pascal Library Procedure

function Get_Primary:integer;

C Library Procedure

```
get_primary()              /* Get what is primary adapter    */
                           /* Return value:                   */
                           /*   0 = Error (undefined)          */
                           /*   1 = EGA is primary             */
                           /*   2 = CGA is primary             */
                           /*   3 = MDA/Hercules is primary   */
```

Example

Listing 6-29. File: PROGC030.C

```
/**********************************************************************/
/* Determine primary adapter and print it                            */
/**********************************************************************/

print_primary()
        {
        static char     *list[] = {"Undefined","EGA/VGA","CGA","MDA/Hercules"};
        int     type;
        type = get_primary();
        printf("\n%s is the primary adapter", list[type]);
        }
```

Listing 6-30. File: PROGP030.PAS

```
{**********************************************************************}
{ Determine primary adapter and print it                             }
{**********************************************************************}

procedure print_primary;
var
display : integer;
begin
    display := Get_Primary;
    case display of
        0 : writeln("The primary adapter is undefined");
        1 : writeln("EGA/VGA is the primary adapter");
        2 : writeln("CGA is the primary adapter");
        3 : writeln("MDA/Hercules is the primary adapter");
    end;
end;
```

Theory

The EGA can-coexist in a system with another display adapter, and either one of the displays can be assigned as the primary display (the display that BIOS video functions direct output to). DOS functions, as well as most application programs, direct all output to the primary adapter.

This library procedure will identify the primary display in the system.

To learn more about the primary adapter see the section on Dual Displays in Chapter 1.

The primary display can be determined by looking at a variable in the BIOS data area known as the Equipment Byte, which is at address 0040:0087h (or 0000:0487h) in system memory.

Listing 6-31. File: PROGC031.C

```
/************************************************************************/
/* Using BIOS data area value at 0:0487H determine                     */
/* primary adapter and print the result.                               */
/************************************************************************/

print_data_primary()
        {
        char    type;
        char    far     *p = 0;                 /* Declare far pointer  */
        type = p[0x487];                        /* Fetch Equipment byte */
        if (!(type & 0x08))                     /* If EGA primary       */
                printf("\nEGA/VGA is primary");
        else if (type & 0x02)                   /* If mono with EGA     */
                printf("\nCGA is primary");
        else                                    /* If color with EGA    */
                printf("\nMDA/Hercules is primary");
        }
```

Assembly Code Example

Listing 6-32. File: PROG031.ASM

```
;************************************************************************
; Determine primary adapter from BIOS variable in segment              *
; zero and return value in AX                                          *
; Exit: AX - Primary adapter type                                      *
;       1 => EGA is primary                                            *
;       2 => CGA is primary                                            *
;       3 => MDA or Hercules is primary                                *
;************************************************************************

        PUBLIC  _Get_Primary

_Get_Primary    PROC NEAR
        PUSH    ES                      ;Preserve ES
        XOR     AX,AX                   ;Move segment zero into ES
        MOV     ES,AX
        MOV     BL,ES:[BIOS_Equipment]  ;Fetch info byte
        MOV     AX,1                    ;Assume EGA is primary
        TEST    BL,08H                  ;Is EGA primary?
        JZ      Primary_Found           ;...Yes, we are done
        MOV     AX,2                    ;...No, assume CGA is primary
        TEST    BL,02H                  ;Is mono attached to EGA?
        JNZ     Primary_Found           ;...Yes, we are done
        MOV     AX,3                    ;...No, must set AX to MDA
Primary_Found:
        POP     ES                      ;Restore ES
        RET
_Get_Primary    ENDP
```

Get Adapter Count

Pascal Library Procedure

function Get_Second_Adapter:integer;

C Library Procedure

```
get_second_adapter()          /* How many adapters installed   */
                              /*    0 - None                   */
                              /*    1 - EGA only               */
                              /*    2 - Two adapters           */
```

Example

This library procedure can be used to determine the number of display adapters in the system.

Listing 6-33. File: PROGC032.C

```
/**********************************************************************/
/* Determine if there is a second video adapter in the system        */
/**********************************************************************/

print_if_second()
        {
        if (get_second_adapter())
                printf("\nSecond adapter is present");
        else
                printf("\nEGA/VGA is the only adapter present");
        }
```

Listing 6-34. File: PROGP032.PAS

```
{**********************************************************************}
{ Determine if there is a second video adapter in the system          }
{**********************************************************************}

procedure print_if_second;
begin
    if Get_Second_Adapter > 0 then writeln("Second adapter is present")
    else  writeln("EGA/VGA is the only adapter present");
end;
```

Theory

Interrogating the BIOS Equipment Byte (0040:0087h or 0000:0487h) will indicate the type of display that is connected to the EGA. If the EGA display is monochrome, the procedure must then test for the presence of a CGA adapter in the system. If the EGA display is color, the procedure must test for the presence of an MDA (or Hercules) adapter in the system.

To test for the presence of a CGA adapter, an attempt is made to write, read, and verify data to the CRT Controller Cursor Position register (one of the few readable registers of the CGA) at I/O address 3D5. To test for the presence of an MDA adapter, an attempt is made to write, read, and verify data to the Cursor Position register located at I/O address 3B5.

```
/*********************************************************/
/* Algorithm for determining presence of second adapter*/
/*********************************************************/

        Determine CRTC address of second adapter
                if EGA is mono then address is 3D4
                otherwise address is 3B4
        Write 55hex to Cursor High register in CRTC
        Read the value back
        Write AAhex to Cursor High register in CRTC
        Read the value back
        If both read back agree with values writen
        then the adapter is present
        otherwise the adapter is absent
```

Assembly Code Example

Listing 6-35. File: PROG032.ASM

```
;*************************************************************************
; Determine if a second video adapter is present                       *
; and return result in AX                                              *
; Exit:  AX = 0 if there is no second adapter                          *
;            = 1 if there is a second adapter                          *
;*************************************************************************

        PUBLIC  _Get_Second_Adapter

_Get_Second_Adapter PROC NEAR
        PUSH    ES                      ;Preserve ES
        XOR     AX,AX                   ;Move segment zero into ES
        MOV     ES,AX
        MOV     DX,03D4H                ;Assume mono attached
        TEST    BYTE PTR ES:[BIOS_Equipment],2   ;Is mono attached?
        JNZ     Find_Second             ;...Yes, go look for CGA
        MOV     DX,03B4H                ;...No, look for MDA
```

```
Find_Second:
        MOV     AL,0FH                  ;Select cursor low
        OUT     DX,AL
        MOV     AL,55H                  ;Write first pattern
        INC     DX
        OUT     DX,AL
        IN      AL,DX                   ;Read pattern back
        JMP     $+2
        CMP     AL,55H                  ;Is pattern same?
        JNE     No_Second               ;...No, adapter not there

        MOV     AL,0AAH                 ;Write second pattern
        OUT     DX,AL
        IN      AL,DX                   ;Read pattern back
        JMP     $+2
        CMP     AL,0AAH                 ;Is pattern same?
        JNE     No_Second               ;...No, adapter not there

        MOV     AX,1                    ;...Yes, return count 1
        POP     ES                      ;Restore ES
        RET

No_Second:
        XOR     AX,AX                   ;Return count 0
        POP     ES
        RET
_Get_Second_Adapter ENDP
```

7

Text Operations

The examples in this chapter perform text related functions, such as setting and reading the cursor shape and position, text scrolling, outputting characters or character strings, reading and writing text attributes, and loading custom character sets. Many of these functions can be performed even if the display is in a graphics mode, allowing text and graphics to be mixed. Text functions executed in graphics mode are much slower, however, since the processor must actually draw each character into the bit-mapped display memory.

Text operations reference character positions on the screen by row number and column number. Row numbers range from 0 to 24, with row 0 at the top of the screen. Column numbers range from 0 to 79, with column zero on the left side of the screen. The first character in the upper left corner of the screen is at row 0, column 0.

Each character on the screen has an attribute code associated with it that defines the character color (both foreground and background), and other attributes such as whether the character is blinking or underlined.

For more information on text characters and attributes, see:

- Standard EGA Operating Modes (Chapter 1).

- Text Modes (Chapter 2).

- Text Attributes (Chapter 2).

- BIOS function 8 (Read Character and Attribute).

- BIOS function 9 (Write Character and Attribute).

Set Cursor Position

Pascal Library Routine

procedure Set_Cursor_Position(row,column:integer);
                                  {desired row and column for the cursor}

C Library Routine

```
set_cursor_position(row, column)  /* set cursor position           */
int   row;                        /* Desired row for the cursor    */
int   column;                     /* Desired column for the cursor */
```

Example

Listing 7-1. File: PROGC040.C

```
/***********************************************************************/
/* Set cursor to the middle of 80x25 screen                          */
/***********************************************************************/

cursor_in_middle()
        {
        clear_screen();
        set_cursor_position(12,40);     /* Cursor in middle          */
        printf("This string starts at row 12 column 40");
        }
```

Listing 7-2. File: PROGP040.PAS

```
{***********************************************************************}
{ Set cursor to the middle of 80x25 screen                            }
{***********************************************************************}

procedure cursor_in_middle;
begin
    Clear_Screen;
    Set_Cursor_Position(12,40);        { Cursor in middle            }
    writeln("This string starts at row 12 column 40");
end;
```

Theory

This procedure will position the cursor to a specific location on the screen. Cursor position is defined in terms of character rows and columns. Standard text modes allow up to 40 rows of 80 columns each. Values outside that range will produce unpredictable results. Cursor position also defines where the next character to be output by the BIOS will appear.

BIOS function 2, Set Cursor Position, will set the cursor position for any given page, whether currently displayed or not. In text modes the hardware generated cursor will appear at the new cursor location.

To learn more about cursor operation, also see:

- Description of CRT controller registers Cursor Location Low and Cursor Location High in Chapter 3.

- BIOS functions Set Cursor Position (2) and Get Cursor Position (3) in Chapter 4.

- BIOS Data Area section in Chapter 4.

- Programming examples in Get Cursor Position in Chapter 7.

Assembly Code Example

Listing 7-3. File: PROG040.ASM

```
;**********************************************************************
; Set current cursor position using BIOS call                        *
; Entry:          Row     - Row for the cursor                       *
;                 Column  - Column for the cursor                     *
;**********************************************************************

Row      EQU     [BP+4]
Column   EQU     [BP+6]

         PUBLIC  _BIOS_Set_Curs_Pos

_BIOS_Set_Curs_Pos    PROC NEAR
         PUSH    BP
         MOV     BP,SP
         MOV     AH,02H                  ;Load BIOS function
         MOV     BH,0                    ;Specify current page to be 0
         MOV     DH,Row                  ;Load desired row
         MOV     DL,Column               ;Load desired column position
         INT     10H                     ;Call BIOS so set position
         POP     BP
         RET
_BIOS_Set_Curs_Pos    ENDP
```

Cursor position can be modified directly by modifying the Cursor Position Register of the CRT Controller. This may confuse the BIOS, however, and is not recommended, unless you also make sure that the BIOS data area is updated to reflect the new cursor position.

Listing 7-4. File: PROG041.ASM

```
;**********************************************************************
; Set current cursor position by changing CRTC registers             *
; Entry:          Row              - Desired row number              *
;                 Column           - Desired column numer             *
;**********************************************************************

Row      EQU     [BP+4]
Column   EQU     [BP+6]

         PUBLIC  _Set_Cursor_Position

_Set_Cursor_Position PROC NEAR
         PUSH    BP
         MOV     BP,SP
         PUSH    ES
         XOR     AX,AX                   ;Point ES to segment 0
         MOV     ES,AX

         ;- Convert (row,column) to absolute address in display buffer
```

```
        MOV     AX,Row                  ;Convert row,column to
        MOV     DX,ES:[BIOS_Columns]    ;absolute address
        MUL     DX
        ADD     AX,Column
        MOV     BX,AX                   ;Save absolute address in BX

        ;- Write absolute address to CRT CURSOR ADDRESS registers (E & F)

        MOV     DX,ES:[BIOS_CRT_Addr]   ;Load CRTC address
        MOV     AL,0EH                  ;Fetch index of cursor high
        OUT     DX,AL                   ;Select index
        INC     DX                      ;Load CRTC address
        MOV     AL,BH                   ;Fetch data value
        OUT     DX,AL                   ;Write data

        DEC     DX                      ;Load CRTC address
        MOV     AL,0FH                  ;Fetch index of cursor low
        OUT     DX,AL                   ;Select index
        INC     DX                      ;Load CRTC address
        MOV     AL,BH                   ;Fetch data value
        OUT     DX,AL                   ;Write data

        ;- Update BIOS data area so that BIOS knows about new position

        MOV     AL,Column               ;Update BIOS data area
        MOV     AH,Row
        MOV     ES:[BIOS_Curs_Pos],AX

        POP     ES
        MOV     SP,BP
        POP     BP
        RET
_Set_Cursor_Position ENDP
```

Get Cursor Position

Read the Current Position of the Cursor

Pascal Library Procedure

procedure   Get_Cursor_Position(row_seg,row_offset,column_seg,column_offset:integer);
            {segment and offset of destinations for row and column}

C Library Procedure

```
    get_cursor_position(Row, Col)    /* Get current cursor pos        */
    int    *Row;                     /* Current cursor row            */
    int    *Col;                     /* Current cursor column         */
```

Example

Listing 7-5. File: PROGC041.C

```
/*************************************************************************/
/* Get cursor position and print it on the screen                       */
/*************************************************************************/

print_cursor_pos()
      {
      int     row, col;
      get_cursor_position(&row,&col);            /* Get position      */
                                                 /* Print it          */
      printf("\nCursor row and column are %d %d", row, col);
      }
```

Listing 7-6. File: PROGP041.PAS

```
{*************************************************************************}
{ Get cursor position and print it on the screen                         }
{*************************************************************************}

procedure print_cursor_pos;
var
row,col : integer;
begin
    Get_Cursor_Position(seg(row),ofs(row),seg(col),ofs(col));
    writeln('Cursor row and column are ', row,', ', col);
end;
```

Theory

BIOS function 3 (Read Cursor Shape and Position) will return the cursor position for a specified page, providing the cursor position was set via a BIOS call.

In text mode, the cursor position for the currently active page can also be read directly from the Cursor Position Register in the CRT Controller. The result will be an absolute memory address which then must be converted into row and column information.

To learn more about cursor operation, also see:

• Description of CRT controller registers Cursor Location Low and Cursor Location High in Chapter 3.

• BIOS functions Set Cursor Position (2) and Get Cursor Position (3) in Chapter 4.

• BIOS Data Area section in Chapter 4.

• Programming examples in Get Cursor Position in Chapter 7.

Assembly Code Examples

Listing 7-7. File: PROG042.ASM

```
;************************************************************************
; Get current cursor position using BIOS call                         *
; and return the values                                               *
; Exit: AL - Column                                                   *
;       AH - Row                                                      *
;************************************************************************

        PUBLIC _BIOS_Get_Cursor_Pos

_BIOS_Get_Cursor_Pos    PROC NEAR
        MOV     AH,03H                  ;Load BIOS function
        MOV     BH,0                    ;Specify current page to be 0
        INT     10H                     ;Call BIOS so get position
        MOV     AH,DH                   ;Save row
        MOV     AL,DL                   ;Save column
        RET
_BIOS_Get_Cursor_Pos    ENDP
```

Listing 7-8. File: PROG043.ASM

```
;************************************************************************
; Get current cursor position by reading CRTC registers               *
; Entry: Row    - Pointer to where to save current cursor row         *
;        Column - Pointer to where to save current cursor column      *
; Exit:  Values at the pointers are set to proper values              *
;************************************************************************

Row     EQU     [BP+4]
Column  EQU     [BP+6]

        PUBLIC  _Get_Cursor_Position

_Get_Cursor_Position PROC NEAR
        PUSH    BP
        MOV     BP,SP
        PUSH    ES
        XOR     AX,AX                   ;Point ES to segment 0
        MOV     ES,AX
        MOV     DX,ES:[BIOS_CRT_Addr]   ;Load CRTC address
        MOV     AL,0EH                  ;Fetch index of cursor high
        OUT     DX,AL                   ;Select index
        INC     DX                      ;Load CRTC address
        IN      AL,DX                   ;Read the high address
        JMP     $+2
        MOV     BH,AL                   ;Save value in BH

        DEC     DX                      ;Load CRTC address
        MOV     AL,0FH                  ;Fetch index of cursor low
        OUT     DX,AL                   ;Select index
        INC     DX                      ;Load CRTC address
        IN      AL,DX                   ;Read the low part of address
        JMP     $+2
```

```
        MOV     AH,BH                   ;Fetch the high byte from earlier
        XOR     DX,DX                   ;convert to row and column
        MOV     BX,ES:[BIOS_Columns]    ;by dividing absolute address
        DIV     BX                      ;with columns
        MOV     BX,Row                  ;Fetch pointer where to save row
        MOV     [BX],AX                 ;Save row number
        MOV     BX,Column               ;Fetch pointer where to save column
        MOV     [BX],DX                 ;Save column number
        POP     ES
        POP     BP
        RET
_Get_Cursor_Position ENDP
```

Set Cursor Size

Set Start and End Scan Lines for Cursor

Pascal Library Procedure

    procedure Set_Cursor_Size(start,stop:integer);

C Library Procedure

```
    set_cursor_size(start, stop)        /* Set cursor shape          */
    int   start;                        /* Starting scan line        */
    int   stop;                         /* Ending scan line          */
```

Example

Listing 7-9. File: PROGC042.C

```
/**************************************************************************/
/* Change cursor to a solid cursor by setting cursor start to           */
/* the first line of a character box.                                   */
/**************************************************************************/

demo_cursor_size()
        {
        set_cursor_size( 0, 13);                /* Full cursor           */
        }
```

Listing 7-10. File: PROGP042.PAS

```
{*********************************************************************}
{ Change cursor to a solid cursor by setting cursor start to          }
{ the first line of a character box.                                  }
{*********************************************************************}

procedure demo_cursor_size;
begin
    Set_Cursor_Size( 0, 13);              { Full cursor             }
end;
```

Theory

This procedure redefines the shape of the hardware text cursor. The default text cursor is a double underline. Another popular cursor is a full block cursor, which fills an entire character cell.

Programs that require more elaborate cursor shapes than are supported by the hardware cursor must generate a "soft" cursor. A common software cursor is generated simply by setting the Reverse Video or Underline attributes on the character at the cursor position.

For a complete explanation of the Cursor Start and End registers, see the CRT Controller section of Chapter 3.

BIOS function 1 (Set Cursor Shape) is the recommended method for changing the cursor shape. Cursor shape can also be changed by directly modifying the Cursor Start and Cursor End registers of the CRT Controller. This may confuse the BIOS, however, unless the BIOS variable at byte address 0040:0060h (or 0000:0460h) is updated as well.

To learn more about cursor operation, also see:

- Description of registers Cursor Start and Cursor End of CRT controller in Chapter 3.

- BIOS functions SET Cursor Size and Get Cursor Size in Chapter 4.

- BIOS Data Area section in Chapter 4.

- Programming examples Set Cursor Size in Chapter 7.

> When working with the Cursor Start and End registers, it is important to note that there are differences in the way that these registers function on the EGA and VGA. With the EGA, the cursor end line will be one less than the value specified in the Cursor End register; with the VGA, it will be the same as the register value.

The EGA and VGA may react differently if the Cursor Start value is greater than the Cursor End value, or if the Cursor End value is greater than the character height.

If CGA Cursor Emulation is enabled in the EGA/VGA BIOS, cursor start and end values will be automatically increased by the BIOS to compensate for the larger size of the enhanced character set. This permits some CGA software that defines cursor size to execute with the enhanced character set. For example, if start and end values of 6 and 7 are stored in the BIOS data area, the values 0Bh and 0Ch will be written to the CRT Controller.

Assembly Code Examples

Listing 7-11. File: PROG044.ASM

```
;*******************************************************************
; Set cursor size using a BIOS function                          *
; Entry:          Start - Starting scan line (0 is at the top)    *
;                 Stop  - Ending scan line for cursor             *
;*******************************************************************

Start   EQU     [BP+4]
Stop    EQU     [BP+6]

        PUBLIC  _BIOS_Set_Curs_Size

_BIOS_Set_Curs_Size PROC NEAR
        PUSH    BP
        MOV     BP,SP
        MOV     AH,01H              ;Load BIOS function
        MOV     CH,Start            ;Start line for cursor
        MOV     CL,Stop             ;End line for cursor
        INT     10H                 ;Call BIOS so set shape
        POP     BP
        RET
_BIOS_Set_Curs_Size ENDP
```

Listing 7-12. File: PROG045.ASM

```
;*******************************************************************
; Set cursor size by writing to CRTC registers                   *
; Entry:          Start - Starting line for cursor               *
;                 Stop  - Ending line for cursor                 *
;*******************************************************************

Start   EQU     [BP+4]
Stop    EQU     [BP+6]

        PUBLIC  _Set_Cursor_Size


_Set_Cursor_Size PROC    NEAR
```

```
        PUSH    BP
        MOV     BP,SP
        PUSH    ES                      ;Preserve ES
        XOR     AX,AX                   ;Select segment zero
        MOV     ES,AX

        MOV     AL,Start                ;Update BIOS data area vars.
        MOV     ES:[BIOS_Curs_Start],AL ;To contain the new cursor shape
        MOV     AL,Stop
        MOV     ES:[BIOS_Curs_Stop],AL

        MOV     DX,ES:[BIOS_CRT_Addr]   ;Load CRTC address
        MOV     AL,0AH                  ;Fetch index of cursor start
        OUT     DX,AL                   ;Select index
        INC     DX                      ;Load CRTC address
        MOV     AL,Start                ;Fetch data value
        OUT     DX,AL                   ;Write the cursor start

        DEC     DX                      ;Load CRTC address
        MOV     AL,0BH                  ;Fetch index of cursor stop
        OUT     DX,AL                   ;Select index
        INC     DX                      ;Load CRTC address
        MOV     AL,Stop                 ;Fetch data value
        OUT     DX,AL                   ;Write cursor stop value

        POP     ES                              ;Restore ES
        POP     BP
        RET
_Set_Cursor_Size ENDP
```

Get Cursor Size

Read Current Cursor Start and Cursor End Values

Get current cursor size (text modes only). See the Get Cursor Size procedure description under Programming Examples - Getting Information.

Scroll Text Window

Scroll an Area of the Screen Up or Down

Pascal Library Procedure

procedure Scroll_Text(up,left,down,right,count:integer);
                    {up,left = upper left corner row and column}
                    {down,right = lower right corner row and column}
                    {count = # of lines to scroll   }
                    {n positive => scroll up}
                    {n negative => scroll down}

C Library Procedure

```
scroll_text(r1,c1,r2,c2,n)      /* Scroll section of screen              */
int    r1,c1;                   /* Upper left corner row and column      */
int    r2,c2;                   /* Lower right corner row and column     */
int    n;                       /* Number of lines to scroll             */
                                /* n positive => scroll up               */
                                /* n negative => scroll down             */
```

Example

Listing 7-13. File: PROGC043.C

```
/*******************************************************************************/
/* Scroll upper left quarter of the 80x25 screen up by  6 lines              */
/*******************************************************************************/

sample_scroll_text()
      {
      int     i,j;
      for (i = 0; i < 25; i++)          /* Fill screen with data        */
            {
            printf("\n");
            for (j = 0; j < 40; j++)
                  printf("%1d",i%10);
            }
      getchar();                        /* Wait for <Enter>             */
      scroll_text(1,3,12,19, 6);        /* Scroll text window           */
      getchar();                        /* Wait for <Enter>             */
      scroll_text(1,3,12,19,-6);        /* Scroll text window           */
      }
```

Listing 7-14. File: PROGP043.PAS

```
{**********************************************************************}
{ Scroll upper left quarter of the 80x25 screen up by   6 lines       }
{**********************************************************************}

procedure sample_scroll_text;
var
i,j : integer;
ch : char;
begin
        for i := 0 to 24 do
            begin
                for j := 0 to 59 do      { Fill screen with data        }
                        Write_Char(Chr(Ord("A")+i), i, j);
            end;
        ch := ReadKey;                    { Wait for key to be pressed   }
        Scroll_Text(1,3,12,19, 6);        { Scroll text window up        }
        ch := ReadKey;
        Scroll_Text(1,3,12,19,-6);        { Scroll text window down      }
end;
```

Theory

This procedure will scroll a text region on the screen. The region is defined in terms of rows and columns. Figure 7–1 shows how the scroll window is specified.

This type of scroll requires the processor to move each line of text from one region in display memory to another. No EGA control registers are used.

BIOS functions 6 and 7, Scroll Text Window Up and Scroll Text Window Down, will perform this scrolling function whether the display is in a text mode or a graphics mode. Smooth scrolling is not supported by the BIOS. A smooth scrolling algorithm will be discussed later (see section Smooth Scroll in this chapter).

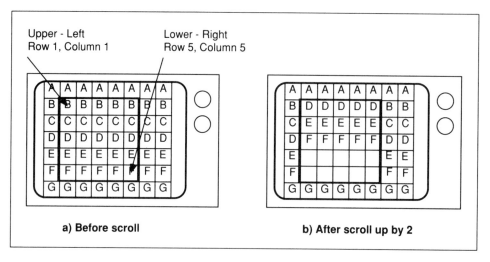

Figure 7-1. Text scroll.

The BIOS scroll function is very complex because the EGA supports such a variety of text modes, and because the BIOS text functions are also supported for graphics modes as well. The scrolling methods are different for each of the modes:

Mode	Scroll Requirement
0,1	80 bytes per line, 1 line per character row
2,3	160 bytes per line, 1 line per character row
4,5	40 bytes per line, 8 interleaved lines per char row
6	80 bytes per line, 8 interleaved lines per char row
7	160 bytes per line, 1 line per char row
D	40 bytes per line, 8 lines per char row
E	80 bytes per line, 8 lines per char row
F	80 bytes per line, 8 or 14 lines per char row
10	80 bytes per line, 8 or 14 lines per char row

Examples are shown for the two most common modes: 80 column text mode with a Color Display (mode 3) or an Enhanced Display (mode 3*), and 80 column text mode with a Monochrome Display (mode 7).

This scrolling method will also work for any nonstandard text mode if it sets correctly all the relevant BIOS variables.

The algorithm used by the BIOS for scrolling depends on the direction of the scroll. A specific sequence must be followed or characters could be overwritten and permanently lost.

For an upward scroll, text characters are moved starting at the top of the window and proceeding downward. To scroll upward N lines, data from row N of the window is moved to the first row of the window. Then, row N+1 is moved to the second row of the window, and so on. Once the last row is moved, the bottom N rows of the window are cleared to blanks.

For a downward scroll, text characters are moved starting at the bottom of the window and proceeding upward. To scroll downward N lines, if R is the bottom row of the window, data from row R-N is moved to row R. Then, row R-N-1 is moved to row R-1, and so on. Once the last (top) row is moved, the top N rows of the window are cleared to blanks.

To learn more about scrolling of text, also see:

- BIOS functions Scroll Text Window Up (6) and Scroll Text Window Down (7) in Chapter 4.

- BIOS Data Area in Chapter 4.

- Scroll Text Page and Smooth Scroll programming examples in this chapter.

Assembly Code Examples

Listing 7-15. File: PROG046.ASM

```
;********************************************************************
; Using BIOS to scroll section of a text screen                   *
; Entry:        Up, Left       - Upper left row and column         *
;               Down, Right    - Lower right row and column        *
;               Count          - Number of lines to scroll         *
;********************************************************************
Up       EQU     BYTE PTR [BP+4]
Left     EQU     BYTE PTR [BP+6]
Down     EQU     BYTE PTR [BP+8]
Right    EQU     BYTE PTR [BP+10]
Count    EQU     BYTE PTR [BP+12]


         PUBLIC  _BIOS_Scroll_Text

_BIOS_Scroll_Text PROC NEAR
         PUSH    BP
         MOV     BP,SP
         MOV     BH,07           ;Attribute for "blank" lines
         MOV     AL,Count        ;Number of lines to scroll
         MOV     CH,Up           ;Upper left corner into CX
         MOV     CL,Left
         MOV     DH,Down         ;Lower right corner into DX
         MOV     DL,Right
         CMP     Count,0         ;Is scroll up?
```

```
        JL      BIOS_Set_Down   ;...No, go scroll down
BIOS_Set_Up:                    ;...Yes, load scroll down fn
        MOV     AH,06H          ;Load service number
        JMP     BIOS_Do_Scroll
BIOS_Set_Down:
        MOV     AH,07H          ;Load service number
        NEG     AL              ;Make scroll value positive
BIOS_Do_Scroll:
        INT     10H                     ;Call BIOS to do the scroll
        POP     BP
        RET
_BIOS_Scroll_Text ENDP
```

Listing 7-16. File: PROG047.ASM

```
;******************************************************************************
; Scrolling text window in text modes                                        *
; Entry:          Up, Left       - Upper left row and column                  *
;                 Down, Right    - Lower right row and column                 *
;                 Count          - Number of lines to scroll                  *
;******************************************************************************

Up       EQU    WORD PTR [BP+4]
Left     EQU    WORD PTR [BP+6]
Down     EQU    WORD PTR [BP+8]
Right    EQU    WORD PTR [BP+10]
Count    EQU    WORD PTR [BP+12]

         PUBLIC  _Scroll_Text

_Scroll_Text    PROC NEAR
        PUSH    BP
        MOV     BP,SP

        PUSH    DS              ;Preserve DS
        PUSH    ES              ;Preserve ES
        PUSH    SI
        PUSH    DI

        ;- Determine and load segment of the display buffer

        XOR     AX,AX           ;Point ES to segment zero
        MOV     ES,AX
        MOV     AX,0B000H       ;Assume monochrome buffer address
        TEST    BYTE PTR ES:[BIOS_Equipment],2   ;Is mono attached?
        JNZ     Scroll_Addr_Ok  ;...Yes, go load segment
        MOV     AX,0B800H       ;...No, change address to color
Scroll_Addr_Ok:
        MOV     DS,AX           ;Set segment of display buffer

        ;- Compute pointers to source and destination

        CMP     Count,0         ;Are we scrolling up?
        JL      Set up_Down     ;...No, set up for scrolling down
Setup_Up:
        MOV     BX,ES:[BIOS_Columns]    ;Compute address of where to move from
```

```
        MOV     AX,Up              ;Compute first byte to move as
        ADD     AX,Count           ;(Upper row + count)*bytes per line
        MUL     BX                 ; + upper column
        ADD     AX,Left
        MOV     SI,AX              ;Save source address in SI
        SHL     SI,1               ;Adjust for two bytes per char

        MOV     AX,Up              ;Compute address of where to move to
        MUL     BX                 ;as Upper row * bytes line + upper
        ADD     AX,Left            ;   + column
        MOV     DI,AX              ;Save destination
        SHL     DI,1               ;Adjust for two bytes per char

        MOV     DX,Right           ;Words to move in each line
        SUB     DX,Left            ;is (Right - Left + 1)
        INC     DX
        SUB     BX,DX              ;Compute "update"
        SHL     BX,1

        MOV     CX,Down            ;Compute number of lines to move
        SUB     CX,Up
        SUB     CX,Count
        INC     CX
        PUSH    DS                 ;Copy DS into ES
        POP     ES
Loop_Up:
        PUSH    CX                 ;Save counter of lines
        MOV     CX,DX              ;Set counter of bytes
        REP     MOVSW              ;Move next line of bytes (word/char)
        ADD     DI,BX              ;Set pointers to next line
        ADD     SI,BX
        POP     CX                 ;Restore line counter
        LOOP    Loop_Up            ;If not done, go move next line
Clear_Up:
        MOV     CX,Count           ;Number of lines to clear
        MOV     AX,0720H           ;Value to use as 'clear'
Loop_Clear_Up:
        PUSH    CX
        MOV     CX,DX              ;Fetch # bytes in each line
        REP     STOSW              ;Clear next line
        ADD     DI,BX              ;Set pointers to next line
        POP     CX
        LOOP    Loop_Clear_Up

        JMP     Scroll_Done

Setup_Down:
        NEG     Count
        MOV     BX,ES:[BIOS_Columns]   ;Compute bytes/line
        MOV     AX,Down            ;Compute first source byte
        SUB     AX,Count           ;(Lower row - count)*bytes per line
        MUL     BX                 ; + upper column
        ADD     AX,Left
        MOV     SI,AX              ;Save source address in SI
        SHL     SI,1               ;Adjust for two bytes per char
```

```
          MOV      AX,Down              ;Compute address of where to move
          MUL      BX                   ;as Lower row * bytes line + left
          ADD      AX,Left              ;    + column
          MOV      DI,AX                ;Save destination
          SHL      DI,1                 ;Adjust for two bytes per char

          MOV      DX,Right             ;Compute words to move in a line
          SUB      DX,Left              ;as (Right - Left + 1)
          INC      DX
          ADD      BX,DX                ;Compute "update"
          SHL      BX,1

          MOV      CX,Down              ;Compute number of lines to move
          SUB      CX,Up
          SUB      CX,Count
          INC      CX
          PUSH     DS                   ;Copy DS into ES
          POP      ES
Loop_Down:
          PUSH     CX                   ;Save counter of lines
          MOV      CX,DX                ;Set counter of bytes
          REP      MOVSW                ;Move next line of bytes
          SUB      DI,BX                ;Set pointers to next line
          SUB      SI,BX
          POP      CX                   ;Restore line counter
          LOOP     Loop_Down            ;If not done, go move next line

Clear_Down:
          MOV      CX,Count             ;Number of lines to clear
          MOV      AX,0720H             ;Value to use as "clear"
Loop_Clear_Down:
          PUSH     CX
          MOV      CX,DX                ;Fetch # bytes in each line
          REP      STOSW                ;Clear next line
          SUB      DI,BX                ;Set pointers to next line
          POP      CX
          LOOP     Loop_Clear_Down

Scroll_Done:
          POP      DI
          POP      SI
          POP      ES
          POP      DS
          POP      BP
          RET
_Scroll_Text     ENDP
```

Scroll Text Page

Scroll Entire Screen Up or Down

Pascal Library Procedure

```
procedure Scroll_Page(count:integer);
                        {count positive => scroll up }
                        {count negative => scroll down}
```

C Library Procedure

```
scroll_page(n)                /* Scroll section of screen      */
int    n;                     /* Number of lines to scroll     */
                              /* n positive => scroll up       */
                              /* n negative => scroll down      */
```

Example

Listing 7-17. File: PROGC044.C

```
/**********************************************************************/
/* Scroll the screen by  6 lines up                                   */
/**********************************************************************/

sample_scroll_page()
        {
        int    i;
        for (i = 0; i < 25; i++)          /* Fill screen with data     */
                printf("\nThis is line %d",i);

        getchar();                        /* Wait for <Enter>          */
        scroll_page( 6);                  /* Scroll page up by  6 rows  */
        }
```

Listing 7-18. File: PROGP044.PAS

```
{**********************************************************************}
{ Scroll the screen by  6 lines up                                    }
{**********************************************************************}

procedure sample_scroll_page;
var
i : integer;
begin
        for i := 1 to 25 do
                writeln("This is line",i);      { Fill screen with data }
        i := integer(ReadKey);                  { Wait for <Enter> key  }
        Scroll_Page( 6);                        { Scroll page up by  6 rows}
end;
```

Theory

This procedure scrolls the entire screen by a specified number of rows. It is similar to the Scroll Text Window procedure described above, except that the window is the entire screen. This permits a faster algorithm to be used.

Assembly Code Examples:

Listing 7-19. File: PROG048.ASM

```
;****************************************************************************
; Use BIOS to scroll whole screen                                         *
; Entry:          Count             - Number of lines to scroll           *
;****************************************************************************

Count   EQU     BYTE PTR [BP+4]

        PUBLIC  _BIOS_Scroll_Page

_BIOS_Scroll_Page PROC NEAR
        PUSH    BP
        MOV     BP,SP
        PUSH    ES
        XOR     AX,AX
        MOV     ES,AX

        MOV     BH,07             ;Attribute for "blank" lines
        MOV     AL,Count          ;Number of lines to scroll
        MOV     CH,0              ;Upper left corner into CX
        MOV     CL,0
        MOV     DH,ES:[BIOS_Rows]     ;Lower right corner into DX
        DEC     DH
        MOV     DL,ES:[BIOS_Columns]
        DEC     DL
        CMP     Count,0           ;Is scroll up?
        JL      B_Page_Down       ;...No, go scroll down
B_Page_Up:                        ;...Yes, load scroll down fn
        MOV     AH,06H            ;Load service number
        JMP     B_Page_Scroll
B_Page_Down:
        MOV     AH,07H            ;Load service number
        NEG     AL
B_Page_Scroll:
        INT     10H               ;Call BIOS to do the scroll
        POP     ES
        POP     BP
        RET
_BIOS_Scroll_Page ENDP
```

Listing 7-20. File: PROG049.ASM

```
;*************************************************************************
; Scrolling 80 column page of text                                      *
; Entry:          Count           - Number of lines to scroll           *
;*************************************************************************

Count     EQU     WORD PTR [BP+4]

          PUBLIC  _Scroll_Page

_Scroll_Page      PROC NEAR
          PUSH    BP
          MOV     BP,SP

          ;- Determine and load segement of the display buffer

          PUSH    DS                      ;Preserve registers
          PUSH    ES
          PUSH    SI
          PUSH    DI

          XOR     AX,AX                   ;Point ES to segment zero
          MOV     ES,AX
          MOV     AX,0B000H               ;Assume monochrome buffer address
          TEST    BYTE PTR ES:[BIOS_Equipment],2   ;Is mono attached?
          JNZ     PAddr_Ok                ;...Yes, go load segment
          MOV     AX,0B800H               ;...No, change address to color
PAddr_Ok:
          MOV     DS,AX                   ;Set segment of display buffer

          ;- Compute pointers to source and destination

          CMP     Count,0                 ;Are we scrolling up?
          JL      P_Set_Down              ;...No, setup for scrolling down
P_Set_Up:
          MOV     BX,ES:[BIOS_Columns]    ;Fetch number of columns
          MOV     AX,Count                ;Fetch number of rows to scroll
          MUL     BX                      ;Compute address of first byte to
          SHL     AX,1                    ;move as Columns*Count*2
          MOV     SI,AX                   ;Save address of first byte to move
          XOR     DI,DI                   ;Address of where to move to
          MOV     AL,ES:[BIOS_Rows]       ;Number of bytes to move is
          XOR     AH,AH
          SUB     AX,Count                ;(Total_Rows-Count)*Columns*2
          MUL     BX                      ;multiply rows*columns
          SHL     AX,1                    ;multipy by 2 (account for attrib)
          MOV     CX,AX                   ;Move count into register CX
          MOV     AX,DS                   ;Point segment register ES to
          MOV     ES,AX                   ;the display buffer segment
          REP     MOVSB                   ;Move rows up
P_Clear_Up:
          MOV     AX,Count                ;Compute number of words to clear
          MUL     BX                      ;as Rows*Columns
          MOV     CX,AX                   ;Save the count in register CX
          MOV     AX,0700H+'              ;Value to use in "cleared" area
                                          ;is attribute 7 and character ' '
```

```
        REP     STOSW                       ;"Clear" the area
        JMP     Page_Scroll_Done

P_Set_Down:
        MOV     BX,ES:[BIOS_Columns]        ;Fetch number of columns
        MOV     AL,ES:[BIOS_Rows]           ;Fetch total number of rows
        XOR     AH,AH
        SUB     AX,Count                    ;Compue address of first byte
        MUL     BX                          ;to move as Total Rows - Count *
        DEC     AX                          ;* Columns * 2 - 2
        SHL     AX,1
        MOV     SI,AX                       ;Save address of first byte to move

        MOV     AL,ES:[BIOS_Rows]           ;Fetch total number of rows
        XOR     AH,AH
        MUL     BX                          ;Compute address of first byte of
        DEC     AX                          ;where the to move bytes to as
        SHL     AX,1                        ;(Total Rows * Columns - 1) * 2
        MOV     DI,AX                       ;Save address in register DI

        MOV     AL,ES:[BIOS_Rows]           ;Compute number of byte to
        XOR     AH,AH
        SUB     AX,Count                    ;move as
        MUL     BX                          ;(Total Rows - Count) * Columns * 2
        SHL     AX,1
        MOV     CX,AX                       ;Put count into register CX
        STD                                 ;Set direction flag to "decrement"
        REP     MOVSB                       ;Move rows up

P_Clear_Down:
        MOV     AX,Count                    ;Compute number of words to clear
        MUL     BX                          ;as Rows*Columns
        MOV     CX,AX                       ;Save the count in register CX
        MOV     AX,0700H+' '                ;Value to use in "cleared" area
                                            ;is attribute 7 and character ' '
        REP     STOSW                       ;"Clear" the area
        CLD                                 ;Reset the direction flag

Page_Scroll_Done:
        POP     DI
        POP     SI
        POP     ES
        POP     DS

        POP     BP
        RET
_Scroll_Page    ENDP
```

Smooth Scroll

Smoothly Pan Horizontally and Scroll Vertically

Pascal Library Procedures

procedure Smooth_Scroll(x,y:integer);
                    { x pixels horizontally, y pixels vertically}

C Library Procedures

```
smooth_scroll(x,y)          /* set scroll value to x,y                    */
int   x,y;                  /* x pixels horizontally, y pixels vertically */
```

Example

Listing 7-21. File: PROGC055.C

```c
/**************************************************************/
/* Scroll smoothly in 100 column text screen using cursor keys  */
/* Quit on Escape key.                                          */
/**************************************************************/

smooth_text_scroll()
        {
        #define KEY_ESC         0x011B
        #define KEY_UP          0x4800
        #define KEY_DOWN        0x5000
        #define KEY_LEFT        0x4B00
        #define KEY_RIGHT       0x4D00
        #define KEY_ENTER       0x1C0D

        int     x = 0, y = 0, i, key;
        set_more_columns(100);  /* Select 100 text column mode    */
        set_cursor_position(0,0);
        for (i = 0; i < 100;i++)/* Fill newly organized text buffer   */
            write_string(i, 0,
            "This is text line in the new 100 column text buffer");
        while((key = get_key()) != KEY_ENTER)
            switch (key)
                {
                case KEY_RIGHT:                         /* Scroll right */
                    x = (x < 799) ? ++x : 799;
                    smooth_scroll(x,y);
                    break;
                case KEY_LEFT:                          /* Scroll left  */
                    x = ( x > 0) ? -x : 0;
                    smooth_scroll(x, y);
                    break;
                case KEY_UP:                            /* Scroll up    */
                    y = (y > 0) ? -y : 0;
                    smooth_scroll(x, y);
                    break;
```

```
                        case KEY_DOWN:                          /* Scroll down   */
                            y = (y < 1399) ? ++y : 1399;
                            smooth_scroll(x, y);
                            break;
                        default:
                            break;
                    }
            smooth_scroll(0,0);
            }
```

Listing 7-22. File: PROGP055.PAS

```
{*********************************************************************}
{ Scroll smoothly in 100 column text screen using cursor keys        }
{ Quit on Escape key.                                                }
{*********************************************************************}

procedure smooth_text_scroll;
const
MONO = 5;
VMONO = 7;
KEY_ESC =       $1B;
KEY_UP  =       72;
KEY_DOWN =      80;
KEY_LEFT =      75;
KEY_RIGHT =     77;
KEY_ENTER =     $0D;
const
msg : string[53] = "This is a text line in the new 100 column text buffer";
var
x,y,i,key : integer;
begin
        x := 0;
        y := 0;
        Set_More_Columns(100);  { Select 100 text column mode  }
        Set_Cursor_Position(0,0);
        for i := 0 to 99 do      { Fill newly organized buffer  }
                Write_String(i, 0, seg(msg), ofs(msg));
        repeat
                key := integer(readkey);
                case key of

                    KEY_RIGHT:                      { Scroll right }
                        if x < 799 then inc(x);
                    KEY_LEFT:                       { Scroll left  }
                        if x > 0 then dec(x);
                    KEY_UP:                         { Scroll up    }
                        if y > 0 then dec(y);
                    KEY_DOWN:                       { Scroll down  }
                        if y < 1399 then inc(y);
                    end;
                Smooth_Scroll(x,y);
        until key = KEY_ENTER;
        Smooth_Scroll(0,0);                         { Restore to 0 }

        {- Set default text mode                                  }
```

```
        i := Get_Display_Type;
        if i = MONO then        Set_Mode(7)
        else if i = VMONO then Set_Mode(7)
        else                    Set_Mode(3);
end;
```

Theory

Smooth_Scroll takes advantage of the EGA's hardware capability to scroll and pan. The display memory of the EGA can be configured as a "logical" display page which is wider and longer than the display screen. Hardware scrolling/panning can then be used to display desired sections of the logical page on the screen.

The procedure Set_More_Columns (described in the Horizontal Scroll programming example) can be used to set up a screen wider than the default 80 columns. The Smooth_Scroll procedure is then used to scroll horizontally and vertically through the larger screen.

By repetitively calling Smooth_Scroll with different X,Y values, a hardware smooth scroll can be implemented.

To learn more about smooth scroll and pan, also see the description of Start Address, Preset Row Scan registers of CRT controller, and Horizontal Panning register of Attribute controller in Chapter 3, and programming examples Panning and Scrolling in Chapter 5.

Assembly Code Examples

The following example shows how the Smooth_Scroll routine is implemented. The scroll is accomplished by combining values for vertical and horizontal scroll (see description of Vertical_Scroll and Horizontal_Scroll programming examples in Chapter 5).

Listing 7-23. File: PROG071.ASM

```
;**********************************************************************
; Smooth simultaneous scroll in horizontal and vertical direction    *
; Entry:      X_Offset- Current horizontal offset                    *
;             Y_Offset- Current vertical offset                      *
;**********************************************************************

X_Offset        EQU     [BP+4]
Y_Offset        EQU     [BP+6]

        PUBLIC  _Smooth_Scroll

_Smooth_Scroll  PROC    NEAR
        PUSH    BP                      ;Standard entry from high level
        MOV     BP,SP
        PUSH    ES
```

```
        XOR     AX,AX                      ;Point ES to segment zero
        MOV     ES,AX

;- Set CRTC ADDRESS register to offset/8
;- Compute offset into display buffer to be loaded into CRTC
;     START ADDRESS register as:
;     X_Offset/8 + Y_Offset/Char_Height * columns

        MOV     AX,Y_Offset                ;Fetch Y_Offset
        XOR     DX,DX                      ;Clear DX for divide
        MOV     BX,ES:[BIOS_Height]        ;Get character height
        DIV     BX                         ;Divide offset by character height
        MOV     BX,AX                      ;Save number of text lines to skip
        MOV     CX,DX                      ;Save number of scan lines to skip
        MOV     AX,ES:[BIOS_Columns]       ;Fetch number of bytes per text line
        SHL     AH,1                       ; (adjust for attributes)
        MUL     BX                         ;Convert to number of bytes to skip

        MOV     BX,X_Offset                ;Compute how many bytes to skip due
        SHR     BX,1                       ;to X_Offset
        SHR     BX,1
        SHR     BX,1
        ADD     BX,AX                      ;and add to previously computed offset
                                           ;due to Y_Offset

;- Wait for an end of vertical retrace

        MOV     DX,ES:[BIOS_CRT_Addr]      ;Get address of CRT controller
        ADD     DX,6                       ;Wait for retrace to change registers
SS_Wait1:                                  ;Wait for vertical to start
        IN      AL,DX
        JMP     $+2
        TEST    AL,8
        JZ      SS_Wait1
SS_Wait2:                                  ;Wait for vertical to end
        IN      AL,DX
        JMP     $+2
        TEST    AL,8
        JNZ     SS_Wait2

;- Set START ADDRESS register in CRTC to the value just computed

        MOV     DX,ES:[BIOS_CRT_Addr]      ;Fetch address of CRTC
        MOV     AL,0DH                     ;Index for START ADDRESS register LO
        OUT     DX,AL                      ;Select index
        INC     DX
        MOV     AL,BL                      ;Fetch the scroll value we computed
        OUT     DX,AL                      ;Set START register
        DEC     DX
        MOV     AL,0CH                     ;Select index for START ADDRESS hi
        OUT     DX,AL
        INC     DX
        MOV     AL,BH                      ;Set START register
        OUT     DX,AL
        DEC     DX

; Wait for vertical retrace to start
```

```
          ADD       DX,6
SS_Wait3:                               ;Wait for vertical to start
          IN        AL,DX
          JMP       $+2
          TEST      AL,8
          JZ        SS_Wait3
          SUB       DX,6

          ;- Set CRTC PRESET ROW SCAN register to number of scan lines to skip
          ;    it was earlier computed as (Y_Offset MOD Char_Height)

          MOV       AL,8                ;Index of PRESET ROW SCAN register
          OUT       DX,AL               ;Select PRESET ROW SCAN register
          MOV       AL,CL               ;Fetch scan lines to skip
          INC       DX
          OUT       DX,AL               ;Set PRESET ROW SCAN register

          ;- Set Attribute PANNING register to Y_Offset MOD 8

          ADD       DX,5                ;Compute Attr Read register address
          IN        AL,DX               ;Reset Attr index/data flip-flop
          MOV       DX,3C0H             ;Fetch address of Attr write register
          MOV       AL,33H              ;Fetch index
          OUT       DX,AL               ;Select PANNING register
          MOV       AX,X_Offset         ;Fetch offset
          AND       AL,7                ;Keep last 3 bits (offset mod 8)
          OUT       DX,AL               ;Set PANNING register

          POP       ES                  ;Standard exit to high level
          MOV       SP,BP
          POP       BP
          RET
_Smooth_Scroll   ENDP
```

Write Character

Output a Single Text Character to the Display

Pascal Library Procedure

```
procedure Write_Char(chr:char;row,column:integer);
                      {character to display, row and column on screen}
```

C Library Procedure

```
write_char(code, row, column)      /* Display character            */
char   code;                       /* Character code (ASCII value) */
int    row;                        /* Position of the character    */
int    column;                     /* on the screen                */
```

Example

Listing 7-24. File: PROGC045.C

```
/*************************************************************************/
/* Display three consecutive characters starting at the end of the     */
/* 80x25 screen                                                        */
/*************************************************************************/

write_one_char()
    {
        write_char("A", 24, 40);            /* First character      */
        write_char("B", 24, 41);            /* Second character     */
        write_char("C", 24, 42);            /* Third character      */
    }
```

Listing 7-25. File: PROGP045.PAS

```
{*************************************************************************}
{ Display three consecutive characters starting at the end of the       }
{ 80x25 screen                                                          }
{*************************************************************************}

procedure write_one_char;
begin
        Write_Char('A', 24, 40);            { First character      }
        Write_Char('B', 24, 41);            { Second character     }
        Write_Char('C', 24, 42);            { Third character      }
end;
```

Theory

To output a text character to the display screen, an ASCII character code, text attribute, and screen position (row and column) must be specified. Standard EGA text modes use 25 rows (numbered from 0 to 24) and either 40 or 80 columns (numbered 0 to 39 or 0 to 79). The upper left corner of the screen is row 0 , column 0. The bottom right corner of the screen is row 24, column 39 or 79 (see Figure 7-2). The attribute for that character position on the screen will be unchanged (the Write Attribute function can be used to change attributes).

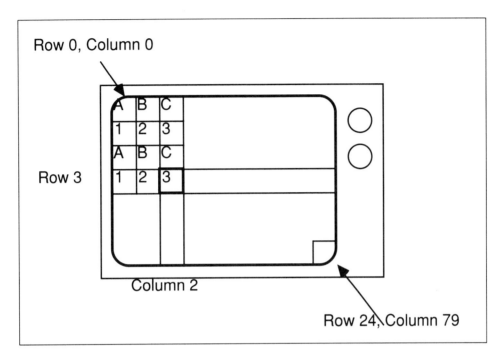

Figure 7-2. Text addressing.

Two BIOS calls are needed to perform this procedure; one to position the cursor and one to output the character. BIOS function 2 (Set Cursor Position) can be used to position the cursor to the desired spot on the screen.

Three BIOS functions are available to place a character into the display buffer at the current cursor position. BIOS function 10 (Write Character Only) will place a character on the screen leaving the character attribute for that screen position unchanged. The new character will have the attributes of the previous character that was at that position. BIOS function 9 (Write Character and Attribute) will place a character on the screen and set its attribute. Neither of these two functions will advance the cursor position.

BIOS function 14 (Write Character and Advance Cursor) will place a character on the screen (without changing the attribute) and advance the cursor position to the next character position. This BIOS function is sometimes called Teletype Mode.

BIOS function 19 (Write Text String) can be used to output an entire string of characters to the display.

For further details on these BIOS functions, see Chapter 4.

ASCII characters and attributes can also be written directly to the display buffer without using the BIOS. Even memory addresses contain ASCII character codes, and odd memory addresses contain attribute bytes. For a complete explanation of display memory usage in text mode, see Display Memory and Text Modes in Chapter 2.

Assembly Code Examples

The following assembly code examples illustrate the use of all four BIOS calls described here, as well as how to access the display buffer directly.

Listing 7-26. File: PROG050.ASM

```
;**********************************************************************
; Display red character "9" on a blue background in the             *
; middle of 80x25 screen using WRITE CHARACTER AND ATTRIBUTE         *
; function in the BIOS                                               *
;**********************************************************************

        PUBLIC _BIOS_Char_9

_BIOS_Char_9    PROC NEAR
        MOV     DH,12                   ;Select row 12
        MOV     DL,40                   ;Select column 40
        MOV     BH,0                    ;Use first page
        MOV     AH,2                    ;Function = SET CURSOR POSITION
        INT     10H                     ;Ask BIOS to set cursor position

        MOV     AL,"9"                  ;Will display character "9"
        MOV     BL,12H                  ;Set character attribute
        MOV     BH,0                    ;Use first page
        MOV     CX,1                    ;Do this character only once
        MOV     AH,9                    ;Function = WRITE CHAR & ATTRIB
        INT     10H                     ;Ask BIOS to display character
        RET
_BIOS_Char_9    ENDP

;**********************************************************************
; Display the character "A" (with attribute same as previous         *
; character in same position) using WRITE CHARACTER ONLY             *
; function in the BIOS                                               *
;**********************************************************************

        PUBLIC _BIOS_Char_A

_BIOS_Char_A    PROC NEAR
        MOV     DH,12                   ;Select row 12
        MOV     DL,41                   ;Select column 41
        MOV     BH,0                    ;Use first page
        MOV     AH,2                    ;Function = SET CURSOR POSITION
        INT     10H                     ;Ask BIOS to set cursor position

        MOV     AL,"A"                  ;Will display character "A"
```

```
        MOV     BH,0                    ;Use first page
        MOV     CX,1                    ;Do this character only once
        MOV     AH,0AH                  ;Function = WRITE CHARACTER
        INT     10H                     ;Ask BIOS to display character
        RET
_BIOS_Char_A    ENDP

;************************************************************************
; Display the characters "FNE" (with attribute same as                 *
; previous charcter in same position) using TELETYPE                    *
; function in the BIOS                                                  *
;************************************************************************

        PUBLIC _BIOS_Char_E

_BIOS_Char_E    PROC NEAR
        MOV     DH,13                   ;Select row 13
        MOV     DL,40                   ;Select column 40
        MOV     BH,0                    ;Use first page
        MOV     AH,2                    ;Function = SET CURSOR POSITION
        INT     10H                     ;Ask BIOS to set cursor position

        MOV     AL,"F"                  ;Will display character "F"
        MOV     BH,0                    ;Use first page
        MOV     AH,0EH                  ;Function = TELETYPE
        INT     10H                     ;Ask BIOS to display character

        MOV     AL,"N"                  ;Will display character "N"
        INT     10H                     ;Ask BIOS to display character

        MOV     AL,"E"                  ;Will display character "E"
        INT     10H                     ;Ask BIOS to display character
        RET
_BIOS_Char_E    ENDP

;************************************************************************
; Display the characters "F13" (with attribute same as                 *
; previous character in same position) using WRITE STRING              *
; function in the BIOS, with blue on red background                     *
;************************************************************************

        PUBLIC _BIOS_Char_13

TestChr DB      "F13"

_BIOS_Char_13   PROC NEAR
        PUSH    ES
        PUSH BP

        MOV     DH,14                   ;Select row 14
        MOV     DL,40                   ;Select column 40
        MOV     BH,0                    ;Use first page
        MOV     CX,4                    ;Display four characters
        MOV     AX,CS                   ;Point ES:BP to the string
        MOV     ES,AX
        LEA     BP,TestChr
        MOV     AH,13H                  ;Function   = WRITE TEXT STRING
```

```
        MOV     AL,1                    ;Subfunction = update cursor
        MOV     BL,12H                  ;BL has attribute
        INT     10H                     ;Ask BIOS to display the string

        POP     BP
        POP     ES
        RET
_BIOS_Char_13   ENDP
```

Listing 7-27. File: PROG051.ASM

```
;***********************************************************************
; Display character Char at position Row, Column (using attributes     *
; already in display buffer)                                           *
; Entry: The following parameters are passed on the stack as words      *
;                   Char, Row, Col                                      *
;***********************************************************************

Char    EQU     [BP+4]
Row     EQU     [BP+6]
Column  EQU     [BP+8]

        PUBLIC  _Write_Char

_Write_Char     PROC NEAR
        PUSH    BP
        MOV     BP,SP
        PUSH    DI                      ;Preserve registers
        PUSH    ES

        ;— Convert row and column to absolute offset within display buffer

        XOR     AX,AX                   ;Point ES to segment zero
        MOV     ES,AX
        MOV     AX,Row                  ;Fetch row number
        MOV     BX,ES:[BIOS_Columns]    ;Fetch columns per screen
        MUL     BX                      ;Compute absolute address as
        ADD     AX,Column               ; Column + Row * Columns)
        SHL     AX,1                    ; Account for attributes
        MOV     DI,AX                   ;Move address into register DI

        ;— Determine and load segement of the display buffer

        MOV     AX,0B000H               ;Assume monochrome buffer address
        TEST    BYTE PTR ES:[BIOS_Equipment],2    ;Is mono attached?
        JNZ     Address_Ok              ;...Yes, go load segment
        MOV     AX,0B800H               ;...No, change address to color
Address_Ok:
        MOV     ES,AX                   ;Set segment of display buffer

        ;— Save the character

        MOV     AL,Char                 ;Get character
        STOSB                           ;Write it into display buffer

        POP     ES                      ;Restore registers
```

```
        POP     DI
        MOV     SP,BP
        POP     BP
        RET
_Write_Char     ENDP
```

Write Attribute

Change the Attribute of a Single Character

Pascal Library Procedure

procedure Write_Attribute(row,column,fore,back:integer);

C Library Procedure

```
write_attribute(row, column, background, foreground)
int    row;                    /* Row and column of character   */
int    column;                 /* to change                     */
int    background;             /* New background color          */
int    foreground;            /* New foreground color          */
```

Example

Listing 7–28. File: PROGC046.C

```
/***********************************************************************/
/* Change 8 characters starting at row 24 and column 40              */
/* to black characters on white background                          */
/***********************************************************************/

make_reverse()
        {
        #define GRAY    7
        #define BLACK   0
        int     i;
        set_cursor_position(24,40);              /* Move cursor to 20,40 */
        printf("Reverse ");                      /* Put a string there   */
        for (i = 0; i < 8 ; i++)                 /* Change its attribute */
                write_attribute(24,40 + i, GRAY, BLACK);
        }
```

Listing 7-29. File: PROGP046.PAS

```
{*******************************************************************}
{ Change 8 characters starting at row 24 and column 40             }
{ to black characters on white background                          }
{*******************************************************************}

procedure make_reverse;
const
GRAY = 7;
BLACK = 0;
var
i : integer;
begin
        Set_Cursor_Position(12,40);       { Move cursor to 20,40 }
        writeln(" Reverse ");             { Put a string there   }
        for i := 0 to 7 do                { Change its attribute }
                Write_Attribute(12,40 + i, GRAY, BLACK);
end;
```

Theory

Many "user friendly" software applications selectively highlight fields of the screen to guide the user during data entry or editing functions. This is performed by modifying the attribute for one or more characters.

No BIOS call is available to change character attributes. The same function can be accomplished, however, by performing one BIOS call to read the current character and a second BIOS call to write that character with a new attribute.

For a description of the BIOS functions to read and write attribute see Read Character and Attribute function 8, and Write Character and Attribute function 9, in Chapter 4.

For a complete description of text attributes, see Standard Color Text Attributes and Monochrome Text Attributes in Chapter 2.

In some applications it may be useful to blank an area of the screen without actually clearing the data from display memory. This can be done by altering attributes. On a monochrome display, an attribute value of zero will blank a character. On a color display, a character is blanked if the foreground color is equal to the background color.

To write an application that will run equally well on monochrome or color displays, choose text attribute values that will work well for either case:

Attribute 07 will appear as white text on a black background on either color or monochrome displays.

Attribute 0F will appear as intensified white on black on either color or monochrome displays.

Attribute 70 will appear as black text on white background on either color or monochrome displays.

Assembly Code Examples

Listing 7-30. File: PROG052.ASM

```
;****************************************************************************
; Change character at the current cursor position to                       *
; "reverse" video character                                                *
;****************************************************************************

        PUBLIC   _BIOS_Invert

_BIOS_Invert    PROC NEAR
        MOV     AH,8                    ;Function = READ CHARACTER & ATTRIBUTE
        MOV     BH,0                    ;from page 0
        INT     10H                     ;Ask BIOS to fetch character
                                        ; AL has a character to write
                                        ; BH still has page to write to
        MOV     BL,AH                   ;Fetch attribute we have just received
        NOT     BL                      ;Invert attribute
        AND     AH,88H                  ;Preserve "blink" & "char gen" bits
        OR      BL,AH
        MOV     CX,1                    ;Number of characters to write
        MOV     AH,9                    ;Function = WRITE CHARACTER & ATTRIBUTE
        INT     10H                     ;Use BIOS to write attribute
        RET
_BIOS_Invert    ENDP
```

Listing 7-31. File: PROG053.ASM

```
;****************************************************************************
; Change attributes of character at Row, Column, using the foreground      *
; Fore and background Back.                                                 *
; Entry: The following parameters are passed on the stack as words          *
;        Row, Col, Back, Fore                                               *
;****************************************************************************

Row     EQU     [BP+4]
Column  EQU     [BP+6]
Back    EQU     [BP+8]
Fore    EQU     [BP+10]

        PUBLIC  _Write_Attribute

_Write_Attribute PROC NEAR
        PUSH    BP
        MOV     BP,SP
        PUSH    DI                      ;Preserve registers
```

```
        PUSH    ES

        ;- Convert row and column to absolute offset within display buffer

        XOR     AX,AX                   ;Point ES to segment zero
        MOV     ES,AX
        MOV     AX,Row                  ;Fetch row number
        MOV     BX,ES:[BIOS_Columns]    ;Fetch columns per screen
        MUL     BX                      ;Compute absolute address as
        ADD     AX,Column               ; Column + Row * Columns)
        SHL     AX,1                    ; Account for attributes
        MOV     DI,AX                   ;Move address into register DI
        INC     DI                      ;Skip character code byte

        ;- Determine and load segment of the display buffer

        MOV     AX,0B000H               ;Assume monochrome buffer address
        TEST    BYTE PTR ES:[BIOS_Equipment],2   ;Is mono attached?
        JNZ     Attr_Addr_Ok            ;...Yes, go load segment
        MOV     AX,0B800H               ;...No, change address to color
Attr_Addr_Ok:
        MOV     ES,AX                   ;Set segment of display buffer

        ;- Compose attribute into a single byte and save into display buffer

        MOV     AH,Back                 ;Get the background attribute
        SHL     AH,1                    ;Shift 4 lower bits into upper nibble
        SHL     AH,1
        SHL     AH,1
        SHL     AH,1
        MOV     AL,Fore                 ;Get the background attribute
        AND     AL,0FH                  ;Keep only lower nibble
        OR      AL,AH                   ;Combine foreground and background
        STOSB                           ;Write it into display buffer

        POP     ES                      ;Restore registers
        POP     DI
        MOV     SP,BP
        POP     BP
        RET
_Write_Attribute ENDP
```

Read Character

Read One Character From Display Memory

Pascal Library Procedure

```
function Read_Char(row,column:integer):byte;
            {read character at row and column}
```

C Library Procedure

```
read_char(row, column)          /* read character           */
int    row;                     /* character position       */
int    column;                  /* on the screen            */
```

Example

Listing 7-32. File: PROGC056.C

```
/***********************************************************************/
/* Read first ten characters at the top of the screen               */
/***********************************************************************/

print_10_chars()
        {
        int     i;
        printf("\Characters read are (in hex): ");
        for (i = 0; i < 10; i++)
                printf("%2X ",read_chara(0, i));
        }
```

Listing 7-33. File: PROGP056.PAS

```
{***********************************************************************}
{ Read first ten characters at the top of the screen                 }
{***********************************************************************}

procedure print_10_chars;
var
i,j : integer;
begin
        writeln("Characters read are: ");
        for i := 0 to 9 do begin
                j := Read_Char(0,i);
                writeln(j);
        end;
end;
```

Theory

To read back a text character from the display screen, the screen position (row and column) must be specified. Standard EGA text modes use 25 rows (numbered from 0 to 24) and 80 colums (numbered 0 to 79). The upper-left corner of the screen is row 0 , column 0. The bottom-right corner of the screen is row 24, column 79.

Assembly Code Examples

Listing 7-34. File: PROG067.ASM

```
;************************************************************************
; Read character code at the cursor position at Row and Col            *
; Entry: Row,Col  Passed on the stack as integers                      *
; Exit:  AX       Character code found                                 *
;************************************************************************

Row       EQU    [BP+4]
Col       EQU    [BP+6]

          PUBLIC  _BIOS_Read_Char

_BIOS_Read_Char PROC NEAR
          PUSH    BP
          MOV     BP,SP

          MOV     DH,Row             ;Set row and column
          MOV     DL,Col
          MOV     BH,0               ;Select page 0
          MOV     AH,2               ;Function = Set cursor position
          INT     10H                ;Ask BIOS to set cursor position

          MOV     AH,8               ;Function = READ CHARACTER & ATTRIBUTE
          MOV     BH,0               ;from page 0
          INT     10H                ;Ask BIOS to fetch character

          XOR     AH,AH              ;Clear upper half of AX

          POP     BP
          RET
_BIOS_Read_Char ENDP
```

Listing 7-35. File: PROG068.ASM

```
;************************************************************************
; Fetch a character at position Row, Column and return its code        *
; Entry: The following parameters are passed on the stack as words     *
;                    Row, Col                                          *
; Exit: AX character code                                              *
;************************************************************************

Row       EQU    [BP+4]
Column    EQU    [BP+6]

          PUBLIC  _Read_Char

_Read_Char     PROC NEAR
          PUSH    BP
          MOV     BP,SP
          PUSH    DI                 ;Preserve registers
          PUSH    ES

          ;- Convert row and column to absolute offset within display buffer
```

```
        XOR     AX,AX                   ;Point ES to segment zero
        MOV     ES,AX
        MOV     AX,Row                  ;Fetch row number
        MOV     BX,ES:[BIOS_Columns]    ;Fetch columns per screen
        MUL     BX                      ;Compute absolute address as
        ADD     AX,Column               ; Column + Row * Columns)
        SHL     AX,1                    ; Account for attributes
        MOV     DI,AX                   ;Move address into register DI

        ;- Determine and load segement of the display buffer

        MOV     AX,0B000H               ;Assume monochrome buffer address
        TEST    BYTE PTR ES:[BIOS_Equipment],2   ;Is mono attached?
        JNZ     Read_Char_Ok            ;...Yes, go load segment
        MOV     AX,0B800H               ;...No, change address to color
Read_Char_Ok:
        MOV     ES,AX                   ;Set segment of display buffer

        ;- Fetch the character

        MOV     AL,ES:[DI]              ;Get character
        XOR     AH,AH                   ;Clear upper half

        POP     ES                      ;Restore registers
        POP     DI
        MOV     SP,BP
        POP     BP
        RET
_Read_Char      ENDP
```

Read Attribute

Get the Attribute for a Single Character

Pascal Library Procedure

function Read_Attribute(row,column:integer):byte;

C Library Procedure

```
read_attribute(row, column)
int   row;                      /* Row and column of character    */
int   column;                   /* to change                      */
```

Example

Listing 7-36. File: PROGC057.C

```
/*****************************************************************************/
/* Read first ten attributes at the top of the screen                      */
/*****************************************************************************/

print_10_attr()
        {
        int     i;
        printf("\Attributes read are (in hex): ");
        for (i = 0; i < 10; i++)
                printf("%2X ",read_attribute(0, i));
        }
```

Listing 7-37. File: PROGP057.PAS

```
{*****************************************************************************}
{ Read first ten attributes at the top of the screen                        }
{*****************************************************************************}

procedure print_10_attr;
var
i : integer;
attr: byte;
begin
        writeln("Attributes read are: ");
        for i := 0 to 9 do
            begin
                attr := Read_Attribute(0, i);
                writeln(attr);
            end;
end;
```

Theory

In some types of screen handling applications, it may be useful to read a character's attribute so that it can be complemented (such as to toggle a highlighted field on and off).

To read back a text attribute from the display screen, the screen position (row and column) must be specified. Standard EGA text modes use 25 rows (numbered from 0 to 24) and 80 colums (numbered 0 to 79). The upper-left corner of the screen is row 0 , column 0. The bottom-right corner of the screen is row 24, column 79.

No BIOS call is available to read character attributes. The same function can be accomplished, however, by performing one BIOS call to set cursor position (see function 2, Set Cursor Position), and a second BIOS call to read that attribute (see function 8, Read Character and Attribute).

For a complete description of text attributes, see Standard Color Text Attributes and Monochrome Text Attributes in Chapter 2.

Assembly Code Examples

Listing 7-38. File: PROG079.ASM

```
;***********************************************************************
; Read character attribute at the cursor position at Row and Col      *
; Entry: Row,Col  Passed on the stack as integers                     *
; Exit:  AX       Backgrouond and foreground colors packed into a byte *
;***********************************************************************

Row     EQU     [BP+4]
Col     EQU     [BP+6]


        PUBLIC  _BIOS_Read_Attr

_BIOS_Read_Attr PROC NEAR
        PUSH    BP
        MOV     BP,SP

        MOV     DH,Row                  ;Set row and column
        MOV     DL,Col
        MOV     BH,0                    ;Select page 0
        MOV     AH,2                    ;Function = Set cursor position
        INT     10H                     ;Ask BIOS to set cursor position

        MOV     AH,8                    ;Function = READ CHARACTER & ATTRIBUTE
        MOV     BH,0                    ;from page 0
        INT     10H                     ;Ask BIOS to fetch attribute

        MOV     AL,AH                   ;Move attribute into lower byte
        XOR     AH,AH                   ;Clear upper byte of return value

        POP     BP
        RET
_BIOS_Read_Attr ENDP
```

Listing 7-39. File: PROG070.ASM

```
;***********************************************************************
; Read attributes of character at Row, Column and return it in AX     *
; Entry: The following parameters are passed on the stack as words     *
;        Row, Col                                                      *
; Exit:  AX       Backgrouond and foreground colors packed into a byte *
;***********************************************************************

Row     EQU     [BP+4]
Column  EQU     [BP+6]


        PUBLIC  _Read_Attribute

_Read_Attribute PROC NEAR
```

```
        PUSH    BP
        MOV     BP,SP
        PUSH    DI                      ;Preserve registers
        PUSH    ES

        ;- Convert row and column to absolute offset within display buffer

        XOR     AX,AX                   ;Point ES to segment zero
        MOV     ES,AX
        MOV     AX,Row                  ;Fetch row number
        MOV     BX,ES:[BIOS_Columns]    ;Fetch columns per screen
        MUL     BX                      ;Compute absolute address as
        ADD     AX,Column               ; Column + Row * Columns)
        SHL     AX,1                    ; Account for attributes
        MOV     DI,AX                   ;Move address into register DI
        INC     DI                      ;Skip character code byte

        ;- Determine and load segment of the display buffer

        MOV     AX,0B000H               ;Assume monochrome buffer address
        TEST    BYTE PTR ES:[BIOS_Equipment],2   ;Is mono attached?
        JNZ     Attr_Read_Ok            ;...Yes, go load segment
        MOV     AX,0B800H               ;...No, change address to color
Attr_Read_Ok:
        MOV     ES,AX                   ;Set segment of display buffer

        ;- Fetch the attribute and return it

        MOV     AL,ES:[DI]              ;Fetch the attribute
        XOR     AH,AH                   ;Clear upper bute of return value

        POP     ES                      ;Restore registers
        POP     DI
        MOV     SP,BP
        POP     BP
        RET
_Read_Attribute ENDP
```

Text Blink

Enable and Disable Text Blinking

Pascal Library Procedure

```
procedure Text_Blink(flag:integer);
            {0 = disable blink, 1 = enable blink}
```

C Library Procedure

```
text_blink(flag)                /* Enable or Disable text blinking   */
int   flag;                     /* 0 => Disable blinking             */
                                /* 1 => Enable blinking              */
```

Example

Listing 7-40. File: PROGC047.C

```c
/********************************************************************/
/* Print "Warning" in last line of the screen and make it blink     */
/********************************************************************/

demo_text_blink()
        {
        #define ENABLE          1
        #define DISABLE         0
        #define BLINKING_BLACK  8
        #define GRAY            7

        int     i;
        static  char    warning[] = "Warning";

        text_blink(ENABLE);                     /* Enable text blinking */
        for (i = 0; warning[i] != 0; i++)       /*Display string        */
                {
                write_char(warning[i],24,40+i);
                write_attribute(24,40+i, BLINKING_BLACK, GRAY);
                }
        }
```

Listing 7-41. File: PROGP047.PAS

```pascal
{********************************************************************}
{ Print "Warning" in last line of the screen and make it blink     }
{********************************************************************}

procedure demo_text_blink;
const
ENABLE = 1;
DISABLE = 0;
BLINKING_BLACK = 8;
GRAY = 7;
warning : array[0..6] of char = "Warning";
var
i : integer;
begin
        Text_Blink(ENABLE);             { Enable text blinking     }
        for i := 0 to 6 do              {Display string            }
            begin
                Write_Char(warning[i],24,40+i);
                Write_Attribute(24,40+i, BLINKING_BLACK, GRAY);
            end;
end;
```

Theory

This procedure will enable or disable the text blink attribute. If blinking is enabled, character attribute bit 7 can be used to blink a character. If blinking is disabled, no characters will blink and attribute bit 7 becomes the Background Intensity instead.

BIOS function 16, subfunction 3 (Blink/Intensity Attribute Control) can be used to enable and disable the blinking of text (for details on BIOS functions see Chapter 4).

Text blinking can also be controlled directly by modifying the Mode Register of the Attribute Controller (See chapter 3.) Care must be taken to preserve the status of other bits in the Mode Register, however. For VGA, the Mode Register is readable; for EGA, it is not. Standard color text modes use a Mode Register value of 08 to enable blinking and 00 to disable blinking. Monochrome text modes use a value of 0Eh to enable blinking and 06 to disable blinking.

To learn more about blinking and attributes, also see:

• Text Attributes section in Chapter 2.

• BIOS functions 8 Read Character and Attribute, 9 Write Character and Attribute, and 16 Set EGA Palette in Chapter 4.

• Write Attribute and Read Attribute programming examples in Chapter 7.

Assembly Code Examples

Listing 7-42. File: PROG055.ASM

```
;*********************************************************************
; Enable text blink by setting Mode Register on EGA                 *
; Entry:        Flag - 0 => disable blinking                        *
;                      1 => enable blinking                         *
;*********************************************************************

Flag     EQU     WORD PTR [BP+4]

         PUBLIC  _Text_Blink

_Text_Blink      PROC NEAR
         PUSH    BP
         MOV     BP,SP
         CMP     Flag,0
         JZ      Blink_Off
         CALL    Enable_Blink
         POP     BP
         RET
Blink_Off:
         CALL    Disable_Blink
         POP     BP
         RET
_Text_Blink      ENDP
```

```
Enable_Blink     PROC NEAR
        PUSH     ES                     ;Preserve register
        XOR      AX,AX                  ;Point to BIOS data area
        MOV      ES,AX
        TEST     BYTE PTR ES:[BIOS_Equipment],2   ;Is mono display attached?
        JZ       Enable_Color           ;...No, go set color blink
Enable_Mono:
        MOV      DX,3BAH                ;Get address of Attrib READ register
        IN       AL,DX                  ;Reset data/index flip-flop
        MOV      DX,3C0H                ;Get address of Attribute controller
        MOV      AL,30H                 ;Select MODE register
        OUT      DX,AL
        MOV      AL,0EH                 ;Enable blink for monochrome text
        OUT      DX,AL
        JMP      Enable_Done
Enable_Color:
        MOV      DX,3DAH                ;Get address of Attrib READ register
        IN       AL,DX                  ;Reset data/index flip-flop
        MOV      DX,3C0H                ;Select Mode register
        MOV      AL,30H
        OUT      DX,AL
        MOV      AL,08H                 ;Enable blink for monochrome text
        OUT      DX,AL
Enable_Done:
        POP      ES
        RET
Enable_Blink     ENDP

;**********************************************************************
; Disable text blink by setting Mode Register on EGA                  *
;**********************************************************************

Disable_Blink    PROC NEAR
        PUSH     ES                     ;Preserve register
        XOR      AX,AX                  ;Point to BIOS data area
        MOV      ES,AX
        TEST     BYTE PTR ES:[BIOS_Equipment],2   ;Is mono display attached?
        JZ       Disable_Color          ;...No, go set color blink
Disable_Mono:
        MOV      DX,3BAH                ;Get address of Attrib READ register
        IN       AL,DX                  ;Reset data/index flip-flop
        MOV      DX,3C0H                ;Get address of Attribute controller
        MOV      AL,30H                 ;Select MODE register
        OUT      DX,AL
        MOV      AL,06H                 ;Enable blink for monochrome text
        OUT      DX,AL
        JMP      Disable_Done
Disable_Color:
        MOV      DX,3DAH                ;Get address of Attrib READ register
        IN       AL,DX                  ;Reset data/index flip-flop
        MOV      DX,3C0H                ;Select Mode register
        MOV      AL,30H
        OUT      DX,AL
        MOV      AL,00H                 ;Enable blink for monochrome text
        OUT      DX,AL
Disable_Done:
        POP      ES
```

```
        RET
Disable_Blink    ENDP
```

Write String

Output a String of Text to the Display

Pascal Library Procedure

procedure Write_String(row,column,string_seg,string_offset:integer);
        {row and column for display, segment and offset of source string}

C Library Procedure

```
write_string(row,column,text)        /*Put text at row,column          */
int    row;                          /* Row number for the text        */
int    column;                       /* Column for the text            */
char   *text;                        /* Ponter to NULL terminated      */
                                     /* string of text                 */
```

Example

Listing 7-43. File: PROGC048.C

```
/********************************************************************/
/* Print "Hello" in the middle of 80x25 screen                      */
/********************************************************************/

print_hello()
        {
        clear_screen();
        write_string(12, 40, "Hello");          /* Display a string    */
        }
```

Listing 7-44. File: PROGP048.PAS.

```
{********************************************************************}
{ Print "Hello" in the middle of 80x25 screen                       }
{********************************************************************}

procedure print_hello;
const
hello : string[5] = "Hello";
begin
        Clear_Screen;
        Write_String(12, 40, seg(hello), ofs(hello));  { Display a string }
end;
```

Theory

This procedure will output a text string to the display without changing display attributes. It will not change cursor position and all ASCII codes 1-255 will be displayed. Text position is specified by row and column. The upper-left corner of the screen is row 0 column 0 (see Figure 7-2).

Inputs to the procedure are display row and column, and a pointer to a text string. For C language compatibility, the text string must be null terminated (terminated by a zero byte); For Turbo Pascal, the text string must begin with a one byte character count specifying the number of characters in the string.

BIOS function 19 (Write Text String) will output a string of text to the display. Depending on which subfunction is selected, cursor position may be advanced after the string is written. The string can be pure ASCII text, or it can have an attribute byte following each character. For a complete description of the BIOS function, see Chapter 4.

The Write Text String function of the BIOS will trap ASCII characters Bell, Backspace, Carriage Return, and Linefeed, and perform the appropriate function rather than attempt to display them.

To learn more about displaying characters, also see Write Character programming example in this chapter.

Assembly Code Examples

Listing 7-45. File: PROG056.ASM

```
;******************************************************************
; Write "Hello" in the middle of the 80x25 screen using          *
; BIOS function 13hex, and move cursor to the start of next       *
; line by including CARRIAGE RETURN and LINEFEED in the text      *
;******************************************************************

CARRIAGE_RETURN EQU     0DH
LINE_FEED       EQU     0AH

Text            DB      "Hello", CARRIAGE_RETURN, LINE_FEED

        PUBLIC  _BIOS_Write_String

_BIOS_Write_String PROC NEAR
        PUSH    ES                      ;Preserve registers
        PUSH    BP

        MOV     AX,CS                   ;Get pointer to the string
        MOV     ES,AX                   ;into register pair ES:BP
        LEA     BP,Text
        MOV     BX,0                    ;Select page 0
        MOV     BL,7                    ;Use normal attribute
```

```
        MOV     CX,5                    ;Display 5 characters
        MOV     DH,12                   ;Start at row 12
        MOV     DL,40                   ;Start at column 40
        MOV     AH,13H                  ;Function = WRITE TEXT STRING
        MOV     AL,0H                   ;Subfunction = Update Cursor Pos.
        INT     10H                     ;Ask BIOS to display the text

        POP     BP
        POP     ES                      ;Restore segment register
        RET
_BIOS_Write_String ENDP
```

Listing 7-46. File: PROG057.ASM

```
;************************************************************************
; Display text at specified row and column                            *
; Entry:          Row             - Starting row of the text          *
;                 Column - Starting column of the text                *
;                 String  - Pointer to a null terminated string of text *
;************************************************************************

Row     EQU     [BP+4]
Column  EQU     [BP+6]
String  EQU     [BP+8]

        PUBLIC  _Write_String

_Write_String   PROC NEAR
        PUSH    BP
        MOV     BP,SP
        PUSH    DI                      ;Preserve registers
        PUSH    ES
        PUSH    SI

        ;- Fetch number of rows and columns on the screen and
        ;   compute absolute address in display buffer

        XOR     AX,AX                   ;Point ES to segment zero
        MOV     ES,AX
        MOV     AX,Row                  ;Fetch row number
        MOV     BX,ES:[BIOS_Columns]    ;Fetch columns per screen
        MUL     BX                      ;Compute absolute address
        ADD     AX,Column               ;in the display buffer as
        SHL     AX,1                    ;((Row*Col_per_row)+Column)*2
        MOV     DI,AX                   ;Move address into register DI

        ;- Determine and load segement of the display buffer

        MOV     AX,0B000H               ;Assume monochrome buffer address
        TEST    BYTE PTR ES:[BIOS_Equipment],2   ;Is mono attached?
        JNZ     Str_Address_Ok         ;...Yes, go load segment
        MOV     AX,0B800H              ;...No, change address to color
Str_Address_Ok:
        MOV     ES,AX                   ;Set segment of display buffer

        ;- Fetch address of the text
```

```
        MOV     SI,String               ;Get pointer to the string
Next_String:
        LODSB                           ;Fetch next character
        OR      AL,AL                   ;Is character the terminating zero?
        JZ      String_Done             ;...Yes, we are done
        STOSB                           ;...No, put it into display buffer
        INC     DI                      ;Skip attribute byte
        JMP     Next_String             ;Go examine next character

String_Done:
        POP     SI
        POP     ES                      ;Restore registers
        POP     DI
        POP     BP
        RET
_Write_String   ENDP
```

Read Character Generator

Read Font Data for Current Character Set

Pascal Library Procedure

> procedure Read_Char_Gen(buffer_seg,buffer_offset:integer);
>   {segment and offset of destination buffer}

C Library Procedure

```
read_char_gen(buffer);  /* Read current character generator   */
char   buffer[256][32];   /* Pointer to buffer      */
```

Example

Listing 7-47. File: PROGC049.C

```
/**********************************************************************/
/* Copy current character generator into a buffer                    */
/* "italicize" the set and make it current set                       */
/**********************************************************************/

italicize()
    {
    static  char    buffer[256][32];        /* Declare temp buffer  */
    int             i, j;

    read_char_gen(buffer);                  /* Get "normal" bitmaps */

    for (i = 0; i < 256; i++)               /* Loop over characters */
            {                               /* Italisize the next   */
            for (j = 0; j < 4; j++)         /* character bitmap      */
```

```
                              {
                              buffer[i][j]    = buffer[i][j   ] >> 1;
                              buffer[i][j+10] = buffer[i][j+10] << 1;
                              }
                   }
            write_char_gen(buffer,0,256);              /* Set new char gen    */
            printf ("\nDisplaying new alphabet:\n"); /* Print new chars      */
            for (i = 32; i < 128; i++) putchar(i);
            }
```

Listing 7-48. File: PROGP049.PAS

```
{***************************************************************************}
{ Copy current character generator into a buffer                          }
{ "italicize" the set and make it current set                             }
{***************************************************************************}

procedure italicize;
var
buffer : array[0..255,0..31] of char;
i,j : integer;
begin
        Read_Char_Gen(seg(buffer),ofs(buffer)); { Get "normal" bitmaps }
        for i := 0 to 255  do                    { Loop over characters }
            begin                                { Italicize the next   }
                for j := 0 to 3  do              { character bitmap     }
                    begin
                        buffer[i,j]    := char(integer(buffer[i,j]) shr 1);
                        buffer[i,j+10] := char(integer(buffer[i,j+10]) shl 1);
                    end;
            end;
        Write_Char_Gen(seg(buffer),ofs(buffer),0,256);   { Set new char gen}
        for i := 32 to 127 do Write_Char(char(i),20,i-31);
end;
```

Theory

This procedure will copy the bitmap definitions from the first character generator in plane 2.

The BIOS cannot return a pointer to the current character generator, but BIOS function 17, type 8, will return pointers to the character generators supplied in ROM for standard text modes. By determining operating mode, the proper character set can be inferred.

It should be noted that most EGA adapters "adjust" the 8 x 14 character set for monochrome mode. If mode 7 is selected, the standard 8 x 14 character set is used but characters ", +, -, M, T, V, W, X, Y, Z, m, v, w, and ASCII codes 1D, 91, 9B, 9D, 9E, F1 and F6 are replaced with improved characters to take advantage of the wider monochrome 9 x 14 character cell. To obtain font data for mode 7 requires pointers to both the 8 x 14 character set and the extended monochrome character subset. Both pointers are returned by BIOS function 17. See Chapter 4 for a complete description of this BIOS function.

For a complete explanation of character generators, see Character Generators in Chapter 2 and the Character Generator Select Register of the Sequencer in Chapter 3.

Assembly Code Examples

Listing 7-49. File: PROG058.ASM

```
;**************************************************************************
; Use BIOS to get a pointer to the ROM base character generator         *
; Works only for standard text modes 0-3 and 7                          *
; returns zero for any other mode                                       *
; Exit: DX,AX   - Pointer to the character generator                    *
;**************************************************************************

        PUBLIC  _BIOS_Get_ROM_CG

_BIOS_Get_ROM_CG PROC NEAR
        ;- Fetch current mode

        PUSH    BP
        PUSH    ES                      ;Preserve segment registers
        XOR     AX,AX                   ;Point to BIOS data area
        MOV     ES,AX
        TEST    BYTE PTR ES:[BIOS_Equipment],2  ;Is mono display attached?
        JNZ     CG_8x14                 ;...Yes, go fetch 8x14 set
        CMP     BYTE PTR ES:[BIOS_Switch],9     ;Is Enhanced display attached?
        JE      CG_8x14                 ;...Yes, go fetch 8x14 set
        CMP     BYTE PTR ES:[BIOS_Switch],3
        JE      CG_8x14

        ;- Return pointer to 8x8 character generator

CG_8x8:
        MOV     AH,11H                  ;Function = CHARACTER GENERATOR
        MOV     AL,30H                  ;Subfunction = GET INFO
        MOV     BH,3
        INT     10H                     ;Ask BIOS to fetch the pointer
        JMP     CG_Done

        ;-- Return pointer to 8x14 character generator
CG_8x14:
        MOV     AH,11H                  ;Function = CHARACTER GENERATOR
        MOV     AL,30H                  ;Subfunction = GET INFO
        MOV     BH,2
        INT     10H                     ;Ask BIOS to fetch the pointer
```

```
        JMP      CG_Done


        XOR      AX,AX                      ;Return zero for unknown modes
        MOV      ES,AX
        MOV      BP,AX

CG_Done:
        MOV      DX,ES                      ;Copy pointer into DX,AX pair
        MOV      AX,BP
        POP      ES
        POP      BP                         ;Restore segment registers
        RET
_BIOS_Get_ROM_CG ENDP
```

In text modes, character generator font data is stored in plane 2 of display memory. The Character Generator Select Register of the EGA Sequencer selects one of up to four RAM resident character generators as the current character set (VGA can have up to eight). On the EGA, this is a write-only register, making it difficult to determine which character generator is current. The default condition uses the first character generator in memory. The following example will enable plane 2 for reading and read all 256 characters from the character set into a buffer, then restore the Read Plane Select register to default.

Listing 7-50. File: PROG059.ASM

```
;*************************************************************************
; Read first character generator from plane 2                          *
; Entry:         DS:Buffer      - Pointer to buffer where to store      *
;                                 32x256 bytes of data                  *
; Exit:          It is assumed that the adapter is in one of the text   *
;                modes 0,1,2,3 or 7 otherwise state is unpredictable    *
;                and will have to be reset by the calling procedure     *
;*************************************************************************

Buffer  EQU      [BP+4]

        PUBLIC   _Read_Char_Gen

_Read_Char_Gen PROC NEAR
        PUSH     BP
        MOV      BP,SP
        PUSH     ES
        PUSH     DS
        PUSH     DI
        PUSH     SI

        ;- Enable for read

        MOV      DX,3C4H                    ;Disable even/odd and text mode
        MOV      AL,4
        OUT      DX,AL
```

```
        INC     DX
        MOV     AL,6
        OUT     DX,AL

        MOV     DX,3CEH                 ;Select plane 2 for read
        MOV     AL,4
        OUT     DX,AL
        MOV     AL,2
        INC     DX
        OUT     DX,AL
        DEC     DX

        MOV     AL,5                    ;Disable odd/even & color compare
        OUT     DX,AL
        INC     DX
        MOV     AL,0
        OUT     DX,AL

        DEC     DX                      ;Map plane to start at A000
        MOV     AL,6
        OUT     DX,AL
        INC     DX
        MOV     AL,05H
        OUT     DX,AL

;- Copy character generator into buffer

        MOV     AX,DS                   ;Point ES:DI to buffer
        MOV     ES,AX
        MOV     DI,Buffer
        MOV     AX,0A000H               ;Point DS:SI to char generator
        MOV     DS,AX
        XOR     SI,SI
        MOV     CX,32*256               ;Number of bytes to move
        REP     MOVSB                   ;Copy the data

;- Restore mode

        MOV     DX,3C4H                 ;Enable even/odd and text mode
        MOV     AL,4
        OUT     DX,AL
        INC     DX
        MOV     AL,3
        OUT     DX,AL

        MOV     DX,3CEH                 ;Restore plane 0 for read
        MOV     AL,4
        OUT     DX,AL
        MOV     AL,0
        INC     DX
        OUT     DX,AL
        DEC     DX

        MOV     AL,5                    ;Restore odd/even
        OUT     DX,AL
        INC     DX
        MOV     AL,10H
```

```
        OUT      DX,AL

        XOR      AX,AX
        MOV      ES,AX
        TEST     BYTE PTR ES:[BIOS_Equipment],2
        JNZ      Set_B000

        MOV      DX,3CEH              ;Map display buffer to B800
        MOV      AL,6
        OUT      DX,AL
        INC      DX
        MOV      AL,0EH
        OUT      DX,AL
        JMP      RCG_Done
Set_B000:
        MOV      DX,3CEH              ;Map display buffer to B000
        MOV      AL,6
        OUT      DX,AL
        INC      DX
        MOV      AL,0AH
        OUT      DX,AL
RCG_Done:
        POP      SI
        POP      DI
        POP      DS
        POP      ES
        MOV      SP,BP
        POP      BP
        RET
_Read_Char_Gen  ENDP
```

Write Character Generator

Write Font Data Into Display Memory

Pascal Library Procedure

procedure Write_Char_Gen(cg_seg,cg_offset,start,count:integer);
                {segment and offset of source buffer for font data,}
                {first character to write,}
                {number of characters to write}

C Library Procedure

```
write_char_gen(ptr, start, count)    /* Change char gen               */
char    far    *ptr;                 /* Pointer to font data          */
int     start;                       /* First character to be written */
int     count;                       /* Number of characters to write */
```

Example

Listing 7-51. File: PROGC050.C

```
/*************************************************************************/
/* Replace capital letter A with a new bitmap                           */
/*************************************************************************/

replace_a()
        {
        static  char    new_A[32] =    {0x7E,
                                        0x42,
                                        0x42,
                                        0x42,
                                        0x7E,
                                        0x42,
                                        0x42,
                                        0xE7,
                                        0,0,0,0,0,0,0,0,
                                        0,0,0,0,0,0,0,0,
                                        0,0,0,0,0,0,0,0};
        write_char_gen(new_A, 'A', 1);          /* Replace 'A' only     */
        printf("\nNew AAAAAAAAA's");
        }
```

Listing 7-52. File: PROGP050.PAS

```
{*************************************************************************}
{ Replace capital letter A with a new bitmap                             }
{*************************************************************************}

procedure replace_a;
const
new_A : array[0..31] of char =    (#126,#66,#66,#126,#66,#66,#103,
                                   #0,#0,#0,#0,#0,#0,#0,#0,#0,#0,#0,#0,#0,
                                   #0,#0,#0,#0,#0,#0,#0,#0,#0,#0);
begin
    Write_Char_Gen(seg(new_A),ofs(new_A),integer("A"),1); { Replace "A" only}
    writeln("New AAAAAAAAAs");
end;
```

Theory

This procedure will load a user defined character set onto the EGA and make it the current character set. The font data for a single character may be loaded, or for a group of characters, or for an entire character set.

Any of the four RAM resident EGA character maps (or eight VGA character maps) may be written using this procedure by specifying the Start Character:

character 0 = start of first character map
character 512 = start of second character map
character 1024 = start of third character map
character 1536 = start of fourth character map

For details on EGA character generators see Character Generators in Chapter 2 and the Character Generator Select Register of the Sequencer in Chapter 3.

Examples in this section assume that the default character set is used (the first character set in plane 2).

Assembly Code Examples

BIOS function 17 (Load Character Generator) can be used to selectively change any or all bitmaps for a character set.

Listing 7-53. File: PROG060.ASM

```
;****************************************************************************
; Replace first 32 characters of character generator                      *
; with a box, using the BIOS function 11hex                               *
;****************************************************************************

Box      DB      0FFH,081H,081H,081H, 081H,081H,081H,0FFH

         PUBLIC  _BIOS_Write_CG

_BIOS_Write_CG  PROC NEAR
         PUSH    BP
         PUSH    ES

         LEA     BP,Box              ;Offset of new bitmap
         MOV     AX,CS               ;Segement of new bitmap into ES
         MOV     ES,AX
         MOV     CX,1                ;Do one character at a time
         MOV     DX,0                ;Start with character 0
         MOV     BL,0                ;Change table 0
         MOV     BH,8                ;8 bytes per character
Replace_Loop:
         MOV     AH,11H              ;Function = LOAD CHARACTER GENERATOR
         MOV     AL,00H              ;Subfunction = CUSTOM CHAR GEN
         INT     10H                 ;Use BIOS to replace next character
         INC     DX                  ;Point to the next character to replace
         CMP     DX,32               ;Are we done with all 32 characters?
         JB      Replace_Loop        ;...No, go do next one

         POP     ES
         POP     BP
         RET
_BIOS_Write_CG  ENDP
```

The following example shows how to download a user supplied character set. The calling procedure passes an array of bitmaps, with 32 bytes for each character (padded if necessary). Some EGA control registers are modified; since the previous value of write-only registers cannot be determined on the EGA, these registers will be set to the default values used for mode 7 if a Monochrome Display is attached to EGA, and to values for mode 3 otherwise.

Listing 7-54. File: PROG061.ASM

```
;********************************************************************
; Load a new character generator into plane 2                    *
; Entry:        Ptr_CG  - Pointer to new character generator     *
;               Start   - First ASCII code to use                *
;               Count   - Number of characters to load           *
;********************************************************************

Ptr_CG   EQU    [BP+4]
Start    EQU    [BP+6]
Count    EQU    [BP+8]

         PUBLIC  _Write_Char_Gen

_Write_Char_Gen PROC     NEAR
         PUSH   BP
         MOV    BP,SP
         PUSH   ES
         PUSH   DS
         PUSH   DI
         PUSH   SI

         ;- Enable memory for write into plane 2

         MOV    DX,03C4h              ; sequencer enable map 2 for write
         MOV    AL,2
         OUT    DX,AL
         INC    DX
         MOV    AL,4
         OUT    DX,AL

         DEC    DX                    ; sequencer no chaining
         MOV    AL,4
         OUT    DX,AL
         INC    DX
         MOV    AL,6
         OUT    DX,AL

         MOV    DX,03CEh              ; graphics use data from processor
         MOV    AL,1
         OUT    DX,AL
         INC    DX
         MOV    AL,0
         OUT    DX,AL
```

```
       DEC      DX                        ; graphics read and write modes
       MOV      AL,5
       OUT      DX,AL
       INC      DX
       MOV      AL,0
       OUT      DX,AL

       DEC      DX                        ; graphics address mapped to A000
       MOV      AL,6
       OUT      DX,AL
       INC      DX
       MOV      AL,05h
       OUT      DX,AL

       DEC      DX                        ; graphics enable 8 bits per write
       MOV      AL,8
       OUT      DX,AL
       INC      DX
       MOV      AL,0FFh
       OUT      DX,AL

;- load the character generator into plane 2

       MOV      AX,0A000h                 ;Point to segment A000
       MOV      ES,AX
       MOV      AX,Start                  ;Compute offset into char gen plane
       MOV      CL,5                      ;as index * bytes_per_char
       SHL      AX,CL                     ;which is index * 32
       MOV      DI,AX                     ;Copy offset in char gen plane into DI
       MOV      SI,Ptr_CG                 ;Fetch pointer to new characters
       MOV      AX,Count                  ;Fetch number of characters to copy
       SHL      AX,CL                     ;Compute how many bytes to copy
       SHR      AX,1                      ;Divide by two so we can use MOV WORD
       MOV      CX,AX                     ;Copy count into CX

       REP      MOVSW                     ;Copy the data

;- Restore Sequencer and Graphics Controller

       MOV      DX,03C4h                  ; Enable plane 0 & 1 for write
       MOV      AL,2
       OUT      DX,AL
       INC      DX
       MOV      AL,03H
       OUT      DX,AL

       DEC      DX                        ; sequencer even/odd & text
       MOV      AL,4
       OUT      DX,AL
       INC      DX
       MOV      AL,3
       OUT      DX,AL

       MOV      DX,3CEH                   ; graphics read and write modes
       MOV      AL,5
       OUT      DX,AL
       INC      DX
```

```
        MOV     AL,10H
        OUT     DX,AL
        DEC     DX

        XOR     AX,AX
        MOV     ES,AX
        TEST    BYTE PTR ES:[BIOS_Equipment],2
        JNZ     WCG_Set_B000

        MOV     DX,3CEH                 ;Map display buffer to B800
        MOV     AL,6
        OUT     DX,AL
        INC     DX
        MOV     AL,0EH
        OUT     DX,AL
        JMP     WCG_Done
WCG_Set_B000:
        MOV     DX,3CEH                 ;Map display buffer to B000
        MOV     AL,6
        OUT     DX,AL
        INC     DX
        MOV     AL,0AH
        OUT     DX,AL

        ;- Clean up and exit
WCG_Done:
        POP     SI
        POP     DI
        POP     DS
        POP     ES
        MOV     SP,BP
        POP     BP
        RET
_Write_Char_Gen ENDP
```

512 Character Set

Enable Use of 512 Characters

Pascal Library Procedure

```
procedure Enable_Second_Set;
procedure Disable_Second_Set;
```

C Library Procedure

```
enable_second_set()
disable_second_set()
```

Example

Listing 7-55. File: PROGC051.C

```
/*************************************************************************/
/* Display 512 different characters at a time                          */
/*************************************************************************/

print_512_chars()
    {
    #define MONO    5
    #define VMONO   7
    #define ON      1                   /* Flag values               */
    #define OFF     0
    static  char    buffer[256][32];/* Buffer for char gen          */
    int     i, j;

    /*- Set default text mode                                       */

    if (get_display_type() == VMONO ||
        get_display_type() == MONO) set_mode(7);
    else                            set_mode(3);

    /*- Download a second 256 character set                         */

    read_char_gen(buffer);          /* Read old character generator */
    for (i = 0; i < 255; i++)       /* Create a new char set        */
            for (j = 0; j < 4; j++) /* from the old by "italicizing"*/
                    {
                    buffer[i][j] = buffer[i][j] >> 1;
                    buffer[i][j+10] = buffer[i][j+10] << 1;
                    }
                                    /* Download new char gen        */
    write_char_gen(buffer, 512, 256);

    /*- Enable the 512 character set generation                     */

    enable_second_set();            /* Enable 512 char set          */

    /*- Display 512 characters and attributes                       */

    for (i = 0; i < 256; i++)       /* Display chars 0 - 255        */
            {
            write_attribute(i/64, i%64, 0, 7);
            write_char(i, i/64, i%64);
            }

    for (i = 0; i < 256; i++)       /* Display chars 256-512        */
            {
            write_attribute(4 + i/64, i%64, 0,15);
            write_char(i, 4 + i/64, i%64);
            }

    /*- Wait for <Enter> and then disable the second character set*/

    getchar();
```

```
        disable_second_set();
        }


Listing 7-56.  File: PROGP051.PAS

{***********************************************************************}
{ Display 512 different characters at a time                            }
{***********************************************************************}

procedure print_512_chars;
const
MONO = 5;
VMONO = 7;
ON = 1;
OFF = 0;
var
buffer : array[0..255,0..31] of char;    { Buffer for char gen            }
i,j : integer;
c : char;
begin
        {- Set default text mode                                         }

        i := Get_Display_Type;
        if i = MONO then         Set_Mode(7)
        else if i = VMONO then Set_Mode(7)
        else                     Set_Mode(3);

        {- Download a second 256 character set                           }

        Read_Char_Gen(seg(buffer),ofs(buffer)); {Read old character generator}
        for i := 0 to 254 do begin              {Create a new char set   }
            for j := 0 to 3 do begin            {from the old by slewing}
                    buffer[i,j] := char(integer(buffer[i,j]) shr 1);
                    buffer[i,j+10] := char(integer(buffer[i,j+10]) shl 1);
            end;                                { Download new char gen }
        end;
        Write_Char_Gen(seg(buffer),ofs(buffer), 512, 256);
        Enable_Second_Set;              { Enable 512 char set            }

        for i := 0 to 255 do            { Display chars 0 - 255 }
            begin
                Write_Attribute(i div 64, i mod 64, 0, 7);
                Write_Char(char(i), i div 64, i mod 64);
            end;
        for i := 0 to 255 do            { Display chars 256-512 }
            begin
                Write_Attribute(4 + i div 64, i mod 64, 0,15);
                Write_Char(char(i), 4 + i div 64, i mod 64);
            end;

        {- Wait for <Enter> and then disable the second character set}

        c := readkey;
        Disable_Second_Set;
end;
```

Theory

EGA/VGA character sets contain 256 different characters, permitting the display of at most 256 different characters on the screen at a time. EGA and VGA include a mechanism to double this number to 512 simultaneous characters, however. Two character sets can be enabled at the same time, and a character attribute bit selects from which of the two character sets each character is drawn.

After two character sets are loaded into memory plane 2, both character sets must be enabled via the Character Generator Select Register. Text attribute bit 3 then determines which character generator is used for each character. Attribute bit 3 normally controls foreground intensity; to avoid intensity variation between the two character sets, the intensity function should be disabled. To disable foreground intensity, reload the last 8 palette registers of the Attribute Controller (registers 8 through 15) so that they match the first 8 palette registers (registers 0 through 7).

The following example uses several of the procedures that were described earlier. Read_Char_Gen is used to read character generator data from the EGA. Write_Char_Gen is used to load character generator data onto the EGA. Put_Char places a character on the screen at a specifed row and column.

For details on character generators see Character Generators in Chapter 2, and the Character Generator Select Register of the Sequencer in Chapter 3.

The steps to configure a 512 character font are:

1. Download two 256 character sets into memory plane 2. BIOS function 17 (Load Custom Character Generator) can be used to download the character generators.

2. Set the Character Generator Select Register of the Sequencer to a value of 4 to select character sets 0 and 1. This enables character attribute bit 3 to select the first or second sets of 256 characters. BIOS function 17 (Select Active Character Set) can be used to set this register.

3. Reload the upper 8 palette registers to disable the foreground intensify function, which also uses character attribute bit 3. The upper 8 palette registers should match the lower 8 palette registers. BIOS function 16 (Set EGA Palette Registers) can be used.

4. When writing character codes to display memory, set character attribute bit 3 to select from which character set each character should be drawn. BIOS function 19 (Write Text String) can be used to place characters and attributes into the display buffer and advance the cursor position.

Assembly Code Examples

Listing 7-57. File: PROG062.ASM

```
;*************************************************************************
; Use BIOS to set up the EGA to display 512 different characters        *
; Entry:         CG_One  - Pointer to the first character generator     *
;                CG_Two  - Pointer to the second character generator    *
;*************************************************************************

CG_One  EQU     [BP+4]
CG_Two  EQU     [BP+6]

        PUBLIC  _BIOS_512_Set

_BIOS_512_Set   PROC NEAR
        PUSH    BP
        MOV     BP,SP
        PUSH    ES

        ;Download the two character generators

        MOV     AX,DS                   ;Assume both bitmaps are in DS seg
        MOV     ES,AX
        MOV     CX,256                  ;Download 256 characters
        MOV     DX,0                    ;Start with character 0
        MOV     BL,0                    ;Download as bitmaps 0 - 255
        MOV     BH,32                   ;Each bitmap is in 8x32 box
        PUSH    BP
        MOV     BP,CG_One               ;Pointer to first char gen
        MOV     AH,11H                  ;Function = CHARACTER GENERATOR
        MOV     AL,0                    ;Subfunction = LOAD CUSTOM SET
        INT     10H                     ;Ask BIOS to download first set
        POP     BP

        MOV     BL,1                    ;Download as bitmaps 256 - 511
        MOV     BP,CG_Two               ;Pointer to second char gen
        INT     10H                     ;Ask BIOS to download second set
        JMP     Set_Colors

        ;- Since the INTENSIFY BIT will be used as generator select
        ;   we must load palette table to keep two halves the same

Default_Colors DB      0,1,2,3,4,5,6,7, 0,1,2,3,4,5,6,7, 0
Default_Monos  DB      0,8,8,8,8,8,8,8, 0,8,8,8,8,8,8,8, 0
Set_Colors:
        LEA     DX,Default_Colors       ;Load offset of color palette
        XOR     AX,AX                   ;Look if mono display is attached
        MOV     ES,AX                   ;to see if mono palette is needed
        TEST    BYTE PTR ES:[BIOS_Equipment],2
        JZ      Default_In              ;... no, mono is not attached
        LEA     DX,Default_Monos        ;... yes, must use mono palette
Default_In:
        MOV     AX,CS                   ;Load segment of palette
        MOV     ES,AX
        MOV     AH,10H                  ;Function = LOAD PALETTE
        MOV     AL,2                    ;Subfunction = ALL REGS
```

```
        INT     10H                     ;Ask BIOS to load palette

        ;- Enable two character generators

Enable_Two_CGs:
        MOV     BL,0100B                ;Register value for CHAR GEN SELECT
                                        ;This selects 0 for A and 1 for B
        MOV     AH,11H                  ;Function = CHARACTER GENERATOR
        MOV     AL,3                    ;Subfunction = SELECT ACTIVE SET
        INT     10H                     ;Ask BIOS to enable two sets
        JMP     Demo_Text

        ;- Display few characters from each 256 character set

TestStr DB      'A', 7,'B', 7,'C', 7    ;Characters in   0 - 255
        DB      'A',15,'B',15,'C',15    ;Characters in 256 - 511

Demo_Text:
        MOV     AX,CS                   ;Segment of text
        MOV     ES,AX
        LEA     BP,TestStr              ;Offset of text
        MOV     BH,0                    ;Use page 0
        MOV     CX,6                    ;Display 6 characters
        MOV     DH,0                    ;Start at row 0
        MOV     DL,0                    ;and column 0
        MOV     AH,13H                  ;Function = WRITE TEXT STRING
        MOV     AL,03H                  ;Subfunction = CHAR+ATTRIB, UPDATE
        INT     10H                     ;Ask BIOS to write the string

        POP     ES
        POP     BP
        RET
_BIOS_512_Set   ENDP
```

The Character Generator Select Register can be modified directly without using the BIOS, as the following example illustrates:

Listing 7-58. File: PROG063.ASM

```
;**********************************************************************
; Eable use of attribute to select between two                      *
; 256 character generators                                          *
;**********************************************************************

Gen_A   EQU     0                       ;For now we choose A to be first 256
Gen_B   EQU     1                       ;and B to be second 256 bitmaps

        PUBLIC  _Enable_Second_Set

_Enable_Second_Set PROC     NEAR
        MOV     DX,3C4H                 ;Index for SELECT register
        MOV     AL,3
        OUT     DX,AL
        INC     DX                      ;Output value
```

```
        MOV     AL,Gen_B                    ;Shift Gen_B into bits 2 and 3
        SHL     AL,1
        SHL     AL,1
        AND     AL,1100B
        MOV     AH,Gen_A
        AND     AH,11B                      ;Shift Gen_A into bits 0 & 1
        OR      AL,AH
        OUT     DX,AL                       ;Output the value
        RET
_Enable_Second_Set ENDP


;**********************************************************************
; Force generator to be always the first 256 characters              *
; in plane 2                                                         *
;**********************************************************************

        PUBLIC  _Disable_Second_Set

_Disable_Second_Set PROC        NEAR
        MOV     DX,3C4H                     ;Fetch address of SEQUENCER
        MOV     AL,3                        ;Fetch index for CHAR GEN SELECT reg
        OUT     DX,AL                       ;Select index
        INC     DX
        MOV     AL,0                        ;Select value = same for A and B
        OUT     DX,AL                       ;Set register to the value
        RET
_Disable_Second_Set ENDP
```

43 Line Text

Format the Display for 43 Lines of Text

Pascal Library Procedure

procedure Set_43_Lines;

C Library Procedure

set_43_lines();   /* invoke 43 line display   */

Example

This example will set all control registers to work with the 8 x 8 character set.

Listing 7-59. File: PROGC053.C

```
/*************************************************************************/
/* Check display type and if ok, set 43 line mode                       */
/*************************************************************************/

demo_43_lines()
        {
        int     i, mode;
        if (get_scanlines() < 350)
                printf("Cannot use 43 lines with your display");
        else
                {
                mode = get_mode();              /* Get current mode    */
                set_43_lines();                 /* Set 43 text mode    */
                for (i = 0; i < 43; i++)        /* Fill screen with text*/
                        printf("\nThis is line %d in 43 line text mode",i);
                getchar();                      /* Wait for <Enter> key */
                set_mode(mode);                 /* Restore all by      */
                }                               /* setting mode        */
        }
```

Listing 7-60. File: PROGP053.PAS

```
{*************************************************************************}
{ Check display type and if ok, set 43 line mode                         }
{*************************************************************************}

procedure demo_43_lines;
const
MONO = 5;
VMONO = 7;
var
i : integer;
begin
        {- Set default text mode                                         }
        i := Get_Display_Type;
        if i = MONO then        Set_Mode(7)
        else if i = VMONO then Set_Mode(7)
        else                    Set_Mode(3);

        i := Get_Scanlines;
        if i < 350 then writeln("Display will not support 43 lines")
        else
            begin
                set_43_lines;                   { Set 43 text mode      }
                for i := 0 to 42 do             { Fill screen with text }
                    begin
                        Set_Cursor_Position(i,0);
                        write("This is line ',i,' in 43 line text mode");
                    end;
            end;
        i := integer(ReadKey);                  { Wait for <Enter> key  }
end;
```

Theory

Displays with 350 scan lines (the Enhanced Color Display and the Monochrome Display) can support 43 lines of text, as opposed to the standard 25 lines, if an 8 x 8 character set is used instead of the larger 8 x 14 character set (see Figure 7-3). 43 line text cannot be supported on the standard Color Monitor, which uses only 200 scan lines.

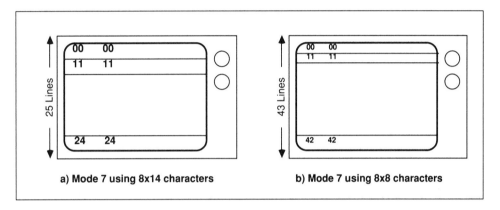

Figure 7–3. Setting up 43 line text.

To invoke a 43 line mode:

1.   Select a text mode that uses 350 scan lines (normally mode 3* or mode 7).

2.   Load the 8 x 8 character set (you can use BIOS function 17, subfunction 2 Load CGA Character Set).

3.   Load the Max Scan Line register of the CRT Controller with a 7 to produce text which is 8 pixels high.

4.   Reduce the value of the Start Vertical Blank register by six. 43 lines of 8 x 8 text requires only 344 scan lines. The remaining six scan lines should be blanked.

To learn more about character generators, also see:

• Character Generator section in Chapter 2.

• Character Generator Select register of Sequencer in Chapter 3.

• BIOS function 17, Load Character Generator in Chapter 4.

• Programming examples Read Character Generator, Write
  Character Generator, and 512 Character Set in this chapter.

Assembly Code Examples

Listing 7-61. File: PROG065.ASM

```
;*************************************************************************
; Select 43 line mode by downloading the 8x8 character generator        *
; This will not work on Color Display (Mono and Enhanced only!)         *
;*************************************************************************

        PUBLIC  _BIOS_43_Lines

_BIOS_43_Lines  PROC    NEAR
        MOV     BL,0                    ;Block to load
        MOV     AH,11H                  ;Function = CHARACTER GENERATOR
        MOV     AL,12H                  ;Subfunction = USE 8x8
        INT     10H                     ;Ask BIOS to load the char gen
        RET
_BIOS_43_Lines  ENDP
```

This example shows how to set control registers on the EGA to work with the 8
x 8 character set. This example can be modified to configure EGA for other character sizes.

Listing 7-62. File: PROG066.ASM

```
;*************************************************************************
; Select 43 line text mode it is assumed that an 8x8 character          *
; generator has been already downloaded                                 *
; This is an example how to set control registers for different         *
; character heights.                                                    *
;*************************************************************************

CHAR_HITE       EQU     8

        PUBLIC  _Set_43_Lines

_Set_43_Lines   PROC    NEAR
        PUSH    ES
        XOR     AX,AX                   ;Point ES to segment zero
        MOV     ES,AX

        ; Set underline location in CRTC 14 to 8

        MOV     DX,FS:[BIOS_CRT_Addr]   ;Fetch address of CRT controller
        MOV     AL,14H                  ;Index for UNDERLINE LOCATION
        OUT     DX,AL                   ;Select UNDERLINE REGISTER
        INC     DX
        MOV     AL,CHAR_HITE            ;Fetch value for underline
        OUT     DX,AL                   ;Set UNDERLINE register
        DEC     DX
```

```
            ; Set character height in CRTC 9 to 7

            MOV    AL,9                    ;Index for CHARACTER HEIGHT
            OUT    DX,AL                   ;Select register for write
            INC    DX
            MOV    AL,CHAR_HITE-1          ;Value is 7
            OUT    DX,AL                   ;Write value into register
            DEC    DX

            ; Set vertical display end in CRTC 12 to 43*8-1
            ; (upper bit in overflow already set)

            MOV    AL,12H                  ;Select index
            OUT    DX,AL
            INC    DX
            MOV    AL,(43*8-1-256)         ;Write value
            MOV    AL,((350/CHAR_HITE)*CHAR_HITE-1-256)
            OUT    DX,AL

            ; Reset constants in segment zero to reflect new dimensions

            MOV    BYTE PTR ES:[BIOS_Rows],(350/CHAR_HITE)-1
            MOV    WORD PTR ES:[BIOS_Columns],80
            MOV    WORD PTR ES:[BIOS_Height],CHAR_HITE

            ; We are forced here to use BIOS function to put 8x8 character
            ; set into plane 2, since we do not have our set to load

            MOV    AX,1112H                ;Function = Load 8x8 character set
            MOV    BL,0                    ;            into first block
            INT    10H                     ;Ask BIOS to use its ROM set


            POP    ES
            RET
_Set_43_Lines   ENDP
```

Split Screen

Divide the Display Into Two Independent Sections

Pascal Library Procedures

procedure Split_Screen(split:integer);
            {Scanline number for the split}

C Library Procedures

```
split_screen(split)             /* Set split screen         */
int   split;                    /* Scan line for split      */
```

Theory

Split_Screen splits the screen into two separate regions.

The split screen capability of the EGA permits the display screen to be split horizontally into 2 regions. The upper region may be panned or scrolled while the lower region remains stationary. The upper screen region can be used to display graphics or text, while the lower region is used for fixed menus or help information.

The Line Compare register of the CRT controller defines at which scan line the upper data region will end and the lower region will begin. Line Compare is a 9 bit register, with its most significant bit located in the Overflow Register of the CRT Controller.

The lower display region always displays data starting from memory address 0 in display memory. The upper display region displays data starting from the memory address defined by the Start Address register of the CRT Controller.

Hardware scrolling cannot be used on the bottom region of a split screen since data displayed in that region always starts at address 0 of the display buffer. The top region of the screen can be scrolled by changing the Start Address register in the CRT Controller.

By setting Line Compare equal to the last scan line, then slowly decrementing its value, the lower screen region can be made to smoothly rise up from the bottom of the display (see Figure 7-4).

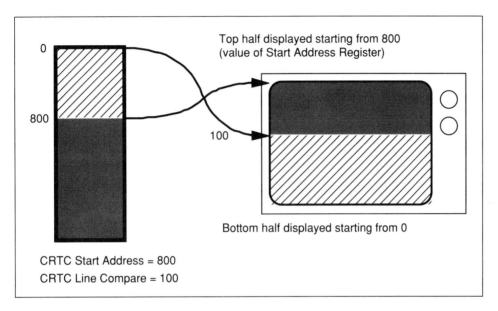

Figure 7-4. Split screen operation.

The total number of scan lines for each display type are:

Display Type	Last Line
Monochrome (mode 7)	349
Color (modes 0 - 3)	199
Enhanced (modes 0 -3)	349
Enhanced VGA modes	479

For example on the Monochrome or Enhanced displays, to establish a split screen with 12 text lines in the top region and 13 text lines in the bottom region, the Line Compare register should be set to a value of 168 (12 x 14) since each of the 12 text lines is 14 scan lines high (using the 8 x 14 character set).

In the C example below, the display memory is first filled with a data pattern. The split screen is smoothly scrolled into place by slowly decrementing the value of the Line Compare register (performed by calling the "split_screen" library procedure). The top region of the split screen can then be scrolled up or down one line at a time by pressing either the up or down arrow keys on the keypad. Scrolling is performed by incrementing or decrementing the Start Address register of the CRT controller in increments of 80 bytes.

Pressing the ESC or Enter keys will cause the split screen to be smoothly scrolled off the screen before the program terminates.

Example:

Listing 7-63. File: PROGC052.C

```
/***************************************************************************/
/* Fill 'display buffer' with text then display it                         */
/* in a split screen.  Use cursor keys to scroll the top half              */
/***************************************************************************/

demo_split_screen()
        {
        #define KEY_ESC         0x011B
        #define KEY_UP          0x4800
        #define KEY_DOWN        0x5000
        #define KEY_LEFT        0x4B00
        #define KEY_RIGHT       0x4D00
        #define KEY_ENTER       0x1C0D
        #define MONO            5
        #define VMONO           7

        static  char    digits[] = {"0123456789"};
        static  char    text[]   = {"This is line 000"};
        int             i, line, key, size, port;

        /*- Fill display buffer with text  -                    */
        /* (cannot use printf since we want to go below line 25)      */

        for (i = 0; i < 400; i++)
                {
                text[15] = digits[i % 10];       /* Add line number      */
                text[14] = digits[(i/10)%10];
                text[13] = digits[(i/100)%10];
                write_string(i, 0, text);        /* Draw next text line  */
                }

        /*- Smoothly move in the split line -                       */

        size = get_scanlines()/2;                /* Last split to do     */
        for (i = get_scanlines(); i > size; i-)/* Loop over scanline   */
                split_screen(i);                 /* to smoothly move in  */

        /*- Use cursor keys to control the scroll -                 */
        /* Each line of text takes 80 bytes, so to scroll down one   */
        /* line, we set START ADDRESS register in CRTC to 80 more     */

        line = 0;                                /* Initialize line pos  */
                                                 /* Set CRTC address     */
        if (get_display_type() == MONO || get_display_type() == VMONO)
                port = 0x3B4;
        else
                port = 0x3D4;

        while((key = get_key()) != KEY_ENTER)
                {
                switch (key)
                        {
                        case KEY_UP:             /* Scroll up one line   */
```

```
                                line = (line > 0) ? -line : 0;
                                break;
                        case KEY_DOWN:              /* Scroll down one line */
                                line++;
                                break;
                        default:
                                break;
                        }
                write_register(port,0x0D);          /* Select CRTC START LO */
                write_register(port+1, line * 80);      /* Write low      */
                write_register(port,0x0C);          /* Select CRTC START HI */
                write_register(port+1,(line * 80)>>8);  /* Write high     */
                }

        /* Reset CRT START ADDRESS to 0 (no scroll)                        */

        write_register(port,0x0D);                  /* Select CRTC START LO */
        write_register(port+1,0);                       /* Write low      */
        write_register(port,0x0C);                  /* Select CRTC START HI */
        write_register(port+1,0);                       /* Write high     */

        /* Remove the split                                                */

        size = get_scanlines();                     /* Last split to do   */
        for (i = get_scanlines()/2; i <= size; i++)     /* Loop over      */
                split_screen(i);                    /* to smoothly move out */
        }
```

Listing 7-64. File: PROGP052.PAS

```
{***********************************************************************}
{ Fill "display buffer" with text then display it                     }
{ in a split screen                                                   }
{***********************************************************************}

procedure demo_split_screen;
const
MONO = 5;
VMONO = 7;

KEY_ESC = $1B;
KEY_UP = 72;
KEY_DOWN = 80;
KEY_LEFT = 75;
KEY_RIGHT = 77;
KEY_ENTER = $0D;

digits : array[0..9] of char = "0123456789";
text : string[16] = "This is line 000";
var
split, i, line, key, size, port : integer;
c : char;
begin
        {- Set default text mode                                        }
        i := Get_Display_Type;
        if i = MONO then
```

```
        begin
            Set_Mode(7);
            port := $3B4;
        end
    else if i = VMONO then
        begin
            Set_Mode(7);
            port := $3B4;
        end
    else
        begin
            Set_Mode(3);
            port := $3D4;
        end;

    {- Fill display buffer with text  -                        }

    for i := 0 to 99 do
        begin
            text[16] := digits[i mod 10];{ Add line number       }
            text[15] := digits[(i div 10) mod 10];
            text[14] := digits[(i div 100) mod 10];
            write_string(i, 0, seg(text),ofs(text));{ Add next line}
        end;

    {- Smoothly move in the split line -                       }

    size := Get_Scanlines div 2;    { Get number of lines       }
    for i := Get_Scanlines downto size do
            Split_Screen(i);
    line := 0;

    {- Use cursor keys to control the scroll               - }
    {- Each line of text takes 80 words so to scroll down 1 line}
    {- we increment CRTC start register by 80              - }
    repeat
    key := integer(readkey);
    case key of
                                            { Scroll up one scanline}
            KEY_UP: if line > 0 then line := line - 1
                    else line := 0;
            KEY_DOWN: line := line+1;        { Scroll down one line }
        end;
    Write_Register(port,$0D);                {Select CRTC start low }
    Write_Register(port+1,line*80);          {Write low }
    Write_Register(port,$0C);                {Select CRTC start hi  }
    Write_Register(port+1,(line*80) shr 8); {Write hi              }

    until key = KEY_ENTER;

    { - Reset CRTC start address to zero                     -}

    Write_Register(port,$0D);                {Select CRTC start low }
    Write_Register(port+1,0);                {Write low             }
    Write_Register(port,$0C);                {Select CRTC start hi  }
    Write_Register(port+1,0);                {Write hi              }
```

```
        { - Remove split                                    - }

        size := Get_Scanlines;
        for i := (Get_Scanlines div 2) to size do
                Split_Screen(i);
end;
```

Assembly Code Example

The following example will establish a split screen by loading the Line Compare register. The Overflow register in the CRT must also be loaded if the value of Line Compare is greater than 255. Working with the Overflow Register can be difficult since the register is write-only on the EGA. Software must either keep Overflow status stored elsewhere or assume the register is at a default value. A default value is assumed here. For the VGA a ninth bit is also available, and should be set to zero for standard modes. Notice that for the VGA we can read back the Overflow and Maximum Scan Line registers and change only the appropriate bit in each.

Listing 7-65. File: PROG064.ASM

```
;************************************************************************
; Enable the split screen                                              *
; Enter:        Split   - Scan line for the split                      *
; Works only for "standard" EGA modes                                  *
;************************************************************************

Split           EQU     [BP+4]

        PUBLIC  _Split_Screen

_Split_Screen   PROC    NEAR
        PUSH    BP                              ;Setup pointer to parameters
        MOV     BP,SP
        CALL    _Vertical_Retrace               ;Wait for vertical retrace
        PUSH    ES                              ;Get pointer to BIOS data area
        XOR     AX,AX
        MOV     ES,AX
        MOV     DX,3B4H                         ;Assume CRTC address is mono address
        TEST    BYTE PTR ES:[BIOS_Equipment],2  ;Is mono display attached?
        JNZ     SS_CRT_Ok                       ;...Yes, keep DX as is
        MOV     DX,3D4H                         ;...No, change DX to 3D4
SS_CRT_Ok:
        MOV     AL,18H                          ;Get index for LINE COMPARE register
        OUT     DX,AL                           ;Select register
        INC     DX
        MOV     AX,Split                        ;Get split line bits 0-7
        OUT     DX,AL                           ;Set LINE COMPARE register
        DEC     DX

        ; Split bits beyond 7 (8 and maybe 9) are handled differently
        ; for EGA and VGA.  Here we decide which case to handle
```

```
              CALL     _Get_Scanlines         ;If we have up to 480 lines
              CMP      AX,480                 ;then can do VGA processing
              JL       EGA_Split              ;...otherwise do EGA processing
VGA_Split:
              MOV      AL,7                   ;Select OVERFLOW register
              OUT      DX,AL
              INC      DX
              IN       AL,DX                  ;Get current overflow value
              MOV      BL,Split+1             ;Fetch bit 8 from split
              AND      BL,1
              MOV      CL,4
              SHL      BL,CL
              AND      AL,NOT 10H             ;Clear bit in data just read in
              OR       AL,BL                  ;Add the bit 8 from split
              OUT      DX,AL                  ;Write to new value to OVERFLOW reg
              DEC      DX
              MOV      AL,9                   ;Get MAX SCAN LINE register value
              OUT      DX,AL
              INC      DX
              IN       AL,DX
              AND      AL,NOT 40H             ;Clear bit (since split bit 9 is 0)
              OUT      DX,AL                  ;Set the new value
              JMP      Split_Done
EGA_Split:
              MOV      BL,Split+1             ;Fetch split bit 8 for overflow reg
              AND      BL,1
              MOV      CL,4                   ;Shift bit 8 into proper position
              SHL      BL,CL
              CMP      DX,3B4H                ;Monochrome mode?
              JE       display_350            ;...Yes,350 line mode
              MOV      AL,ES:[BIOS_Switch]    ;Get display type from
              CMP      AL,3                   ;switch setting
              JE       Display_350            ;Enhanced display?
              CMP      AL,9                   ;...Yes, 350 line mode
              JE       Display_350
Display_200:                                 ;...No, use 200 line mode
              OR       BL,01H                 ;Get 200 line value
              JMP      Over_Set
Display_350:
              OR       BL,0FH                 ;Get 350 line value
Over_Set:
              MOV      AL,07H                 ;Select OVERFLOW register
              OUT      DX,AL
              INC      DX                     ;Fetch address of OVERFLOW register
              MOV      AL,BL                  ;Fetch value for OVERFLOW register
              OUT      DX,AL                  ;Set OVERFLOW register
Split_Done:
              POP      ES                     ;Restore ES and return
              POP      BP
              RET
_Split_Screen ENDP
```

Line Graphics

Display Graphics Objects in Text Mode

The standard IBM character set used for EGA, CGA, and MDA (see Appendix) includes a set of characters that permit the drawing of simple graphics objects such as boxes around text. These characters are normally called Line Graphics characters (or Block Graphics characters).

These examples show how to use Line Graphics to draw three types of boxes: a single line box, double line box, and a solid line box.

A Line Graphics character (or any of the standard 256 characters on the EGA) can be viewed on the screen by typing its ASCII code in decimal (0-255) while holding down the <Alt> key. Some text editors will also accept the <Alt> sequence to enter character codes into a file. For a complete list of graphics characters see the ASCII table in the Appendix B.

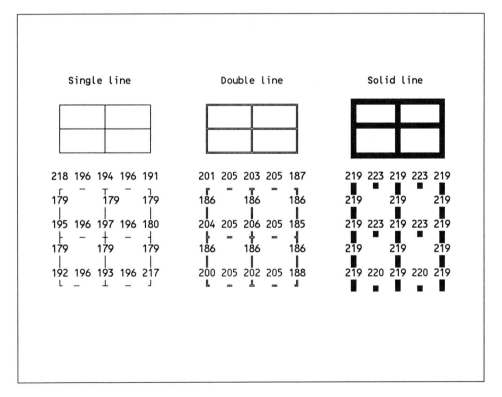

Figure 7-5. Using Line Graphics to create boxes.

Art by mozaics

If you are not completely satisfied with the selection of block (graphics) characters, you can create your own custom block characters. To do that, read the current character generator using the library function 'Read_Character_Generator', and replace as many characters as your artistic heart desires. After you have replaced the characters in the set, write the new character set out using the library function 'Write_Character_Generator'. You can then create your own mozaic pictures using the new block characters.

Listing 7-66. File: PROGC054.C

```
/**************************************************************************/
/* Display "Hello" in a single line box                                  */
/**************************************************************************/

boxed_hello()
        {
        static char line1[] = {218,196,196,196,196,196,196,196,191,0};
        static char line2[] = {179,' ','H','e','l','l','o',' ',179,0};
        static char line3[] = {192,196,196,196,196,196,196,196,217,0};
        write_string(10, 35, line1);    /* Display top of the box      */
        write_string(11, 35, line2);    /* Display middle of the box   */
        write_string(12, 35, line3);    /* Display bottom of the box   */
        }
```

Listing 7-67. File: PROGP054.PAS

```
{**************************************************************************}
{ Display "Hello" in a single line box                                    }
{**************************************************************************}

procedure boxed_hello;
const
MONO = 5;
VMONO = 7;
line1 : string[9] = #218#196#196#196#196#196#196#196#191;
line2 : string[9] = #179' Hello '#179;
line3 : string[9] = #192#196#196#196#196#196#196#196#217;
var
i : integer;
begin
        {- Set default text mode                                         }

        i := Get_Display_Type;
        if i = MONO then        Set_Mode(7)
        else if i = VMONO then  Set_Mode(7)
        else                    Set_Mode(3);


        {- Display the box                                               }
```

```
        Write_String(10, 35, seg(line1),ofs(line1)); { Display top of box }
        Write_String(11, 35, seg(line2),ofs(line2)); { Display middle of box }
        Write_String(12, 35, seg(line3),ofs(line3)); { Display bottom of box }
end;
```

Assembly Code Example

Listing 7-68. File: PROG072.ASM

```
;**************************************************************************
;  Display 'Hello' in a single line box                                   *
;**************************************************************************

line1   DB        218,196,196,196,196,196,196,196,191
line2   DB        179,' ','H','e','l','l','o',' ',179
line3   DB        192,196,196,196,196,196,196,196,217

Boxed_Hello     PROC    NEAR
        PUSH    BP
        PUSH    ES
        MOV     AX,CS                   ;Get pointer to the string
        MOV     ES,AX                   ;into register pair ES:BP
        LEA     BP,Line1
        MOV     BX,0                    ;Select page 0
        MOV     BL,7                    ;Use normal attribute
        MOV     CX,9                    ;Display 9 characters
        MOV     DH,12                   ;Start at row 12
        MOV     DL,35                   ;Start at column 35
        MOV     AH,13H                  ;Function = WRITE TEXT STRING
        MOV     AL,0H                   ;Subfunction = Update Cursor Pos.
        INT     10H                     ;Ask BIOS to display the text

        MOV     DH,13                   ;Next line at row 13
        LEA     BP,Line2
        INT     10H

        MOV     DH,14                   ;Next line at row 14
        LEA     BP,Line3
        INT     10H

        POP     ES
        POP     BP
        RET
Boxed_Hello     ENDP
```

8

Graphics Mode Examples

This chapter is dedicated to the graphics functions of EGA/VGA. The examples will illustrate how to manipulate pixels to draw graphics primitives like lines and circles, and how to preform BITBLTs (Bit BLock Transfers).

These examples all use EGA mode 10 hex, which is the most popular graphics mode for EGA. This mode has a resolution of 640 x 350 and supports sixteen colors. Some mention will be made of how to adapt these algorithms, if needed, for use with mode E (640 x 200 graphics) and mode F (monochrome 640 x 350 graphics).

To comprehend examples in this chapter, you will need to be familiar with basic CRT terminology (pixels, scan lines, rasters). These terms are explained in the section on Operation of CRT Displays in Chapter 2.

Paired numbers represent a coordinate for a pixel on the screen. For example point 300,275 refers to pixel number 300 on scan line 275. Pixel 0,0 is in the upper left corner of the screen (see Figure 8-1).

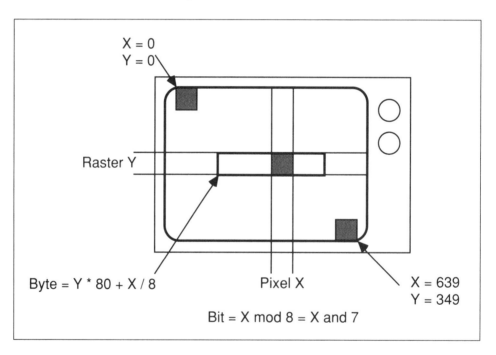

Figure 8-1. Pixel addressing.

All library routines in this chapter assume that a proper graphics mode has already been selected. The mode to select depends on the type of display attached to the EGA. For monochorme display use mode F, for Color display (but not Enhanced) use mode D, and for Enhanced or Multi-scan display use mode 10hex. For VGA use mode 10hex regardless of the display attached. To learn how to select a mode, also see Set Mode programming examples in Chapter 5.

The following short main procedure can be used to run any of the examples in this section:

```
main()
        {
        #define MONO            5
        #define COLOR           4
        #define ENHANCED        3
        int     type;

        /* Get display type and select mode accordingly           */

        type = get_display_type();              /* Get display type        */
        switch (type)                           /* Set mode according to   */
                {                               /* type of display         */
                case MONO:
                        set_mode(0x0F);
                        break;
                case COLOR:
                        set_mode(0x0E);
                        break;
                default:
                        set_mode(0x10);
                        break;
                }

        /* Call procedure to perform the example                  */

        example_proc();                         /* Draw the example        */
        getchar();                              /* Wait for <Enter>        */

        /* Restore the original mode                              */

        if (type == MONO)       setmode(7);     /* Restore text mode       */
        else                    setmode(3);
        exit(0);                                /* Quit                    */
        }
```

Write Pixel

Write a Single Pixel in Display Memory

Pascal Library Procedure

procedure Pixel_Set(x,y,color:integer);
procedure Pixel_Packed_Write(x,y,color:integer);
procedure Pixel_Write(x,y,color:integer);

C Library Procedure

pixel_set(x, y, color)	/* Mode 0 using Set-Reset	*/
pixel_packed_write(x, y, color)	/* Mode 2	*/
pixel_write(x, y, color)	/* Mode 0 using planar write	*/
int x;	/* x coordinate	*/
int y;	/* y coordinate	*/
int value;	/* pixel value	*/

Example

This procedure will change an individual pixel on the screen to a selected color. This represents the most elementary graphics operation.

The following example uses the Write_Pixel procedure to draw sixteen boxes, each in a different color. Each box is 20 pixels wide and 10 pixels high.

This example executes slowly because each pixel write requires a subroutine call. More sophisticated algorithms avoid calling the Write_Pixel procedure for every pixel in favor of faster methods that change several pixels together as a group whenever possible (the Scan Line Fill and Rectangle Fill programming examples demonstrate this). The most common use of the procedure Write_Pixel is in development of new algorithms.

Listing 8-1. File: PROGC080.C

```
/************************************************************************/
/* Draw sixteen boxes using pixel write                               */
/************************************************************************/

pixel_box16()
     {
     #define MONO          5
     #define VMONO         7
     #define COLOR         4
     #define ENHANCED      3
     #define VCOLOR        8
```

```
int     box, i, j, color, x, y;
int     type;

/* Get display type and select mode accordingly            */

type = get_display_type();          /* Get display type    */
switch (type)                       /* Set mode according to*/
        {                           /* type of display      */
        case VMONO:
        case MONO:
                set_mode(0x0F);
                break;
        case COLOR:
                set_mode(0x0E);
                break;
        case VCOLOR:
        case ENHANCED:
        default:
                set_mode(0x10);
                break;
        }

/* Draw boxes using SET/RESET write mode                    */

printf("Drawing pixels using mode 0, SET/RESET method");
for (box = 0; box < 16; box++)          /* Loop over boxes      */
    for (j = 0; j < 10; j++)            /* Loop over rasters    */
                                        /* within box           */
        for (i = 0; i < 100; i++)       /* Loop over pixels     */
            {                           /* within raster        */
            x = i;                      /* Set x                */
            y = j + 10 * box;           /* Compute y            */
            color = box;                /* Set color            */
            pixel_set(x, y, color);     /* Fill next pixel      */
            }
getchar();                              /* Wait for <Enter>     */

/* Draw boxes using PACKED write mode                       */

cls();
printf("Drawing pixels using mode 2, packed write method");
for (box = 0; box < 16; box++)          /* Loop over boxes      */
    for (j = 0; j < 10; j++)            /* Loop over rasters    */
                                        /* within box           */
        for (i = 0; i < 100; i++)       /* Loop over pixels     */
            {                           /* within raster        */
            x = i;                      /* Set x                */
            y = j + 10 * box;           /* Compute y            */
            color = 15 - box;           /* Set color            */
            pixel_packed_write(x, y, color);/*Fill next pix */
            }
getchar();                              /* Wait for <Enter>     */

/* Draw boxes using PLANAR write mode                       */

cls();
printf("Drawing pixels using mode 0, planar write method");
```

```
for (box = 0; box < 16; box++)          /* Loop over boxes      */
    for (j = 0; j < 10; j++)            /* Loop over rasters    */
                                        /* within box           */
        for (i = 0; i < 100; i++)       /* Loop over pixels     */
            {                           /* within raster        */
            x = i;                      /* Set x                */
            y = j + 10 * box;           /* Compute y            */
            color = box;                /* Set color            */
            pixel_write(x, y, color);/*Fill next pixel          */
            }
    }
```

Listing 8-2. File: PROGP080.PAS

```
{***************************************************************}
{ Draw sixteen boxes using three different modes of pixel write }
{***************************************************************}

procedure pixel_box16;
const
MONO = 5;
VMONO = 7;
COLOR = 4;
ENHANCED = 3;
msg1 : array[0..40] of char = "Writing using write mode 0, SET/RESET     ";
msg2 : array[0..40] of char = "Writing using write mode 2, packed pixels";
msg3 : array[0..40] of char = "Writing using write mode 0, planar write ";
var
box,i,j,pixel_color,x,y : integer;
c : char;
begin
        Clear_Screen;
        i := Get_Display_Type;
        if i = MONO then        Set_Mode($0F)
        else if i = VMONO then Set_Mode($0F)
        else if i = COLOR then Set_Mode($0E)
        else                   Set_Mode($10);

        { Draw boxes using SET/RESET write mode                 }

        for j := 0 to 40 do Video_BIOS($E00 + integer(msg1[j]),7,0,0,0,0);

        for box := 0 to 15 do              { Loop over boxes       }
          begin
            for j := 0 to 9 do             { Loop over rasters     }
              begin                        { within box            }
                for i := 0 to 99 do        { Loop over pixels      }
                    begin
                        x := i;            { Set x                 }
                        y := j + 10 ^ box; { Compute y             }
                        pixel_color := box; { Set color            }
                        Pixel_Set(x, y, pixel_color); { Fill next pixel }
                    end;
              end;
          end;
```

```
  c := readkey;                              { Wait for <Enter>        }

  { Draw boxes using PACKED write mode                                 }

  Clear_Screen;
  for j := 0 to 40 do Video_BIOS($E00 + integer(msg2[j]),7,0,0,0,0);

  for box := 0 to 15 do                      { Loop over boxes         }
    begin
      for j := 0 to 9 do                     { Loop over rasters       }
        begin                                { within box             }
          for i := 0 to 99 do                { Loop over pixels        }
              begin                          { within raster          }
                  x := i;                    { Set x                  }
                  y := j + 10 * box;         { Compute y              }
                  pixel_color := 15-box;     { Set color              }
                  Pixel_Packed_Write(x, y, pixel_color);{Fill next pix }
              end;
        end;
    end;
  c := readkey;                              { Wait for <Enter>        }

  { Draw boxes using planar write mode                                 }

  Clear_Screen;
  for j := 0 to 40 do Video_BIOS($E00 + integer(msg3[j]),7,0,0,0,0);

  for box := 0 to 15 do                      { Loop over boxes         }
    begin
      for j := 0 to 9 do                     { Loop over rasters       }
        begin                                { within box             }
          for i := 0 to 99 do                { Loop over pixels        }
              begin                          { within raster          }
                  x := i;                    { Set x                  }
                  y := j + 10 * box;         { Compute y              }
                  pixel_color := box;        { Set color              }
                  Pixel_Write(x, y, pixel_color);{Fill next pixel }
              end;
        end;
    end;

  {- Set default text mode                                            }

  c := readkey;                              { Wait for <Enter>        }

  i := Get_Display_Type;
  if i = MONO then        Set_Mode(7)
  else if i = VMONO then Set_Mode(7)
  else                    Set_Mode(3);
end;
```

Theory

Even though the procedure library contains procedures for writing and reading pixels, practical graphics drawing algorithms must write directly to display memory to achieve acceptable performance. For this reason, it is essential that the graphics programmer understand how to use the hardware of the EGA.

The EGA/VGA is a plane oriented device, but by properly configuring the Graphics Controller either planar or packed pixel data can be written to the planar display memory. For an explanation of packed pixels and planar pixels, see Packed Pixels vs. Color Planes in Chapter 2. For a complete discussion of display memory read and write modes, see the Graphics Controller section of Chapter 3.

Display memory is arranged as 8 pixels per byte. To write a single pixel to display memory, it is necessary to modify a single bit in a byte (in one or more planes). The Mask Register of the Graphics Controller can be used to modify a single pixel while preserving the other seven pixels of the byte.

The Plane Write Enable register of the Sequencer determines which memory planes will be modified by a display memory write. A single plane can be modified, all planes can be modified, or any combination of planes can be modified by a single write operation.

Four types of display memory write operations can be performed with the EGA. These methods can be used to modify the display memory:

1. **Processor Write using Set-Reset:** Write the color pattern defined by the Set/Reset Register to display memory. Useful for memory fill operations, this mode will fill up to 8 pixels (one byte) of each enabled plane with a predefined fill color. Used with the Mask Register, this mode can be used efficiently to write single pixels and is the most efficient method for standard DDA (Digital Differential Analyzer) drawing algorithms. This mode is used in drawing routines such as Draw Line, Scan Line Fill, Rectangle Fill, and the like.

2. **Processor Write using Planar Pixel Write:** Write planar pixel data from processor to display memory. This is the most simple form of display memory write operation. The Write Plane Enable register is used to select the plane(s) to be modified. The Mask Register is used to define which bits (pixels) will be preserved. Then data is written from processor to display memory. This mode is most suitable for loading whole planes, one plane at a time; it is efficient for loading a stored image onto the display, since this is normally done one plane at a time (see the Load Screen programming example). This mode is not efficient for DDA drawing algorithms.

3.   **Latched Data Write:** Write the contents of the processor read latches to display memory. The processor read latch for each plane contains the data from the last display memory read operation. By performing read cycles followed by write cycles, the processor read latches can be used to quickly copy data from one location in display memory to another. Up to 32 bits can be copied in one operation (8 bits for each plane that is write enabled). The Display Cursor programming example uses this mode to save and restore screen data under the cursor.

4.   **Packed Pixel Write:** Write packed pixel data from processor to display memory. The lowest four bits of the processor write data are written into the corresponding four planes. In other words, the value of the processor data is used as the pixel color. One to eight pixels are written at a time, depending on the value of the Mask Register. This mode can be used to efficiently load an image that is stored in a packed pixel format, such as TIFF (Tag Image File Format).

The last three modes are illustrated in Figure 8-2.

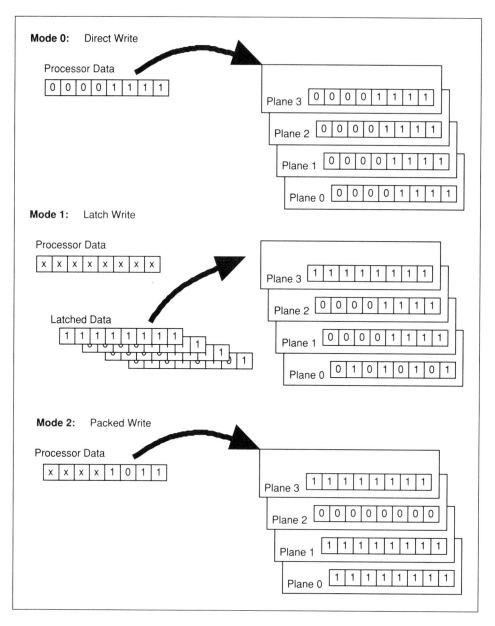

Figure 8-2. Write modes.

To modify a single pixel without destroying surrounding pixels, a Read-Write sequence is used. First, the Mask register is loaded to define which pixel will be modified. Next, a byte is read by the processor and latched into the processor read latches. This step is required for the Mask register to work properly. Finally, a write is performed to modify the pixel. This same sequence must also be used when using the logical functions of the EGA (AND, OR or XOR). This sequence is summarized in Figure 3-15.

To learn more about memory organization, also see Display Memory in Graphics Modes in Chapter 2.

To learn more about write modes, logical functions and masking, see description of Graphics Controller in Chapter 2 and Chapter 3, and programming examples BITBLT and Display Cursor in this chapter.

Assembly Code Examples

The following example uses BIOS function 12 (Write Graphics Pixel) to fill a single 100 x 100 square in the upper left corner of the screen. BIOS function 12 is actually too slow for practical use, however.

Listing 8-3. File: PROG080.ASM

```
;**********************************************************************
; Draw a box in upper left corner using BIOS function              *
; WRITE PIXEL                                                       *
;**********************************************************************

BIOS_Write_Pix  EQU     OCH

        PUBLIC  _BIOS_Pixel_Write

_BIOS_Pixel_Write PROC    NEAR

        ; We use CX as a pixel counter as well as pixel address
        ; and use DX as a raster counter as well as raster address

        MOV     DX,100                  ;Want to draw 100 rasters
Box_Raster_Loop:                        ;Loop over rasters
        MOV     CX,100                  ;Want to draw 100 pixels across
Box_Pixel_Loop:                         ;Loop over pixels within raster
        MOV     AL,1                    ;Set color to be 1
        MOV     AH,BIOS_Write_Pix       ;Function = WRITE PIXEL
        INT     10H                     ;Ask BIOS to write pixel

        DEC     CX                      ;Update column number
        JGE     Box_Pixel_Loop          ;If not last do it again
        DEC     DX                      ;Update row number
        JGE     Box_Raster_Loop         ;If not last row do it again
        RET
_BIOS_Pixel_Write ENDP
```

The next example contains three routines that can be used to modify single pixel in the display memory. Each routine uses different write method. The routine Pixel_Set uses the Set-Reset method, the routine Packed_Pixel_Write uses the Packed Pixel Write method, and Pixel_Write uses the Planar Write method (the three methods are described earlier, in the Theory section).

Listing 8-4. File: File: PROG081.ASM

```
;**************************************************************************
; Common definitions for the next five routines                        *
;**************************************************************************

GRAPHICS_CTL    EQU     3CEH            ;Address of Graphics controller
SEQUENCE_CTL    EQU     3C4H            ;Address the Sequencer

XSIZE   EQU     640                     ;Assume 640 pixels across
HBYTES  EQU     (XSIZE/8)               ;Compute bytes per raster
GRAPH_SEG       EQU     0A000H          ;Segment of display buffer


;**************************************************************************
; Set pixel at X,Y to color COLOR                                       *
; using SET-RESET method                                               *
;**************************************************************************

X               EQU     [BP+4]          ;Formal parameters on stack
Y               EQU     [BP+6]
COLOR           EQU     [BP+8]

        PUBLIC  _Pixel_Set

_Pixel_Set      PROC    NEAR
        PUSH    BP
        MOV     BP,SP
        PUSH    ES

        ; Convert x,y address into OFFSET:SEGMENT and get MASK

        MOV     BX,X                    ;Fetch X coordinate
        MOV     AX,Y                    ;Fetch Y coordinate
        CALL    Get_Address             ;Compute SEGMENT:OFFSET address
                                        ;in ES:BX, Mask in CL

        MOV     DX,GRAPHICS_CTL

        ; Enable set/reset and load value into reset register

        MOV     AL,00H                  ;Select SET/RESET register
        UUI     UX,AL
        INC     DX
        MOV     AL,COLOR                ;Fetch color passed on the stack
        OUT     DX,AL                   ;Set SET register to color
        DEC     DX
        MOV     AL,01H                  ;Select ENABLE RESET
        OUT     DX,AL
```

```
            INC     DX
            MOV     AL,0FH                  ;Enable all four planes for SET
            OUT     DX,AL
            DEC     DX

            ; Set mask register to preserve unused 7 bits in a byte

            MOV     AL,08H                  ;Select BIT MASK register
            OUT     DX,AL
            MOV     AL,CL                   ;Fetch mask returned earlier
            INC     DX                      ;and set MASK register to it
            OUT     DX,AL
            DEC     DX

            ; Set the pixel to new color

            MOV     AL,ES:[BX]              ;Must latch to preserve old bits
            MOV     ES:[BX],AL              ;Set pixel color to new value

            ; Restore SET/RESET and MASK registers

            MOV     AL,01H                  ;Select ENABLE RESET
            OUT     DX,AL
            INC     DX
            MOV     AL,00H                  ;Disable all four planes for SET
            OUT     DX,AL
            DEC     DX

            MOV     AL,08H                  ;Select BIT MASK register
            OUT     DX,AL
            MOV     AL,0FFH                 ;Enable all 8 bits for write
            INC     DX                      ;(default)
            OUT     DX,AL
            DEC     DX

            ; Restore segment registers and return

            POP     ES
            MOV     SP,BP
            POP     BP
            RET
_Pixel_Set      ENDP

;*********************************************************************
; Set pixel at X,Y to color COLOR                                   *
; using the PACKED PIXEL WRITE method                              *
;*********************************************************************

X               EQU     [BP+4]              ;Formal parameters on stack
Y               EQU     [BP+6]
COLOR           EQU     [BP+8]

        PUBLIC  _Pixel_Packed_Write

_Pixel_Packed_Write PROC    NEAR
        PUSH    BP
        MOV     BP,SP
```

```
        PUSH    ES

        ; Convert x,y address into OFFSET:SEGMENT and get MASK

        MOV     BX,X                    ;Fetch X coordinate
        MOV     AX,Y                    ;Fetch Y coordinate
        CALL    Get_Address             ;Compute SEGMENT:OFFSET address
                                        ;in ES:BX, Mask in CL

        MOV     DX,GRAPHICS_CTL

        ; Select write mode to be "PACKED PIXEL WRITE"

        MOV     AL,05H                  ;Select MODE register
        OUT     DX,AL
        INC     DX
        MOV     AL,02H                  ;Select write mode to be PACKED WRITE
        OUT     DX,AL
        DEC     DX

        ; Set mask register to preserve unused 7 bits in a byte

        MOV     AL,08H                  ;Select BIT MASK register
        OUT     DX,AL
        MOV     AL,CL                   ;Fetch mask returned earlier
        INC     DX                      ;and set MASK register to it
        OUT     DX,AL
        DEC     DX

        ; Set the pixel to new color

        MOV     AL,COLOR                ;Fetch color passed on the stack
        MOV     AH,ES:[BX]              ;Must read to preserve old bits
        MOV     ES:[BX],AL              ;Set pixel color to new value

        ; Restore MODE and MASK registers

        MOV     AL,05H                  ;Select MODE register
        OUT     DX,AL
        INC     DX
        MOV     AL,00H                  ;Select default write mode
        OUT     DX,AL
        DEC     DX

        MOV     AL,08H                  ;Select BIT MASK register
        OUT     DX,AL
        MOV     AL,0FFH                 ;Enable all 8 bits for write
        INC     DX                      ;(default)
        OUT     DX,AL
        DEC     DX

        ; Restore segment registers and return

        POP     ES
        MOV     SP,BP
        POP     BP
```

```
        RET
_Pixel_Packed_Write ENDP


;************************************************************************
; Set pixel at X,Y to color COLOR                                      *
; using the PLANAR PIXEL WRITE method                                  *
;************************************************************************

X               EQU     [BP+4]          ;Formal parameters on stack
Y               EQU     [BP+6]
COLOR           EQU     [BP+8]

        PUBLIC  _Pixel_Write

_Pixel_Write    PROC    NEAR
        PUSH    BP
        MOV     BP,SP
        PUSH    ES

        ; Convert x,y address into OFFSET:SEGMENT and get MASK

        MOV     BX,X            ;Fetch X coordinate
        MOV     AX,Y            ;Fetch Y coordinate
        CALL    Get_Address     ;Compute SEGMENT:OFFSET address
                                ;in ES:BX, Mask in CL

        ; Set mask register to preserve unused 7 bits in a byte

        MOV     DX,GRAPHICS_CTL
        MOV     AL,08H          ;Select BIT MASK register
        OUT     DX,AL
        MOV     AL,CL           ;Fetch mask returned earlier
        INC     DX              ;and set MASK register to it
        OUT     DX,AL
        DEC     DX

        ; Set MAP MASK register to enable all planes and set pixel to 0
        ; then set MAP MASK to enable planes coresponding to color

        MOV     DX,SEQUENCE_CTL
        MOV     AL,02           ;Select MAP MASK (PLANE SELECT) reg.
        OUT     DX,AL
        INC     DX
        MOV     AL,0FH          ;Enable all four planes for write
        OUT     DX,AL

        MOV     AH,ES:[BX]      ;Latch data to preserve unused bits
        XOR     AL,AL           ;Make sure that proper bit is CLEAR
        MOV     ES:[BX],AL      ;Clear all four planes

        MOV     AL,COLOR        ;Fetch color passed on the stack
        AND     AL,0FH          ;Clear unused bits (use first four)
        OUT     DX,AL           ;Enable planes as specified in color
        DEC     DX              ;(MAP MASK reg is still selected)
```

```
        ; Set the pixel to new color

        MOV     AL,0FFH                 ;Make sure that proper bit is ON
        MOV     ES:[BX],AL              ;Set pixel color to new value

        ; Restore MASK registers

        MOV     DX,GRAPHICS CTL
        MOV     AL,08H                  ;Select BIT MASK register
        OUT     DX,AL
        MOV     AL,0FFH                 ;Enable all 8 bits for write
        INC     DX                      ;(default)
        OUT     DX,AL

        MOV     DX,SEQUENCE_CTL
        MOV     AL,02                   ;Select MAP MASK (PLANE SELECT) reg
        OUT     DX,AL
        INC     DX
        MOV     AL,0FH                  ;Enable all four planes for write
        OUT     DX,AL

        ; Restore segment registers and return

        POP     ES
        MOV     SP,BP
        POP     BP
        RET
_Pixel_Write    ENDP


;*********************************************************************
; Compute SEGMENT:OFFSET pair from a given x,y address             *
; of a pixel.  We know that there is HBYTES bytes in each          *
; raster and that each byte  contains eight pixels.                *
; To find offset of pixel x,y we use the following formula         *
;                                                                  *
;       OFFSET = HBYTES * y + x/8                                  *
;                                                                  *
; To compute which bit within byte is to be changed we get        *
; (x mod 8) which is remainder when x is divided by 8.             *
; Which is same as keeping last three bits of x.  We use           *
; position within a byte to rotate value 80H so that the          *
; single bit matches the position in a byte.                      *
; Recall that bit 7 in a byte represents left most pixel.          *
; Thus MASK is computed as follows:                               *
;                                                                  *
;       MASK = ROTATE 80H TO THE RIGHT BY (X AND 7)               *
;                                                                  *
; Entry:        BX - X coordinate (pixel)                          *
;               AX - Y coordinate (raster)                         *
; Exit:         CL - Mask (x mod 8)                                *
;               BX - Absolute offset in display buffer             *
;*********************************************************************

Get_Address     PROC    NEAR

        ; Compute SEGMENT:OFFSET pair from x,y pair
```

```
        MOV     CX,HBYTES               ;Fetch bytes per raster
        MUL     CX                      ;Compute offset past y rasters
        MOV     CL,BL                   ;Keep copy of x for later
        SHR     BX,1                    ;Get offset within raster as x mod 8
        SHR     BX,1
        SHR     BX,1
        ADD     BX,AX                   ;Add offsets together and keep in BX
        MOV     AX,GRAPH_SEG            ;Fetch segment and copy it into ES
        MOV     ES,AX

      ; Compute MASK within byte from x coordinate

        AND     CL,07H                  ;Compute which bit in a byte
        MOV     AL,80H                  ;and use it to rotate mask into positio
        ROR     AL,CL
        MOV     CL,AL                   ;Keep mask in CL

        RET
Get_Address     ENDP
```

Read Pixel

Read a Single Pixel From Display Memory

Pascal Library Procedure

function Pixel_Read(x,y:integer):byte;

C Library Procedure

```
pixel_read(x,y)       /* Return value of the pixel at x,y               */
int    x;             /* Pixel x coordinate                            */
int    y;             /* Pixel y coordinate                            */
                      /* Returns: pixel at x,y, one bit per plane for planes 0-3 */
```

This procedure reads one pixel from display memory and returns a four-bit pixel, packed into a byte. Pixels are addressed by scan line and pixel number; pair (x,y) refers to pixel x on scan line y (see Figure 8-1).

Example

Listing 8-5. File: PROGC081.C

```
/****************************************************************************/
/* Read back ten pixels and print their values                             */
/****************************************************************************/


read_10_pixels()
        {
        int     x, y, color;
        printf("\nValues in raster 19 are: ");
        y = 19;                               /* 20th raster from top      */
        for (x = 0; x < 10; x++)              /* Loop over pixels          */
                {
                pixel_write(x, y, x);   /* Put in known value        */
                color = pixel_read(x,y);/* Read next value           */
                printf(" %2d", color);  /* Print value just read     */
                }
        }
```

Listing 8-6. File: PROGP081.PAS

```
{****************************************************************************}
{ Read back ten pixels and print their values                              }
{****************************************************************************}

procedure read_10_pixels;
const
MONO = 5;
VMONO = 7;
COLOR = 4;
ENHANCED = 3;
var
i,x,y,color : integer;
begin
        i := Get_Display_Type;
        if i = MONO then        Set_Mode($0F)
        else if i = VMONO then  Set_Mode($0F)
        else if i = COLOR then  Set_Mode($0E)
        else                    Set_Mode($10);

        writeln("Values in raster 19 are: ");
        y := 19;                         { 20th raster line from top  }
        for x := 0 to 9 do               { Loop over pixels           }
            begin
                Pixel_Set(x, y, x);      { Put in dummy value         }
                color := Pixel_Read(x,y);{ Read next value            }
                writeln(color);          { Print value just read      }
            end;
        i := integer(readkey);

        {- Set default text mode                                      }

        i := Get_Display_Type;
```

```
      if i = MONO then       Set_Mode(7)
      else if i = VMONO then Set_Mode(7)
      else                   Set_Mode(3);
end;
```

BIOS function 13 (Read Pixel) will return the value of a given pixel. This function is too slow, however, for practical use. Also, the BIOS Read Pixel function does not always properly set and restore the values of EGA control registers.

Theory

A single byte read from display memory accesses 32 bits of data (one byte per plane times four planes). Only one byte can be returned to the processor as read data. How this byte relates to the 32 bits of read data depends on the current read mode.

The simplest, and most common, read mode is a Single Plane Read. The byte is read from one designated plane and is returned as read data to the processor. The Read Plane Select Register of the Graphics Controller defines which plane will be read. The read data represents one bit of color information for eight pixels. To retrieve all four bits of color information for a specific pixel, four read and mask operations are required (one for each plane). This process is illustrated in Figure 8-3.

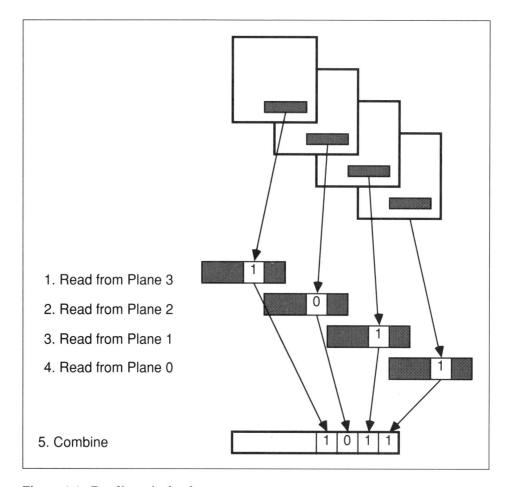

1. Read from Plane 3

2. Read from Plane 2

3. Read from Plane 1

4. Read from Plane 0

5. Combine

Figure 8-3. Reading pixel value.

Another read mode, called Color Compare Mode, will compare all four bits of color information for each pixel to a four bit reference color and return a one bit if a match occured. A single byte read operation returns true/false status for eight pixels tested for a color match. This mode is used for searching for a specified color in display memory. The Color Compare Register of the Graphics Controller is loaded with the four bit color value to search for. This mode is not useful for reading pixels.

To learn more about read plane select and read modes, alse see registers Read Plane Select (4), Mode Select (5), and Color Compare (2) of Graphics controller in Chapter 3.

Assembly Code Examples

Listing 8-7. File: PROG082.ASM

```
;**********************************************************************
; Read value of the pixel at 100,50 and return value in AX         *
; Use BIOS function READ PIXEL to get the value.                   *
;**********************************************************************

X               EQU     [BP+4]          ;Formal parameters on stack
Y               EQU     [BP+6]

        PUBLIC  _BIOS_Pixel_Read

_BIOS_Pixel_Read PROC    NEAR
        PUSH    BP
        MOV     BP,SP
        MOV     CX,X            ;Load pixel (column)
        MOV     DX,Y            ;Load raster (row)
        MOV     AH,0DH          ;Function = READ PIXEL
        INT     10H             ;Ask BIOS to read the pixel
        XOR     AH,AH           ;Clear upper bits of AX (since value in
        POP     BP
        RET
_BIOS_Pixel_Read ENDP
```

Listing 8-8. File: PROG083.ASM

```
;**********************************************************************
; Parameter and constant definitions                               *
;**********************************************************************

GRAPHICS_CTL    EQU     3CEH            ;Address of Graphics controller
SEQUENCE_CTL    EQU     3C4H            ;Address the Sequencer

XSIZE   EQU     640                     ;Assume 640 pixels across
HBYTES  EQU     (XSIZE/8)               ;Compute bytes per raster
GRAPH_SEG       EQU     0A000H          ;Segment of display buffer


;**********************************************************************
; Read value of the pixel at x,y and return value in AX            *
;**********************************************************************

X               EQU     [BP+4]          ;Formal parameters on stack
Y               EQU     [BP+6]

        PUBLIC  _Pixel_Read

_Pixel_Read     PROC    NEAR
        PUSH    BP
        MOV     BP,SP
        PUSH    ES
        PUSH    SI

        ; Convert x,y address into OFFSET:SEGMENT and get MASK
```

```
        MOV     BX,X                    ;Fetch X coordinate
        MOV     AX,Y                    ;Fetch Y coordinate
        CALL    Get_Address             ;Compute SEGMENT:OFFSET address
                                        ;in ES:BX, Mask in CL

        ; Set MAP MASK register to read next plane and read next plane

        MOV     DX,GRAPHICS_CTL
        MOV     AL,04H                  ;Select MAP MASK register
        OUT     DX,AL
        INC     DX

        MOV     SI,BX                   ;Copy offset into register SI
        XOR     BH,BH                   ;Clear color
        MOV     BL,CL                   ;Copy mask into register CL
        MOV     CX,4                    ;Initialize loop counter
Read_Plane_Loop:
        SHL     BH,1
        MOV     AL,CL                   ;Select next plane for read
        DEC     AL
        OUT     DX,AL

        MOV     AH,ES:[SI]              ;Fetch values for 8 pixels in plane 0
        AND     AH,BL                   ;Mask of the bit for our pixel (mask in
        JZ      Zero_Value              ;Put 0 into next color bit
        OR      BH,1                    ;Put 1 into next color bit
Zero_Value:
        LOOP    Read_Plane_Loop

        MOV     AL,BH                   ;Put result into AX
        XOR     AH,AH

        ; Restore segment registers and return

        POP     SI
        POP     ES                      ;Restore registers
        MOV     SP,BP
        POP     BP
        RET
_Pixel_Read     ENDP
```

Scan Line Fill

Fill Section of a Scan Line

Pascal Library Procedure

procedure Scanline(start,stop,scanline,color:integer);
              {start pixel, end pixel,scan line,color}

C Library Procedure

```
scanline(x_start,x_end,y,color)      /* Fill section of scan line with color */
int    x_start, x_end;               /* Starting and ending pixel          */
int    y;                            /* scan line                          */
int    color;                        /* Color to be used                   */
```

Theory

This procedure fills all pixels between two points on the same scan line. This type of operation represents the heart of most "fill" algorithms. In a typical polygon fill algorithm, for every scan line the intersection of each edge of the polygon with the scan line is computed. The sections between consecutive intersections are then filled with the color of the polygon.

The following example will fill the triangle whose vertices lie at (10, 10), (0, 20), and (30, 20). Note that this triangle has one edge parallel to a scan line. We have taken advantage of this fact, and this example code cannot be used for the general case of any triangle. Any triangle can be reduced, however, to two triangles of this type (see Figure 8-4). At the end of the C programming example is a routine to divide a general triangle into two base triangles and to fill each.

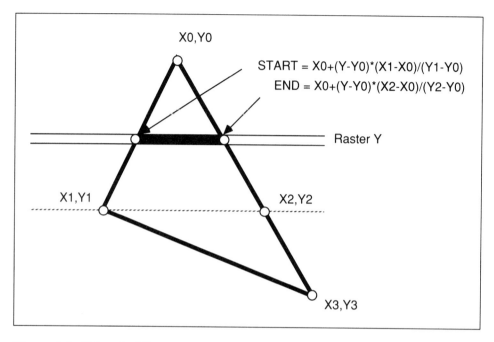

Figure 8-4. Triangle fill.

A triangle, being composed of straight lines, has sides of constant slope. By using the slope of each side, the intersection points can be calculated for each scan line.

For the vertices of the triangle $(x0,y0)$, $(x1,y1)$, and $(x2,y2)$ ordered as in Figure 8-4, an arbitrary point (x,y) located on the left edge of the triangle must satisfy the following equations:

$$(x - x0)/(y - y0) = (x1 - x0)/(y1 - y0)$$

And a point (x,y) on the right edge of the triangle must satisfy a similar algebraic equation:

$$(x - x0)/(y - y0) = (x2 - x0)/(y2 - y0)$$

For a given scan line y, the intersection points of the triangle can be calculated from these formulas, then used as inputs to the Scan Line Fill procedure:

```
y      = y
x_start = x0 + ((y - y0) * (x1 - x0))/(y1 - y0)
x_end  = x0 + ((y - y0) * (x2 - x0))/(y2 - y0)
```

Listing 8-9. File: PROGC082.C

```
/***********************************************************************/
/* Fill a base triangle using scan-line function                     */
/* and then fill a general triangle (using triangle fill routine)    */
/***********************************************************************/


fill_triag()
       {

       /* Fill a base line triangle                                  */

       int    x0 = 100,x1 = 0, x2 = 300, y0 = 10, y1 = 100, y2 = 100;
       int    y, color = 15, start, end;
       for (y = y0; y <= y1; y++)        /* Loop over raster lines    */
              {                          /* Compute intercepts        */
              start = x0 + ((y - y0)*(x1 - x0))/(y1 - y0);
              end   = x0 + ((y - y0)*(x2 - x0))/(y2 - y0);
              scanline(start,end,y,color);   /* Fill next section     */
              }

       /* Fill a general triangle                                    */

       triangle(400,100, 500,0, 630,200, color);
       }

/***********************************************************************/
/*                                                                   */
/*  triangle(x0,y0,x1,y1,x2,y2,color) - Fill a general triangle with */
/*          color "color".  This routine will call the scanline      */
/*          procedure to fill scanlines between two edges of the     */
/*          triangle.                                                */
/*                                                                   */
/*          First vertices are ordered so that vertex "a" is the     */
/*          left most top vertex, and "b" is the left most bottom    */
/*          vertex.  Triangle is than split into two "baseline"      */
/*          triangles, and each triangle is filled separately.       */
/*          One triangle is an upward pointing arrow and the second  */
/*          Triangle is a downward pointing arrow.                   */
/*                                                                   */
/***********************************************************************/

triangle(x0,y0, x1,y1, x2,y2, color)
int    x0,y0, x1,y1, x2,y2,color;
       {
       int    x[4],y[4],a,b,c,temp;
       x[0] = x0;
       x[1] = x1;
       x[2] = x2;
       y[0] = y0;
       y[1] = y1;
       y[2] = y2;

       /* Order the vertices */
       a = 0;                                   /* Get lowest left in a */
       if (y[0] > y[1]) a = 1;
       if (y[a] > y[2]) a = 2;
```

```
            b = (a+1)%3;
            c = (b+1)%3;
            if (y[a] == y[b] && x[a] > x[b]) a = b;
            if (y[a] == y[c] && x[a] > x[c]) a = c;
            b = (a+1)%3;
            c = (b+1)%3;
            if (y[b] < y[c])                           /* Get highest left in b*/
                  {
                  temp = b;
                  b = c;
                  c = temp;
                  }
            if (y[b] == y[c] && x[b] > x[c])
                  {
                  temp = b;
                  b = c;
                  c = temp;
                  }
            /* fill 'base' triangles */
            if (y[a] == y[b])                          /* Fill degenerates     */
                  {
                  scanline(x[a],x[b],y[b],color);
                  scanline(x[a],x[c],y[c],color);
                  }
            else if (y[a] == y[c])               /* Fill down arrow     */
                  fill_dw(x[a],y[a],x[b],y[b],x[c],y[c],x[b],y[b],y[c],color);
            else if (y[b] == y[c])               /* Fill up arrow       */
                  fill_up(x[a],y[a],x[b],y[b],x[a],y[a],x[c],y[c],y[c],color);
            else
                  {                              /* Split into two bases */
                  y[3] = y[c];                   /* one up and one down  */
                  x[3] = x[a] + ((y[3] - y[a])*(long int)(x[b] - x[a]))/(y[b] -
y[a]);

                  if (x[3] < x[c])               /* 'c' is to the right  */
                      {
                      fill_up(x[a],y[a],x[b],y[b],x[a],y[a],x[c],y[c],y[c],color);
                      fill_dw(x[a],y[a],x[b],y[b],x[c],y[c],x[b],y[b],y[c],color);
                      }
                  else                           /* 'c' is to the left   */
                      {
                      fill_up(x[a],y[a],x[c],y[c],x[a],y[a],x[b],y[b],y[c],color);
                      fill_dw(x[c],y[c],x[b],y[b],x[a],y[a],x[b],y[b],y[c],color);
                      }
                  }
            }

fill_up(ax,ay, bx,by, cx,cy, dx,dy,y0,color)      /* Fill up arrow        */
int     ax,ay,bx,by,cx,cy,dx,dy,y0,color;
        {
        int     dyab,dycd,y,d1,d2;
        dycd = dy - cy;
        dyab = by - ay;
        for (y = ay; y <= y0; y++)
                {
                d1 = ((y - ay)*(long)(bx - ax))/dyab;
                d2 = ((y - cy)*(long)(dx - cx))/dycd;
                scanline(ax+d1, cx+d2, y,color);
                }
```

```
                }
            }
fill_dw(ax,ay, bx,by, cx,cy, dx,dy,y0,color)      /* Fill down arrow      */
int     ax,ay,bx,by,cx,cy,dx,dy,y0,color;
        {
        int     dyab,dycd,y,d1,d2;
        dycd = dy - cy;
        dyab = by - ay;
        for (y = dy; y >= y0; y-)
                {
                d1 = ((y - ay)*(long)(bx - ax))/dyab;
                d2 = ((y - cy)*(long)(dx - cx))/dycd;
                scanline(ax+d1, cx+d2, y, color);
                }
        }
```

Listing 8-10. File: PROGP082.PAS

```
{*********************************************************************}
{ Fill a triangle using scan-line function                          }
{*********************************************************************}

procedure fill_triag;
const
x0 = 100;
x1 = 0;
x2 = 300;
y0 = 10;
y1 = 100;
y2 = 100;
line_color = 15;
const
MONO = 5;
VMONO = 7;
COLOR = 4;
ENHANCED = 3;
var
i,y,line_start,line_end : integer;
begin
        Clear_Screen;
        i := Get_Display_Type;
        if i = MONO then        Set_Mode($0F)
        else if i = VMONO then  Set_Mode($0F)
        else if i = COLOR then  Set_Mode($0E)
        else                    Set_Mode($10);

        for y := y0 to y1 do              { Loop over raster lines        }
            begin                         { Compute intercepts            }
                line_start := x0 + ((y - y0)*(x1 - x0)) div (y1 - y0);
                line_end   := x0 + ((y - y0)*(x2 - x0)) div (y2 - y0);
                Scanline(line_start,line_end,y,line_color); {Fill section}
            end;
        y := integer(readkey);

        {- Set default text mode                                    }
```

```
        i := Get_Display_Type;
        if i = MONO then        Set_Mode(7)
        else if i = VMONO then  Set_Mode(7)
        else                    Set_Mode(3);
end;
```

One approach for an implementation of scan line fill would be to call the Write Pixel procedure for every pixel. This would work but would be too slow to be practical. A more intelligent approach is to write eight pixels in each write operation. In general, the first few and last few pixels to be filled do not use a full byte and require special attention. In between, pixels can be written eight at a time.

For example, section {12,42} (a section starting at pixel 12 and ending at pixel 42) can be broken into three parts:

1.   Four pixels at the start (pixels 12, 13, 14, and 15).

2.   Three bytes of aligned pixels (pixels 16–23, 24–31, and 32–39).

3.   Three pixels at the end (pixels 40, 41, and 42).

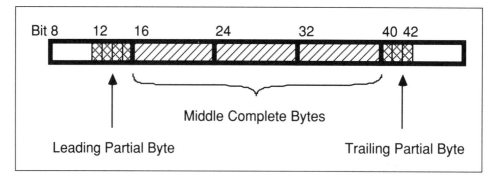

Figure 8-5. Scan Line fill.

Only five write operations are required for the fill (versus 21 calls to the Write Pixel procedure). To perform the fill the following sequence is used:

1.   Load Set/Reset register with the fill color, and enable Set/Reset.

2.   Compute a mask for the first four pixels and set Mask register.

3.   Write to the byte containing the first section of pixels.

4.   Set Mask register to enable writing of all 8 bits.

5.   Write the three middle bytes.

6. Compute a mask for the last three pixels and set Mask register.

7. Write to the byte containing the last section of pixels.

8. Restore Set/Reset Enable and Mask registers to default values.

Note that steps 3 and 7 first require a memory read (to fill the EGA read latches) before writing the partial bytes, otherwise the Mask register will not operate properly.

Assembly Code Example

The following example shows an implementation of the fill algorithm described above.

Listing 8-11. File: PROG084.ASM

```
;***************************************************************
;                                                            *
;   Scanline(start, end, raster, color):draw line from (start,y) to  *
;        (end,y) with a color 'color'.                       *
;   Entry :sp + 2 = Start                                    *
;          sp + 4 = Stop                                     *
;          sp + 6 = y                                        *
;          sp + 8 = color                                    *
;          ....                                              *
;                                                            *
;***************************************************************

XSIZE   EQU     640
HBYTES  EQU     (XSIZE/8)
GRFSEG  EQU     0A000H

Start   EQU     [BP+4]
Stop    EQU     [BP+6]
Raster  EQU     [BP+8]
Color   EQU     [BP+10]

        PUBLIC  _ScanLine

_ScanLine       PROC NEAR
        PUSH    BP
        MOV     BP,SP

        PUSH    DI                      ;Preserve segment registers
        PUSH    SI
        PUSH    DS
        PUSH    ES

        ;- Load SET/RESET registers with current color

        MOV     DX,03CEh                ; move color into reset register
        XOR     AL,AL
```

```
        OUT     DX,AL
        INC     DX
        MOV     AL,Color
        OUT     DX,AL
        DEC     DX                      ; enable use of reset register
        MOV     AL,1
        OUT     DX,AL
        INC     DX
        MOV     AL,0Fh
        OUT     DX,AL
        MOV     DX,03C4h                ; enable all four planes for writing
        MOV     AL,2
        OUT     DX,AL
        INC     DX
        MOV     AL,0Fh
        OUT     DX,al

        ;- COMPUTE ADDRESS AND MASK FOR FIRST PIXEL -----
SL_Address:
        ;- Convert (x,y) to absolute address in display buffer

        MOV     AX,Raster               ;Compute offset as 80*y+x/8
        MOV     BX,HBYTES
        MUL     BX
        MOV     DI,Start                ; + x/8
        MOV     CL,3
        SHR     DI,CL
        ADD     DI,AX

        MOV     DX,GRFSEG               ;Point DS and ES into display buffer
        MOV     DS,DX
        MOV     ES,DX

        MOV     CX,Stop                 ;Compute dx
        SUB     CX,Start

        ;- Compute bit mask for the leading partial byte

        MOV     AX,Start                ;Fetch x0
        AND     AX,07H                  ;Check if there is leading partial byte
        JZ      SL_Complete             ;...No, bypass this step
        MOV     BX,0FFH                 ;Compute mask for the first byte by
        PUSH    CX                      ;shifting FF pattern to the right
        MOV     CX,AX                   ;until only partial leading bits are
        SHR     BX,CL                   ;on
        POP     CX
        ADD     CX,AX                   ;Update counter of bits completed
        SUB     CX,8
        JGE     SL_SetMask              ;Modify mask if only one byte
        NEG     CX
        SHR     BX,CL
        SHL     BX,CL
        XOR     CX,CX                   ; restore counter
SL_SetMask:
        MOV     DX,3CEH                 ;Set mask by loading BIT MASK
        MOV     AL,08h                  ;register in the GRAPHICS controller
        OUT     DX,AL
```

```
        INC     DX
        MOV     AL,BL
        OUT     DX,AL

        ;- Draw pixels from the leading partial byte

        MOV     AL,[DI]                 ;Latch data
        STOSB                           ;Write new data

        ;- Draw pixels from the middle complete bytes

SL_Complete:                            ; check if any bytes to set
        MOV     BX,CX                   ;Check if there is more than 7 bits
        CMP     CX,8                    ;left to draw
        JL      SL_Trailing             ;... If not, skip this part

        SHR     CX,1                    ;Divide bits by 8 to get byte count
        SHR     CX,1
        SHR     CX,1
        MOV     DX,03CEH                ; Enable all 8 bits for write
        MOV     AL,08h                  ; by writing to BIT MASK register in
        OUT     DX,AL                   ; the SEQUENCER
        INC     DX
        MOV     AL,0FFH
        OUT     DX,AL

        REP     STOSB                   ;Write new data

        ;- Compute mask for the trailing partial byte

SL_Trailing:
        AND     BX,07H                  ;Check if there are any bits left to do
        JZ      SL_Done                 ;...No, quit
        MOV     AX,0FFFFH               ;...Yes, compute mask by shifting FFFF
        MOV     CX,BX                   ;by number of bits to be drawn
        SHR     AX,CL
        XOR     AH,0FFH
        MOV     DX,03CEH                ;Set BIT MASK register in GRAPHICS
        MOV     AL,08h                  ;controller to the mask
        OUT     DX,AL
        INC     DX
        MOV     AL,AH
        OUT     DX,AL

        ;- Draw pixels from the trailing partial byte

        MOV     AL,[DI]                 ;Latch data
        STOSB                           ;Write new data

        ;- Restore PLANE ENABLE and BIT MASK registers
SL_Done:
        MOV     DX,03CEh                ; Enable all 8-bits in a byte for write
        MOV     AL,08h                  ; by setting BIT MASK register to Fhex
        OUT     DX,AL
        INC     DX
        MOV     AL,0FFh
        OUT     DX,AL
```

```
        DEC     DX                      ; Disable SET/RESET function
        MOV     AL,1
        OUT     DX,AL
        INC     DX
        XOR     AX,AX
        OUT     DX,AL

        POP     ES                      ;Restore segment registers
        POP     DS
        POP     SI
        POP     DI
        MOV     SP,BP
        POP     BP
        RET
_ScanLine       ENDP
```

Solid Rectangular Fill

Fill a Rectangle with a Color

Pascal Library Procedure

procedure Solid_Box(x0,y0,x1,y1,color:integer);
        {x0,y0 = upper left corner; x1,y1 = lower right corner; color=color}

C Library Procedure

```
solid_box(x0,y0,x1,y1,color)    /* fill a rectangle        */
int    x0, y0;                  /* Upper left corner       */
int    x1, y1;                  /* Lower right corner      */
int    color;                   /* Color of the box        */
```

Theory

This procedure fills a rectangle with a solid color. A common use for this routine is to clear a region of the screen to a desired background color. The rectangle is defined by its upper left corner (x,y) and by its width and height (dx,dy).

In the following example a 640 x 350 rectangle is used to clear the screen, then 16 rectangles are displayed, each in a different color. The sixteen boxes will be arranged in four rows, with four boxes in each row. To ensure that the boxes can fit onto a standard Color Display (as well as Enhanced Color and Monochrome displays), only 200 lines of the screen are used.

Listing 8-12. File: PROGC083.C

```
/**********************************************************************/
/* Clear screen and then draw 16 boxes                               */
/**********************************************************************/

solid_box16()
        {
        int     i, j, x, y, color;
        solid_box(0,0,640,350,0);                   /* Clear screen      */
        for (j = 0; j < 4; j++)                     /* Loop over rows of b's*/
                for (i = 0; i < 4; i++)             /* Loop over columns   */
                        {
                        y     = j * 200/4;          /* Draw the box        */
                        x     = i * 640/4;
                        color = i + j * 4;
                        solid_box(x, y, x + 640/4, y + 200/4, color);
                        }
        }
```

Listing 8-13. File: PROGP083.PAS

```
{**********************************************************************}
{ Clear screen and then draw 16 boxes                                 }
{**********************************************************************}

procedure solid_box16;
const
MONO = 5;
COLOR = 4;
VMONO = 7;
var
i, j, x, y, box_color : integer;
begin
        Clear_Screen;
        i := Get_Display_Type;
        if i = MONO then        Set_Mode($0F)
        else if i = VMONO then Set_Mode($0F)
        else if i = COLOR then Set_Mode($0E)
        else                    Set_Mode($10);

        Solid_Box(0,0,640,350,0);                   { Clear screen  }
        for j := 0 to 3 do                          { Loop over rows of b's}
            begin
                for i := 0 to 3 do                  { Loop over columns     }
                    begin
                        y := j * 200 div 4;         { Draw the box  }
                        x := i * 640 div 4;
                        box_color := i + j * 4;
                        Solid_Box(x,y,x + 640 div 4,y + 200 div 4,box_color);
                    end;
            end;
        i := integer(readkey);

        {- Set default text mode                                        }
```

```
        i := Get_Display_Type;
        if i = MONO then        Set_Mode(7)
        else if i = VMONO then Set_Mode(7)
        else                    Set_Mode(3);
end;
```

The simplest way to implement the solid rectangle procedure is to repetitively call the Scan Line Fill procedure described previously. The resulting procedure operates quite efficiently:

Listing 8-14. File: PROGC084.C

```
/********************************************************************/
/* C implementation of a box draw algoritm using scanline          */
/********************************************************************/

slow_solid_box(x, y, dx, dy, color)
        {
        int i;
        cls();
        for (i = 0; i < dy; i++)
                scanline(x, x + dx - 1, y + i, color);
        }
```

An improvement can be made by dividing the box into three vertical strips to separate the nonbyte-aligned edges from the byte-aligned middle (similar to the division that was done inside the Scan Line Fill procedure). The left strip contains all leading partial bytes, the middle strip contains all the full bytes, and the right strip contains all the trailing partial bytes (see Figure 8-6). For example box (x=3,y=5,dx=14,dy=18) would be divided into strips (3-7), (8-15), and (16-16). If each strip is drawn separately, the Mask register does not have to be reloaded as frequently and a starting pixel does not have to be recomputed for each scan line.

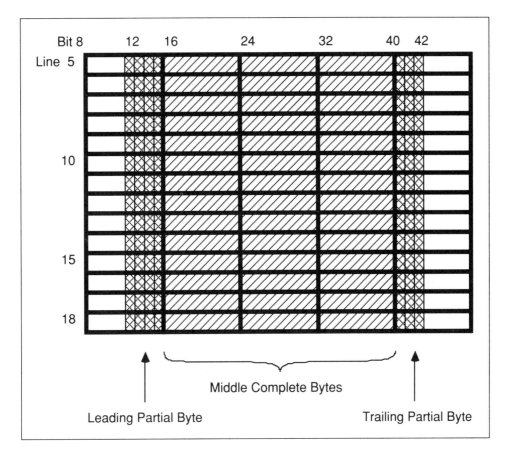

Figure 8-6. Solid rectangle fill.

Assembly Code Example

Listing 8-16. File: PROG085.ASM

```
;*****************************************************************
; solid_box(x0,y0,x1,y1,color)   fill a rectangle defined by    *
;           upper-left "x0,y0", and lower-right "x1,y1"          *
;           with the specified color "Color".                    *
;           Each pixel on the display corresponds to one bit in memory.  *
;           Thus one byte represents 8 different pixles.          *
;           A rectangle, in general, will consist of three vertical  *
;           strips. The middle strip will be composed entirely from pixels  *
;           forming a complete byte. The left strip has pixels only in  *
;           last few bits of a byte, and right strip only in first few bits.*
;           This routine will draw each strip in a separate loop.  *
;*****************************************************************

x0      EQU     [BP+4]
y0      EQU     [BP+6]
x1      EQU     [BP+8]
y1      EQU     [BP+10]
Color   EQU     [BP+12]

        PUBLIC  _Solid_Box

_Solid_Box      PROC NEAR
        PUSH    BP
        MOV     BP,SP
        PUSH    DI                      ;Preserve segment registers
        PUSH    SI
        PUSH    DS
        PUSH    ES

        ;- Rearrange corners so that x0<x1 and y0<y1

        MOV     AX,X1                   ; make x0 < x1
        MOV     BX,X0
        CMP     AX,BX
        JGE     xfine
        MOV     X0,AX
        MOV     X1,BX
xfine:  MOV     AX,Y1                   ; make y0 < y1
        MOV     BX,Y0
        CMP     AX,BX
        JGE     yfine
        MOV     Y0,AX
        MOV     Y1,BX
yfine:

        ;- COMPUTE ADDRESS AND MASK FOR FIRST PIXEL ------

        MOV     cl,4                    ; offset = 80 * y + x/8
        MOV     AX,Y0
        SHL     AX,CL
        MOV     BX,AX
        SHL     AX,1
        SHL     AX,1
```

```
        ADD     AX,BX
        MOV     BX,X0                   ; + x/8
        MOV     CL,3
        SHR     BX,CL
        ADD     AX,BX
        MOV     DI,AX                   ; save offset in register di

        ;- Load SET/RESET registers with current color

        MOV     DX,03CEh                ; move color into reset register
        XOR     AL,AL
        OUT     DX,AL
        INC     DX
        MOV     AL,Color
        OUT     DX,AL
        DEC     DX                      ; enable use of reset register
        MOV     AL,1
        OUT     DX,AL
        INC     DX
        MOV     AL,0Fh
        OUT     DX,AL
        MOV     DX,03C4h                ; enable all four planes for writing
        MOV     AL,2
        OUT     DX,AL
        INC     DX
        MOV     AL,0Fh
        OUT     DX,al

        ;-      load segment register

        MOV     DX,0A000h
        MOV     ES,DX
        MOV     DX,DX

;--------- FILL LEADING PARTIAL BYTES ------------
; in this section first strip of the rectangle is drawn

        MOV     CX,X0                   ; check for partial leading byte by
        AND     CX,07h                  ; checking that x0 is not a multiple
        JZ      endlead                 ; of 8

        MOV     AX,X0                   ; update x0 to start in the middle strip
        SUB     AX,CX
        ADD     AX,8
        MOV     X0,AX                   ;...and save it for later

        MOV     BX,0FFh                 ; compute the mask (bits to change)
        SHR     BX,CL

        SUB     AX,X1                   ; check if whole rectangle is in
        DEC     AX                      ; this byte
        JLE     bitmask                 ; modify mask if it is the only byte
        MOV     CX,AX
        SHR     BX,CL
        SHL     BX,CL

bitmask:MOV     DX,03CEh                ; set the mask in EGA control registers
```

```
          MOV      AL,08h
          OUT      DX,AL
          INC      DX
          MOV      AL,BL
          OUT      DX,AL
                                          ; Loop to fill the whole strip
          MOV      CX,Y1                   ; set counter over rasters
          SUB      CX,Y0
          INC      CX
          MOV      BX,80                   ; byte in next raster is 80 bytes
                                          ; further
          PUSH     DI
looplead:
          MOV      AH,[DI]                 ; latch data(preserve unused bits in a
                                          ; byte)
          MOV      [DI],AL                 ; write new data(mask register will do
                                          ; right bits)
          ADD      DI,BX                   ; address of byte in next raster
          LOOP     looplead

          POP      DI
          INC      DI                      ; address next to first byte in this
                                          ; strip
endlead:
;————— FILL FULL BYTES —————
; in this section the strip containing  full bytes is drawn

          MOV      CX,X1                   ; check if any more to do
          SUB      CX,X0
          JL       endtrail
          INC      CX                      ; check if any full bytes
          CMP      CX,8
          JL       endfull

          MOV      BX,Y1                   ; set counter of rasters to fill
          SUB      BX,Y0
          INC      BX

          SHR      CX,1                    ;Converts bits fill into bytes to fill
          SHR      CX,1
          SHR      CX,1

          MOV      DX,03CEh                ; set the mask in EGA control registers
          MOV      AL,08h
          OUT      DX,AL
          INC      DX
          MOV      AL,0FFH
          OUT      DX,AL

          MOV      DX,80                   ; byte in next raster is 80 bytes
                                          ; further
          PUSH     DI
loopfull:
          PUSH     CX                      ; loop over rasters
          PUSH     DI

          REP      STOSB                   ; set all full bytes in the same raster
```

```
            POP     DI                      ; address of first byte in next raster
            ADD     DI,DX
            POP     CX                      ; restore counter of bytes in a raster
            DEC     BX                      ; check if more rasters to do
            JG      loopfull

            POP     DI                      ; address of byte next to last one
            ADD     DI,CX                   ; in this strip
endfull:
;--------- FILL TRAILING PARTIAL BYTES -----------

            MOV     CX,X1                   ; check for trailing partial byte
            INC     CX
            AND     CX,07h
            JZ      endtrail

            MOV     AX,00FFh                ; compute mask
            ROR     AX,CL


            MOV     DX,03CEh                ; set the mask
            MOV     AL,08h
            OUT     DX,AL
            INC     DX
            MOV     AL,AH
            OUT     DX,AL

            MOV     CX,Y1                   ; set counters
            SUB     CX,Y0
            INC     CX
            MOV     BX,80
looptrail:
            MOV     AL,[DI]                 ; latch data (to preserve other bits)
            MOV     [DI],AL                 ; set new data
            ADD     DI,BX
            LOOP    looptrail

            ;- Restore PLANE ENABLE and BIT MASK registers
endtrail:
            MOV     DX,03CEh                ; Enable all 8-bits in a byte for write
            MOV     AL,08h                  ; by setting BIT MASK register to Fhex
            OUT     DX,AL
            INC     DX
            MOV     AL,0FFh
            OUT     DX,AL

            DEC     DX                      ; Disable SET/RESET function
            MOV     AL,1
            OUT     DX,AL
            INC     DX
            XOR     AX,AX
            OUT     DX,AL

;------- CLEAN UP AND EXIT ---------------------

            POP     ES
            POP     DS
```

```
        POP     SI
        POP     DI
        MOV     SP,BP
        POP     BP
        RET
_Solid_Box      ENDP
```

Draw Line

Draw a Solid Straight Line Between Two Points

Pascal Library Procedure

procedure Line(x0,y0,x1,y1,color:integer);
         {x0,y0 = start; x1,y1 = end; color = color}

C Library Procedure

```
line(x0,y0,x1,y1,color)         /* Draw a solid line       */
int   x0,y0;                    /* Starting point          */
int   x1,y1;                    /* Ending point            */
int   color;                    /* Color of the line       */
```

Example

Listing 8-17. File: PROGC085.C

```
/***********************************************************************/
/* Draw a set of radial lines from center of the screen to the outside  */
/***********************************************************************/

radial_lines()
        {
        int     i;
        clear_screen();
        for (i = 0; i < 640; i += 20) line(320,100,i,  0,i/20);
        for (i = 0; i < 640; i += 20) line(320,100,i,199,i/20);
        for (i = 0; i < 200; i += 10) line(320,100,0,  i,i/10);
        for (i = 0; i < 200; i += 10) line(320,100,639,i,i/10);
        }
```

```
{**********************************************************************}
{ Draw a set of radial lines from center of the screen to the outside  }
{**********************************************************************}

procedure radial_lines;
const
MONO = 5;
COLOR = 4;
VMONO = 7;
var
i : integer;
begin
        Clear_Screen;
        i := Get_Display_Type;
        if i = MONO then        Set_Mode($0F)
        else if i = VMONO then Set_Mode($0F)
        else if i = COLOR then Set_Mode($0E)
        else                    Set_Mode($10);

        for i := 0 to 31 do Line(320,100,20*i,0,i);
        for i := 0 to 31 do Line(320,100,20*i,199,i);
        for i := 0 to 19 do Line(320,100,0,10*i,i);
        for i := 0 to 19 do Line(320,100,639,10*i,i);

        i := integer(readkey);

        {- Set default text mode                                       }

        i := Get_Display_Type;
        if i = MONO then        Set_Mode(7)
        else if i = VMONO then Set_Mode(7)
        else                    Set_Mode(3);
end;
```

Theory

The easiest way to draw a line in Figure 8-7 is simply to calculate pixel positions using the algebraic equation for a line defined by two end points (x0,y0), (x1,y1):

$$(x - x1)/(y - y1) = (x0 - x1)/(y0 - y1)$$

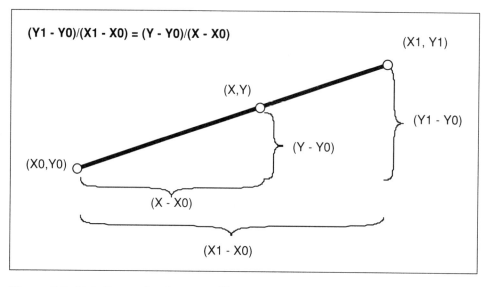

Figure 8-7. Relations of points on a line.

Depending on the end points of the line (x0,y0) and (x1,y1), one of the following four methods can be used to compute points along the line:

1) If x0 = x1 and y0 = y1, draw a single pixel at x0,y0.
2) If y0 = y1 but x0 <> x1, then for each x from x0 to x1, draw pixel at (x,y0)
3) If y0 <> y1 but x0 = x1, then for each y from y0 to y1, draw pixel at (x0,y)
4) If x0 <> x1 and y0 <> y1, compare their differences:

If abs(x0 - x1) >= abs(y0 - y1), then for each x from x0 to x1,
compute y = y0 + ((x - x0) * (y1 - y0))/(x1 - x0)
draw pixel at (x,y)

If abs(x0 - x1) < abs(y0 - y1), then for each y from y0 to y1,
compute x = x0 + ((y - y0) * (x1 - x0))/(y1 - y0)
draw pixel at (x,y)

This approach, though simple, requires many multiplications and divisions making it slow and cumbersome. If this technique is used, 32 bit multiplication should be used, and multiplication should be performed before division to assure sufficient precision.

In C language the implementation would look like this:

Listing 8-19. File: PROGC086.C

```
/*****************************************************************/
/* Drawing line with brute force algorithm                      */
/*****************************************************************/

slow_line(x0, y0, x1, y1, color)
int     x0, y0, x1, y1, color;
        {
        int   x, y;

        /*- Draw degenerate line (pixel)                        */

        if (x0 == x1 && y0 == y1)          /* Draw a single pixel */
             pixel_write(x0, y0, color);

        /*- Draw lines with dx > dy                             */

        else if (abs(x1 - x0) >= abs(y1 - y0))
                    {                                          /* Swap end point      */
             if (x1 < x0)
                    {
                    x = x1;
                    y = y1;
                    x1 = x0;
                    y1 = y0;
                    x0 = x;
                    y0 = y;
                    }
             for (x = x0; x <= x1; x++)     /* Loop over x coord    */
                    {                        /* Compute y using x    */
                    y = y0 + ((x - x0)*(long)(y1 - y0))/(x1 - x0);
                    pixel_write(x,y,color);   /* Draw next point     */
                    }
                    }

        /*- Draw lines with dy > dx                             */

        else
                    {
             if (y1 < y0)                    /* Swap end points     */
                    {
                    x = x1;
                    y = y1;
                    x1 = x0;
                    y1 = y0;
                    x0 = x;
                    y0 = y;
                    }
             for (y = y0; y <= y1; y++)      /* Loop over y coord    */
                    {                        /* Compute x using y    */
                    x = x0 + ((y - y0)*(long)(x1 - x0))/(y1 - y0);
```

```
                pixel_write(x,y,color);      /* Draw next point      */
                }
            }
        }
```

The same algorithm in Pascal looks like this:

Listing 8-20. File: PROGP086.PAS

```
{**********************************************************************}
{ Drawing line with brute force algorithm                            }
{**********************************************************************}

procedure Slow_Line(x0, y0, x1, y1, color:integer);
var
i,x,y : integer;
l : longint;
begin
        {- Draw degenerate line (pixel)                              }

        if (x0 = x1) and (y0 = y1) then
                Pixel_Set(x0,y0,color)

        {- Draw lines with dx > dy                                   }

        else if abs(x1-x0) >= abs(y1-y0) then
            begin
                if x1<x0 then
                    begin
                        x := x1;              { Swap end points      }
                        y := y1;
                        x1 := x0;
                        y1 := y0;
                        x0 := x;
                        y0 := y;
                    end;

            for x := x0 to x1 do
                begin                    { Loop over x coord, computing y}
                    l := longint(y1 - y0) * longint(x - x0);
                    l := l div longint(x1 - x0);
                    y := y0 + integer(l);

                    Pixel_Set(x,y,color);   { Draw next point        }
                end;
        end

        {- Draw lines with dy > dx                                   }

        else
            begin
                if y1<y0 then
                    begin                          { Swap end points      }
                        x := x1;
                        y := y1;
```

```
                    x1 := x0;
                    y1 := y0;
                    x0 := x;
                    y0 := y;
            end;
        for y := y0 to y1 do
                    begin  { Loop over y coord, computing x}
                    l := longint(y - y0) *  longint(x1 - x0);
                    l := l div longint(y1 - y0);
                    x := x0 + integer(l);

                    Pixel_Set(x,y,color);   { Draw next point       }
                    end;
        end;
end;
```

Faster drawing for adjacent pixels:

Most drawing algorithms for curves, do at some point of the algorithm generate a set of adjacent (x,y) pixels. One of the coordinates is incrementing, and the second is being computed from the first coordinate. For example when a line from (5, 10) to (100, 20) is generated, the y coordinate is computed for each of the x's at 5, 6, 7,...,100. The x coordinate is incrementing, and the y coordinate is computed from x.

Using a proper method to modify such generated (x,y) pixels can greatly influence the drawing speed. EGA does not support addressing in terms of x and y. To change a pixel at (x,y), we must know the absolute byte address (which is = 80 * y+x/8) and a mask for the bit within the byte (it is = x mod 8). An address and mask can be computed for each (x,y) pair, but to speed up the drawing, the next address and mask can be obtained from the previous one. After the address has been computed for the first pixel, the address does not have to be computed again as long as the pixels falls within a same byte. All that needs to be done, is to rotate the mask by one to the right for each new x coordinate. After the mask reaches the right-most bit, a 1 must be added to the address. This process is much faster than computing address and mask for each pixel from scratch. As pixels along the line are generated, every so often the y will also need to change. At such point 80 is added to the address (or subtracted if y is getting smaller).

A further improvement is made by isolating vertical and horizontal lines. The horizontal lines can be drawn very fast by using the technique in "Scanline Fill" programming example. The vertical lines can also be done much more efficiently, since the mask is the same for whole line, and since to get from one pixel to the next, the address needs to be increased by 80.

A more efficient (but more complex) algorithm was developed by J. E. Bresenham. It is adapted here from "J. E. Bresenham, IBM System Journal, 4 1965", and it is the standard incremental algorithm used in many text books on computer graphics.

Note: abs(x) represents the absolute value of x.

To draw a line from point (x0,y0) to point (x1,y1):

    1) If x0=x1 and y0=y1 then draw a single pixel at (x0,y0)

    2) If y0=y1 then:
        Ensure that x0 < x1 (reverse endpoints if needed)
        Draw scanline from x0 to x1

    3) If x0=x1, then:
        For y = y0 to y1 draw pixel at (y,x0)

    4) If abs(x1 - x0) >= abs(y1 - y) then do the following:
        Ensure that x0 < x1 (reverse endpoints if needed)
        Compute error = 2 * abs(y1 - y0) + abs(x1 - x0)
        Draw pixel at (x0,y0) and set x = x0, y = y0
        If y1 > y0 then dy=1, otherwise dy=-1
        While x < x1:
            Increment x (x = x + 1)
            If error < 0, then
           error = error + 2 * abs(y1 - y0)
           and y = y + dy
            Else if error >= 0, then
           error = error + 2 * (abs(x1-x0) + abs(y1-y0))
            Draw pixel at (x,y)

    5) If abs(y1 - y0) > abs(x1 - x0) then do the following:
        Ensure that y0 < y1 (reverse endpoints if needed)
        Compute error = 2 * abs(x1 - x0) + abs(y1 - y0)
        Draw pixel at (x0,y0) and set x=x0, and y = y0
        If x1 > x0 then dx=1, otherwise dx=-1
        While y < y1:
            Increment y (y = y + 1)
            If error < 0, then
           error = error + 2 * abs(x1 - x0)

and x = x + dx
Else if error >= 0, then
error = error + 2 * (abs(x1 - x0) + abs(y1 - y0))
Draw pixel at (x,y)

Multiplication and division tend to be time consuming operations. When performing drawing operations that involve repeated multiplication or division, it may in some cases be faster to substitute Shift and Add instructions. For instance, a one bit left shift is equivalent to multiplying by 2. A three bit left shift is equivalent to multiplying by 8.

In many drawing algorithm an address computation involves a multiplication by 80. This can be reduced to Shift and Add instructions using the following relation:

$$80 * y = (64 + 16) * y = (y \text{ SHL } 6) + (y \text{ SHL } 4)$$

An assembly code to compute (80 * y) is:

```
MOV    AX,Y              ;Fetch y
MOV    CX,4              ;Load shift counter
SHL    AX,CL             ;Compute y * 16
MOV    BX,AX             ;and save it
SHL    BX,1              ;Compute (y * 16) * 2 = y * 32
SHL    BX,1              ;Compute (y * 16) * 2 * 2 = y * 64
ADD    AX,BX             ;Add (y * 64) + (y * 16)
```

Assembly Code Example

This example is not the shortest routine for line drawing, but it is a very fast implementation for the EGA and VGA. It uses Bresenham algorithm, as described above.

Listing 8-21. File: PROG086.ASM

```
;*********************************************************************
; Line (x0, y0, x1, y1,c ): draw line from (x0,y0) to (x1,y1)        *
;                with a color (c).                                    *
;                This routine is divided into three parts. Horizontal *
;                lines are done in the first part, vertical lines in  *
;                second part, and rest in the third part.  The lines  *
;                in the third part are done using the Bresenham       *
;                algorithm.                                           *
; entry : sp + 2 = x0                                                 *
;          sp + 4 = y0                                                *
;          sp + 6 = x1                                                *
;          sp + 8 = y1                                                *
;          sp + 10= color                                             *
;*********************************************************************

X0       EQU      [BP+4]
Y0       EQU      [BP+6]
X1       EQU      [BP+8]
Y1       EQU      [BP+10]
Color    EQU      [BP+12]

         PUBLIC   _Line

_Line    PROC     NEAR
         PUSH     BP
         MOV      BP,SP
         SUB      SP,6                    ;Declare three local variables

         PUSH     DI
         PUSH     SI
         PUSH     DS
         PUSH     ES

         MOV      AX,X0                   ; make sure that x1 >= x0
         MOV      CX,X1
         CMP      CX,AX
         JGE      Get_Offset
         MOV      BX,Y0
         MOV      DX,Y1
         MOV      X0,CX
         MOV      Y0,DX
         MOV      X1,AX
         MOV      Y1,BX

;---COMPUTE ADDRESS AND MASK FOR FIRST PIXEL ------
Get_Offset:
         ;- Compute offset and save on stack
         MOV      CL,4                    ; offset = 80 * y + x/8
         MOV      AX,Y0
         SHL      AX,CL
         MOV      BX,AX
         SHL      AX,1
         SHL      AX,1
         ADD      AX,BX
         MOV      BX,X0                   ; + x/8
```

```
        MOV     CL,3
        SHR     BX,CL
        ADD     AX,BX
        PUSH    AX                      ; save offset on stack, later pop to DI

        ;- Compute mask and save on the stack

        MOV     CX,X0                   ; compute which bit (x mod 8) to modify
        AND     CL,7
        MOV     BX,80h
        SHR     BX,CL
        PUSH    BX                      ; save mask on stack, later pop to SI
        MOV     DX,03CEh                ; enable only the bit(within a byte)
        MOV     AL,08H                  ; to be changed
        OUT     DX,AL
        INC     DX
        MOV     AL,BL                   ; ... reg-bx has the correct bit
        OUT     DX,AL

        ;- Load set/reset registers with current color

        MOV     DX,03CEh                ; move color into reset register
        XOR     AL,AL
        OUT     DX,AL
        INC     DX
        MOV     AX,Color
        OUT     DX,AL
        DEC     DX                      ; enable use of reset register
        MOV     AL,1
        OUT     DX,AL
        INC     DX
        MOV     AL,0FH
        OUT     DX,AL
        MOV     DX,03C4h                ; enable all four planes for writing
        MOV     AL,2
        OUT     DX,AL
        INC     DX
        MOV     AL,0FH
        OUT     DX,AL

        ;- Load segment register

        MOV     DX,0A000h
        MOV     DS,DX
        MOV     ES,DX

;---COMPUTE  DX AND DY --------------------
;       DETERMINE IF HORIZONTAL, VERTICAL OR DIAGONNAL LINE

        MOV     AX,80                   ; set raster increment
        MOV     [bp-6],AX
        MOV     SI,X1                   ; compute dx          reg-si
        SUB     SI,X0
        MOV     DI,Y1                   ; compute dy          reg-di
        SUB     DI,Y0
        JGE     DyIsPos
        NEG     AX
```

```
        MOV     [bp-6],AX
        NEG     DI
DyIsPos:
        CMP     SI,0                        ; jump according to type of line
        JZ      Vert
        CMP     DI,0
        JZ      Horiz
        JMP     Diag

;----GENERATE A VERTICAL LINE ---------

Vert:   MOV     cx,di                       ; set up counter
        INC     cx
        MOV     bx,[bp-6]

        POP     SI                          ; fetch mask
        MOV     DX,03CEh                    ; set mask
        MOV     AL,08h
        OUT     DX,AL
        INC     DX
        MOV     AX,SI
        OUT     DX,AL

        POP     DI                          ; fetch offset
LoopVert:
        MOV     AL,[DI]                     ; latch data(to preserve other 7 bits i
        MOV     [DI],AL                     ; write new data (only one bit will be
        ADD     DI,BX                       ; update offset
        LOOP    LoopVert
        JMP     LineDone

;----GENERATE A HORIZONTAL LINE --------

Horiz:  MOV     CX,SI                       ; set counter of pixels
        POP     SI                          ; fetch mask
        POP     DI                          ; fetch offset

        ;-   draw pixels from the leading partial byte

        MOV     AX,X0
        AND     AX,07h                      ; check for partial byte
        JZ      FullBytes
        MOV     BX,0FFh                     ; compute the mask
        PUSH    CX
        MOV     CX,AX
        SHR     BX,CL
        POP     CX
        ADD     CX,AX                       ; update counter
        SUB     CX,08h
        JGE     MaskSet                     ; modify mask if only one byte
        NEG     CX
        SHR     BX,CL
        SHL     BX,CL
        XOR     CX,CX                       ; restore counter
MaskSet:
        MOV     DX,03CEh                    ; set the mask
        MOV     AL,08h
```

```
            OUT     DX,AL
            INC     DX
            MOV     AL,BL
            OUT     DX,AL
            MOV     AH,[DI]                 ; latch data
            MOV     [DI],AL                 ; write new data
            INC     DI                      ; update offset

            ;—      draw pixels from the middle complete bytes
FullBytes:                                  ;
            MOV     BX,CX                   ; check if any bytes to set
            CMP     BX,8
            JL      TrailBytes
            SHR     CX,1                    ; compute count
            SHR     CX,1
            SHR     CX,1
            MOV     DX,03CEh                ; set the mask
            MOV     AL,08h
            OUT     DX,AL
            INC     DX
            MOV     AL,0FFh
            OUT     DX,AL

            REP     STOSB                   ; fill complete bytes

            ;—      draw pixels from the trailing partial byte
TrailBytes:
            AND     BX,07h
            JZ      HorizDone
            MOV     AX,0FFFFh               ; compute mask
            MOV     CX,BX
            SHR     AX,CL
            XOR     AH,0FFh                 ; set the mask
            MOV     DX,03CEh
            MOV     AL,08h
            OUT     DX,AL
            INC     DX
            MOV     AL,AH
            OUT     DX,AL
            MOV     AL,[DI]                 ; latch data
            MOV     [DI],AL                 ; set new data
HorizDone:
            JMP     LineDone

;——————— GENERATE A DIAGONAL LINE ———————

            ;— figure out which quarter does the line lie in

Diag:       CMP     SI,DI                   ; Is dy > dx
            JLE     oct12                   ; ...Yes, do processing in octants
                                            ;     1 and 2
            ; Compute constants for octant zero and three
            ; This is where x is the major direction and y is minor

oct03:      MOV     CX,SI                   ; set counter to dx+1
            INC     CX
            SAL     DI,1                    ; d1 = dy*2              reg-di
```

```
        MOV     BX,DI            ; d  = dy*2-dx          reg-bx
        SUB     BX,SI
        NEG     SI               ; d2 = dy*2-dx-dx       reg-si
        ADD     SI,BX

        MOV     [bp-2],di        ; save d1
        MOV     [bp-4],si        ; save d2
        MOV     DX,03CEh         ; select BIT MASK register
        MOV     AL,08h
        OUT     DX,AL
        INC     DX
        POP     AX               ; fetch mask
        POP     DI               ; fetch address

;------- GENERATE LINE IN THE OCTANT ZERO AND THREE ---

next0:  OUT     DX,AL            ; enable a bit in a byte
        MOV     AH,[DI]          ; latch old data
        MOV     [DI],AH          ; modify (enabled bits)

        ROR     AL,1             ; update mask
        ADC     DI,0             ; update byte address

        TEST    BX,8000H         ; if d >= 0 then ...
        JNZ     dneg0
        ADD     BX,[BP-4]        ; ... d = d + d2
        ADD     DI,[BP-6]        ; update offset to next scan line
        LOOP    next0
        JMP     LineDone

dneg0:  ADD     BX,[BP-2]        ; if d < 0 then d = d + d1
        LOOP    next0
        JMP     LineDone

        ;------------------------------

        ;-  Compute constants for octant one and two

oct12:  MOV     CX,DI            ; set counter to dy+1
        INC     CX
        SAL     SI,1             ; d1 = dx * 2
        MOV     BX,SI            ; d  = dx * 2 - dy
        SUB     BX,DI
        NEG     DI               ; d2 = -dy + dx * 2 - dy
        ADD     DI,BX

        MOV     [BP-4],DI        ; save d2
        MOV     [BP-2],SI        ; save d1
        MOV     dx,03CEh         ; select BIT MASK register
        MOV     al,08h
        OUT     DX,AL
        INC     DX
        POP     AX               ; fetch mask
        POP     DI               ; fetch address
        OUT     DX,AL            ; enable a bit in a byte
```

```
                ;--GENERATE A LINE IN THE OCTANT ONE AND TWO --------

next1:  MOV     AH,[DI]                 ; latch old data
        MOV     [DI],AH                 ; modify (enabled bits)

        ADD     DI,[BP-6]               ; update offset (y = y+1)

        TEST    BX,8000H                ; if d >= 0 then ...
        JNZ     dneg1

        ADD     BX,[BP-4]               ; ... d = d + d2
        ROR     AL,1                    ; ... update mask (x = x+1)
        ADC     DI,0                    ; ... update offset
        OUT     DX,AL                   ; Enable next bit within a byte
        LOOP    next1
        JMP     LineDone

dneg1:  ADD     BX,[BP-2]               ; if d < 0 then d = d + d1
        LOOP    next1


                ;---------------------------------
                ;- Restore PLANE ENABLE and BIT MASK registers
LineDone:
        MOV     DX,03CEh                ; Enable all 8-bits in a byte for write
        MOV     AL,08h                  ; by setting BIT MASK register to Fhex
        OUT     DX,AL
        INC     DX
        MOV     AL,0FFh
        OUT     DX,AL

        DEC     DX                      ; Disable SET/RESET function
        MOV     AL,1
        OUT     DX,AL
        INC     DX
        XOR     AX,AX
        OUT     DX,AL

        POP     ES
        POP     DS
        POP     SI
        POP     DI
        MOV     SP,BP
        POP     BP
        RET
_Line   ENDP
```

Patterned Lines

Draw a Line Using a Given Pattern

This function is not apart of the EGALIB.OBJ Library. Use PROGC088.C or PROGP088.PAS source code instead.

Pascal Library Procedure

```
PROCEDURE    pattern_line(x0,y0,x1,y1,color,pattern:integer);
                {x0,y0 = start point, x1,y1 = end point}
                {color = color, pattern = pattern mask}
```

C Library Procedure

```
pattern_line(x0,y0,x1,y1,color,pattern)   /* Draw patterned line           */
int    x0,y0;                             /* Starting point                */
int    x1,y1;                             /* Ending point                  */
int    color;                             /* Color for ON pixels           */
                                          /* (OFF pixels are unchanged)    */
int    pattern;                           /* Pattern for the line          */
                                          /* for each pattern bit,         */
                                          /* 0 => do not draw pixel        */
                                          /* 1 => draw pixel               */
```

Theory

It is often desirable to draw lines that are not solid (dotted or dashed lines). In graphs and charts, lines for different variables might be distinguished by different line styles. In Computer Aided Design (CAD) programs, line styles are used to identify special element of objects, center of symmetry, or interior lines.

The next example will superimpose an eight bit pattern onto a line. To draw a dashed line, the eight bit pattern 0F hex (00001111 bin) might be used. For a dotted line, a 55 hex (01010101 bin) might be used.

All patterns used in this section will be byte aligned eight bit patterns. Besides simplifying the algorithm, this guarantees that a sequence of short connected line segments will appear as one continuous patterned curve.

Example

Listing 8-22. File: PROGC087.C

```c
/********************************************************************/
/* Draw a triangle with dot-dashed lines                        */
/********************************************************************/

pattern_triag()
        {
        #define DOT_DASH           0x30FC
        #define WHITE              15
        slow_pattern_line(420,0,0,200,WHITE,DOT_DASH);
        slow_pattern_line(0,200,639,200,WHITE,DOT_DASH);
        slow_pattern_line(420,0,639,200,WHITE,DOT_DASH);
        }

/********************************************************************/
/* Draw a box with checkerboard pattern using patterned lines    */
/********************************************************************/

checkers()
        {
        #define EVEN_DOTS          0xAAAA
        #define ODD_DOTS           0x5555
        #define WHITE              15
        int     i;
        for (i = 0; i < 100; i += 2)
                {
                slow_pattern_line(300,i  ,500,i  ,WHITE,EVEN_DOTS);
                slow_pattern_line(300,i+1,500,i+1,WHITE, ODD_DOTS);
                }
        }
```

Listing 8-23. File: PROGP087.PAS

```pascal
{************************************************************}
{ Draw a triangle with dot-dashed lines                   }
{************************************************************}

procedure pattern_triag;
const
MONO = 5;
COLOR = 4;
VMONO = 7;
DOT_DASH = $30FC;
WHITE = 15;
var
i : integer;
begin
        Clear_Screen;
        i := Get_Display_Type;
        if i = MONO then        Set_Mode($0F)
        else if i = VMONO then Set_Mode($0F)
        else if i = COLOR then Set_Mode($0E)
        else                   Set_Mode($10);
```

```
        Slow_Pattern_Line(210,0,0,100,WHITE,DOT_DASH);
        Slow_Pattern_Line(0,100,320,100,WHITE,DOT_DASH);
        Slow_Pattern_Line(210,0,320,100,WHITE,DOT_DASH);

        i := integer(readkey);

        {- Set default text mode                                         }

        i := Get_Display_Type;
        if i = MONO then        Set_Mode(7)
        else if i = VMONO then Set_Mode(7)
        else                    Set_Mode(3);
end;

{**********************************************************************}
{ Draw a box with checkerboard pattern using patterned lines         }
{**********************************************************************}

procedure checkers;
const
MONO = 5;
COLOR = 4;
VMONO = 7;
EVEN_DOTS = $AAAA;
ODD_DOTS = $5555;
WHITE = 15;
var
i : integer;
begin
        Clear_Screen;
        i := Get_Display_Type;
        if i = MONO then        Set_Mode($F)
        else if i = VMONO then Set_Mode($F)
        else if i = COLOR then Set_Mode($E)
        else                    Set_Mode($10);

        for i := 0 to 49 do
            begin
                Slow_Pattern_Line(300,2*i,500,2*i,WHITE,EVEN_DOTS);
                Slow_Pattern_Line(300,2*i+1,500,2*i+1,WHITE, ODD_DOTS);
            end;

        i := integer(readkey);

        {- Set default text mode                                         }

        i := Get_Display_Type;
        if i = MONO then        Set_Mode(7)
        else if i = VMONO then Set_Mode(7)
        else                    Set_Mode(3);
end;
```

The line drawing procedure described earlier in this chapter (Draw_Line) demonstrates how to calculate the individual pixel positions for a solid line. A slight modification of that procedure can provide the ability to draw patterned lines.

To generate a patterned line, the procedure could count the number of pixels on the line that have been generated, using the pixel count (modulo 8) as a bit index into the pattern. If the resulting bit is one the pixel is drawn; if it is zero, the pixel is not.

This method works well for one line, but when multiple connected lines are drawn there will be no continuity of pattern from one line to the next. To gain pattern continuity, the absolute x or y coordinate of each pixel (modulo 8) is used as the pattern index instead. The proper state (on or off) of any pixel on any line is then defined by the absolute coordinate of that pixel, and is independent of end points of the line itself. For lines of steep slope, the y coordinate is used; for lines of small slope, the x coordinate is used.

A side effect of this approach is that the actual size of the pattern (the length of each dot or dash) will change as the slope of the line changes. This is usually considered acceptable.

For a line of no slope (either straight horizontal or straight vertical) with pattern 0xCC Hex (11001100B), the results for the first four pixels would be:

pixel 0 = pattern[0] = 1 = draw pixel
pixel 1 = pattern[1] = 1 = draw pixel
pixel 2 = pattern[2] = 0 = do not draw pixel
pixel 3 = pattern[3] = 0 = do not draw pixel

A more general case line and pattern is illustrated in Figure 8-8.

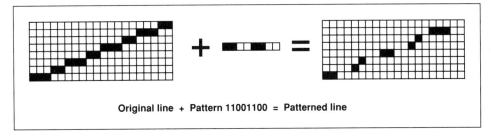

Original line + Pattern 11001100 = Patterned line

Figure 8-8. Pattern line.

Since the processors used in IBM compatible personal computers do not support bit indexing (only byte or word indexing are supported), an array of sixteen mask words will be used to convert a word index into a bit value. For example, to test if pattern bit number 7 is On or Off:

| if (mask[7] & pattern) then | bit 7 is ON |
| else | bit 7 is OFF |

The algorithm can be implemented in C as follows:

Listing 8-24. File: PROGC088.C

```
/****************************************************************************/
/* Draw a line with a pattern using the "slow" algorithm                    */
/****************************************************************************/

slow_pattern_line(x0, y0, x1, y1, color,pattern)
int     x0, y0, x1, y1, color, pattern;
        {
        int     x, y;
        static int mask[16] = {
                            0x8000,0x4000,0x2000,0x1000,
                            0x0800,0x0400,0x0200,0x0100,
                            0x0080,0x0040,0x0020,0x0010,
                            0x0008,0x0004,0x0002,0x0001};

        /*- Draw degenerate line (pixel)                            */

        if (x0 == x1 && y0 == y1)               /* Draw a single pixel  */
                {
                if (mask[x0 & 15] & pattern)
                        pixel_write(x0, y0, color);
                }

        /*- Draw lines with dx > dy                                 */

        else if (abs(x1 - x0) >= abs(y1 - y0))
                {                                       /* Swap end points      */
                if (x1 < x0)
                        {
                        x = x1;
                        y = y1;
                        x1 = x0;
                        y1 = y0;
                        x0 = x;
                        y0 = y;
                        }
                for (x = x0; x <= x1; x++)      /* Loop over x coord    */
                        {                               /* Compute y using x    */
                        y = y0 + ((x - x0)*(long)(y1 - y0))/(x1 - x0);
                        if (mask[x & 15] & pattern)
                                pixel_write(x,y,color); /* Draw next point      */
                        }
```

```
              }
     /*- Draw lines with dy > dx                              */

     else
          {
          if (y1 < y0)                    /* Swap end points     */
               {
               x = x1;
               y = y1;
               x1 = x0;
               y1 = y0;
               x0 = x;
               y0 = y;
               }
          for (y = y0; y <= y1; y++)       /* Loop over y coord   */
               {                           /* Compute x using y   */
               x = x0 + ((y - y0)*(long)(x1 - x0))/(y1 - y0);
               if (mask[y & 15] & pattern)
                    pixel_write(x,y,color);  /* Draw next point     */
               }
          }
     }
```

Listing 8-25. File: PROGP088.PAS

```
{***********************************************************************}
{ Draw a line with a pattern using the "slow" algorithm                 }
{***********************************************************************}

procedure slow_pattern_line(x0, y0, x1, y1, color,pattern:word);
const
mask : array[0..15] of word = (
                                 $8000,$4000,$2000,$1000,
                                 $0800,$0400,$0200,$0100,
                                 $0080,$0040,$0020,$0010,
                                 $0008,$0004,$0002,$0001);
var
i,x,y : integer;
l : longint;
begin
        {- Draw degenerate line (pixel)                               }

        i := x0 - x1;
        if i = 0 then i := y0 - y1;
        if i = 0 then
            begin                                { Draw a single pixel  }
                if (mask[x0 and $0F] and pattern)>0 then Pixel_Set(x0,y0,color);
            end

        {- Draw lines with dx > dy                                    }

        else if abs(x1 - x0) >= abs(y1 - y0) then
        begin
                if x1 < x0 then                  { Swap end points      }
                    begin
```

```
                         x  := x1;
                         y  := y1;
                         x1 := x0;
                         y1 := y0;
                         x0 := x;
                         y0 := y;
                    end;
               for x := x0 to x1 do            { Loop over x coord      }
                    begin                       { Compute y using x       }
                         y := x - x0;
                         l := y1;
                         l := l - y0;
                         l := l * y;
                         l := l div (x1 - x0);
                         y := y0 + l;

                         if (mask[x and $0f] and pattern) > 0 then
                                 Pixel_Set(x,y,color); { Draw next point}
                    end;
          end

     {- Draw lines with dy > dx                                       }

     else
          begin
               if y1 < y0 then                  { Swap end points         }
                    begin
                         x  := x1;
                         y  := y1;
                         x1 := x0;
                         y1 := y0;
                         x0 := x;
                         y0 := y;
                    end;
               for y := y0 to y1 do            { Loop over y coord       }
                    begin                       { Compute x using y       }
                         x := y - y0;
                         l := x1;
                         l := l - x0;
                         l := l * x;
                         l := l div (y1 - y0);
                         x := x0 + l;
                         if (mask[y and $0f] and pattern) > 0 then
                             Pixel_Set(x,y,color);{ Draw next point       }
                    end;
          end;
end;
```

Assembly Code Example

The assembly language implementation of Bresenham's line drawing algorithm, developed as an earlier programming example, can be modified to support
patterned lines. The lengthy procedure will not be shown here.

Draw Arc

This function is not part of the library EGALIB.OBJ. Use PROGC090.C or PROGP090.PAS source code instead.

Draw a Section of a Circle

Pascal Library Procedure

```
PROCEDURE arc(xc,yc,xp,yp,a0,a1,color:integer);
            {xc,yc = center point; xp,yp = point on circumference}
            {a0 = start angle; a1 = end angle (in degrees); color = color}
```

C Library Procedure

```
arc(xc,yc,xp,yp,a0,a1,color)    /* Draw circular arc          */
int    xc,yc;                   /* Center of the arc          */
int    xp,yp;                   /* Any point on full circle   */
int    a0,a1;                   /* Starting and ending angle  */
                                /* in degrees                 */
int    color;                   /* Color of the arc           */
```

Example

There are several methods for defining circles, including:

1.   Three points on the circumference of the circle.

2.   A center point plus two points on the circumference.

3.   A radius plus two points on the circumference.

4.   A center, a circumference point, start angle, and stop angle.

Each method has unique advantages and disadvantages. Method four (center, point, start angle, stop angle) will be used here. A major reason for selecting method four is because of the aspect ratio of the EGA screen.

It should be noted that the point xp,yp does not have to lie on the segment of arc between the two angles (the segment of arc to be drawn).

Listing 8-26. File: PROGC089.C

```
/**********************************************************************/
/* A set of concentric circles and four sets of symmetric arcs      */
/**********************************************************************/

arc_demo()
        {
        #define WHITE    15
        int     r;
        cls();
        for (r = 100; r > 70; r -= 5)               /* Draw 6 circles    */
                arc(320,100,320+r,100,0,360,WHITE);
        for (r = 70; r > 0; r -= 5)                 /* Loop over size    */
                {                                   /* Draw next four arcs */
                arc(320,100,320+r,100, 22, 66,WHITE);
                arc(320,100,320+r,100,112,156,WHITE);
                arc(320,100,320+r,100,202,246,WHITE);
                arc(320,100,320+r,100,292,336,WHITE);
                }
        }

arc(xc,yc,xp,yp,a0,a1,color)
int     xc,yc;                  /* Center of the arc                 */
int     xp,yp;                  /* Any point on full circle          */
int     a0,a1;                  /* Starting and ending angle in degrees */
int     color;                  /* Color of the arc                  */
        {
        brute_arc(xc,yc,xp,yp,a0,a1,color);
        }
```

Listing 8-27. File: PROGP089.PAS

```
{**********************************************************************}
{ A set of concentric circles and four sets of symmetric arcs        }
{**********************************************************************}

procedure arc_demo;
const
MONO = 5;
COLOR = 4;
VMONO = 7;
WHITE = 15;
var
i,r : integer;
begin
        Clear_Screen;
        i := Get_Display_Type;
        if i = MONO then        Set_Mode($0F)
        else if i = VMONO then  Set_Mode($0F)
        else if i = COLOR then  Set_Mode($0E)
        else                    Set_Mode($10);

        for r := 20 downto 15 do                   { Draw 6 circles     }
                Arc(320,100,320+5*r,100,0,360,WHITE);
        for r := 14 downto 1 do                    { Loop over size     }
```

```
        begin                              { Draw next four arcs   }
            Arc(320,100,320+5*r,100, 22, 66,WHITE);
            Arc(320,100,320+5*r,100,112,156,WHITE);
            Arc(320,100,320+5*r,100,202,246,WHITE);
            Arc(320,100,320+5*r,100,292,336,WHITE);
        end;

    i := integer(readkey);

    {- Set default text mode                                    }

    i := Get_Display_Type;
    if i = MONO then        Set_Mode(7)
    else if i = VMONO then Set_Mode(7)
    else                    Set_Mode(3);
end;
```

Theory

An arc made from a set of points that are the same distance (in pixels) from a center point will appear on the EGA as an ellipse, not a circle (this is also true of CGA and Hercules). This is illustrated in Figure 8-9. To generate something that looks like a circle, the arc drawing procedure must correct for aspect ratio. The example routine allows the user to specify a center and one circumference point, then the procedure calculates all other points while adjusting for aspect ratio.

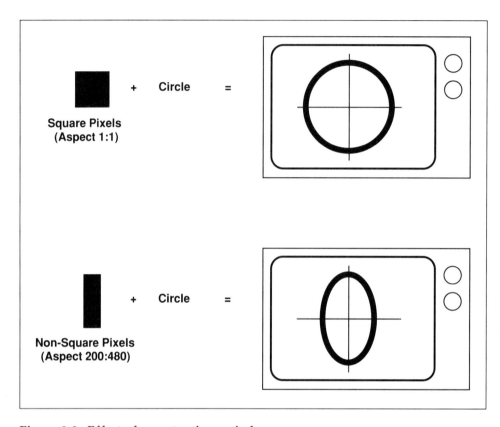

Figure 8-9. Effect of aspect ratio on circles.

Arc drawing algorithms tend to be rather esoteric in nature, especially algorithms for elliptical (noncircular) arcs (as this one must be, to correct for aspect ratio). It is beyond the scope of this book to derive an efficient incremetal algorithm for elliptical arc generation. Such an exercise could easily fill an entire chapter. A simple but inefficient algorithm will be given here instead.

The aspect ratio in graphics modes F and 10 is x:y=350:480 and in mode E is 200:480. An ellipse that has the opposite aspect ratio will appear circular. For example, to display a circle with its center at pixel 100,200 and going through pixel 200,200 we must draw the ellipse that is generated by the following formula:

$$(x - 100)^2 / (100)^2 + (y - 200)^2 / (100 * 350/480)^2 = 1$$

The most simplistic approach to drawing this ellipse would be to evaluate this equation for all necessary values of x and y. This would be too slow, however, to be of any practical use. Instead we shall approximate the ellipse with a polygon. To compute vertices of this polygon we use the trigonometric representation of the ellipse:

$$x = A * \cos (alpha)$$
$$y = B * \cos (alpha)$$

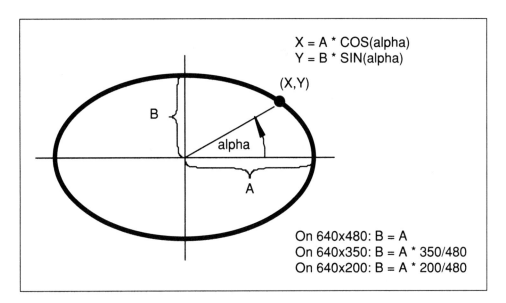

Figure 8-10. Points on an ellipse.

For the VGA operating at 640 x 480 resolution the aspect ratio of the display is true 1:1 (square pixels) and and a circle can be drawn without a correction for aspect ratio.

The following example uses short line segments to draw the circle. If each line segment is short enough (which is dependent on display resolution), the result will appear circular. We have arbitrarily chosen one line segment for each six pixels of the arc.

Listing 8-28. File: PROGC090.C

```
/*************************************************************************/
/* Brute force arc generation                                          */
/*************************************************************************/

brute_arc(xc,yc,xp,yp,a0,a1,color)
int     xc,yc;                   /* Center of the arc                  */
int     xp,yp;                   /* Any point on full circle           */
int     a0,a1;                   /* Starting and ending angle in degrees */
int     color;                   /* Color of the arc                   */
        {
        #include <math.h>
        #define PI 3.1415926
        float   a,b,f,dx,dy;
        int     xa,ya,xb,yb,alpha,delta;

        if (xp - xc == 0 && yp - yc == 0)/* Process degenerate case    */
                {
                pixel_write(xc,yc,color);
                return;
                }
                                        /* Compute major & minor axis  */
        if (get_scanlines() > 200)      f = 480./350.;
        else                            f = 480./200.;
        dx= xp - xc;
        dy=(yp - yc)*f;
        a = sqrt(dx * dx + dy * dy);
        b  = a/f;
                                        /* Compute first point         */
        xa = xc + a * cos((double)(a0 * PI/180.));
        ya = yc + b * sin((double)(a0 * PI/180.));
        delta = 6 * 180./(PI * a);      /* Force 6 pixels per segment   */
                                        /* Loop over segment on ellipse */
        for (alpha = a0; alpha <= a1; alpha = alpha + delta)
                {                       /* Compute next point on ellipse*/
                xb = xc + a * cos(alpha * PI/180.);
                yb = yc + b * sin(alpha * PI/180.);
                line (xa, ya, xb, yb, color);   /* Draw to previous pt */
                xa = xb;
                ya = yb;
                }
                                        /* Do the last segment          */
        xb = xc + a * cos(a1 * PI/180.);
        yb = yc + b * sin(a1 * PI/180.);
        line (xa, ya, xb, yb, color);
        }
```

Listing 8-29. File: PROGP090.PAS

```pascal
{**********************************************************************}
{ Brute force arc generation                                         }
{**********************************************************************}

procedure arc(xc,yc,xp,yp,a0,a1,color:word);
                {xc,yc - Center of the arc                           }
                {xp,yp - Any point on full circle                    }
                {a0,a1 - Starting and ending angle in degrees        }
                {color - Color of the arc                            }

var
a,b,f,s,dx,dy,pi : real;
i,sl,xa,ya,xb,yb,alpha,delta : integer;
begin
    pi := 3.1415926;
    i := xp-xc;
    if i = 0 then i := yp-yc;
    if i = 0 then Pixel_Set(xc,yc,color)            { degenerate case    }
    else
        begin
            sl := Get_Scanlines;
            s := sl;
            f := 480/s; { Compute major & minor axis}
            dx := xp - xc;
            dy := (yp - yc)*f;
            a := sqrt(dx * dx + dy * dy);
            b := a/f;
                                                { Compute first point  }
            xa := round(xc + a * cos(a0 * PI/180));
            ya := round(yc + b * sin(a0 * PI/180));
            delta := round(6 * 180/(PI * a));   { Force 6 pixels per segment}
                                                { Loop over segment on ellipse }
            alpha := a0;
            while alpha < a1 do                 { Compute next point on ellipse}
                begin
                    xb := round(xc + a * cos(alpha * PI/180));
                    yb := round(yc + b * sin(alpha * PI/180));
                    Line(xa, ya, xb, yb, color);{ Draw to previous pt  }
                    xa := xb;
                    ya := yb;
                    alpha := alpha + delta;
                end;
                                                { Do the last segment  }
            xb := round(xc + a * cos(a1 * PI/180));
            yb := round(yc + b * sin(a1 * PI/180));
            Line(xa, ya, xb, yb, color);
        end;
end;
```

Block Transfer (BITBLT)

Copy a Rectangular Region of Memory

Pascal Library Procedure

```
procedure Bitblt(x_src,y_src,x_dst,y_dst,width,height,fun:integer);
            {x_src,y_src = top left corner of source}
            {x_dst,y_dst = top left corner of destination}
            {width,height = dimensions, fun = logical functions}
```

C Library Procedure

```
bitblt(xs,ys,xd,yd,dx,dy,fn)    /* Bit Aligned Block Transfer               */
int xs, ys;                     /* Upper left corner of the source block to transfer */
int xd, yd;                     /* Upper left corner of the destination   block    */
int dx, dy;                     /* Dimension of the block to transfer        */
int fn;                         /* Logical operation to be performed         */
                                /*    0 - COPY                               */
                                /*    1 - AND                                */
                                /*    2 - OR                                 */
                                /*    3 - XOR                                */
```

Example

This example will "slide" a 100 x 100 pixel block from the upper left corner. The slide is done in 50 steps and in each step the block is copied 2 pixels lower and to the right.

Listing 8-30. File: PROGC095.C

```
/**********************************************************************/
/* Copy a 100,100 block from upper left corner of the screen          */
/* and move it successively 50 times, two pixels at a time            */
/**********************************************************************/

slide_block()
    {
        #define COPY    0
        int     i,j,x,y,color;

        /* First draw interesting background                        */

        clear_screen();
```

```
        for (i = 0; i < 25; i++)
                for (j = 0; j < 80; j++)
                        printf("%c",'A'+i);

        /* Here we use BITBLT to copy a block 50 times                    */

        for (i = 0; i < 100; i += 2)      /* Copy next block
*/
                bitblt(0,0, 320+i, 0+i, 100, 100, COPY);
        }
```

Theory

This function is popularly known as BIT aligned Block Transfer or BITBLT. It is the basic building block of modern graphical user interfaces (such as GEM by Digital Research and Microsoft Windows). BITBLTs are used for window manipulations, pop-up and pull-down menus, and text generation in graphics modes.

BITBLTs transfer data from a Source block to a Destination block. There are many variations of BITBLT depending on the number of planes in the source, number of planes in the destination, and logical operations (such as AND, OR, XOR) between source and destination. This section will concentrate on transfers where both the source and destination are in EGA display memory, and will use only the logical operations that are supported by EGA:

CLEAR   Clear Destination to given color
COPY   Replace Destination with Source
OR   OR Source with Destination and place result in Destination
XOR   XOR Source with Destination and place result in Destination
AND   AND Source with Destination and place result in Destination

Note that the Solid_Box procedure described earlier can be used to perform Clear functions.

At first glance, the idea of copying a block of data may seem simple, but the problem is much more difficult than it sounds. A rectangular block on the display does not generally represent a contiguous block of memory. Different scan lines in the rectangle are located in different areas of the display memory. The edges of the rectangle may not even be byte aligned.

If the source block overlaps the destination block, the data transfered to the destination will overwrite some of the pixels in the source block. This can result in a permanent loss of data unless the transfer is done in the proper sequence to insure that pixels in the source block are not destroyed until they have already been tranferred. Depending on the location of the overlap, the BITBLT transfer may need to begin from one specific corner of the source block. This is illustrated in Figure 8-11.

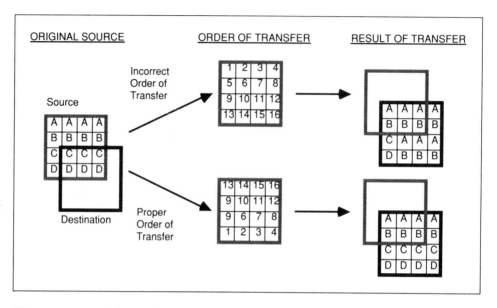

Figure 8-11. Problems of overlapped source and destination.

It is the responsibility of the BITBLT procedure to detect overlaps and perform the transfer in a safe sequence. In the example above, this can be accomplished by starting with the bottom raster line of the source and transferring one raster line at a time until the top row is reached.

The BITBLT procedure must choose one of four ways to traverse the source to guarantee that overlapping source and destination do not result in data loss. The proper choice of traversal is determined by the relative positions of source and destination. Labeling the upper-left corner of the source block as (xs,ys) and the upper-left corner of the destination as (xd,yd), the four options are as follows:

- yd < ys: Start in upper-left corner, transferring pixels from left to right, top to bottom.

- yd > ys: Start in lower-left corner, transferring pixels from left to right, bottom to top.

- yd = ys and xd <= xs: Start in upper-left corner, transferring pixels from left to right, top to bottom.

- yd = ys and xd > xs: Start in upper-right corner, transferring pixels from right to left, top to bottom.

A rather simplistic, and rather slow, implementation of BITBLT transfers one pixel at a time:

Listing 8-31. File: PROGC091.C

```
/****************************************************************/
/* Transfer source block of dimension DX x DY from XS,YS        */
/* to XD, YD                                                    */
/****************************************************************/

slow_bitblt(xs, ys, xd, yd, dx, dy, fn)
int     xs, ys;                         /* Source upper left corner   */
int     xd, yd;                         /* Destination upper left     */
int     dx, dy;                         /* Dimensions of the block    */
int     fn;                             /* Logical operation          */
        {
        #define COPY    0
        #define CLEAR   1
        #define OR      2
        #define XOR     3
        #define AND     4
        int     x_incr, y_incr, x_max, y_max, x, y, i, j, value;

        /****************************************************************/
        /* Compute starting points and directions of transfer          */
        /****************************************************************/

        x = 0;                          /* Assume no overlap or ++    */
        y = 0;                          /* i.e. xs > xd && ys > yd    */
        x_incr = 1;
        y_incr = 1;

        if (xs <= xd && xs + dx >= xd)  /* Reverse x direction if source*/
                {                       /* overlaps left half of dest. */
                x = dx - 1;
                x_incr = -1;
                }

        if (ys > yd && ys <= yd + dy)   /* Revers y direction if source */
                {                       /* overlaps bottom half of dest */
                y = dy - 1;
                y_incr = -1;
                }

        /****************************************************************/
        /* Transfer the block                                           */
        /****************************************************************/

        for (j = 0; j < dy; j++)                /* Loop over rasters   */
                {
                for (i = 0; i < dx; i++)        /* Loop over pixels    */
                        {
                        switch (fn)             /* Select logical op   */
                                {
                                case COPY:
```

```
                                        value = pixel_read(xs+x,ys+y);
                                        pixel_write(xd+x,yd+y,value);
                                        break;
                                case CLEAR:
                                        value = 0;
                                        pixel_write(xd+x,yd+y,value);
                                        break;
                                case OR:
                                        value = pixel_read(xs+x,ys+y) |
                                                pixel_read(xd+x,yd+x);
                                        pixel_write(xd+x,yd+y,value);
                                        break;
                                case XOR:
                                        value = pixel_read(xs+x,ys+y) ^
                                                pixel_read(xd+x,yd+x);
                                        pixel_write(xd+x,yd+y,value);
                                        break;
                                case AND:
                                        value = pixel_read(xs+x,ys+y) &
                                                pixel_read(xd+x,yd+x);
                                        pixel_write(xd+x,yd+y,value);
                                        break;
                                default:
                                        break;
                                }
                        x += x_incr;                    /* Update pixel pointer */
                        }
                y += y_incr;                    /* Update raster pointer*/
                x -= dx * x_incr;               /* Reset pixel pointer  */
                }
        }
```

Listing 8-32. File: PROGP091.PAS

```
{********************************************************************}
{ Transfer source block of dimension DX x DY from XS,YS            }
{ to XD, YD                                                         }
{********************************************************************}

procedure slow_bitblt(xs, ys, xd, yd, dx, dy, fn:word);
{xs, ys Source upper left corner}
{xd, yd Destination upper left  }
{dx, dy Dimensions of the block }
{fn Logical operation           }
const
COPY =  0;
CLEAR = 1;
FUN_OR = 2;
FUN_XOR = 3;
FUN_AND = 4;
var
x_incr, y_incr, x_max, y_max, x, y, i, j, value : integer;
begin
```

```
{*****************************************************************}
{ Compute starting points and directions of transfer             }
{*****************************************************************}
x := 0;                            { Assume no overlap or ++       }
y := 0;                            { i.e. xs > xd && ys > yd       }
x_incr := 1;
y_incr := 1;

if xs <= xd then if xs+dx >= xd then
    begin
      { Reverse x direction if source overlaps left half of dest.}
        x := dx - 1;
        x_incr := -1;
    end;

if ys > yd then if ys <= yd+dy then
    begin
      { Reverse y direction if source overlaps bottom half of dest}
        y := dy - 1;
        y_incr := -1;
    end;

{*****************************************************************}
{ Transfer the block                                             }
{*****************************************************************}

for j := 0 to dy-1 do                  { Loop over rasters    }
    begin
        for i := 0 to dx-1 do          { Loop over pixels     }
            begin
                case fn of             { Select logical op    }

                COPY :
                    begin
                        value := Pixel_Read(xs+x,ys+y);
                        Pixel_Set(xd+x,yd+y,value);
                    end;

                CLEAR:
                    begin
                        value := 0;
                        Pixel_Set(xd+x,yd+y,value);
                    end;

                FUN_OR:
                    begin
                        value := Pixel_Read(xs+x,ys+y) or
                                 Pixel_Read(xd+x,yd+x);
                        Pixel_Set(xd+x,yd+y,value);
                    end;

                FUN_XOR:
                    begin
                        value := Pixel_Read(xs+x,ys+y) xor
                                 Pixel_Read(xd+x,yd+x);
                        Pixel_Set(xd+x,yd+y,value);
                    end;
```

```
             FUN_AND:
                begin
                    value := Pixel_Read(xs+x,ys+y) and
                                Pixel_Read(xd+x,yd+x);
                        Pixel_Set(xd+x,yd+y,value);
                    end;
                end;

             x := x + x_incr;          { Update pixel pointer }
         end;
      y := y + y_incr;                 { Update raster pointer}
      x := x - dx * x_incr;            { Reset pixel pointer   }
   end;
end;
```

To learn more about memory organization see Display Memory in Graphics Modes in Chapter 2.

To learn more about logical operations, masking and rotate, see Graphics Controller register description for Set/Reset registers 0 and 1, Data Rotate/Function Select register 3, Mode register 5, and Mask register 8, in Chapter 3.

Also see programming examples Pixel Write and Scanline Fill in this chapter.

Assembly Language Example

A faster BITBLT algorithm transfers pixels up to eight at a time, rather than one at a time. The result is at least an order of magnitude improvement in execution time. An additional improvement in speed can be achieved by using the logical functions built into the EGA hardware (SET/CLEAR, OR, XOR and AND).

The Scan Line Fill procedure, described earlier in the chapter used a technique of dividing the line into three regions: a partial byte (0-6 bits) on the front, a partial byte on the back, and a number of full bytes in the middle. A similar technique is used by this algorithm.

A byte of data read from the source block will usually not be byte aligned in the destination; it will "straddle" a byte boundary. The byte must be split into two sections and written into two bytes of the destination. In general, these steps are required as each byte is transferred:

1.   Read a source byte.

2.   Determine which bits go into the current destination byte.

3.   Combine these bits with the bits "left over" from the previous source byte.

4.   Determine which bits must be saved for the next destination byte.

This is illustrated in Figure 8-12.

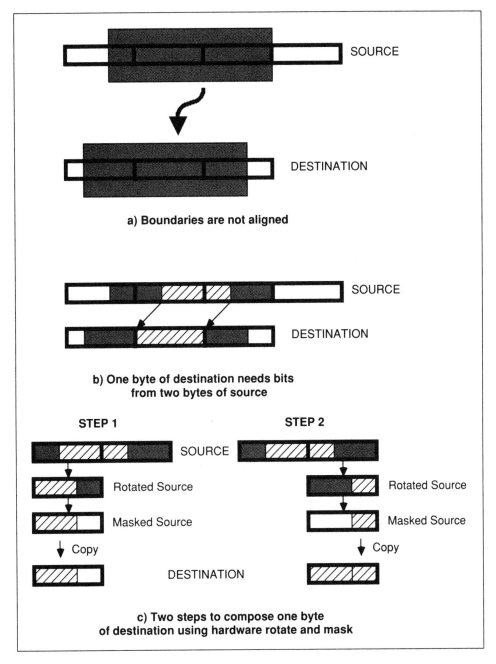

Figure 8-12. Nonaligned source and destination.

The overall sequence is as follows:

First byte of scan line:

Get byte from source (may have to get data from two bytes)
Align with destination
Mask partial bits
Write one byte of destination
 Save unused bits for next transfer

Middle bytes of scan line:

Get byte from source
Combine with unused bits from previous source byte
Write one byte of destination
Save unused bits for next transfer

Last byte of scan line:

Mask partial bits
Write unused bits from previous source byte

If the data transfer involves only one memory plane, this technique requires only one read from display memory and one write to display memory for each eight bits that are transferred (except for the partial bytes at the beginning and end of each scan line). If multiple planes are involved, the algorithm must be repeated for each plane.

The EGA hardware rotate capability is used to align source and destination, and EGA logical functions are used to perform AND, OR, and XOR functions.

Listing 8-33. File: PROG087.ASM

```
;**********************************************************************
; Transfer Bit Aligned Block of dimensions Width x Height, from       *
; source, with upper left corner at (X_Src,Y_Src), to destination with *
; upper left corner at (X_Dst,Y_Dst), using function fn.              *
; Entry:       X_Srs, Y_Src  - Source upper left                      *
;              X_Dst, Y_Dst  - Destination upper left                 *
;              BWidth,BHeight- Dimensions of the block                *
;              Fn            - Logical function (Copy, AND, OR, XOR)   *
;**********************************************************************

;xxxx add later traversing x in reverse for overlapped src and dst

X_Src   EQU     [BP+4]                  ;Formal parameters on the stack
Y_Src   EQU     [BP+6]
```

```
X_Dst     EQU      [BP+8]
Y_Dst     EQU      [BP+10]
BWidth    EQU      [BP+12]
BHeight   EQU      [BP+14]
Fn        EQU      [BP+16]

HBYTES    EQU      80                       ;Number of bytes per scanline
GRF_SEG   EQU      0A000H                   ;Segment for display buffer

Y_Incr           EQU       WORD PTR [BP-2]  ;Local variables
First_Mask       EQU       BYTE PTR [BP-4]
InFirst          EQU       WORD PTR [BP-6]
Last_Mask        EQU       BYTE PTR [BP-8]
Read_Plane       EQU       BYTE PTR [BP-10]
Lower_Mask       EQU       BYTE PTR [BP-12]
Upper_Mask       EQU       BYTE PTR [BP-14]
Src_Address      EQU       WORD PTR [BP-16]
Dst_Address      EQU       WORD PTR [BP-18]
Block_Dx         EQU       WORD PTR [BP-20]
Block_Dy         EQU       WORD PTR [BP-22]

          PUBLIC   _BitBlt

_BitBlt PROC     NEAR
        PUSH     BP
        MOV      BP,SP

        SUB      SP,24                      ;Setup local variables

        PUSH     DS                         ;Presrve segment registers
        PUSH     ES
        PUSH     DI
        PUSH     SI

        ;*********************************************************************
        ;- COMPUTE MASKS FOR FIRST AND LAST BYTE WITHIN A RASTER            *
        ;    ROTATION FACTOR, AND MASKS FOR HI AND LOW BITS AFTER ROTATION  *
        ;    ENABLE ROTATION AND LOGICAL FUNCTIONS IN GRAPHICS CONTROLLER   *
        ;*********************************************************************

        MOV      CX,X_Dst                   ; NUMBER OF CLEAR BITS IN FIRST BYTE
        AND      CX,7
        MOV      First_Mask,0FFH            ; COMPUTE MASK TO CLEAR LEADING BITS
        SHR      First_Mask,CL
        MOV      AX,8
        SUB      AX,CX
        MOV      InFirst,AX

        ;MASK TO KEEP BITS IN LAST BYTE (PARTIAL BYTE)

        MOV      CX,X_Dst                   ; GET ADDRESS OF LAST BIT
        ADD      CX,BWidth
        AND      CX,7                       ; POSITION JUST AFTER LAST BIT
        MOV      Last_Mask,0FFH             ; COMPUTE MASK TO KEEP BITS AFTER
        SHR      Last_Mask,CL
        NOT      Last_Mask                  ; COMPLEMENT TO KEEP LEADING BITS
```

```
;*********************************************************************
;BITS FROM SOURCE BYTE MUST BE ALLIGNED WITH BITS IN THE         *
;DESTINATION BYTE.  THE ROTATION IS COMPUTED HERE AND THE        *
;TWO MASKS NEEDED TO ISOLATE TWO HALVES OF THE BYTE              *
;*********************************************************************

    ; COMPUTE ROTATION

    MOV     CX,X_Dst            ; COMPUTE BIT DISTANCE BETWEEN
    SUB     CX,X_Src            ;... BIT POSITIONS IN FIRST BYTES
    AND     CX,7                ; ... OF SOURCE AND DESTINATION BYTES
                                ; ... AS (SRC-DST)&7
    MOV     AX,00FFH            ;Compute masks for nonzero rotation
    ROR     AX,CL
    MOV     Lower_Mask,AL       ;Save the masks
    MOV     Upper_Mask,AH

    MOV     DX,3CEH             ;Address of GRAPHICS controller
    MOV     AL,3                ;Index for DATA ROTATE & FN SELECT
    OUT     DX,AL               ;Select DATA ROTATE & FN SELECT REG
    INC     DX
    MOV     AL,CL               ;Fetch rotate count
    MOV     AH,Fn               ;Fetch logical function
    AND     AH,3                ;Move logical function into
    SHL     AH,1                ;bits 3 and 4
    SHL     AH,1
    SHL     AH,1
    OR      AL,AH
    OUT     DX,AL               ;Write value into DATA ROTATE... reg

;*********************************************************************
;- COMPUTE ABSOLUTE ADDRESS OF SOURCE AND DESTINATION            *
;*********************************************************************

    MOV     WORD PTR Y_Incr,HBYTES  ;Initialize y traversal as normal

;Because of possible overlap we must adjust direction of traversal
;If source block is above the destination then reverse Y traversal
;If source block is to the left, then reverse X traversal

    MOV     AX,Y_Src            ;Compare source and destination Y
    MOV     BX,Y_Dst
    CMP     AX,BX
    JLE     Compute_Address     ;...Leave alone if src <= dst
    ADD     AX,BHeight          ;Begin with last raster in block
    DEC     AX
    ADD     BX,BHeight
    DEC     BX
    MOV     Y_Src,AX
    MOV     Y_Dst,BX
    NEG     WORD PTR Y_Incr     ;And traverse backward
Compute_Address:
    MOV     AX,Y_Src            ;Compute offset for source
    MOV     BX,HBYTES           ;as offset = y * 80 + x/8
    MUL     BX
    MOV     SI,X_Src
    SHR     SI,1
```

```
           SHR     SI,1
           SHR     SI,1
           ADD     SI,AX
           MOV     Src_Address,SI

           MOV     AX,Y_Dst               ;Compute offset for destination
           MOV     BX,HBYTES              ;as offset = y * 80 + x/8
           MUL     BX
           MOV     DI,X_Dst
           SHR     DI,1
           SHR     DI,1
           SHR     DI,1
           ADD     DI,AX
           MOV     Dst_Address,DI

           MOV     AX,GRF_SEG             ;Setup segment
           MOV     ES,AX
           MOV     DS,AX

           ;****************************************************************
           ;- ENABLE NEXT PLANE FOR READ AND WRITE                       *
           ;****************************************************************

           MOV     AL,3                   ;Initialize counter of planes
           MOV     Read_Plane,AL
Plane_Loop:
           MOV     AX,BWidth              ;Copy dimensions of the block
           MOV     Block_Dx,AX
           MOV     AX,BHeight
           MOV     Block_Dy,AX
           MOV     SI,Src_Address         ;Fetch source address
           MOV     DI,Dst_Address         ;Fetch destination address
           MOV     CL,Read_Plane          ;Fetch next plane to do
           MOV     AH,1                   ;Use plane number to setup value
           SHL     AH,CL                  ;for WRITE PLANE SELECT register
           MOV     DX,3C4H                ;Fetch address of SEQUENCER
           MOV     AL,2                   ;Index for WRITE PLANE SELECT register
           OUT     DX,AL                  ;Select register
           INC     DX
           MOV     AL,AH                  ;Fetch value
           OUT     DX,AL                  ;Write value into register
           MOV     DX,3CEH                ;Fetch address of GRAPHICS controller
           MOV     AL,4                   ;Index for READ PLANE SELECT register
           OUT     DX,AL                  ;Select register
           INC     DX
           MOV     AL,CL                  ;Fetch plane number
           OUT     DX,AL                  ;Write plane number into register
           DEC     DX
           MOV     AL,8                   ;Index for BIT MASK register
           OUT     DX,AL                  ;Select BIT MASK register
           INC     DX
```

```
        ;**********************************************************************
        ; RASTER LOOP IS DONE IN FOUR STEPS                                   *
        ; (1) MASKS AND ROTATION FACTOR IS COMPUTED TO ALIGN SRC AND DEST     *
        ; (2) LEADING PARTIAL BYTE OF DESTINATION IS MODIFIED                 *
        ; (3) FULL BYTES OF DESTINATION ARE MODIFIED                          *
        ; (4) TRAILING PARTIAL BYTE OF DESTINATION IS MODIFIED                *
        ;**********************************************************************


        ;**********************************************************************
        ;- GET ENOUGH BITS FROM SOUCE TO CONSTRUCT FIRST PARTIAL BYTE OF DST  *
        ;**********************************************************************
Raster_Loop:
        MOV     CX,Block_Dx             ;Number of bits to copy
        PUSH    SI                      ;Preserve addresses for next raster loop
        PUSH    DI

        MOV     AX,X_Src                ;Check if need one or two bytes
        AND     AX,7                    ;for first byte of destination
        MOV     BX,X_Dst
        AND     BX,7
        CMP     AX,BX
        JG      Get_2_Bytes
Get_1_Byte:
        MOV     AL,First_Mask           ;Fetch mask for first partial byte
        AND     AL,Lower_Mask           ;Combine with "lower mask"
        OUT     DX,AL                   ;Write mask into BIT MASK register
        LODSB                           ;Fetch first source byte
        MOV     AH,[DI]                 ;Latch destination
        STOSB                           ;Write first byte of destination
        MOV     AH,AL                   ;Save AL since it will be trashed by OU
        JMP     Leading_Done

Get_2_Bytes:
        MOV     AL,First_Mask           ;Fetch mask for first partial byte
        AND     AL,Upper_Mask           ;Combine with "upper mask"
        OUT     DX,AL                   ;Write mask into BIT MASK register
        LODSB
        MOV     AH,[DI]                 ;Latch destination bits
        MOV     ES:[DI],AL              ;Write first byte

        MOV     AL,First_Mask           ;Fetch mask for first partial byte
        AND     AL,Lower_Mask           ;Combine with "lower mask"
        OUT     DX,AL                   ;Write mask into BIT MASK register
        LODSB
        MOV     AH,[DI]                 ;Latch destination bits
        STOSB                           ;Write first byte
        MOV     AH,AL                   ;Save AL since it will be trashed by OU

Leading_Done:
        SUB     CX,InFirst              ;Update number of bits to transfer
        JLE     Raster_Done

        ;**********************************************************************
        ;- LOOP OVER COMPLETE BYTES WITHIN A SINGLE SOURCE RASTER             *
        ;**********************************************************************
```

```
Full_Loop:
        CMP     CX,8                    ;If less then 8 bits to do
        JL      Full_Done               ;quit this loop

        MOV     AL,Upper_Mask           ;Fetch the "upper mask"
        OUT     DX,AL                   ;Write mask into BIT MASK register
        MOV     AL,[DI]                 ;Latch destination bits
        MOV     [DI],AH                 ;Write half 2 for src to half 1 of dst

        MOV     AL,Lower_Mask           ;Fetch the lower mask
        OUT     DX,AL                   ;Write mask into BIT MASK register
        LODSB                           ;Fetch next source byte
        MOV     AH,[DI]                 ;Latch destination bits
        STOSB                           ;Write half 1 of src to half 2 of dst
        MOV     AH,AL                   ;Save AL since it will be trashed by OU

        SUB     CX,8                    ; DECREMENT WIDTH BY BITS TO BE DONE
        JMP     Full_Loop
Full_Done:

        ;****************************************************************
        ;- TRANSFER THE LAST PARTIAL BYTE                              *
        ;****************************************************************

Last_Partial:
        CMP     CX,0                    ;Any more bits to transfer?
        JLE     Raster_Done             ;...No, quit this raster

        MOV     AL,Last_Mask            ;Fetch mask for last partial byte
        AND     AL,Upper_Mask           ;Combine with "upper mask"
        OUT     DX,AL                   ;Write mask into BIT MASK register
        MOV     AL,[DI]                 ;Latch destination bits
        MOV     [DI],AH                 ;Write half 2 for src to half 1 of dst

        MOV     AL,Last_Mask            ;Fetch mask for last partial byte
        AND     AL,Lower_Mask           ;Combine with "upper mask"
        OUT     DX,AL                   ;Write mask into BIT MASK register
        LODSB                           ;Fetch next source byte
        MOV     AH,[DI]                 ;Latch destination bits
        STOSB                           ;Write half 1 of src to half 2 of dst

        ;- ADVANCE TO THE NEXT RASTER

Raster_Done:
        POP     DI                      ;Pointers to current raster
        POP     SI
        ADD     SI,Y_Incr               ;Update pointer to point to the next
        ADD     DI,Y_Incr               ;raster
        DEC     WORD PTR Block_Dy       ;Update number of rasters to do
        JLE     Test_Plane
        JMP     Raster_Loop             ;And repeat if not all done

Test_Plane:
        DEC     Read_Plane              ;Update number of planes to do
        JL      Blit_Done
        JMP     Plane_Loop              ;And do next plane if any left to do
```

```
        ;************************************************************************
        ;- Clean up and exit                                                   *
        ;************************************************************************
Blit_Done:
        ;restore rotate value
        MOV     DX,3CEH                 ;Address of GRAPHICS controller
        MOV     AL,3                    ;Index for ROTATE & FN SELECT
        OUT     DX,AL                   ;Select ROTATE & FN SELECT register
        INC     DX
        XOR     AL,AL                   ;Disable rotate and set fn=copy
        OUT     DX,AL                   ;Write value into register
        ;restore bit mask
        DEC     DX
        MOV     AL,8                    ;Index for BIT MASK register
        OUT     DX,AL                   ;Select BIT MASK register
        INC     DX
        MOV     AL,0FFH                 ;Enable all 8 bits for write
        OUT     DX,AL                   ;Write value into register
        ;enable all four planes for write
        MOV     DX,3C4H                 ;Address of SEQUENCER
        MOV     AL,2                    ;Index for PLANE ENABLE register
        OUT     DX,AL                   ;Select register
        INC     DX
        MOV     AL,0FH                  ;Value to enable all four planes
        OUT     DX,AL                   ;Write value into register

        POP     SI                      ;Restore segment registers
        POP     DI
        POP     ES
        POP     DS
        MOV     SP,BP
        POP     BP
        RET
_BitBlt ENDP
```

Display Cursor

Draw a Graphics Cursor (Sprite)

SET_CURSOR is used to define shape, color, and alignment of the cursor.
MOVE_CURSOR is used to control motion of the cursor.
REMOVE_CURSOR is used to remove the cursor from the screen.

Pascal Library Procedure

```
procedure Set_Cursor(andmask,xormask,backgnd,foregnd:integer);
                {offset of AND mask and XOR mask, foreground and back-
                ground}
procedure Move_Cursor(x,y:integer);
                {new position of a cursor}
procedure Remove_Cursor;
```

C Library Procedures

```
set_cursor(and_mask, xor_mask, fg, bg)    /* Define cursor shape          */
int   and_mask[16];                       /* 16x16 array with AND mask    */
int   or_mask[16];                        /* 16x16 array with XOR mask    */
int   fg;                                 /* Color for 1 bits in masks    */
int   bg;                                 /* Color for 0 bits in masks    */

move_cursor(x, y)                         /* Move cursor to x,y           */
int   x,y;                                /* New position                 */

remove_cursor()                           /* Restore area under the last cursor  */
```

Theory

The Display Cursor procedure will rapidly move a 16 x 16 pixel object around the screen without destroying the background area. The most common application for this function is in cursor display. This technique is also used in games to manipulate Sprites (small objects of fixed appearance that move rapidly around the screen).

Three types of cursor operations are needed:

Define Shape: Cursor shape is defined by two structures: the AND mask and the XOR mask. Each structure is a 16 x 16 pixel array of bits defining the cursor shape. By properly setting the bits of the AND mask and the XOR mask, the cursor square can be defined to have white regions, black regions, and regions of transparency. A typical cursor might have a black border with a white outline and a transparent interior; another might have a black arrow with a white outline, with the rest of the cursor box transparent. This is illustrated in Figure 8-13. The following table shows how to define the masks for each pixel to establish the desired result.

AND Mask	XOR Mask	Result
0	0	Black
0	1	White
1	0	Transparent
1	1	Inverted

Cursor color is defined in terms of background and foreground color. The single plane (monochrome) arrays for AND Mask and XOR Mask are Color Expanded into four plane deep arrays using the background and foreground colors.

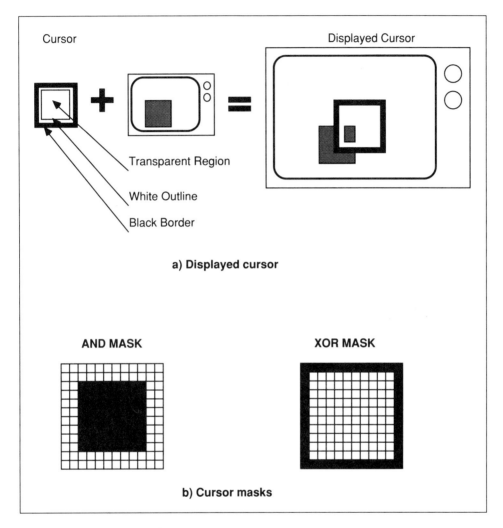

Figure 8-13. Cursor regions.

Move Cursor: First the background data at the previous cursor position is re-stored by being copied back in from the "save" area in offscreen memory, where it was saved during the previous Move Cursor operation. Next the background data at the new cursor position is copied into the save area. Then the AND and XOR masks are used to draw the cursor (see Figure 8-14).

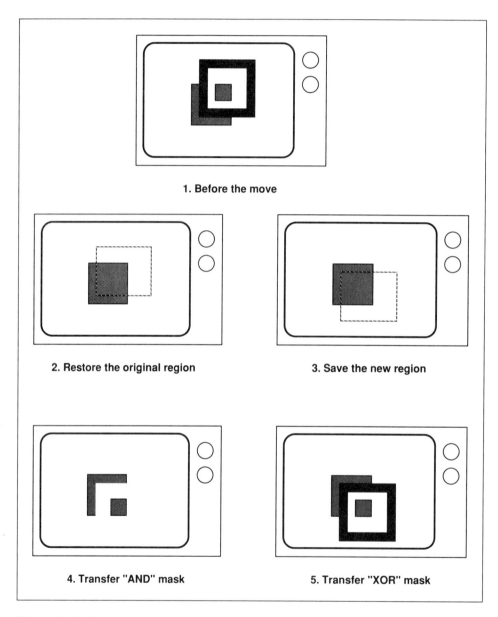

Figure 8-14. Steps in cursor move.

Remove Cursor: This step is performed to completely remove the cursor from the screen. The background data at the cursor position is restored by being copied back in from the "save" area.

> When working with graphics cursors, it is important to ensure that no drawing function will ever attempt to draw over the current cursor position. If this occurs, that data will be lost when the cursor is moved and the background data is restored. For safety, it is best to remove the cursor from the display when a drawing function is in progress.

Example

Listing 8-34. File: PROGC092.C

```
/**********************************************************************/
/* Display black and white sprite and move it using arrow keys       */
/**********************************************************************/

demo_cursor()
       {
       #define MAX_X            (640 - 16)
       #define MAX_Y            (350 - 16)

       #define KEY_ESC          0x011B
       #define KEY_UP           0x4800
       #define KEY_DOWN         0x5000
       #define KEY_LEFT         0x4B00
       #define KEY_RIGHT        0x4D00
       #define KEY_ENTER        0x1C0D

       static  char    and_mask[] = {
               0x00,0x00, 0x00,0x00, 0x00,0x00, 0x1F,0xF8,
               0x1F,0xF8, 0x1F,0xF8, 0x1F,0xF8, 0x1F,0xF8,
               0x1F,0xF8, 0x1F,0xF8, 0x1F,0xF8, 0x1F,0xF8,
               0x1F,0xF8, 0x00,0x00, 0x00,0x00, 0x00,0x00};
       static  char    xor_mask[] = {
               0xFF,0xFF, 0x80,0x01, 0xBF,0xFD, 0xA0,0x05,
               0xA0,0x05, 0xA0,0x05, 0xA0,0x05, 0xA0,0x05,
               0xA0,0x05, 0xA0,0x05, 0xA0,0x05, 0xA0,0x05,
               0xA0,0x05, 0xBF,0xFD, 0x80,0x01, 0xFF,0xFF};
       int     key, x, y, i;

       /* Draw a background pattern  and a solid white box          */

       clear_screen();
       for (i = 0; i < 640; i += 20) line(320,100,i,  0,i/20);
       for (i = 0; i < 640; i += 20) line(320,100,i,199,i/20);
       for (i = 0; i < 200; i += 10) line(320,100,0,  i,i/10);
       for (i = 0; i < 200; i += 10) line(320,100,639,i,i/10);
       solid_box(320,100,150,150,15);
```

```
/* Set cursor shape and color, and display the first cursor      */

set_cursor(and_mask, xor_mask, 0, 15);
x = 320;                                /* initial position of cursor   */
y = 100;
move_cursor(x,y);                       /* show cursor at initial pos   */

/* Loop while keys are pressed
*/

do
    {
    switch (key = get_key())/* Move cursor according to key */
        {
        case KEY_ESC:
        case KEY_ENTER:
                remove_cursor();
                break;
        case KEY_UP:
                y = (y -1) > 0 ? -y : 0;
                move_cursor(x, y);
                break;
        case KEY_DOWN:
                y = (y + 1) < MAX_Y ? ++y : MAX_Y;
                move_cursor(x, y);
                break;
        case KEY_RIGHT:
                x = (x + 1) < MAX_X ? ++x : MAX_X;
                move_cursor(x, y);
                break;
        case KEY_LEFT:
                x = (x - 1) > 0 ? -x : 0;
                move_cursor(x, y);
                break;
        default:
                break;
        }
    } while (key != KEY_ENTER);
}
```

Listing 8-35. File: PROGP092.PAS

```
{*************************************************************************}
{ Display black and white sprite and move it using arrow keys           }
{*************************************************************************}

procedure demo_cursor;
const
MAX_X = 624;
MAX_Y = 334;
KEY_ESC = $1B;
KEY_UP   = 72;
KEY_DOWN = 80;
KEY_LEFT = 75;
KEY_RIGHT = 77;
KEY_ENTER = $0D;
```

```
MONO = 5;
COLOR = 4;
VMONO = 7;

arrow_and_mask : array[0..31] of byte = (
                0,0, 0,0, 0,0, $1F,$F8,
                $1F,$F8, $1F,$F8, $1F,$F8, $1F,$F8,
                $1F,$F8, $1F,$F8, $1F,$F8, $1F,$F8,
                $1F,$F8, 0,0, 0,0, 0,0);

arrow_xor_mask : array[0..31] of byte = (
                $FF,$FF, $80,$01, $BF,$FD, $A0,$05,
                $A0,$05, $A0,$05, $A0,$05, $A0,$05,
                $A0,$05, $A0,$05, $A0,$05, $A0,$05,
                $A0,$05, $BF,$FD, $80,$01, $FF,$FF);

var
i,key,x,y : integer;
begin
        Clear_Screen;
        i := Get_Display_Type;
        if i = MONO then        Set_Mode($0F)
        else if i = VMONO then  Set_Mode($0F)
        else if i = COLOR then  Set_Mode($0E)
        else                    Set_Mode($10);

        { Draw white box to see how cursor looks on white background   }

        for i := 0 to 31 do Line(320,100,20*i,0,i);     { Fill background}
        for i := 0 to 31 do Line(320,100,20*i,199,i);
        for i := 0 to 19 do Line(320,100,0,10*i,i);
        for i := 0 to 19 do Line(320,100,639,10*i,i);
        Solid_Box(220,100,150,150,15);                  { and draw a box}


        { Set cursor shape and color, and display the first cursor       }

        Set_Cursor(ofs(arrow_and_mask),ofs(arrow_xor_mask), 0, 15);
        x := 220;                         { initial position of cursor    }
        y := 100;
        Move_Cursor(x,y);                 { show cursor at initial pos    }

        { Loop while keys are pressed }

        repeat
                key := integer(readkey);
                case key of      { Move cursor according to key }

                KEY_ESC : Remove_Cursor;
                KEY_ENTER : Remove_Cursor;

                KEY_UP:
                    begin
                        if y > 0 then dec(y);
                        Move_Cursor(x, y);
                    end;
```

```
            KEY_DOWN:
                begin
                    if y < MAX_Y then inc(y);
                    Move_Cursor(x, y);
                end;

            KEY_RIGHT:
                begin
                    if x < MAX_X then inc(x);
                    Move_Cursor(x, y);
                end;

            KEY_LEFT:
                begin
                    if x > 0 then dec(x);
                    Move_Cursor(x, y);
                end;
            end;
    until key = KEY_ENTER;

    i := integer(readkey);

    {- Set default text mode                                     }

    i := Get_Display_Type;
    if i = MONO then        Set_Mode(7)
    else if i = VMONO then  Set_Mode(7)
    else                    Set_Mode(3);
end;
```

Assembly Code Example

The **Set_Cursor** procedure will color expand the two cursor masks into four planes by the following procedure. The expanded masks will be stored at the start of off-screen memory, just above the visible section of the display memory.

1.   Fill all 32 bytes (16 bits x 16 bits) of both masks with the background color using the Set/Reset register of the Graphics Controller.

2.   Use each of the 32 bytes of the monochrome AND mask as a bit mask in the Mask register of the Graphics Controller, with the foreground color in the Set/Reset register, to set desired bits to foreground color in both masks.

3.   Copy data from the initial cursor position (upper left corner of the screen) to a "save" area to be used as restore data on the first call to Move_Cursor. For each byte, read display data into the read latches (using any read mode), and write the data to the save area (using Write Latch Data as the write mode). All four planes must be write enabled, with all mask bits set (default settings). Since 16 horizontal pixels can span up to three bytes, three bytes are always copied from each scan line.

4. Save the initial cursor position as the "previous" cursor position.

The **Move_Cursor** procedure will move the cursor from one location to another by these steps:

1. Restore data at previous cursor position by copying the data from the "save" area. For each byte, read data from "save" area using any read mode (to load read latches), and write the data to on-screen display memory using Write Latch Data as the write mode. All four planes must be write enabled, with all mask bits set (default settings).

2. Compute next location for cursor block.

3. Set up logical operation AND, use BITBLT function to copy cursor AND mask. Set up logical operation XOR and use BITBLT function to copy cursor XOR mask.

The **Remove_Cursor** procedure will erase the cursor from the screen and restore the background data from the "save" area.

To learn more about memory organization see Display Memory in Graphics Modes in Chapter 2.

To learn more about logical operations, masking, and rotate, see register description for Set/Reset registers 0 and 1, Data Rotate/Function Select register 3, Mode register 5, and Mask register 8, in Chapter 3.

Also see programming examples Pixel Write and Scanline Fill in this chapter.

Listing 8-36. File: PROG088.ASM

```
;**********************************************************************
; Set Cursor:                                                       *
; This procedure will expand the two cursor masks into              *
; four planes.  The expanded masks will be stored                   *
; after the last visible scan line at A000:(640/8*350).             *
; Entry:        AND_Mask - 2x16 bytes with AND mask                 *
;               XOR_Mask - 2x16 bytes with XOR mask                 *
;               FG_Color - Foreground color                         *
;               BG_Color - Background color                         *
;**********************************************************************


YSIZE          EQU       350
HBYTES         EQU       80
CUR_HEIGHT     EQU       16
GRFSEG         EQU       0A000H

AND_SAVE       EQU       (YSIZE*HBYTES+0)
```

```
XOR_SAVE          EQU     (YSIZE*HBYTES+2)
CUR_SAVE          EQU     (YSIZE*HBYTES+4)

AND_Mask          EQU     [BP+4]
XOR_Mask          EQU     [BP+6]
BG_Color          EQU     [BP+8]
FG_Color          EQU     [BP+10]

Last_Cursor       DW      0

        PUBLIC  _Set_Cursor

_Set_Cursor       PROC NEAR
        PUSH    BP
        MOV     BP,SP
        PUSH    SI
        PUSH    DI
        PUSH    ES                      ; always save seg regs
        PUSH    DS

        MOV     AX,GRFSEG               ;Point ES to video ram.
        MOV     ES,AX

        ;Set EGA to use SET/RESET register to fill with background color

        MOV     DX,3CEH                 ; enable use of reset register
        MOV     AL,1
        OUT     DX,AL
        INC     DX
        MOV     AL,0Fh
        OUT     DX,AL
        DEC     DX                      ; move color into reset register
        XOR     AL,AL
        OUT     DX,AL
        INC     DX
        MOV     AX,BG_Color
        OUT     DX,AL

        ; Fill with background

        MOV     DI,AND_SAVE             ;Pointer to save area (AND and XOR)
        MOV     CX,CUR_HEIGHT           ;Number of scanlines to do
Back_Loop1:
        STOSW                           ;16 bits for AND mask
        STOSW                           ;16 bits for XOR mask
        ADD     DI,HBYTES-4             ;Point to next scanline
        LOOP    Back_Loop1

        ; Change foreground bits for the AND mask save area

        MOV     AX,FG_Color             ;Load SET/RESET with foreground color
        OUT     DX,AL
        DEC     DX                      ;Select BIT MASK register
        MOV     AL,8
        OUT     DX,AL
        INC     DX
```

```
        MOV     CX,CUR_HEIGHT           ;Initialize counter
        MOV     DI,AND_Save             ;Get pointer to AND save area
        MOV     SI,AND_Mask             ;Get pointer to AND mask

Fore_Loop1:
        LODSB                           ;Fetch next byte from the mask
        OUT     DX,AL                   ;Set BIT MASK register using cursor mas
        MOV     AH,ES:[DI]              ;Latch data
        STOSB                           ;Write next 8 bits
        LODSB                           ;Fetch next byte from the mask
        OUT     DX,AL                   ;Set BIT MASK register using cursor mas
        MOV     AH,ES:[DI]              ;Latch data
        STOSB                           ;Write next 8 bits
        ADD     DI,HBYTES-2
        LOOP    Fore_Loop1

        ; Change foreground bits for the XOR mask save area

        MOV     CX,CUR_HEIGHT           ;Initialize counter
        MOV     DI,XOR_Save             ;Get pointer to XOR save area
        MOV     SI,XOR_Mask             ;Get pointer to XOR mask

Fore_Loop2:
        LODSB                           ;Fetch next byte from the mask
        OUT     DX,AL                   ;Set BIT MASK register using cursor mas
        MOV     AH,ES:[DI]              ;Latch data
        STOSB                           ;Write next 8 bits
        LODSB                           ;Fetch next byte from the mask
        OUT     DX,AL                   ;Set BIT MASK register using cursor mas
        MOV     AH,ES:[DI]              ;Latch data
        STOSB                           ;Write next 8 bits
        ADD     DI,HBYTES-2
        LOOP    Fore_Loop2

        ;Setup EGA registers for data copy (WRITE LATCH write mode)

        MOV     DX,3CEH                 ;Restore graphics controller
        MOV     AL,1                    ;Disable use of SET/RESET
        OUT     DX,AL
        INC     DX
        XOR     AL,AL
        OUT     DX,AL
        DEC     DX
        MOV     AL,8                    ;Enable all 8 bits for write
        OUT     DX,AL
        INC     DX
        MOV     AL,0FFH
        OUT     DX,AL
        DEC     DX
        MOV     AL,5                    ;Select WRITE LATCH write mode
        OUT     DX,AL
        INC     DX
        MOV     AL,1
        OUT     DX,AL

        ;Copy upper left corner into save area (this is needed for first
        ;call to Move_Cursor procedure because it always restores and
```

```
                ;we need meaningfull data for the first restore).

        MOV     SI,0                    ;Copy from upper left
        MOV     CS:Last_Cursor,SI       ;Keep where it came from
        MOV     DI,CUR_SAVE             ;Copy to cursor save area
        MOV     AX,ES                   ;Point DS to display buffer
        MOV     DS,AX
        MOV     CX,CUR_HEIGHT           ;Number of lines to copy
Set_Copy_Loop:
        MOVSB                           ;Copy 24 bits from next raster
        MOVSB
        MOVSB
        ADD     DI,HBYTES-3             ;Update pointers to next raster
        ADD     SI,HBYTES-3
        LOOP    Set_Copy_Loop

                ;Restore normal write mode

        XOR     AL,AL                   ;WRITE MODE register is still selected
        OUT     DX,AL                   ;so load it with value 0

                ;Clean up and return

        POP     DS                      ;Restore segment registers
        POP     ES
        POP     DI
        POP     SI
        MOV     SP,BP
        POP     BP
        RET
_Set_Cursor     ENDP

;********************************************************************
; Move_Cursor:                                                     *
; This procedure is used to move the cursor from one              *
; location to another.                                            *
; Entry:          Curs_X - Position of the new cursor             *
;                 Curs_Y                                          *
;********************************************************************

FUNC_AND        EQU     1
FUNC_XOR        EQU     3

Curs_X          EQU     [BP+4]
Curs_Y          EQU     [BP+6]

        PUBLIC  _Move_Cursor

_Move_Cursor    PROC    NEAR
        PUSH    BP
        MOV     BP,SP
        PUSH    SI
        PUSH    DI
        PUSH    ES                      ; always save seg regs
        PUSH    DS

        CALL    _Remove_Cursor          ;Restore last location
```

```
        ;Setup EGA registers for data copy (WRITE LATCH write mode)

        MOV     DX,3CEH                 ;Address of GRAPICS controller
        MOV     AL,5                    ;Select WRITE LATCH write mode
        OUT     DX,AL
        INC     DX
        MOV     AL,1
        OUT     DX,AL

        ;Copy next location of the cursor to the save area

        MOV     AX,Curs_Y               ;Convert cursor X,Y to offset
        MOV     BX,HBYTES
        MUL     BX
        MOV     SI,Curs_X
        SHR     SI,1
        SHR     SI,1
        SHR     SI,1
        ADD     SI,AX
        MOV     CS:Last_Cursor,SI       ;Keep location so we can restore later
        MOV     AX,GRFSEG               ;Point ES and DS to display buffer
        MOV     DS,AX
        MOV     ES,AX
        MOV     DI,CUR_SAVE             ;Pointer to save area
        MOV     CX,CUR_HEIGHT           ;Number of lines to copy
Move_Copy_Loop:
        MOVSB                           ;Copy 16 bits from next raster
        MOVSB
        MOVSB
        ADD     DI,HBYTES-3             ;Update pointers to next raster
        ADD     SI,HBYTES-3
        LOOP    Move_Copy_Loop

        ;Restore normal write mode

        MOV     DX,3CFH
        MOV     AL,0                    ;WRITE MODE register is still selected
        OUT     DX,AL                   ;so load it with value 0

        ;Use BITBLT procedure to copy AND and XOR masks of the cursor

        MOV     AX,FUNC_AND             ;Push function on the stack
        PUSH    AX
        MOV     AX,CUR_HEIGHT           ;Push width and height
        PUSH    AX
        PUSH    AX
        PUSH    WORD PTR Curs_Y         ;Push x and y of destination
        PUSH    WORD PTR Curs_X
        MOV     AX,YSIZE                ;Push x and y of source
        PUSH    AX
        MOV     AX,0
        PUSH    AX
        CALL    _BitBlt
        ADD     SP,14

        MOV     AX,FUNC_XOR             ;Push function on the stack
        PUSH    AX
```

```
        MOV     AX,CUR_HEIGHT            ;Push width and height
        PUSH    AX
        PUSH    AX
        PUSH    WORD PTR Curs_Y          ;Push x and y of destination
        PUSH    WORD PTR Curs_X
        MOV     AX,YSIZE                 ;Push x and y of source
        PUSH    AX
        MOV     AX,16
        PUSH    AX
        CALL    _BitBlt
        ADD     SP,14

        ;Clean up and return

        POP     DS                       ;Restore segment registers
        POP     ES
        POP     DI
        POP     SI
        MOV     SP,BP
        POP     BP
        RET
_Move_Cursor    ENDP

;**************************************************************************
; Remove_Cursor:                                                         *
; This procedure is used to remove the cursor from the screen            *
; and to restore the screen to its original appearance                   *
;**************************************************************************

        PUBLIC  _Remove_Cursor

_Remove_Cursor  PROC NEAR
        PUSH    BP
        MOV     BP,SP
        PUSH    SI
        PUSH    DI
        PUSH    ES                       ; always save seg regs
        PUSH    DS

        ;Setup EGA registers for data copy (WRITE LATCH write mode)

        MOV     DX,3CEH                  ;Address of GRAPICS controller
        MOV     AL,5                     ;Select WRITE LATCH write mode
        OUT     DX,AL
        INC     DX
        MOV     AL,1
        OUT     DX,AL

        ;Copy save area back to last location of the cursor

        MOV     AX,0A000H                ;Set up segment pointers
        MOV     ES,AX
        MOV     DS,AX
        MOV     DI,CS:Last_Cursor        ;Copy to last X,Y of cursor
        MOV     SI,CUR_SAVE              ;Copy form cursor save area
        MOV     CX,CUR_HEIGHT            ;Number of lines to copy
Rest_Copy_Loop:
```

```
        MOVSB                            ;Copy 16 bits from next raster
        MOVSB
        MOVSB
        ADD     DI,HBYTES-3              ;Update pointers to next raster
        ADD     SI,HBYTES-3
        LOOP    Rest_Copy_Loop

        ;Restore normal write mode

        MOV     AL,0                     ;WRITE MODE register is still selected
        OUT     DX,AL                    ;so load it with value 0

        ;Clean up and return

        POP     DS                       ;Restore segment registers
        POP     ES
        POP     DI
        POP     SI
        MOV     SP,BP
        POP     BP
        RET
_Remove_Cursor  ENDP
```

Dump Screen

Save Contents of the Display Buffer Into a File

Pascal Library Procedure

function Screen_Dump:integer;

C Library Procedure

screen_dump()   /* Save display buffer into a file   */

Example

Listing 8-37. File: PROGC093.C

```
/*********************************************************************/
/* Save content of screen into a file "picture.001"                 */
/*********************************************************************/

save_screen()
      {
      int     i, j, x, y, color;

      /* Display a pattern on the screen                       */

      cls();                                 /* Clear screen        */
      for (j = 0; j < 4; j++)                /* Loop over rows of b's*/
            for (i = 0; i < 4; i++)          /* Loop over columns   */
```

```
                        {
                        y       = j * 200/4;        /* Draw the box          */
                        x       = i * 640/4;
                        color = i + j * 4;
                        solid_box(x, y, x + 640/4, y + 200/4, color);
                        }
              /* Save it into a file                                         */

              if (!screen_dump())
                      printf("\n...Error while saving screen\n");
              else
                      printf("\n...Picture sucessfully saved\n");
              }
```

Listing 8-38. File: PROGP093.PAS

```
{**********************************************************************}
{ Save content of screen into a file "picture.001"                    }
{**********************************************************************}

procedure save_screen;
const
MONO = 5;
COLOR = 4;
VMONO = 7;
var
i,j,x,y,pcolor : integer;
begin   { Display a pattern on the screen                        }
        Clear_Screen;                                { Clear screen  }
        i := Get_Display_Type;
        if i = MONO then        Set_Mode($0F)
        else if i = VMONO then Set_Mode($0F)
        else if i = COLOR then Set_Mode($0E)
        else            Set_Mode($10);

        for j := 0 to 3 do begin              { Loop over rows of b's}
              for i := 0 to 3 do begin        { Loop over columns    }
                      y := j * 200 div 4;     { Draw the box         }
                      x := i * 640 div 4;
                      pcolor := i + j * 4;
                      Solid_Box(x, y, x+640 div 4, y+200 div 4, pcolor);
              end;
        end;
        i := Screen_Dump;
        if i = 0 then writeln('...Error while saving screen')
        else writeln('...Picture sucessfully saved');

        i := integer(readkey);

        {- Set default text mode                                     }

        i := Get_Display_Type;
        if i = MONO then        Set_Mode(7)
        else if i = VMONO then Set_Mode(7)
        else            Set_Mode(3);
end;
```

Theory

The most efficient way to save and restore data on the EGA/VGA is to read one memory plane at a time. The screen save is done in these steps:

1. Open an output file for writing.

2. Enable Plane 0 for reading. Transfer 28,000 bytes from display memory, starting at address A000:0000, to the output file.

3. Repeat step 2 for planes 1, 2, and 3.

4. Close the output file.

To save a full screen of high resolution graphics data requires 112,000 bytes of storage. It may be desirable to compress the data while saving it, and decompress the data when redisplaying it. Besides saving disk space, compression can also speedup the save and display process since it reduces time consuming disk accesses.

Assembly Code Examples

Listing 8-39. File: PROG089.ASM

```
;**********************************************************************
; Save current screen into a file PICTURE.001                       *
; Assumes default settings of EGA registers for modes E,F,10        *
;**********************************************************************
;
Save_Name      DB      "PICTURE.000",0
Save_Handle    DW      0
Save_Counter   DB      0

        PUBLIC   _Screen_Dump

_Screen_Dump   PROC     NEAR
        PUSH    DS                      ;Preserve DS

        ;- Open next file (*.001 first time, *.002 next,  ...)

        MOV     AX,CS                   ;Setup pointer to file name
        MOV     DS,AX                   ;into DS:DX

        INC     Save_Name[10]           ;Change name so that we can call
                                        ;this routine several times
        LEA     DX,Save_Name
        MOV     CX,0                    ;Normal attribute for the file
        MOV     AH,3CH                  ;DOS function to open file
        INT     21H                     ;Ask DOS to open the file
        JC      Dump_Error              ;Quit on open error
        MOV     Save_Handle,AX          ;Save the handle to the opened file
```

```
            ;- Enable next plane and write the 28,000 bytes into a file

        MOV     Save_Counter,3          ;Initialize counter of planes done
        MOV     DX,3CEH                 ;Select READ MAP SELECT register
        MOV     AL,4                    ;in graphics controller
        OUT     DX,AL
        MOV     AX,0A000H               ;Point DS:DX to display buffer
        MOV     DS,AX
Dump_Plane_Loop:
        MOV     AL,CS:Save_Counter      ;Select next plane for read
        MOV     DX,3CFH
        OUT     DX,AL
        XOR     DX,DX
        MOV     CX,28000                ;Number of bytes to write
        MOV     BX,CS:Save_Handle       ;File handle
        MOV     AH,40H                  ;DOS function to write into a file
        INT     21H                     ;Ask DOS to write data into a file
        JC      Close_Dump_File         ;Quit on error
        CMP     AX,28000
        JNE     Close_Dump_File
        DEC     CS:Save_Counter         ;Check if all planes are done
        JGE     Dump_Plane_Loop ;and if not go do next plane

            ;- Close the file

Close_Dump_File:
        MOV     BX,CS:Save_Handle       ;Fetch handle
        MOV     AH,3EH                  ;DOS function to close a file
        INT     21H                     ;Ask DOS to close the file
Dump_Done:
        MOV     DX,3CEH                 ;Restore plane 0 for read by
        MOV     AL,3                    ;setting READ MAP register
        OUT     DX,AL                   ;in GRAPHICS controller
        INC     DX
        MOV     AL,0
        OUT     DX,AL

        POP     DS                      ;Restore DS
        RET
Dump_Error:                             ;This is where we can add error
        JMP     Dump_Done               ;reporting
_Screen_Dump    ENDP
```

The above procedure can be used as a "terminate and stay resident" program that is installed to service the "print screen" interrupt, INT 5. A listing for such a program is shown below.

To use this program, first run it to make it memory resident, then generate a picture. Press the <Shift> and <PrtScreen> keys to save the picture. Each time <Shift><PrtScreen> is pressed, the display buffer (at address A000:0000) will be saved in a file "PICTURE.nnn", where nnn starts at 000 and is advanced after each save.

Listing 8-40. File: PROG090.ASM

```
;************************************************************************
; Terminate and stay resident program to intercept INT 5, caused by     *
; <Shift>+<PrtSc>, and to save graphics screen into a file.             *
;************************************************************************


_TEXT     SEGMENT BYTE PUBLIC 'CODE'
          ASSUME  CS:_TEXT,DS:_TEXT

          ORG    100H
Screen_Dump:
          JMP    Init_Dump

          ;************************************************************
          ; This is where we get when the <Shift>+<PrtSc> is detected  *
          ;************************************************************

Print_Int       PROC FAR
          STI
          PUSH   AX                    ;Save registers
          PUSH   BX
          PUSH   CX
          PUSH   DX

          CALL   _Screen_Dump          ;Call routine to save video buffer

          POP    DX                    ;Restore registers
          POP    CX
          POP    BX
          POP    AX
          IRET
Print_Int       ENDP

          ;!!!!!!!!!!!!!!!!!!!!!!!!!!!!!!!!!!!!
          ;INSERT THE SCREEN_DUMP ROUTINE HERE
          ;!!!!!!!!!!!!!!!!!!!!!!!!!!!!!!!!!!!!
          INCLUDE PROG089.ASM
Last_Byte:
          ;************************************************************
          ; THIS IS THE INITIALIZATION DONE ONLY WHEN LOADED INTO MEMORY
          ;************************************************************

Message   DB     "Screen Dump Utility Loaded",0Ah,0Dh,0

Init_Dump:

          ;- Print a message telling user that we are installed

          PUSH   CS                    ;Fetch pointer to sign on message
          POP    DS
          LEA    SI,Message
          MOV    BH,0                   ;Use BIOS to print the message
          MOV    BL,7
          LODSB                         ;Fetch first character of message
Write:  MOV    AH,0EH                  ;Output the next character
```

```
        INT     10H                     ;using BIOS function E
        LODSB                           ;Fetch next character of the message
        CMP     AL,0                    ;Is it the terminating zero?
        JNZ     WRITE                   ;...No, go output next one

        ;- Use DOS services to revector Interrupt 5

        MOV     BX,CS                   ;Use service 25 to set vector 5
        MOV     DS,BX
        MOV     DX,OFFSET Print_Int
        MOV     AL,05H
        MOV     AH,25H
        INT     21H

        ;Terminate but stay resident

        MOV     BX,CS                   ;Use DOS service 31 to leave us resident
        MOV     DS,BX
        MOV     DX,OFFSET Last_Byte
        SHR     DX,1
        SHR     DX,1
        SHR     DX,1
        SHR     DX,1
        INC     DX
        MOV     AX,3100H
        INT     21H

        RET
_TEXT   ENDS
        END     Screen_Dump
```

Load Screen

Load Display Buffer From a File

This Procedure is the Converse of Dump Screen

Pascal Library Procedure

function Screen_Load(name_seg,name_ofs:integer):integer;

C Library Procedure

```
screen_load(filename)           /* Display content of a file on    */
char *filename;                 /* the screen                      */
```

Example

Listing 8-41. File: PROGC094.C

```
/***********************************************************************/
/* Display content of file "PICTURE.001" on the screen                */
/***********************************************************************/

restore_screen()
        {
        clear_screen();
        screen_load("picture.001");                   /* Copy file to screen  */
        }
```

Listing 8-42. File: PROGP094.PAS

```
{***********************************************************************}
{ Display content of file "PICTURE.001" on the screen                  }
{***********************************************************************}

procedure restore_screen;
const
MONO = 5;
COLOR = 4;
VMONO = 7;
picture_name : array [0..11] of char = 'PICTURE.001 ';
var
i : integer;
begin
        picture_name[11] := chr(0);
        Clear_Screen;
        i := Get_Display_Type;
        if i = MONO then      Set_Mode($0F)
        else if i = VMONO then Set_Mode($0F)
        else if i = COLOR then Set_Mode($0E)
        else                  Set_Mode($10);

        i := Screen_Load(seg(picture_name),ofs(picture_name));
                                           { Copy file to screen  }
        i := integer(readkey);             { Wait for <Enter>     }

        {- Set default text mode                                  }

        i := Get_Display_Type;
        if i = MONO then      Set_Mode(7)
        else if i = VMONO then Set_Mode(7)
        else                  Set_Mode(3);
end;
```

Theory

The most efficient way to save and restore data on the EGA/VGA is to access one plane at a time. The screen restore is done in the following steps:

1.   Open an input file for reading.

2.   Enable plane 0 for writing. Transfer 28,000 bytes from the input file to display memory starting at A000:0000.

3.   Repeat step 2 for planes 1, 2, and 3.

4.   Close the file.

Assembly Code Example

Listing 8-43. File: PROG091.ASM

```
;********************************************************************************
; Restore screen from a file PICTURE.001                                      *
; Assumes default settings of EGA registers for modes E,F,10                  *
;********************************************************************************

Load_Name       EQU     [BP+4]
Load_Handle     DW      0
Load_Counter    DB      0

        PUBLIC  _Screen_Load

_Screen_Load    PROC    NEAR
        PUSH    BP                      ;Standard high level entry
        MOV     BP,SP
        PUSH    DS                      ;Preserve DS

        ;- Open the file

        MOV     DX,Load_Name            ;Fetch pointer to the file name
        MOV     CX,0                    ;Normal attribute for the file
        MOV     AH,3DH                  ;DOS function to open file
        MOV     AL,0                    ;Open file for READ
        INT     21H                     ;Ask DOS to open the file
        JC      Load_Error              ;Quit on open error
        MOV     CS:Load_Handle,AX       ;Save the handle to the opened file

        ;- Enable next plane and read 28,000 bytes into it

        MOV     CS:Load_Counter,8       ;Initialize counter of planes done
        MOV     AX,0A000H               ;Point DS:DX to display buffer
        MOV     DS,AX
        MOV     DX,3C4H                 ;Select PLANE ENABLE register
        MOV     AL,2                    ;in SEQUENCER
        OUT     DX,AL
Load_Loop:
        MOV     AL,CS:Load_Counter      ;Select next plane for write
```

```
        MOV     DX,3C5H
        OUT     DX,AL
        XOR     DX,DX
        MOV     CX,28000            ;Number of bytes to read
        MOV     BX,CS:Load_Handle   ;File handle
        MOV     AH,3FH              ;DOS function to read from a file
        INT     21H                 ;Ask DOS to read data from a file
        JC      Close_Load_File     ;Quit on error
        CMP     AX,28000
        JNE     Close_Load_File
        SHR     CS:Load_Counter,1   ;Check if all planes are done
        JNZ     Load_Loop           ;and if not go do next plane

        ;- Close the file

Close_Load_File:
        MOV     BX,CS:Load_Handle   ;Fetch handle
        MOV     AH,3EH              ;DOS function to close a file
        INT     21H                 ;Ask DOS to close the file
Load_Done:
        MOV     DX,3C4H             ;Restore all four planes for write
        MOV     AL,2                ;By loading PLANE ENABLE register
        OUT     DX,AL               ;in the SEQUENCER
        INC     DX
        MOV     AL,0FH
        OUT     DX,AL

        POP     DS                  ;Restore DS
        POP     BP
        RET
Load_Error:                         ;This is where we can add error
        JMP     Load_Done           ;reporting
_Screen_Load    ENDP
```

Appendix A

Function Summaries

A-1. Summary of BIOS Functions

Function 0 - Mode Select
Function 1 - Set Cursor Size
Function 2 - Set Cursor Position
Function 3 - Read Cursor Size and Position
Function 4 - Get Light Pen Position
Function 5 - Select Active Page
Function 6 - Scroll Text Window Up (or Blank Window)
Function 7 - Scroll Text Window Down (or Blank Window)
Function 8 - Read Character and Attribute at Cursor Position
Function 9 - Write Character and Attribute at Cursor Position
Function 10 (0Ah) - Write Character Only at Current Cursor Position
Function 11 (0Bh) - Set CGA Color Palette (Modes 4, 5, 6)
Function 12 (0Ch) - Write Graphics Pixel
Function 13 (0Dh) - Read Graphics Pixel
Function 14 (0Eh) - Write Character and Advance Cursor
Function 15 (0Fh) - Get Current Display Mode
Function 16 (10h) - Set EGA Palette Registers
   Sub-Function 0 - Set A Single Palette Register
   Sub-Function 1 - Set Border Color
   Sub-Function 2 - Set All Palette Registers
   Sub-Function 3 - Blink/Intensity Attribute Control
   Sub-Function 7 - Read Single Palette Register (VGA Only)
   Sub-Function 8 - Read Border Color Register (VGA Only)
   Sub-Function 9 - Read All Palette Registers (VGA Only)
   Sub-Function 10h - Set a Single DAC Register (VGA Only)
   Sub-Function 12h - Set Block of DAC Registers (VGA Only)
   Sub-Function 13h - Select Color Subset (VGA Only)
   Sub-Function 15h - Read a Single DAC Register (VGA Only)
   Sub-Function 17h - Read Block of DAC Registers(VGA Only)
   Sub-Function 1Ah - Read Subset Status (VGA Only)
   Sub-Function 1Bh - Convert DAC Regs to Gray Scale (VGA)
Function 17 (11h) - Load Character Generator
   Sub-Function 0 - Load Custom Character Generator
   Sub-Function 1 - Load Monochrome Character Set
   Sub-Function 2 - Load CGA Character Set
   Sub-Function 3 - Select Active Character Set(S)
   Sub-Function 4 - Load VGA 16 Line Character Set
   Sub-Function 20h - Initialize INT 1FH Vector
   Sub-Function 21h - Set Graphics Mode For Custom Char Set

A-2. Summary of C Library Functions

Direct Access to Registers

write_register(register, data)	Output data to register
write_register_set(list_ptr)	Output data to all registers
read_register(register)	Read data from register
load_palette(table_pointer)	Load palette registers from table
vertical_retrace()	Wait for start of retrace
set_more_columns(columns)	Set wider logical text page width
horizontal_scroll(x)	Scroll horizontally by x pixels
vertical_scroll(y)	Scroll vertically by y pixels
clear_screen()	Clear display memory
set_mode(mode)	Select video mode
video_BIOS(AX,BX,CX,DX,ES,BP)	C interface to video BIOS

Getting Information

get_mode()	Get current display mode
get_rows_n_cols (&x, &y)	Get current resolution
get_cursor_size(&start, &stop)	Get cursor size put result at pointers start, stop
get_page_size()	Get number of bytes in each page
get_display_type()	Get current display type
get_scanlines()	Get maximum number of scan lines
get_memory_size()	Get amount of RAM on EGA (64, 128, 256)
get_primary()	Get type of primary adapter (EGA=1, CGA=2, MDA=3)
get_second_adapter()	Get number of adapters installed

Text Mode Operations

set_cursor_position(row, column)	Set cursor position
get_cursor_position(&row, &column)	Get current cursor position
set_cursor_size(&start, &stop)	Set cursor size
scroll_text(r1,c1,r2,c2,n)	Scroll section of screen n lines
scroll_page(n)	Scroll entire screen n lines

smooth_scroll(x,y)	Smooth scroll x pixels horizontally, y pixels vertically
write_char(char, row, column)	Display character at row and column
write_attribute (row, column, background, foreground)	Change attribute at row, column
read_char(row, column)	Read character at row, column
read_attribute(row, column)	Read attribute at row, column)
text_blink(flag)	Enable or Disable text blinking - 0=disable, 1=enable
write_string(row,column,text_ptr)	Put text string at row,column
read_char_gen(buffer_pointer)	Read current character generator
write_char_gen(ptr, start, count)	Write data at ptr to character generator
enable_second_set()	Enable 512 character font
disable_second_set()	Disable 512 character font
set_43_lines()	Invoke 43 line display
split_screen(scanline)	Create split screen, split at scanline

Graphics Operations

pixel_set(x, y, color)	Set color of a pixel using write Mode 0 with Set-Reset
pixel_packed_write(x,y,color)	Set color of a pixel using write Mode 2
pixel_write(x, y, color)	Set color of a pixle using write Mode 0 with planar pixel write
pixel_read(x,y)	Return value of the pixel at x,y
scanline(x0,x1,y,color)	Fill section of scan line y from x0 to x1
solid_box(x0,y0,x1,y1,color)	Fill rectangle with color - x0,y0=top left,x1,y1=bottom right
line(x0,y0,x1,y1,color)	Draw a solid line from x0,y0 to x1,y1
pattern_line (x0,y0,x1,y1,color,pattern)	Draw patterned line from x0,y0 to x1,y1
arc(xc,yc,xp,yp,a0,a1,color)	Arc-xc,yc=center,xp,yp=point on arc,a0=start angle,a1=end angle
bitblt(xs,ys,xd,yd,dx,dy,fn)	Copy block from xs,ys to xd,yd of size dx,dy, using function fn
set_cursor (and_mask_ptr,xor_mask_ptr,fg,bg)	Set graphics cursor shape and color
move_cursor(x, y)	Move graphics cursor to x,y

remove_cursor()	Remove graphics cursor
screen_dump()	Save display buffer into a file
screen_load(file_name_ptr)	Display content of a file on the screen

Alphabetical List

arc(xc,yc,xp,yp,a0,a1,color)	Arc-xc,yc=center,xp,yp=point on arc,a0=start angle,a1=end angle
bitblt(xs,ys,xd,yd,dx,dy,fn) dx,dy, using function fn	Copy block from xs,ys to xd,yd of size
clear_screen()	Clear display memory
disable_second_set()	Disable 512 character font
enable_second_set()	Enable 512 character font
get_mode()	Get current display mode
get_rows_n_cols (x, y)	Get current resolution
get_cursor_size(&start, &stop)	Get cursor size
get_page_size()	Get number of bytes in each page
get_display_type()	Get current display type
get_scanlines()	Get maximum number of scan lines
get_memory_size()	Get amount of RAM on EGA (64, 128, 256)
get_primary()	Get type of primary adapter (EGA=1, CGA=2, MDA=3)
get_second_adapter()	Get number of adapters installed
set_cursor_position(row, column)	Set cursor position
get_cursor_position(&row, &column)	Get current cursor position
horizontal_scroll(x)	Scroll horizontally by x pixels
line(x0,y0,x1,y1,color)	Draw a solid line from x0,y0 to x1,y1
load_palette(table_pointer)	Load palette registers from table
move_cursor(x, y)	Move graphics cursor to x, y
pattern_line (x0,y0,x1,y1,color,pattern)	Draw patterned line from x0,y0 to x1,y1
pixel_set(x, y, color)	Set color of a pixel using write Mode 0 with Set-Reset
pixel_packed_write(x,y,color)	Set color of a pixel using write Mode 2

pixel_write(x, y, color)	Set color of a pixel using write Mode 0 with planar pixel write
pixel_read(x,y)	Return value of the pixel at x,y
read_char_gen(buffer_pointer)	Read current character generator
read_register(port)	read one byte from port
read_char(row, column)	Read character at row, column
read_attribute(row, column)	Read attribute at row, column)
remove_cursor()	Remove graphics cursor
set_cursor (and_mask_ptr,xor_mask_ptr,fg,bg)	Set graphics cursor shape and color
set_more_columns(columns)	Set wider logical text page width
set_mode(mode)	Select video mode
set_cursor_size(&start, &stop)	Set cursor size
scroll_text(r1,c1,r2,c2,n)	Scroll section of screen n lines - r1,c1=top left, r2,c2 = bottom right
scroll_page(n)	Scroll entire screen n lines
smooth_scroll(x,y)	Smooth scroll x pixels horizontally, y pixels vertically
set_43_lines()	Invoke 43 line display
split_screen(scanline)	Create split screen, split at scan line
scanline(x0,x1,y,color)	Fill section of scan line y from x0 to x1
solid_box(x0,y0,x1,y1,color)	Fill rectangle with color
screen_dump()	Save display buffer into a file
screen_load(file_name_ptr)	Display content of a file on the screen
text_blink(flag)	Enable or Disable text blinking - 0=disable, 1=enable
vertical_scroll(y)	Scroll vertically by y pixels
video_BIOS(AX,BX,CX,DX,ES,BP)	C interface to video BIOS
write_register(register, data)	Output data to register
write_register_set(list_ptr)	Output data to all registers
vertical_retrace()	Wait for start of retrace
write_char(char, row, column)	Display character at row and column
write_attribute (row, column, background, foreground)	Change attribute at row, column
write_string(row,column,text_ptr)	Put text string at row,column
write_char_gen(ptr, start, count)	Write data at ptr to character generator

A-3. Summary of Pascal Library Functions

Routines marked with a "*" are functions, rest of the routines are procedures

Direct Access to Registers

Write_Register(register,data)	Output data to register
Write_Register_Set (table_seg,table_offset)	Write all registers from table at segment:offset
*Read_Register(register)	Read data from register
Write_Palette(table_seg,table_offset)	Write palette registers from table
*Vertical_Retrace	Wait for start of retrace
Horizontal_Scroll(dx)	Scroll horizontally x pixels
Vertical_Scroll(dy)	Scroll vertically y pixels
Clear_Screen	Clear display memory
Set_Mode(Mode)	Select a standard display mode
Video_BIOS(AX,BX,CX,DX,ES,BP)	Perform a BIOS call

Getting Information

*Get_Mode	Get current display mode
Get_Rows_n_Cols (x_seg,x_offset,y_seg,y_offset)	Return resolution at destination specified
Get_Cursor_Size (start_seg,start_offset,stop_seg,stop_offset)	Return cursor size at destination
*Get_Page_Size	Get # of bytes in a display page
*Get_Display_Type	Get current display type
*Get_Scanlines	Get total # of scan lines on display
*Get_Memory_Size	Get amount of RAM on EGA (64, 128, 256)
*Get_Primary	Get type of primary adapter (EGA=1, CGA=2, MDA=3)
*Get_Second_Adapter	Get # of adapters installed

Text Mode Operations

Set_Cursor_Position(row,column)	Position cursor at row,column
Get_Cursor_Position (row_seg,row_offset,col_seg,col_offset)	Return cursor position at dest.
Set_Cursor_Size(start,stop)	Set cursor size
Scroll_Text(up,left,down,right,n)	Scroll section of text n lines

Scroll_Page(n)	Scroll entire page n lines
Smooth_Scroll(x,y)	Smooth scroll x pixels horizontally and y pixels vertically
Write_Char(chr,row,column)	Display character at row,column
Write_Attribute (row,column,background,foreground)	Change attribute at row,column
*Read_Char(row,column)	Read character at row,column
*Read_Attribute(row,column)	Read attribute at row,column
Text_Blink(flag)	0 = disable blink, 1 = enable blink
Write_String (row,column,string_seg,string_offset)	Output a text string at row,column
Read_Char_Gen (buffer_seg,buffer_offset)	Read current character generator
Write_Char_Gen (cg_seg,cg_offset,start,count)	Write character generator
Enable_Second_Set	Enable 512 character font
Disable_Second_Set	Disable 512 character font
Set_43_Lines	Invoke 43 line display
Split_Screen(scanline)	Create split screen at scan line

Graphics Operations

Pixel_Set(x,y,color)	Set color of a pixel using write mode 0 with Set-Reset
Pixel_Packed_Write(x,y,color)	...using write mode 2
Pixel_Write(x,y,color)	...using write mode 0 with planar pixel write
*Pixel_Read(x,y)	Read pixel at (x,y)
Scanline(x0,x1,y,color)	Fill section of scan line y
Solid_Box(x0,y0,x1,y1,color)	Fill a rectangle with color}
Line(x0,y0,x1,y1,color)	Draw a solid line from x0,y0 to x1,y1
Pattern_Line(x0,y0,x1,y1,color,pattern)	Draw a patterned line
Arc(xc,yc,xp,yp,a0,a1,color)	Draw arc}
Bitblt(xs,ys,xd,yd,dx,dy,fn)	Copy block from xs,ys to xd,yd of dimentions dx,dy using function fn
Set_Cursor (andmask,xormask,backgnd,foregnd)	Define graphics cursor shape and color
Move_Cursor(x,y)	Move graphics cursor from current position to x,y

Remove_Cursor   Remove graphics cursor
Screen_Dump   Save display buffer to a file
Screen_Load   Restore display buffer from a file
   (filename_seg,filename_offset)

Alphabetical List

Arc(xc,yc,xp,yp,a0,a1,color)   Draw arc
Bitblt(xs,ys,xd,yd,dx,dy,fn)   Copy block from xs,ys to xd,yd of
                                                  dimentions dx,dy using function fn

Clear_Screen   Clear display memory
Disable_Second_Set   Disable 512 character font
Enable_Second_Set   Enable 512 character font
*Get_Mode   Get current display mode
Get_Rows_n_Cols   Return resolution at destination
   (x_seg,x_offset,y_seg,y_offset)   specified
Get_Cursor_Size   Return cursor size at destination
   (start_seg,start_offset,stop_seg,stop_offset)
*Get_Page_Size   Get # of bytes in a display page
*Get_Display_Type   Get current display type
*Get_Scanlines   Get total # of scan lines on display
*Get_Memory_Size   Get amount of RAM on EGA
                                                  (64, 128, 256)

*Get_Primary   Get type of primary adapter
                                                  (EGA=1, CGA=2, MDA=3)

*Get_Second_Adapter   Get # of adapters installed
Get_Cursor_Position   Return cursor position at dest.
   (row_seg,row_offset,col_seg,col_offset)
Horizontal_Scroll(dx)   Scroll horizontally x pixels
Line(x0,y0,x1,y1,color)   Draw a solid line from x0,y0 to x1,y1
Move_Cursor(x,y)   Move graphics cursor to x,y
Pattern_Line(x0,y0,x1,y1,color,pattern)   Draw a patterned line
Pixel_Set(x,y,color)   Set color of a pixel using write mode 0
                                                  with Set-Reset

Pixel_Packed_Write(x,y,color)   ...using write mode 2
Pixel_Write(x,y,color)   ...using write mode 0 with planar pixel
                                                  write

*Pixel_Read(x,y)   Read pixel at (x,y)}
*Read_Char(row,column)   Read character at row,column

*Read_Attribute(row,column)	Read attribute at row,column
*Read_Register(register)	Read data from register
Read_Char_Gen (buffer_seg,buffer_offset)	Read current character generator
Remove_Cursor	Remove graphics cursor}
Set_Mode(Mode)	Select a standard display mode
Set_Cursor_Position(row,column)	Position cursor at row,column
Set_Cursor_Size(start,stop)	Set cursor size
Scroll_Text(up,left,down,right,n)	Scroll section of text n lines
Scroll_Page(n)	Scroll entire page n lines
Smooth_Scroll(x,y)	Smooth scroll x pixels horizontally and y pixels vertically
Set_43_Lines	Invoke 43 line display
Split_Screen(scanline)	Create split screen at scan line
Scanline(x0,x1,y,color)	Fill section of scan line y
Solid_Box(x0,y0,x1,y1,color)	Fill a rectangle with color
Screen_Dump	Save display buffer to a file
Screen_Load (filename_seg,filename_offset)	Restore display buffer from a file
Set_Cursor (andmask,xormask,backgnd,foregnd)	Define graphics cursor shape and color
Text_Blink(flag)	0 = disable blink, 1 = enable blink
*Vertical_Retrace	Wait for start of retrace
Vertical_Scroll(dy)	Scroll vertically y pixels
Video_BIOS(AX,BX,CX,DX,ES,BP)	Perform a BIOS call
Write_Register(register,data)	Output data to register

Write_Register_Set
    (table_seg,table_offset)
	Write all registers from table at
	    segment:offset

Write_Palette(table_seg,table_offset)	Write palette registers from table
Write_Char(chr,row,column)	Display character at row,column
Write_Attribute (row,column,background,foreground)	Change attribute at row,column
Write_String (row,column,string_seg,string_offset)	Output a text string at row,column

Write_Char_Gen
    (cg_seg,cg_offset,start,count)
	Write character generator from source
	    buffer

Appendix B

Useful Tables

B-1. ASCII Codes

Char	DEC HEX	Char	DEC HEX	Char	DEC HEX	Char	DEC HEX	Char	DEC HEX	Char	DEC HEX	Char	DEC HEX	Char	DEC HEX
	0 0		32 20	@	64 40	`	96 60	Ç	128 80	á	160 A0	└	192 C0	α	224 E0
☺	1 1	!	33 21	A	65 41	a	97 61	ü	129 81	í	161 A1	┴	193 C1	ß	225 E1
☻	2 2	"	34 22	B	66 42	b	98 62	é	130 82	ó	162 A2	┬	194 C2	Γ	226 E2
♥	3 3	#	35 23	C	67 43	c	99 63	â	131 83	ú	163 A3	├	195 C3	π	227 E3
♦	4 4	$	36 24	D	68 44	d	100 64	ä	132 84	ñ	164 A4	─	196 C4	Σ	228 E4
♣	5 5	%	37 25	E	69 45	e	101 65	à	133 85	Ñ	165 A5	┼	197 C5	σ	229 E5
♠	6 6	&	38 26	F	70 46	f	102 66	å	134 86	ª	166 A6	╞	198 C6	µ	230 E6
•	7 7	'	39 27	G	71 47	g	103 67	ç	135 87	º	167 A7	╟	199 C7	τ	231 E7
◘	8 8	(	40 28	H	72 48	h	104 68	ê	136 88	¿	168 A8	╚	200 C8	Φ	232 E8
○	9 9	)	41 29	I	73 49	i	105 69	ë	137 89	⌐	169 A9	╔	201 C9	Θ	233 E9
◙	10 A	*	42 2A	J	74 4A	j	106 6A	è	138 8A	¬	170 AA	╩	202 CA	Ω	234 EA
♂	11 B	+	43 2B	K	75 4B	k	107 6B	ï	139 8B	½	171 AB	╦	203 CB	δ	235 EB
♀	12 C	,	44 2C	L	76 4C	l	108 6C	î	140 8C	¼	172 AC	╠	204 CC	∞	236 EC
♪	13 D	-	45 2D	M	77 4D	m	109 6D	ì	141 8D	¡	173 AD	═	205 CD	φ	237 ED
♫	14 E	.	46 2E	N	78 4E	n	110 6E	Ä	142 8E	«	174 AE	╬	206 CE	ε	238 EE
☼	15 F	/	47 2F	O	79 4F	o	111 6F	Å	143 8F	»	175 AF	╧	207 CF	∩	239 EF
►	16 10	0	48 30	P	80 50	p	112 70	É	144 90	░	176 B0	╨	208 D0	≡	240 F0
◄	17 11	1	49 31	Q	81 51	q	113 71	æ	145 91	▒	177 B1	╤	209 D1	±	241 F1
↕	18 12	2	50 32	R	82 52	r	114 72	Æ	146 92	▓	178 B2	╥	210 D2	≥	242 F2
‼	19 13	3	51 33	S	83 53	s	115 73	ô	147 93	│	179 B3	╙	211 D3	≤	243 F3
¶	20 14	4	52 34	T	84 54	t	116 74	ö	148 94	┤	180 B4	╘	212 D4	⌠	244 F4
§	21 15	5	53 35	U	85 55	u	117 75	ò	149 95	╡	181 B5	╒	213 D5	⌡	245 F5
▬	22 16	6	54 36	V	86 56	v	118 76	û	150 96	╢	182 B6	╓	214 D6	÷	246 F6
↨	23 17	7	55 37	W	87 57	w	119 77	ù	151 97	╖	183 B7	╫	215 D7	≈	247 F7
↑	24 18	8	56 38	X	88 58	x	120 78	ÿ	152 98	╕	184 B8	╪	216 D8	°	248 F8
↓	25 19	9	57 39	Y	89 59	y	121 79	Ö	153 99	╣	185 B9	┘	217 D9	∙	249 F9
→	26 1A	:	58 3A	Z	90 5A	z	122 7A	Ü	154 9A	║	186 BA	┌	218 DA	·	250 FA
←	27 1B	;	59 3B	[	91 5B	{	123 7B	¢	155 9B	╗	187 BB	█	219 DB	√	251 FB
∟	28 1C	<	60 3C	\	92 5C	|	124 7C	£	156 9C	╝	188 BC	▄	220 DC	ⁿ	252 FC
↔	29 1D	=	61 3D	]	93 5D	}	125 7D	¥	157 9D	╜	189 BD	▌	221 DD	²	253 FD
▲	30 1E	>	62 3E	^	94 5E	~	126 7E	₧	158 9E	╛	190 BE	▐	222 DE	■	254 FE
▼	31 1F	?	63 3F	_	95 5F	⌂	127 7F	ƒ	159 9F	┐	191 BF	▀	223 DF		255 FF

B-2. EGA/VGA Memory Map

Table B-2. EGA/VGA Memory Map

Location	Size	Description
0000:0040	DWORD	Interrupt Vector 10h - EGA/VGA BIOS Video Services
0000:0108	DWORD	Interrupt Vector 42h - Old BIOS Video Services
0000:010C	DWORD	Interrupt Vector 43h - Pointer to CGA 8 x 8 Char Set
0000:007C	DWORD	Interrupt Vector 1Fh - Optional Pointer to Upper 128 CGA 8 x 8 characters
0000:0410	BYTE	EQUIPMENT_FLAG

Bits D4 and D5 of this byte identify the current primary display device:

D5	D4	Adapter
0	0	EGA (or none)
0	1	CGA 40x25
1	0	CGA 80x25
1	1	MDA

Location	Size	Description	
0000:0449	BYTE	VIDEO_MODE	Current mode
0000:044A	WORD	COLUMNS	Number of text columns
0000:044C	WORD	PAGE_LENGTH	Length of each page in bytes
0000:044E	WORD	START_ADDR	Start Address Register value
0000:0450	8 WORDS	CURSOR_POSITION	Cursor positions for all pages
0000:0458	WORD	CURSOR_SHAPE	Cursor Start and End Registers
0000:045A	BYTE	ACTIVE_PAGE	Current active page number
0000:045B	WORD	CRTC_ADDRESS	3B4 or 3D4
0000:045D	BYTE	MODE_REG_DATA	CGA Mode Register setting
0000:045E	BYTE	PALETTE	CGA palette setting
0000:0484	BYTE	ROWS	Number of text rows - 1
0000:0485	WORD	CHAR_HEIGHT	Bytes per character
0000:0487	BYTE	EGA_INFO_1	

(continued)

Table B-2. EGA/VGA Memory Map *(continued)*.

		D7 - equals bit D7 from AL register on most recent mode select. (a one indicates display memory was not cleared by mode select)
		D6,D5 - Display memory size (00=64K, 01=128K, 10=192K, 11=256K)
		D4 - reserved
		D3 - A zero indicates EGA is the primary display
		D2 - A one will force the BIOS to wait for Vertical Retrace before memory write
		D1 - A one indicates that EGA is in monochrome mode.
		D0 - A zero means that CGA cursor emulation is enabled. The cursor shape will be modified if enhanced text is used.
0000:0488	BYTE	EGA_INFO_2
		D4-D7 - Feature Control Bits (from Feature Control Register)
		D0-D3 - EGA Configuration Switch settings
0000:04A8	DWORD	ENVIRON_PTR Pointer to environment table
A000:0000-FFFF		Display Memory (Graphics Modes)
B000:0000-7FFF		Display Memory (Monochrome Text Mode) Hercules Graphics Page 0
B800:0000-7FFF		Display Memory (Color Text and CGA Graphics) Hercules Graphics Page 1
C000:0000-3FFF		EGA/VGA BIOS

B-3. Summary of Control Registers

3BB - Clear Light Pen Latch (EGA Only)

3BC - Set Light Pen Latch (EGA Only)

3C2 - Miscellaneous Output Register

D7 - Vertical Sync Polarity
D6 - Horizontal Sync Polarity
D5 - Odd/Even Page Bit
D4 - Disable Video
D3 - Clock Select 1
D2 - Clock Select 0
D1 - Enable Display RAM
D0 - I/O address select

3DA or 3BA - Feature Control Register (EGA Only)

D7 - D2 - reserved (0)
D1 - Feature control bit 1
D0 - Feature control bit 0

3C2 - Input Status Register 0

D7 - Vertical retrace interrupt pending
D6 - Feature sense bit 1 (EGA only)
D5 - Feature sense bit 0 (EGA only)
D4 - Switch Sense
D3 - unused
D2 - unused
D1 - unused
D0 - unused

3DA or 3BA - Input Status Register 1

D7 - unused
D6 - unused
D5 - Diagnostic
D4 - Diagnostic
D3 - Vertical Retrace
D2 - Light Pen switch (EGA only)

D1 - Light Pen strobe (EGA only)
D0 - Display Enable

3C3 - VGA Enable Register (VGA Only)

D7-D1 - Reserved
D0 - VGA Enable/Disable

3D4,3D5 or 3B4,3B5 - CRT Controller Registers

INDEX 0 - HORIZONTAL TOTAL
INDEX 1 - HORIZONTAL DISPLAY ENABLE
INDEX 2 - START HORIZONTAL BLANKING
INDEX 3 - END HORIZONTAL BLANKING
        D7 - must be 0 for EGA
        must be 1 for VGA
        D6,D5 - Display Enable Skew Control
        D4-D0 - End Horizontal Blanking
INDEX 4 - START HORIZONTAL RETRACE
INDEX 5 - END HORIZONTAL RETRACE
        D7 - Start on Odd Memory Address (EGA only)
        D7 - End Horizontal Blanking Overflow bit (VGA only)
        D6,D5 - Horizontal Retrace Delay
        D4-D0 - End Horizontal Retrace
INDEX 6 - VERTICAL TOTAL
INDEX 7 - OVERFLOW REGISTER
        D7 - VGA Only - Vertical Retrace Start (Bit 9)
        D6 - VGA Only - Vertical Display Enable End (Bit 9)
        D5 - VGA Only - Vertical Total (Bit 9)
        D4 - Line Compare (Bit 8)
        D3 - Start Vertical Blank (Bit 8)
        D2 - Vertical Retrace Start (Bit 8)
        D1 - Vertical Display Enable End (Bit 8)
        D0 - Vertical Total (Bit 8)
INDEX 8 - PRESET ROW SCAN
        D7 - reserved (0)
        D6,D5 - byte panning control (VGA only)
        D4-D0 - Preset Row Scan
INDEX 9 - MAXIMUM SCAN LINE/TEXT CHARACTER HEIGHT
        D7 - Double Scan (VGA only)
        D6 - Bit 9 of Line Compare register (VGA only)
        D5 - Bit 9 of Start Vertical Blank register (VGA only)

D4-D0 - Maximum Scan Line
INDEX 0AH - CURSOR START
      D7,D6 - reserved (0)
      D5 - Cursor Off (VGA only)
      D4-D0 - Cursor Start
INDEX 0BH - CURSOR END
      D7 - reserved (0)
      D6,D5 - Cursor Skew
      D4-D0 - Cursor End
INDEX 0CH - START ADDRESS (HIGH BYTE)
INDEX 0DH - START ADDRESS (LOW BYTE)
INDEX 0EH - CURSOR LOCATION (HIGH BYTE)
INDEX 0FH - CURSOR LOCATION (LOW BYTE)
INDEX 10H - LIGHT PEN REGISTER (HIGH BYTE)
INDEX 11H - LIGHT PEN REGISTER (LOW BYTE)
INDEX 10 - VERTICAL RETRACE START
INDEX 11 - VERTICAL RETRACE END
      D7 - Write Protect Index 0-7 (VGA Only)
      D6 - Alternate Refresh Rate (VGA Only)
      D5 - Enable Vertical Interrupt (0 = enable)
      D4 - Clear Vertical Interrupt (0 = clear)
      D3-D0 - Vertical Retrace End
INDEX 12 - VERTICAL DISPLAY ENABLE END
INDEX 13H - OFFSET REGISTER/LOGICAL SCREEN WIDTH
INDEX 14H - UNDERLINE LOCATION REGISTER
      D7 - reserved (0)
      D6 - Doubleword mode (VGA only)
      D5 - Count by 4 (VGA only)
      D4-D0 - Underline Location
INDEX 15 - START VERTICAL BLANKING
INDEX 16 - END VERTICAL BLANKING
INDEX 17 - Mode CONTROL Register
      D7 - Hardware Reset
      D6 - Word/Byte Address Mode
      D5 - Address Wrap
      D4 - Output Control
      D3 - Count by Two
      D2 - Horizontal Retrace Select
      D1 - CGA Graphics Compatibility Mode
      D0 - Hercules Graphics Compatibility Mode
INDEX 18H - LINE COMPARE REGISTER

3C4,3C5 - Sequencer Registers

INDEX 0 - RESET REGISTER
        D7-D2 - reserved (0)
        D1 - Synchronous reset
        D0 - Asynchronous reset
INDEX 1 - THE CLOCK MODE REGISTER
        D5 - Display Off
        D1 - Bandwidth Control
        D0 - 8/9 Dot Clocks
INDEX 2 - THE COLOR PLANE WRITE ENABLE REGISTER
        D7-D4 - reserved (0)
        D3 - plane 3 write enable (1 = enabled)
        D2 - plane 2 write enable (1 = enabled)
        D1 - plane 1 write enable (1 = enabled)
        D0 - plane 0 write enable (1 = enabled)
INDEX 3 - CHARACTER GENERATOR SELECT REGISTER
        D7 - reserved (0)
        D6 - reserved (0)
        D5 - VGA Only - Character generator table select A (MSB)
        D4 - VGA Only - Character generator table select B (MSB)
        D3-D2 - Character generator table select A
        D1-D0 - Character generator table select B
INDEX 4 - MEMORY MODE REGISTER
        D7-D3 - reserved
        D2 - Odd/Even
        D1 - Extended Memory
        D0 - Text Mode (EGA Only)

3CE,3CF - Graphics Controller Registers

INDEX 0 - SET/RESET REGISTER (INDEX 0)
        D7-D4 - reserved (0)
        D3 - fill data for plane 3
        D2 - fill data for plane 2
        D1 - fill data for plane 1
        D0 - fill data for plane 0
INDEX 1 - SET/RESET ENABLE REGISTER
        D7-D4 - reserved (0)
        D3 - enable Set/Reset for plane 3 (1 = enable)
        D2 - enable Set/Reset for plane 2

D1 - enable Set/Reset for plane 1

D0 - enable Set/Reset for plane 0

INDEX 2 - COLOR COMPARE REGISTER

    D7-D4 - reserved (0)

    D3 - Color Compare value for plane 3

    D2 - Color Compare value for plane 2

    D1 - Color Compare value for plane 1

    D0 - Color Compare value for plane 0

INDEX 3 - DATA ROTATE AND FUNCTION SELECT REGISTER

    D7-D5 - reserved (0)

    D4,D3 - Function Select

    D2-D0 - Rotate Count

    D4-D3 - Function

        0 0   Write data unmodified

        0 1   Write data AND processor latches

        1 0   Write data OR processor latches

        1 1   Write data XOR processor latches

INDEX 4 - READ PLANE SELECT REGISTER

    D7-D2 - reserved (0)

    D1,D0 - defines color plane for reading (0-3)

INDEX 5 - MODE REGISTER

    D7 - reserved (0)

    D6 - 256 color mode (VGA Only)

    D5 - Shift Register Mode

    D4 - Odd/Even Mode

    D3 - Color Compare Mode Enable (1 = enable)

    D2 - reserved (0)

    D1,D0 - Write Mode

        0 0   Direct write

                    (Data Rotate, Set/Reset may apply)

        0 1   Use processor latches as write data

        1 0   Color plane n (0-3) is filled with the

                    value of bit n in the write data

        1 1   Not used

INDEX 6 - MISCELLANEOUS REGISTER

    D7-D4 - reserved (0)

    D3,D2 - Memory Address Select

    D1 - Chain Odd and Even Maps

    D0 - Graphics Enable

INDEX 7 - COLOR DON'T CARE REGISTER

    D7-D4 - reserved (0)

D3 - Plane 3 don't care
D2 - Plane 2 don't care
D1 - Plane 1 don't care
D0 - Plane 0 don't care
INDEX 8 - BIT MASK REGISTER
D7 - mask data bit 7
D6 - mask data bit 6
D5 - mask data bit 5
D4 - mask data bit 4
D3 - mask data bit 3
D2 - mask data bit 2
D1 - mask data bit 1
D0 - mask data bit 0

3C7 - DAC Status (Read) (VGA Only)

3C7 - DAC Look-up Table Read Index (Write) (VGA Only)

3C8 - DAC Look-up Table Write Index (VGA Only)

3C9 - DAC Look-up Table Data (VGA Only)

3C0 - Attribute Controller Registers

INDEX REGISTER
D7 - reserved (0)
D6 - reserved (0)
D5 - Palette address source
0 = palette can be modified, screen is blanked
1 = screen is enabled, palette cannot be modified
D4-D0 - Register address (0-13H)

PALETTE REGISTERS (INDEX 0 THROUGH F)

For Enhanced Color Displays:

D7 - reserved (0)
D6 - reserved (0)
D5 - Secondary Red
D4 - Secondary Green
D3 - Secondary Blue

D2 - Red
D1 - Green
D0 - Blue

For Standard Color Displays:

D7 - Reserved
D6 - Reserved
D5 - Reserved
D4 - Intensity
D3 - Reserved
D2 - Red
D1 - Green
D0 - Blue

For Monochrome Displays:

D7 - Reserved
D6 - Reserved
D5 - Reserved
D4 - Intensity
D3 - Video Out
D2 - Reserved
D1 - Reserved
D0 - Reserved

For VGA:

D7 - Reserved
D6 - Reserved
D5 = P5
D4 = P4
D3 = P3
D2 = P2
D1 = P1
D0 = P0

INDEX 10 - MODE CONTROL REGISTER
D7 - P4,P5 source select (VGA Only)
D6 - Pixel Width (VGA Only)
D5 - Horizontal Pan Compatibility (VGA Only)

D4 - reserved (0)

D3 - Background Intensity or Enable Blink

D2 - Enable Monochrome Line Graphics

D1 - Display Type

D0 - Graphics/Text Mode

INDEX 11 - SCREEN BORDER COLOR (OVERSCAN)

INDEX 12 - COLOR PLANE ENABLE REGISTER

D7,D6 - reserved (0)

D5,D4 - Video Status Mux

D3 - Enable color Plane 3

D2 - Enable Color Plane 2

D1 - Enable Color Plane 1

D0 - Enable Color Plane 0

INDEX 13 - HORIZONTAL PANNING REGISTER

D7-D4 - reserved (0)

D3-D0 - Horizontal Pan

INDEX 14 - COLOR SELECT REGISTER (VGA ONLY)

D7-D4 - reserved (0)

D3 - color 7

D2 - color 6

D1 - color 5

D0 - color 4

B-4. Default Register Values

Table B-4. Default Register Values (256K RAM).

	Color							Enhanced								Monochrome	
	1	3	4	5	6	D	E	1*	3*	4	5	6	D	E	10	7	F
EXTERNAL REGISTERS																	
3C2 - MISCELLANEOUS OUTPUT REGISTER	23	23	23	23	23	23	23	A7	A7	23	23	23	23	23	A7	A6	A2
3D4,3D5/3B4,3B5 - CRT CONTROLLER REGISTERS																	
INDEX 0 - HORIZONTAL TOTAL	37	70	37	37	70	37	70	2D	5B	37	37	70	37	70	5B	60	60
INDEX 1 - HORIZONTAL DISPLAY ENABLE	27	4F	27	27	4F	27	4F	27	4F	27	27	4F	27	4F	4F	4F	4F
INDEX 2 - START HORIZONTAL BLANKING	2D	5C	2D	2D	59	2D	59	2B	53	2D	2D	59	2D	59	53	56	56
INDEX 3 - END HORIZONTAL BLANKING	37	2F	37	37	2D	37	2D	2D	37	37	37	2D	37	2D	37	3A	3A
INDEX 4 - START HORIZONTAL RETRACE	31	5F	30	30	5E	30	5E	28	51	30	30	5E	30	5E	52	51	50
INDEX 5 - END HORIZONTAL RETRACE	15	07	14	14	06	14	06	6D	5B	14	14	06	14	06	00	60	60
INDEX 6 - VERTICAL TOTAL	04	04	04	04	04	04	04	6C	6C	04	04	04	04	04	6C	70	70
INDEX 7 - OVERFLOW REGISTER	11	11	11	11	11	11	11	1F	1F	11	11	11	11	11	1F	1F	1F
INDEX 8 - PRESET ROW SCAN	00	00	00	00	00	00	00	00	00	00	00	00	00	00	00	00	00
INDEX 9 - MAXIMUM SCAN LINE/CHAR HEIGHT	07	07	01	01	01	00	00	0D	0D	01	01	01	00	00	00	0D	00
INDEX Ah - CURSOR START	06	06	00	00	00	00	00	06	06	00	00	00	00	00	00	0B	00
INDEX Bh - CURSOR END	07	07	00	00	00	00	00	07	07	00	00	00	00	00	00	0C	00
INDEX Ch - START ADDRESS (HIGH BYTE)	00	00	00	00	00	00	00	00	00	00	00	00	00	00	00	00	00
INDEX Dh - START ADDRESS (LOW BYTE)	00	00	00	00	00	00	00	00	00	00	00	00	00	00	00	00	00
INDEX Eh - CURSOR LOCATION (HIGH BYTE)	00	00	00	00	00	00	00	00	00	00	00	00	00	00	00	00	00
INDEX Fh - CURSOR LOCATION (LOW BYTE)	00	00	00	00	00	00	00	00	00	00	00	00	00	00	00	00	00
INDEX 10h - VERTICAL RETRACE START	E1	E1	E1	E1	E0	E1	E0	5E	5E	E1	E1	E0	E1	E0	5E	5E	5E
INDEX 11h - VERTICAL RETRACE END	24	24	24	24	23	24	23	2B	2B	24	24	23	24	23	2B	2E	2E
INDEX 12h - VERTICAL DISPLAY ENABLE END	C7	C7	C7	C7	C7	C7	C7	5D	5D	C7	C7	C7	C7	C7	5D	5D	5D
INDEX 13h - OFFSET REGISTER/LOGICAL WIDTH	14	28	14	14	28	14	28	14	28	14	14	28	14	28	28	28	28
INDEX 14h - UNDERLINE LOCATION REGISTER	08	08	00	00	00	00	00	0F	0F	00	00	00	00	00	0F	0D	0D
INDEX 15h - START VERTICAL BLANKING	E0	E0	E0	E0	DF	E0	DF	5E	5E	E0	E0	DF	E0	DF	5F	5F	5E
INDEX 16h - END VERTICAL BLANKING	F0	F0	F0	F0	EF	F0	EF	0A	0A	F0	F0	EF	F0	EF	0A	6E	6E
INDEX 17h - MODE CONTROL REGISTER	A3	A3	A2	A2	C2	E3	E3	A3	A3	A2	A2	C2	E3	E3	E3	A3	E3
INDEX 18h - LINE COMPARE REGISTER	FF	FF	FF	FF	FF	FF	FF	FF	FF	FF	FF	FF	FF	FF	FF	FF	FF
3C4,3C5 - SEQUENCER REGISTERS																	
INDEX 0 - RESET REGISTER	00	00	00	00	00	00	00	00	00	00	00	00	00	00	00	00	00
INDEX 1 - THE CLOCK MODE REGISTER	0B	01	0B	0B	01	0B	01	0B	01	0B	0B	01	0B	01	01	00	01
INDEX 2 - THE COLOR PLANE WRITE ENABLE	03	03	03	03	01	0F	0F	03	03	03	03	01	0F	0F	0F	03	0F
INDEX 3 - CHARACTER GENERATOR SELECT REGISTER	00	00	00	00	00	00	00	00	00	00	00	00	00	00	00	00	00
INDEX 4 - MEMORY MODE REGISTER	03	02	02	02	06	06	06	03	03	02	02	06	06	06	06	03	06
3CE,3CF - GRAPHICS CONTROLLER REGISTERS																	
INDEX 0 - SET/RESET REGISTER (INDEX 0)	00	00	00	00	00	00	00	00	00	00	00	00	00	00	00	00	00
INDEX 1 - SET/RESET ENABLE REGISTER	00	00	00	00	00	00	00	00	00	00	00	00	00	00	00	00	00
INDEX 2 - COLOR COMPARE REGISTER	00	00	00	00	00	00	00	00	00	00	00	00	00	00	00	00	00
INDEX 3 - DATA ROTATE AND FUNCTION SELECT	00	00	00	00	00	00	00	00	00	00	00	00	00	00	00	00	00
INDEX 4 - READ PLANE SELECT REGISTER	00	00	00	00	00	00	00	00	00	00	00	00	00	00	00	00	00
INDEX 5 - MODE REGISTER	10	10	30	30	00	00	00	10	10	30	30	00	00	00	00	10	00
INDEX 6 - MISCELLANEOUS REGISTER	0E	0E	0F	0F	0D	05	05	0E	0E	0F	0F	0D	05	05	05	0A	05
INDEX 7 - COLOR DON'T CARE REGISTER	00	00	00	00	00	0F	0F	00	00	00	00	00	0F	0F	0F	00	0F
INDEX 8 - BIT MASK REGISTER	FF	FF	FF	FF	FF	FF	FF	FF	FF	FF	FF	FF	FF	FF	FF	FF	FF

(continued)

Table B-4. Default Register Values (256K RAM) *(continued)*.

```
        3CO - ATTRIBUTE CONTROLLER REGISTERS
INDEX  0 - PALETTE REGISTER  0      00 00 00 00 00 00 00    00 00 00 00 00 00 00 00    00 00
INDEX  1 - PALETTE REGISTER  1      01 01 13 13 17 01 01    01 01 13 13 17 01 01 01    08 08
INDEX  2 - PALETTE REGISTER  2      02 02 15 15 17 02 02    02 02 15 15 17 02 02 02    08 00
INDEX  3 - PALETTE REGISTER  3      03 03 17 17 17 03 03    03 03 17 17 17 03 03 03    08 00
INDEX  4 - PALETTE REGISTER  4      04 04 02 02 17 04 14    04 04 02 02 17 04 14 04    08 18
INDEX  5 - PALETTE REGISTER  5      05 05 04 04 17 05 15    05 05 04 04 17 05 15 05    08 18
INDEX  6 - PALETTE REGISTER  6      06 06 06 06 17 06 06    14 14 06 06 17 06 06 14    08 00
INDEX  7 - PALETTE REGISTER  7      07 07 07 07 17 07 07    07 07 07 07 17 07 07 07    08 00
INDEX  8 - PALETTE REGISTER  8      10 10 10 10 17 10 10    38 38 10 10 17 10 10 38    10 00
INDEX  9 - PALETTE REGISTER  9      11 11 11 11 17 11 11    39 39 11 11 17 11 11 39    18 08
INDEX  Ah- PALETTE REGISTER  Ah     12 12 12 12 17 12 12    3A 3A 12 12 17 12 12 3A    18 00
INDEX  Bh- PALETTE REGISTER  Bh     13 13 13 13 17 13 13    3B 3B 13 13 17 13 13 3B    18 00
INDEX  Ch- PALETTE REGISTER  Ch     14 14 14 14 17 14 14    3C 3C 14 14 17 14 14 3C    18 00
INDEX  Dh- PALETTE REGISTER  Dh     15 15 15 15 17 15 15    3D 3D 15 15 17 15 15 3D    18 18
INDEX  Eh- PALETTE REGISTER  Eh     16 16 16 16 17 16 16    3E 3E 16 16 17 16 16 3E    18 00
INDEX  Fh- PALETTE REGISTER  Fh     17 17 17 17 17 17 17    3F 3F 17 17 17 17 17 3F    18 00
INDEX 10h- MODE CONTROL REGISTER   08 08 01 01 01 01 01    08 08 01 01 01 01 01 01    0E 0B
INDEX 11h- SCREEN BORDER COLOR (OVERSCAN)  00 00 00 00 00 00 00    00 00 00 00 00 00 00 00    00 00
INDEX 12h- COLOR PLANE ENABLE REGISTER     0F 0F 03 03 01 0F 0F    0F 0F 03 03 01 0F 0F 0F    0F 05
INDEX 13h- HORIZONTAL PANNING REGISTER     00 00 00 00 00 00 00    00 00 00 00 00 00 00 00    08 00
```

Note: Modes 4,5,6,D,E are 200 line modes, and are same on Color Display and Enhanced display

	Double Scan						350 lines					480 lines					200
VGA DISPLAY (SCAN LINES)																	
Mode																	
	1	3	4	5	6	D	E	1*	3*	7	F	10	1+	3+	7+	11	12	13
Register Value																	

```
        EXTERNAL REGISTERS
3C3 - VGA ENABLE REGISTER (VGA ONLY)       01 01 01 01 01 01 01    01 01 01 01 01    01 01 01 01 01    01
3C2 - MISCELLANEOUS OUTPUT REGISTER        63 63 63 63 63 63 63    A3 A3 A6 A2 A3    67 67 66 E3 E3    63
   3D4,3D5/3B4,3B5 - CRT CONTROLLER REGISTERS
INDEX  0 - HORIZONTAL TOTAL                2D 5F 2D 2D 5F 2D 5F    2D 5F 5F 5F 5F    2D 5F 5F 5F 5F    5F
INDEX  1 - HORIZONTAL DISPLAY ENABLE       27 4F 27 27 4F 27 4F    27 4F 4F 4F 4F    27 4F 4F 4F 4F    4F
INDEX  2 - START HORIZONTAL BLANKING       28 50 28 28 50 28 50    28 50 50 50 50    28 50 50 50 50    50
INDEX  3 - END HORIZONTAL BLANKING         90 82 90 90 82 90 82    90 82 82 82 82    90 82 82 82 82    82
INDEX  4 - START HORIZONTAL RETRACE        2B 55 2B 2B 54 2B 54    2B 55 55 54 54    2B 55 55 54 54    54
INDEX  5 - END HORIZONTAL RETRACE          A0 81 80 80 80 80 80    A0 81 81 80 80    A0 81 81 80 80    80
INDEX  6 - VERTICAL TOTAL                  BF BF BF BF BF BF BF    BF BF BF BF BF    BF BF BF 0B 0B    BF
INDEX  7 - OVERFLOW REGISTER               1F 1F 1F 1F 1F 1F 1F    1F 1F 1F 1F 1F    1F 1F 1F 3E 3E    1F
INDEX  8 - PRESET ROW SCAN                 00 00 00 00 00 00 00    00 00 00 00 00    00 00 00 00 00    00
INDEX  9 - MAXIMUM SCAN LINE/CHAR HEIGHT   C7 C7 C1 C1 C1 C0 C0    4D 4D 4D 40 40    4F 4F 4F 40 40    41
INDEX  Ah- CURSOR START                    06 06 00 00 00 00 00    0B 0B 0B 00 00    0D 0D 00 00 00    00
INDEX  Bh- CURSOR END                      07 07 00 00 00 00 00    0C 0C 0C 00 00    0E 0E 0E 00 00    00
INDEX  Ch- START ADDRESS (HIGH BYTE)       00 00 00 00 00 00 00    00 00 00 00 00    00 00 00 00 00    00
INDEX  Dh- START ADDRESS (LOW BYTE)        00 00 00 00 00 00 00    00 00 00 00 00    00 00 00 00 00    00
INDEX  Eh- CURSOR LOCATION (HIGH BYTE)     00 00 00 00 00 00 00    00 00 00 00 00    00 00 00 00 00    00
INDEX  Fh- CURSOR LOCATION (LOW BYTE)      00 00 00 00 00 00 00    00 00 00 00 00    00 00 00 00 00    00
INDEX 10h- VERTICAL RETRACE START          9C 9C 9C 9C 9C 9C 9C    83 83 83 83 83    9C 9C 9C EA EA    9C
INDEX 11h- VERTICAL RETRACE END            8E 8E 8E 8E 8E 8E 8E    85 85 85 85 85    8E 8E 8E 8C 8C    8E
INDEX 12h- VERTICAL DISPLAY ENABLE END     8F 8F 8F 8F 8F 8F 8F    5D 5D 5D 5D 5D    8F 8F 8F DF DF    8F
INDEX 13h- OFFSET REGISTER/LOGICAL WIDTH   14 28 14 14 28 14 28    14 28 28 28 28    14 28 28 28 28    28
INDEX 14h- UNDERLINE LOCATION REGISTER     1F 1F 00 00 00 00 00    1F 1F 0D 0F 0F    1F 1F 0F 00 00    40
```

(continued)

Table B-4. Default Register Values (256K RAM) *(continued)*.

INDEX 15h - START VERTICAL BLANKING	96	96	96	96	96	96	96	63	63	63	63	63	96	96	96	E7	E7	96
INDEX 16h - END VERTICAL BLANKING	B9	B9	B9	B9	B9	B9	B9	BA	BA	BA	BA	BA	B9	B9	B9	04	04	B9
INDEX 17h - MODE CONTROL REGISTER	A3	A3	A2	A2	C2	E3	E3	A3	A3	A3	E3	E3	A3	A3	A3	C3	E3	A3
INDEX 18h - LINE COMPARE REGISTER	FF	FF	FF	FF	FF	FF	FF	FF	FF	FF	FF	FF	FF	FF	FF	FF	FF	FF
3C4,3C5 - SEQUENCER REGISTERS																		
INDEX 0 - RESET REGISTER	00	00	00	00	00	00	00	00	00	00	00	00	00	00	00	00	00	00
INDEX 1 - THE CLOCK MODE REGISTER	09	01	09	09	01	09	01	09	01	00	01	01	08	00	00	01	01	01
INDEX 2 - THE COLOR PLANE WRITE ENABLE	03	03	03	03	01	0F	0F	03	03	03	0F	0F	03	03	03	0F	0F	0F
INDEX 3 - CHARACTER GENERATOR SELECT REGISTER	00	00	00	00	00	00	00	00	00	00	00	00	00	00	00	00	00	00
INDEX 4 - MEMORY MODE REGISTER	02	02	02	02	06	06	06	02	02	03	06	06	02	02	02	06	06	0E
3CE,3CF - GRAPHICS CONTROLLER REGISTERS																		
INDEX 0 - SET/RESET REGISTER (INDEX 0)	00	00	00	00	00	00	00	00	00	00	00	00	00	00	00	00	00	00
INDEX 1 - SET/RESET ENABLE REGISTER	00	00	00	00	00	00	00	00	00	00	00	00	00	00	00	00	00	00
INDEX 2 - COLOR COMPARE REGISTER	00	00	00	00	00	00	00	00	00	00	00	00	00	00	00	00	00	00
INDEX 3 - DATA ROTATE AND FUNCTION SELECT	00	00	00	00	00	00	00	00	00	00	00	00	00	00	00	00	00	00
INDEX 4 - READ PLANE SELECT REGISTER	00	00	00	00	00	00	00	00	00	00	00	00	00	00	00	00	00	00
INDEX 5 - MODE REGISTER	10	10	30	30	00	00	00	10	10	10	00	00	10	10	10	00	00	40
INDEX 6 - MISCELLANEOUS REGISTER	0E	0E	0F	0F	0D	05	05	0E	0E	0A	05	05	0E	0E	0A	05	05	05
INDEX 7 - COLOR DON'T CARE REGISTER	00	00	00	00	00	0F	0F	00	00	00	05	0F	00	00	00	01	0F	0F
INDEX 8 - BIT MASK REGISTER	FF	FF	FF	FF	FF	FF	FF	FF	FF	FF	FF	FF	FF	FF	FF	FF	FF	FF
3C0 - ATTRIBUTE CONTROLLER REGISTERS																		
INDEX 0 - PALETTE REGISTER 0	00	00	00	00	00	00	00	00	00	00	00	00	00	00	00	00	00	00
INDEX 1 - PALETTE REGISTER 1	01	01	13	13	17	01	01	01	01	08	08	01	01	01	08	3F	01	01
INDEX 2 - PALETTE REGISTER 2	02	02	15	15	17	02	02	02	02	08	00	02	02	02	08	3F	02	02
INDEX 3 - PALETTE REGISTER 3	03	03	17	17	17	03	03	03	03	08	00	03	03	03	08	3F	03	03
INDEX 4 - PALETTE REGISTER 4	04	04	02	02	17	04	14	04	04	08	18	04	04	04	08	3F	04	04
INDEX 5 - PALETTE REGISTER 5	05	05	04	04	17	05	15	05	05	08	18	05	05	05	08	3F	05	05
INDEX 6 - PALETTE REGISTER 6	06	06	06	06	17	06	06	14	14	08	00	14	14	14	08	3F	14	06
INDEX 7 - PALETTE REGISTER 7	07	07	07	07	17	07	07	07	07	08	00	07	07	07	08	3F	07	07
INDEX 8 - PALETTE REGISTER 8	10	10	10	10	17	10	10	38	38	10	00	38	38	38	10	3F	38	08
INDEX 9 - PALETTE REGISTER 9	11	11	11	11	17	11	11	39	39	18	00	39	39	39	18	3F	39	09
INDEX Ah- PALETTE REGISTER Ah	12	12	12	12	17	12	12	3A	3A	18	00	3A	3A	3A	18	3F	3A	0A
INDEX Bh- PALETTE REGISTER Bh	13	13	13	13	17	13	13	3B	3B	18	00	3B	3B	3B	18	3F	3B	0B
INDEX Ch- PALETTE REGISTER Ch	14	14	14	14	17	14	14	3C	3C	18	00	3C	3C	3C	18	3F	3C	0C
INDEX Dh- PALETTE REGISTER Dh	15	15	15	15	17	15	15	3D	3D	18	18	3D	3D	3D	18	3F	3D	0D
INDEX Eh- PALETTE REGISTER Eh	16	16	16	16	17	16	16	3E	3E	18	00	3E	3E	3E	18	3F	3E	0E
INDEX Fh- PALETTE REGISTER Fh	17	17	17	17	17	17	17	3F	3F	18	00	3F	3F	3F	18	3F	3F	0F
INDEX 10h- MODE CONTROL REGISTER	08	08	01	01	01	01	01	08	08	0E	0B	01	0C	0C	0E	01	01	41
INDEX 11h- SCREEN BORDER COLOR (OVERSCAN)	00	00	00	00	00	00	00	00	00	00	00	00	00	00	00	00	00	00
INDEX 12h- COLOR PLANE ENABLE REGISTER	0F	0F	03	03	01	0F	0F	0F	0F	0F	05	0F	0F	0F	0F	0F	0F	0F
INDEX 13h- HORIZONTAL PANNING REGISTER	00	00	00	00	00	00	00	00	00	08	00	00	00	00	00	00	00	00
INDEX 14h- COLOR SELECT REGISTER	00	00	00	00	00	00	00	00	00	00	00	00	08	08	08	00	00	00

Note: With VGA displays, modes 1, 3, 4, 5, D, E are double scanned (8 x 8 character box)
and modes 1+,3+ use 480 lines (9 x 16 character box)

Register values are courtesy of Quadtel Corporation.

B-5. Configuration Switches

SW4	SW3	SW2	SW1	PRIMARY ADAPTER	SECONDARY ADAPTER
Off	Off	Off	Off	— INVALID —	
Off	Off	Off	On	— INVALID —	
Off	Off	On	Off	— INVALID —	
Off	Off	On	On	— INVALID —	
Off	On	Off	Off	EGA - Monochrome	CGA - 80 x 25
Off	On	Off	On	EGA - Monochrome	CGA - 40 x 25
Off	On	On	Off	EGA-80 x 25-Enhanced	Monochrome
Off	On	On	On	EGA-40 x 25-Enhanced	Monochrome
On	Off	Off	Off	EGA-80 x 25-CGA Text	Monochrome
On	Off	Off	On	EGA-40 x 25-CGA Text	Monochrome
On	Off	On	Off	CGA - 80 x 25	EGA - Monochrome
On	Off	On	On	CGA - 40 x 25	EGA - Monochrome
On	On	Off	Off	Monochrome	EGA-80 x 25-Enhanced
On	On	Off	On	Monochrome	EGA-40 x 25-Enhanced
On	On	On	Off	Monochrome	EGA-80 x 25-CGA Text
On	On	On	On	Monochrome	EGA-40 x 25-CGA Text

B-6. Standard Modes

Table B-6. Standard IBM video modes.

Mode	Type	Colors	Resolution	Compatible Displays
0, 1	Color text	16	40 x 25 8 x 8 char cell	CD, ED, VGA Multifrequency
0*, 1*	Color text	16	40 x 25 8 x 14 char cell	ED, VGA Multifrequency
0+, 1+	Color text	16	40 x 25 9 x 16 char cell	VGA Multifrequency
2,3	Color text	16	80 x 25 8 x 8 char cell	CD, ED, VGA Multifrequency
2*, 3*	Color text	16	80 x 25 8 x 14 char cell	ED, VGA Multifrequency
2+, 3+	Color text	16	80 x 25 9 x 16 char cell	VGA Multifrequency
4, 5	Color graphics	4	320 x 200	CD, ED, VGA Multifrequency
6	Color graphics	2	640 x 200	CD, ED, VGA Multifrequency
7	Monochrome text	2	80 x 25 8 x 14 char cell	Monochrome VGA
7+	Monochrome text	2	80 x 25 9 x 16 char cell	VGA only

(continued)

Table B-6. Standard IBM video modes *(continued)*.

8, 9, A	PC jr only			
D	Color graphics	16	320 x 200	CD, ED, VGA Multifrequency
E	Color graphics	16	640 x 200	CD, ED, VGA Multifrequency
F	Mono graphics	2	640 x 350	Monochrome VGA
10	Color graphics	16	640 x 350	ED, VGA Multifrequency
11	Color graphics	2	640 x 480	VGA Multifrequency
12	Color graphics	16	640 x 480	VGA Multifrequency
13	Color graphics	256	320 x 200	VGA Multifrequency

Most multifrequency displays are VGA compatible.
The original NEC Multisync is not.

CD = Color Display.
ED = Enhanced Color Display.

Appendix C

Programming Hints

C-1. Assembly Language Programming

Many programmers see assembly language as a kind of dark, mystical art that is somehow beyond their grasp. This is really not the case; the concepts behind assembly language are no more difficult than those of any other computer language. The information in this appendix will not make anyone an expert at assembly language programming, but it will help them to understand the simple assembly language routines needed to interface a high level language with the EGA and VGA. The assembly language described here is that of the Intel 8086 family of processors, which are used in all IBM PC/AT compatible computers, as well as IBM PS/2 computers.

Assembly language is really the "natural" language of a computer. One assembly language instruction corresponds to one instruction cycle of the processor. Assembly language therefore gives the programmer direct control over what the processor does, cycle by cycle, and this is why it provides flexibility and performance that cannot be matched by a high-level language. The task of interfacing directly with hardware, such as a display adapter, frequently can only be accomplished with assembly language.

Assembly language programs process words of data and move them between the processor's internal Registers, system Memory, and system I/O Ports.

Data Registers

Registers are used inside the processor to hold data. In the Intel 8086 family of processors, each register holds 16 Bits (two Bytes, or one Word) of data. Some registers are general purpose, and others have special functions. The general purpose registers are registers AX, BX, CX, and DX. For byte wide data manipulation, these registers can be referenced by their upper and lower halves as AH and AL, BH and BL, CH and CL, DH and DL.

Two special purpose registers, SI and DI, are called Index Registers. SI and DI can be used to hold memory addresses that point into system memory. (SI and DI can also be used as general purpose data registers if desired.)

System Memory

System memory is where all program code and data is stored. The processor reads and writes to memory as required, referencing data with a 16 bit memory address. A 16 bit address is only sufficient to reference 64K bytes of memory; however, system memory is usually much larger than 64K bytes. The system memory is therefore broken up into several Segments. Reads and writes to memory must specify which segment is being accessed.

Segment Registers

A particular segment of memory is referenced by setting a processor segment register with the address of that segment. The segment registers are the CS (code segment) register, which defines from which segment instruction codes are fetched; the DS (data segment) register, which defines which segment data is read from and written to; the ES (extra segment) register, which is used when transferring data from one memory segment to another; and the SS (stack segment), which defines where in memory the processor stack is located.

I/O Ports

Input/Output ports provide a means of sensing and controlling peripheral hardware in the computer system. There are 65,536 byte-wide I/O port addresses, addressable by the processor (this is referred to as the 64K byte I/O address space).

Access to I/O ports is simple. The port address is placed in the DX register, and data is input or output from the AL register. The instruction sequence looks like this:

To input:

```
        mov     dx,IO_ADDR
        in      al,dx
```

To output:

```
        mov     dx,IO_ADDR
        out     dx,al
```

The Instruction Set

The instructions that can be performed by the processor are logically divided into the following groups:

Data Movement - MOV instructions move data from register to register, register to memory, or memory to register. The first argument of the instruction is the destination for the move. For instance:

```
Data         DW      27
             ...
             MOV     AX,BX      ;register to register - 16 bit
             MOV     AH,AL      ;register to register - 8 bit
             MOV     CX,Data    ;memory to register
             MOV     [SI],AX    ;register to memory indirect
                                ;(SI points to memory location)
```

Data processing - instructions that process data in registers or memory (addition, subtraction, anding, oring, etc.). The first argument in the instruction is the destination for the result. For instance:

```
             ADD     AX,DX      ;put the sum of AX and DX in AX
             AND     BX,[DI]    ;put AND of BX and memory in BX
             SUB     [SI],3     ;subtract 3 from data in memory
             INC     SI         ;increment SI register
             DEC     CL         ;decrement CL register
```

Program control - instructions that control program flow, such as:

```
             JMP     Loop_Point  ;absolute program jump
             CALL    Subroutine1 ;subroutine call
             RET                 ;return from subroutine call
             JZ      Test_Fail   ;jump if zero flag set
             JC      Test_Pass   ;jump if carry flag set
             JNC     Test_Fail   ;jump if carry flag not set
```

Status Flags

Processor status flags show the result of the most recent logical or arithmetic process. The Zero flag indicates if the result of the last processing instruction was zero. The Carry flag indicates if an arithmetic operation generated a carry. These flags can be tested with conditional jumps to modify program flow.

Not all instructions modify the status flags. The following instruction sequence is permissible, for instance:

```
             CMP     AX,BX      ;compare-are AX and BX equal?
             MOV     AX,[SI]
             MOV     BX,[DI]    ;load parameters
             JNZ     TEST_FAIL  ;jump if test failed
```

C-2. Interfacing with High Level Language

When assembly language subroutines are defined, the assembler must be instructed as to what memory segments will be used by the program. The use of segment registers is usually dictated by the high level language that is being used.

When using Microsoft C (small model) with the Microsoft Macro-assembler, the following format should be used for assembly language subroutines to match segment usage:

```
_TEXT    SEGMENT BYTE    PUBLIC   "CODE"
ASSUME   CS:_TEXT, DS:NOTHING

MYPROC   PROC     NEAR                   ;(MYPROC is any subroutine name)

         Assembly
         language
         code

         RET
MYPROC   ENDP
_TEXT    ENDS
         END
```

When using the Microsoft Macro-assembler with Turbo Pascal, this format should be used to match segment usage:

```
CODE     SEGMENT BYTE    PUBLIC   "CODE"
ASSUME   CS:CODE, DS:NOTHING

MYPROC   PROC     FAR                    ;(MYPROC is any subroutine name)

         Assembly
         language
         code

         RET     2*N                    ;N is number of parameters passed
MYPROC   ENDP
CODE     ENDS
         END
```

Parameters are normally passed on the stack when a call is made from a high level language. Assume a subroutine will be called in the format:

```
MyProc(P1,P2,P3);
```

With Microsoft C (small model), the following example shows how to enter and exit a routine and get parameters:

```
_MyProc PROC    NEAR
        PUSH    BP
        MOV     BP,SP          ;get pointer to parameters
        PUSH    SI             ;save critical registers
        PUSH    DI             ;(BP, SI, DI, ES and DS must be preserved)
        ...
        MOV     AX,[BP+4]      ;get p1
        MOV     BX,[BP+6]      ;get p2
        MOV     CX,[BP+8]      ;get p3
        ...
        POP     DI
        POP     SI
        MOV     SP,BP
        POP     BP
        RET
_MyProc ENDP
```

With Turbo Pascal, parameters are passed on the stack in the reverse order. Also, the subroutine is responsible for removing the parameters from the stack before exiting. Subroutines must also be defined as FAR instead of NEAR. The following format works with Turbo Pascal:

```
_MyProc PROC    FAR
        PUSH    BP
        MOV     BP,SP          ;Get pointer to parameters
        PUSH    SI             ;Save critical registers
        PUSH    DI             ;(BP, SI, DI, DS and ES must be preserved)
        ...
        MOV     AX,[BP+10]     ;get p1
        MOV     BX,[BP+8]      ;get p2
        MOV     CX,[BP+6]      ;get p3
        ...
        POP     DI
        POP     SI
        MOV     SP,BP
        POP     BP
        RET     6              ;remove 6 bytes from stack on exit
_MyProc ENDP
```

C-3. Compiling with In-Line Assembly Code

To achieve the fastest possible execution time, many high level language compilers allow assembly language instructions to be imbedded directly into the high level code and compiled with it. This can be especially useful for executing video BIOS calls that return data via the ES:BP register pair.

In Turbo C, in-line assembly language statements can be added to a program by prefacing each statement with the "asm" directive; for example:

```
main ()                              /* get pointer to 8x8 character genenerator  */
      {
      char     far     *p;

      asm      push    bp        /* preserve registers                  */
      asm      push    es
      asm      mov     ah,11h  /* load BIOS function #                 */
      asm      mov     al,30h
      asm      mov     bh,3
      asm      int     10h       /* call BIOS function                  */
      asm      mov     word ptr p,bp
      asm      mov     word ptr p+1,es
      asm      pop     es
      asm      pop     bp

      printf("\n8x8 character generator is at %lx\n",p);
      }
```

In Turbo Pascal, in-line code is more difficult because the programmer must assemble the code himself and place the resulting binary instruction codes into his program using the "in-line" directive:

```
procedure SetMode(Mode:byte);
begin
      inline  ($8A/$86/Mode/       {MOV AL,Mode[BP]      ;Load mode number}
               $B4/$00/            {MOV AH,0             ;Load function code}
               $CD/$10);           {INT 10H              ;Call BIOS}
end;
```

C-4. Debugging Video Software

Some special precautions are necessary when debugging programs that interface with a video display adapter.

Most software debugging tools output debugging information to the system console device. If the software being debugged is also outputting information to the console, the resulting interaction between the program and the debugger may produce totally unpredictable results. The debugger itself may even cease to function.

One way around this problem is to install a secondary display adapter in the system. If the program under debug outputs to the secondary display, it will not interfere with the debugger's use of the primary (console) display. If, for instance, the software under debug is outputting color graphics to an EGA, an MDA monochrome adapter can be installed. The Mode Mono command can be used to declare the monochrome display as the console device for the debugger. This method is not guaranteed to eliminate problems if the program under debug uses any DOS or BIOS functions that output to the console device.

Another approach is to connect a CRT terminal to a serial port, then redirect console I/O to the serial port by using the CTTY COM1 command. This method also may not be reliable if the software being debugged outputs data to the console device.

In cases where only one display adapter is available, or if the debugger and program under debug must both output to the console device, special precautions must be taken. Program single stepping or setting of breakpoints must be done with great care. When the debugger is activated by a breakpoint, it will output data to the console, thereby altering the state of the display adapter. This may destroy any adapter configuration that was done by the program under debug.

For EGA and VGA, register access is usually a two step process of outputting first an index and then register data. If a breakpoint is set between the output of the index and data, it is virtually guaranteed that the debugger will overwrite the index and the subsequent data output will be performed incorrectly.

Above all, bear in mind that if the display adapter is left in an invalid state for more than a few seconds, damage to the display may result.

Glossary

40 x 25:

A text mode of operation that displays 25 lines of text with 40 character columns per line.

80 x 25:

A text mode of operation that displays 25 lines of text with 80 character columns per line.

80 x 86:

The Intel family of microprocessors, including the 8086, 8088, 80186, 80286, and 80386, which are all software compatible.

320 x 200, 640 x 350, etc.:

Graphics screen resolutions, expressed as the number of pixels displayed horizontally across the screen by the number of pixels displayed vertically; i.e. 320x200 means 320 horizontal pixels by 200 vertical pixels.

Adapter or Display Adapter:

A circuit board designed to interface a display device to a computer system, such as MDA, CGA, EGA, or VGA.

All Points Addressable (APA):

IBM terminology for a graphics mode, so called because each dot on the display screen may be controlled independently.

Analog Display:

A display device that uses an analog interface.

Analog Interface:

A type of interface used between video controller and video display in which colors are determined by the voltage levels on three output lines, normally called the RED, GREEN, and BLUE (or RGB) lines. A theoretically unlimited number of colors can be supported by this method. Output voltage normally varies between zero volts (for black) to one volt (for maximum brightness). Load impedance is normally 75 ohms.

ASCII:

American Standard Code for Information Interchange, the most common method of digitally encoding alphanumeric data.

Aspect Ratio:

The ratio of height to width of a single pixel on a display screen. High resolution displays usually have a 1:1 aspect ratio, or are said to have Square Pixels. Graphics drawing algorithms must compensate for the aspect ratio of the display if it is not 1:1; otherwise, circles will appear elliptical and squares will appear rectangular.

Attribute Controller:

The section of logic on EGA and VGA that generates display attributes (see Display Attribute).

Background:

In text mode, the area of a character cell that is not illuminated by the character. The rest of the character cell is referred to as the Foreground. In graphics mode, the area of the screen that is not illuminated by a graphics object.

BIOS:

Basic Input Output System; in IBM compatible personal computers, this is a set of ROM based firmware routines that control the resources of the system and make them available to applications programs in an orderly fashion.

BIOS Data Area:

An area in system memory where the EGA/VGA BIOS stores data defining the display resolution, cursor position, etc.

BITBLT:

Bit oriented Transfer; this is a type of graphics drawing routine that moves a rectangle of display data from one area of display memory to another. This can be difficult because the data to be moved is usually neither contiguous nor byte aligned. Graphics controllers frequently include varying levels of hardware assist to help speed BITBLT operations.

Bit Mapped Graphics:

A graphics display mode in which each pixel on the display surface is represented by one or more bits in display memory. All EGA and VGA graphics modes are bit mapped.

Bit Plane:
See Color Planes.

Blanking, Blank Pulse:

For CRT displays, a timing signal which shuts off the electron beam during retrace intervals to prevent unwanted diagonal lines of light from appearing on the screen.

Block Graphics (Or Line Graphics):

In text mode, a set of primitive graphics objects that can be used as text characters to create simple graphics such as borders and lines.

CGA:

Color Graphics Adapter, the first IBM color graphics product for personal computers (EGA was the second). CGA can produce 4 color graphics or 8 color text at a resolution of 640 pixels horizontally by 200 pixels vertically.

Character Cell:

In text mode, the area of display used to display one character. On EGA, character cells are either 8 or 9 pixels wide and usually either 8 or 14 pixels high.

Character Code:

A one byte code representing a text character (usually ASCII).

Character Generator:

A translation table used to translate an ASCII character code into character font information for display. Some display adapters use ROM based character generators; for EGA and VGA, the character generator is loaded into a section of display RAM.

Character Set:

The set of characters that a display adapter is capable of displaying. In text mode, this is determined by the contents of the Character Generator. The EGA character set contains 256 characters.

Color Palette:

The set of colors that are available with a given display system.

Color Planes:

In plane oriented graphics adapters, color planes are overlapping pages or sections of memory which control different display colors.

Composite Display:

A display device that uses a composite sync signal (combined horizontal and vertical sync) as opposed to separate sync signals.

Console Device:

The keyboard and display that are used to control the computer. In multiple display systems, the console device can usually be assigned to be any one of the display devices.

CPU:

Central Processing Unit, another name for the system processor.

CRT Controller (CRTC):

On the EGA and VGA, as well as many other video display adapters, the CRT Controller is the circuit that is responsible for generating the timing signals required to operate a CRT display (including blanking and retrace sync pulses).

CRT Display:

Cathode Ray Tube Display; all of the display devices discussed in this book fall into this category.

Digital Display:

A display device that uses a digital interface.

Digital Interface:

A type of interface used between video controller and video display in which display color is controlled by digital color control lines switching on and off. The number of colors that can be supported depends on the number of signal lines in the interface. Most digital interfaces are TTL (Transistor-Transistor Logic) compatible. CGA and EGA both use digital interfaces.

Display Attribute:

A programmable display characteristic. In graphics modes, color is usually the only display attribute. In text modes, attributes may include blinking, underlining, or reverse video.

Display Refresh (or Screen Refresh):

An image drawn on a CRT display will only remain visible for a few milliseconds (the presistence of the screen phosphor), unless it is redrawn continuously. This process is called Display Refresh or Screen Refresh. Different displays use different refresh rates, but display refresh is normally required between 50 and 70 times a second to avoid any visible screen flickering. Sixty times a second is a common refresh rate.

Dot Clock (or Pixel Clock):

The timing signal on a display adapter that controls the serial output of pixels to the display device.

Double Scan:

A technique used by VGA to gain compatibility with the lower resolution CGA. Each horizontal scan line is drawn twice, which converts a CGA 200 line image into a VGA 400 line image. This also partially compensates (actually over-compensates) for the different aspect ratio of the VGA.

Driver:

A software module that interfaces a particular display device to an application program. EGA drivers have been written for programs such as Microsoft Windows, DRI GEM, Lotus 1-2-3, etc.

Electron Beam:

In a CRT display, a moving beam of electrons creates the display image seen on the display screen. Timing and modulation of the electron beam are controlled by the display adapter.

Emulation:

A technique for making one type of display device appear to operate as if it were a different display device. Emulations improve the usefulness of a product by making it compatible with other products. EGA is capable of emulating MDA and sometimes CGA and Hercules. VGA is capable of emulating EGA, CGA, and MDA.

Feature Connector:

An expansion connector on the EGA that can be used to combine other video signals with EGA video output. It is not widely used.

Font:

This term originated in the publishing industry. A font is a character set of one particular size and style (such as 14 point Helvetica).

Foreground:

In text mode, the portion of a character cell that is illuminated by the character font (as opposed to Background).

Graphics Controller:
On EGA and VGA, a section of circuitry that can provide hardware assist for graphics drawing algorithms by performing logical functions on data written to display memory.

Graphics Mode:
A display mode in which all pixels on the display screen can be controlled independently to draw graphics objects (as opposed to Text Mode, in which only a pre-defined set of characters can be displayed).

Hercules Graphics:
Graphics programs that are compatible with the monochrome graphics adapter produced by Hercules Corporation.

HGC:
Hercules monochrome Graphics Adapter.

Horizontal Retrace:
In CRT displays, the time interval when the electron beam returns from the right side of the display screen to the left side of the display screen. The electron beam is turned off during this time (Horizontal Blanking).

IBM Color Display (CD):
The display device marketed by IBM for use with the CGA display adapter.

IBM Enhanced Color Display (ECD):
The display device marketed by IBM for use with the EGA display adapter.

Index Register:
A register used to indirectly address other registers.

I/O Register:
A data register (either read only, write only, or read-write), which is mapped into the I/O space of the processor.

Latch:
In electronics, a type of memory device that captures and holds several bits of data.

Light Pen:

A device that allows an operator to input commands to the computer by placing the pen tip to a certain position on the display screen (such as touching an item on a menu). The application software must be written to support the use of a light pen. Light pens have not become nearly as popular as mice or joysticks for this purpose.

Line Graphics:

See Block Graphics.

MDA:

Monochrome Display Adapter; the original display adapter marketed by IBM for personal computers. MDA has no bit-mapped graphics capability.

Monochrome Display:

A one color display device; often referred to as a black and white display, even though the color used is often amber or green. Sometimes referred to as a two color display (the second color being black).

Monitor:

Another term for a CRT Display.

Multisync Display:

A display marketed by NEC Corporation. The Multisync is EGA compatible, and also supports higher resolutions. Many displays operate only at a single horizontal scanning rate. The Multisync display can operate over a range of scanning frequencies and screen resolutions.

Palette:

The choice of available colors with a color graphics display system. The term Palette is sometimes used to refer to a color look-up table.

Panning:

A technique by which the display screen is made to appear to be a viewport into a larger display, and then the viewport is moved around so that different areas of the display come into view.

PEL:

IBM terminology for a pixel.

PGC or PGA:

Professional Graphics Controller, a high resolution color display adapter sold by IBM. The PGC was not highly successful as a product.

Pixel:

A single dot on the the display surface. The smallest independently program-mable display element.

Primary Display:

An IBM term for the console device; the display where DOS displays prompts and messages.

Raster:

The left-to-right, top-to-bottom scanning pattern made on the screen by the elec-tron gun in a CRT display.

Resolutoin:

A measure of the quality of image that can be shown on a particular display; usually expressed as the number of pixels that can be displayed horizontally across the display screen by the number of pixels that can be displayed verti-cally on the display screen.

RGB:

A type of interface used with color displays which uses three color signals (Red, Green and Blue).

Scan Line:

One horizontal scan of the electron beam in a CRT display.

Scrolling:

On a text display, the process of moving the displayed text up or down (usually up) on the display screen, normally to make room for new text to be displayed. This allows a large block of text to be viewed a small amount at a time. Scrolling is usually done in an upward direction one line at a time so that the text appears to roll smoothly upward on the screen.

Secondary Display:

An IBM term for a display device that is not the console device, but that may be used by an application program to display data.

Sequencer:

The section of circuitry on EGA and VGA that controls timing for the board. The sequencer also contains memory plane enabling and disabling functions.

Serializer:

On display adapters, the section of circuitry that converts words of display refresh data into a serial bit stream to be output to the display.

Set/Reset:

A function on EGA and VGA (poorly named) that permits a fill pattern to be quickly written into display memory. The Set/Reset function is part of the Graphics Controller.

Simultaneous Colors:

The number of colors in a display system that can be displayed on the screen at one time. This number is limited by the circuitry of the display adapter, and is usually much smaller than the number of colors the display device can actually support. The number of simultaneous colors a display adapter will support is normally determined by the number of color planes, or bits per pixel, that it uses. For example, a device with four bits per pixel will support 16 simultaneous colors.

Smooth Scrolling:

A scrolling process by which text characters scroll up or down smoothly one pixel at a time, rather than scrolling one full character line at a time, which tends to appear slightly jerky. Smooth scrolled text can easily be read while scrolling is in process. EGA and VGA provide hardware support to assist in smooth scrolling.

Sync, Sync Pulse:

Another term for horizontal and vertical retrace pulses to a CRT display.

Teletype Mode:

An EGA/VGA BIOS call that displays text as if the display screen were a page in a teletype machine. The cursor is advanced after each character, scrolling and line wrap are performed as needed, carriage return, line feed bell, and backspace characters are recognized.

Text Mode:

On EGA and VGA, a display mode in which the display adapter converts ASCII character data into display information directly. Text mode displays impose very little overhead on the system processor, but do not support graphics.

Vertical Retrace:

On CRT displays, the time interval after a raster scan has been completed when the electron beam returns to the top of the display screen for the next scan. The electron beam is blanked during this time. Retrace occurs between 50 and 70 times a second, depending on the display.

VGA:

The IBM Virtual Graphics Array display adapter.

VLSI:

Very Large Scale Integration - the technology of manufacturing Integrated Circuits (chips) with thousands of transistors on a single device. The personal computer was made possible because of VLSI technology.

Wait State:

When a system processor is reading or writing a memory or peripheral device that cannot respond fast enough, a time interval (usually a fraction of a microsecond) is inserted during which the processor does nothing but wait for the slower device. This has a detrimental effect on system throughout, but is often necessary. Because of the constant requirement to perform screen refresh, many display adapters, including EGA and VGA, impose wait states on the processor.

Window:

As commonly used in personal computers, the term Window refers to a section of the display screen (usually rectangular) that displays data independently of the reset of the screen. Several windows may be present at once on the display. In advanced computer graphics, the terms Window and Viewport are used to refer to the content and position of display information. The section of data that is to be displayed is referred to as a Window (as if looking at a scene through a window, and only part of the scene is visible). The position and scaling of the information on the screen is referred to as a Viewport.

Index

About the Authors

George Sutty of Huntington Beach, California received his BA in mathematics from Vassar College and his MA in mathematics/computer science from UCLA. As an independent consultant in the field of computer graphics, he has developed software for such companies as AST Research, Western Digital, and Basic Four.

Steve Blair of Alta Loma, California is an independent engineering consultant who operates Digital Resources in Alta Loma. He has worked for such companies as AST Research, Emulex Corporation, General Automation, and Computer Automation.

Important! Read Before Opening Sealed Diskette
END USER LICENSE AGREEMENT

The software in this package is provided to You on the condition that You agree with SIMON & SCHUSTER, INC. ("S&S") to the terms and conditions set forth below. **Read this End User Agreement carefully. You will be bound by the terms of this agreement if you open the sealed diskette.** If You do not agree to the terms contained in this End User License Agreement, return the entire product, along with your receipt, to *Brady, Simon & Schuster, Inc., One Gulf + Western Plaza, New York, NY 10023, Attn: Refunds,* and your purchase price will be refunded.

S&S grants, and You hereby accept, a personal, nonexclusive license to use the software program and associated documentation in this package, or any part of it ("Licensed Product"), subject to the following terms and conditions:

1. *License*
The license granted to You hereunder authorizes You to use the Licensed Product on any single computer system. A separate license, pursuant to a separate End User License Agreement, is required for any other computer system on which You intend to use the Licensed Product.

2. *Term*
This End User License Agreement is effective from the date of purchase by You of the Licensed Product and shall remain in force until terminated. You may terminate this End User License Agreement at any time by destroying the Licensed Product together with all copies in any form made by You or received by You. Your right to use or copy the Licensed Product will terminate if You fail to comply with any of the terms or conditions of this End User License Agreement. Upon such termination You shall destroy the copies of the Licensed Product in your possession.

3. *Restriction Against Transfer*
This End User License Agreement, and the Licensed Product, may not be assigned, sublicensed or otherwise transfered by You to another party unless the other party agrees to accept the terms and conditions of this End User License Agreement. If You transfer the Licensed Product, You must at the same time either transfer all copies whether in printed or machine-readable form to the same party or destroy any copies not transferred.

4. *Restrictions Against Copying or Modifying the Licensed Product*
The Licensed Product is copyrighted and except for certain limited uses as noted on the copyright page, may not be further copied without the prior written approval of S&S, except that You may make one copy for backup purposes provided You reproduce and include the complete copyright notice on the backup copy. Any unauthorized copying is in violation of this Agreement and may also constitute a violation of the United States Copyright Law for which You could be liable in a civil or criminal suit. **You may not use, transfer, copy or otherwise reproduce the Licensed Product, or any part of it, except as expressly permitted in this End User License Agreement.**

5. *Protection and Security*
You shall take all reasonable steps to safeguard the Licensed Product and to ensure that no unauthorized person shall have access to it and that no unauthorized copy of any part of it in any form shall be made.

6. **Limited Warranty**
If You are the original consumer purchaser of a diskette and its found to be defective in materials or workmanship (which shall not include problems relating to the nature or operation of the Licensed Product) under normal use, S&S will replace it free of charge (or, at S&S's option, refund your purchase price) within 30 days following the date of purchase. Following the 30-day period, and up to one year after purchase, S&S will replace any such defective diskette upon payment of a $5 charge (or, at S&S's option, refund your purchase price), provided that the Limited Warranty Registration Card has been filed within 30 days following the date of purchase. Any request for replacement of a defective diskette must be accompanied by the original defective diskette and proof of date of purchase and purchase price. S&S shall have no obligation to replace a diskette (or refund your purchase price) based on claims of defects in the nature or operation of the Licensed Product.

The software program is provided "as is" without warranty of any kind, either expressed or implied, including but not limited to the implied warranties of merchantability and fitness for a particular purpose. The entire risk as to the quality and performance of the program is with You. Should the program prove defective, You (and not S&S) assume the entire cost of all necessary servicing, repair or correction.

Some states do not allow the exclusion of implied warranties, so the above exclusion may not apply to You. This warrant gives You specific legal rights, and You may also have other rights which vary from state to state.

S&S does not warrant that the functions contained in the program will meet your requirements or that the operation of the program will be uninterrupted or error free. Neither S&S nor anyone else who has been involved in the creation or production of this product shall be liable for any direct, indirect, incidental, special or consequential damages, whether arising out of the use or inability to use the product, or any breach of a warranty, and S&S shall have no responsibility except to replace the diskette pursuant to this limited warranty (or, at its option, provide a refund of the purchase price).

No sales personnel or other representative of any party involved in the distribution of the Licensed Product is authorized by S&S to make any warranties with respect to the diskette or the Licensed Product beyond those contained in this Agreement. **Oral statements do not constitute warranties,** shall not be relied upon by You, and are not part of this Agreement. The entire agreement between S&S and You is embodied in this Agreement.

7. *General*
If any provision of this End User License Agreement is determined to be invalid under any applicable statute of rule of law, it shall be deemed omitted and the remaining provisions shall continue in full force and effect. This End User License Agreement is to be governed by the construed in accordance with the laws of the State of New York.